D1715464

Highlife Saturday Night

AFRICAN EXPRESSIVE CULTURES

Patrick McNaughton, editor

Associate editors
Catherine M. Cole
Barbara G. Hoffman
Eileen Julien
Kassim Koné
D. A. Masolo
Elisha Renne
Zoë Strother

 **Ethnomusicology Multimedia**

Ethnomusicology Multimedia (EM) is a collaborative publishing program, developed with funding from the Andrew W. Mellon Foundation, to identify and publish first books in ethnomusicology, accompanied by supplemental audiovisual materials online at www.ethnomultimedia.org.

A collaboration of the presses at Indiana and Temple universities, EM is an innovative, entrepreneurial, and cooperative effort to expand publishing opportunities for emerging scholars in ethnomusicology and to increase audience reach by using common resources available to the presses through support from the Andrew W. Mellon Foundation. Each press acquires and develops EM books according to its own profile and editorial criteria.

EM's most innovative features are its dual web-based components, the first of which is a password-protected Annotation Management System (AMS) where authors can upload peer-reviewed audio, video, and static image content for editing and annotation and key the selections to corresponding references in their texts. Second is a public site for viewing the web content, www.ethnomultimedia.org, with links to publishers' websites for information about the accompanying books. The AMS and website were designed and built by the Institute for Digital Arts and Humanities at Indiana University. The Indiana University Digital Library Program (DLP) hosts the website and the Indiana University Archives of Traditional Music (ATM) provides archiving and preservation services for the EM online content.

Highlife SATURDAY Night

POPULAR MUSIC AND SOCIAL CHANGE IN URBAN GHANA

NATE PLAGEMAN

INDIANA UNIVERSITY PRESS

Bloomington and Indianapolis

This book is a publication of

INDIANA UNIVERSITY PRESS
601 North Morton Street
Bloomington, Indiana 47404-3797 USA

iupress.indiana.edu

Telephone orders   800-842-6796
Fax orders   812-855-7931

Manufactured in the
United States of America

Library of Congress
Cataloging-in-Publication Data

Plageman, Nate, [date]
  Highlife Saturday night : popular music
and social change in urban Ghana / Nate
Plageman.
     p. cm. — (African expressive cul-
tures) (Ethnomusicology multimedia)
  Includes bibliographical references, dis-
cography, and index.
  ISBN 978-0-253-00725-4 (cloth : alk.
paper) — ISBN 978-0-253-00729-2 (pbk. :
alk. paper) — ISBN 978-0-253-00733-9
(e-book) 1. Dance music—Social as-
pects—Ghana. 2. Highlife (Music)—
Ghana—History and criticism. 3. Ghana
—Social conditions. I. Title. II. Series:
African expressive cultures. III. Series:
Ethnomusicology multimedia.
  ML3917.G43P53 2013
  306.4'8409667—dc23
                              2012026045

1 2 3 4 5 18 17 16 15 14 13

FOR

JOHN HANSON

Contents

Acknowledgments

This book, like every other, has a history. As I remember, it was born alongside a pair of speakers playing highlife music at a funeral in Ghana in 1998, gained salience in a library cafeteria in Bloomington, Indiana, and then began to travel—in words, thoughts, and computer hard drives—with me over many years and countless miles. To tell its full story here would be difficult and tedious. I also wouldn't blame those who didn't read it. At the same time, there are elements of this project's evolution that deserve notice and recognition. Writing a book is an endeavor that requires much more than a lonely academic, a stack of notes and documents, and a dimly lit computer screen. This particular one is the product of many thought-provoking conversations, invaluable advice, practical assistance, and unending encouragement, all of which came at the hands of other people. To acknowledge the enormous role that they had in its conceptualization and making, I want to mention them briefly and offer a word of thanks.

One of my largest debts is to the many individuals and institutions that helped transform a somewhat naïve young man from Lincoln, Nebraska, into a historian of Africa. My engagement with the historical discipline, Ghana, and the broader confines of African studies started at both Saint Olaf College and the University of Ghana, where I benefited from the tutelage of Joseph Mbele, Joan Hepburn, Michael Fitzgerald, Michael Williams, and Kofi Agyekum. A fortunate string of events led me to Bloomington, where I began my graduate studies at Indiana University. While there, I grew as both a person and a scholar at the hands of John Hanson, Phyllis Martin, George Brooks, Marissa Moorman, Daniel Reed, Claude Clegg, and many others. I owe a considerable debt to John and Phyllis, both of whom placed considerable faith in my project and helped orient it in the right directions, as well as my African studies cohort, who helped me expand my knowledge and satiate my intellectual curiosity. Perhaps one day I'll get to gather around a table with Cyprian Adupa, Ebenezer Ayesu, Katie Boswell, Jeremy Brooke, Matt Carotenuto, R. David Goodman, Muzi Hadebe, Jennifer Hart, Liz McMahon, Peter Mwesige, Hannington Ochwada, Elizabeth Perrill, Paul Schauert, Kate Schroeder, Cullen Strawn, Richard Wafula, and Craig Waite not simply to reminisce, but to again benefit from their collective acumen. The administrators and staff of the African Studies Program and History Department at Indiana University helped me jump many hurdles en route to my PhD. Support for my graduate work and writing of the PhD came from the Indiana University Graduate School, History Department, Office of International Programs, and U.S. Department of Education Foreign Language and Area Studies Fellowship program. The U.S. Department of Education Fulbright Hays Doctoral Dissertation Research Abroad program and Indiana University History Department funded the research that informs much of this book.

I also have accumulated many debts in Ghana, the largest of which undoubtedly go to the many men and women who spoke with me about their daily lives, their engagement with popular music, and the connections that existed between them. Their names are listed in the notes as well as the bibliography, but I owe particular appreciation to those who were instrumental to its progression: Jerry Hansen, Kofi Lindsay, Koo Nimo, Stan Plange, and Ebo Taylor. John Collins deserves special mention for all that he did to make this book a reality. During the last decade, John invited me for innumerable chats, offered access to his writings and materials housed in his Bookor African Popular Musical Archives Foundation, provided contact information for several musicians, and patiently considered my many questions. I consider him a great colleague and friend. Apetsi Amenumey spent countless hours at my side, tirelessly arranging visits, helping me conduct interviews, and scouring out records and other source materials. I owe him a great deal. Much of what I've learned about Ghanaian music over the last fourteen years is due to the efforts of Francis Akotua, and his stamp is on these pages. I'm grateful to Eddie Bruce, Miles Cleret, Peter Marfo, Edmund Mensah, and Stan Plange for supporting the inclusion of the songs on the website that accompanies this book. In Bloomington and Legon, Seth Ofori, Kofi Saah, and Kofi Agyekum helped me (with great patience) improve my Twi. At the University of Ghana, I benefited from the assistance of Kofi Baku, Takyiwaa Manuh, Owusu Brempong, Willie Anku, Judith Botchwey, Edward Apenteng-Sackey, Christopher Frimpong, Baning Peprah, Seth

Allotey, and Kafui Ofori, as well as the staff of the Balme Library, the Institute of African Studies Library, and the International Center for African Music and Dance. The staff at the Public Records and Archives Administration Department in Accra, Cape Coast, Sekondi, and Kumasi offered great aid and insight, as did the staff at the Information Services Department Photograph Library. The kindness and hospitality of Gavin and Comfort Webb, Michael Williams, Nana and Mercy Sekyere, Sarpei Nunoo, Mutala Karim, Sam Bathrick, Isaac Hirt-Manheimer and Gloria Manheimer, Yaw Gyamfi, Elikem Nyamuame, Nii Okai Aryeetey, and Gidi Agbeko, made Accra truly feel like my home away from home.

I now live in Winston Salem, North Carolina, a place that has become home only on account of another set of people. Many of my colleagues at Wake Forest University, including Lisa Blee, Simon Caron, Monique O'Connell, Emily Wakild, and Charles Wilkins, have provided meals, opened their homes, and eased my transition from graduate student to professor. Fellow members in the Department of History read and commented on parts of this book and have shared numerous comparative insights that have made it better. I am particularly grateful to Lisa Blee, John Hayes, Charles McGraw, Monique O'Connell, Nathan Roberts, and Emily Wakild for their engagement with my ideas and writing as well as their willingness to join in conversations about the study of history, gender, and popular music. Funding from the Wake Forest University Archie Fund for the Arts and Humanities as well as the Creative and Research Development and Enrichment initiative enabled me to return to Ghana, conduct additional research, and complete the book.

At Indiana University Press, I owe much to Dee Mortensen and Patrick McNaughton, each of whom believed in the project. Working with Dee has been a tremendous pleasure, and the book has improved considerably as a result of her ideas and efforts. I am extremely grateful to Suzanne Gott and Stephan Miescher for their careful reading and comments on the manuscript. Invaluable assistance also came from Carol Kennedy, Sarah Jacobi, Raina Polivka, and June Silay. Clara Henderson was my ever-patient guide through all things related to the Ethnomusicology Multimedia website. Bill Nelson produced the maps. Many individuals and institutions, including Bailey's African History Archives, the Basel Mission, Bookor African Popular Music Archives Foundation, Ghana Information Services Department, and Isaac Hudson Bruce Vanderpuije, enabled the inclusion of the photographs that appear in the book as well as on the accompanying website. Matt Carotenuto read the manuscript in its entirety, poked at its holes, and helped me fill them. I look forward to returning the favor. Many other people have read portions of this work at various times and stages, adding insight and encouragement along the way; thanks to Jean Allman, Steve Feld, Sandra Greene, John Hanson, Stephan Miescher, Richard Waller, Emily Wakild, and Sara Berry and the participants of the Johns Hopkins All-University Seminar on Africa.

Many of the people important to the making of this book are also those who helped me set it aside when I needed it most. There is no way to list them all here, but they are the folks who joined me for a run in the woods, shared a cup of coffee or pint of beer, dipped a canoe paddle in clear water, went out to hear or play music, took aim at a piñata, climbed mountains, waded in the ocean, drove ridiculous distances to watch a football game, or sat around a table to talk, laugh, and relax. Such people live (or have lived) in Accra, Albuquerque, Bloomington, Canton, Charlottesville, Lincoln, Longmont, Memphis, Minneapolis–St. Paul, New York, Saint Louis, Seattle, Tacoma, Washington, D.C., Wausau, and Winston Salem. I have leaned especially hard on members of my family, who have bridged geographical distance to extend tremendous support and ease the burdens of my work. My parents, Ron and Mary, handed me the world and my brother, Brendan, has long helped me explore it. George, Peg, Josh, Lynn, Bridget, and Jenn welcomed me with open arms and have been kind enough to let me be at the front of their family pictures. Pod Twelve might sound like an odd name for a group of family members, but they are as true as any other. At the center of all of this stands Amanda, whose boundless love, endless enthusiasm, and unfailing spirit have given me immeasurable joy and made me a better person. She has shared in, at times endured, this project in its entirety. Much of it, like the rest of me, is hers.

My last words of thanks are especially important. While my early experiences with African history and highlife music made me dream about the prospects of writing such a book, I was woefully unprepared to do so until I came under the tutelage of John Hanson. During my many years in Bloomington, John saw things in me long before I did, and his guidance, as much as anything, led me to where I am today. He opened countless doors, taught me much of what I know about being a historian, and, perhaps unknowingly, embodied every single quality that made me ever want to become a college professor. Over the last few years, he has personified other attributes, such as courage and perseverance, in ways that defy description. It is with great admiration and gratitude that I dedicate this book to him.

Ethnomusicology
Multimedia Series Preface

Each of the audio, video, or still image media examples listed below is associated with specific passages in this book, and each example has been assigned a unique persistent uniform resource identifier, or PURL. The PURL points to the location of a specific audio, video, or still image media example on the Ethnomusicology Multimedia website, accessible at www.ethnomultimedia.org. Within the running text of the book, a "PURL number" in parentheses functions like a citation and immediately follows the text to which it refers, e.g., (PURL 3.1). The numbers following the word "PURL" relate to the chapter in which the media example is found, and the number of PURLs contained in that chapter. For example, PURL 3.1 refers to the first media example found in chapter three; PURL 3.2 refers to the second media example found in chapter three, and so on.

There are two ways to access and playback a specific audio, video, or still image media example. When readers enter into a web browser the full address of the PURL associated with a specific media example, they will be taken to a web page containing that media example as well as a playlist of all of the media examples related to this book. Information about the book and the author is also available through this web page. Once readers have navigated to the Ethnomusicology Multimedia website they may also access media examples by entering into the "Media Segment ID" search field the unique six-digit PURL identifier located at the end of the full PURL address. Readers will be required to electronically sign an end-users license agreement (EULA) the first time they attempt to access a media example on the Ethnomusicology Multimedia Project website.

PURL LIST

PURL 0.1. *"Betu Me Ho Awow"* (Come and keep me warm). Source: Professional Uhuru Dance Band. http://purl.dlib.indiana.edu/iudl/em/Plageman/910140

PURL 0.2. *"Medzi Me Sigya"* (I prefer to be a bachelor). Source: Professional Uhuru Dance Band. http://purl.dlib.indiana.edu/iudl/em/Plageman/910144

PURL 0.3. *"Alome"* (Death will come in your sleep). Source: Ramblers Dance Band. http://purl.dlib.indiana.edu/iudl/em/Plageman/910137

PURL 0.4. *"Ama Bonsu"* [a woman's name]. Source: Ramblers Dance Band. http://purl.dlib.indiana.edu/iudl/em/Plageman/910155

PURL 0.5. "Knock on Wood." Source: Ramblers Dance Band. http://purl.dlib.indiana.edu/iudl/em/Plageman/910141

PURL 0.6. *"Awusa Dzi Mi"* (I am an orphan). Source: Ramblers Dance Band. http://purl.dlib.indiana.edu/iudl/em/Plageman/910139

PURL 1.1. *"Homowo Ese"* (Homowo is here). Source: Osu Selected Union. http://purl.dlib.indiana.edu/iudl/em/Plageman/910143

PURL 1.2. *"Nkyrinna"* (This generation). Source: B. E. Sackey Band. http://purl.dlib.indiana.edu/iudl/em/Plageman/910148

PURL 2.1. "The Surviving Members of the Excelsior Orchestra." Source: Bookor African Popular Musical Archives Foundation. http://purl.dlib.indiana.edu/iudl/em/Plageman/910097

PURL 2.2. "Dance Program for the Cape Coast Social and Literary Club Ball." Source: photograph by the author. http://purl.dlib.indiana.edu/iudl/em/Plageman/910106

PURL 2.3. *"Nana Kwesi Wade Kwahu"* (Nana Kwesi what have you done for me). Source: Mexico Rhythm Band. http://purl.dlib.indiana.edu/iudl/em/Plageman/910157

PURL 2.4. "The Cape Coast Light Orchestra (Sugar Babies) in Enugu, Nigeria, 1937." Source: Bookor African Popular Musical Archives Foundation. http://purl.dlib.indiana.edu/iudl/em/Plageman/910099

PURL 3.1. *"Medzi Medzi"* (I will enjoy). Source: courtesy of E. T. Mensah and the Tempos Dance Band. http://purl.dlib.indiana.edu/iudl/em/Plageman/910149

PURL 3.2. *"Essie Attah"* [a woman's name]. Source: The Red Spots. http://purl.dlib.indiana.edu/iudl/em/Plageman/910152

PURL 3.3. "The Rhythm Aces onstage, 1950s." Source: Isaac Hudson Bruce Vanderpuije, Deo Gratias Studio, Accra. http://purl.dlib.indiana.edu/iudl/em/Plageman/910100

PURL 3.4. "Members of Accra's Rhythm and Sounds Dancing School before an evening out on the town, 1950s." Source: Margaret Acolatse. http://purl.dlib.indiana.edu/iudl/em/Plageman/910101

PURL 3.5. "205." Source: E. T. Mensah and the Tempos Dance Band. http://purl.dlib.indiana.edu/iudl/em/Plageman/910153

PURL 3.6. *"Odo Anigyina"* (Love sickness). Source: E. T. Mensah and the Tempos Dance Band. http://purl.dlib.indiana.edu/iudl/em/Plageman/910138

PURL 3.7. *"Medaho Mao"* (I am there for you). Source: King Bruce and the Black Beats. http://purl.dlib.indiana.edu/iudl/em/Plageman/910154

PURL 3.8. "Auntie Christie" [a woman's name]. Source: Ramblers Dance Band. http://purl.dlib.indiana.edu/iudl/em/Plageman/910150

PURL 3.9. *"Agodzi"* (Money). Source: King Bruce and the Black Beats. http://purl.dlib.indiana.edu/iudl/em/Plageman/910146

PURL 3.10. *"Misumo Bo Tamo She"* (I love you like Sugarcane). Source: King Bruce and the Black Beats. http://purl.dlib.indiana.edu/iudl/em/Plageman/910159

PURL 3.11. *"Enya Wo Do Fo"* (You have got your lover). Source: King Bruce and the Black Beats. http://purl.dlib.indiana.edu/iudl/em/Plageman/910156

PURL 4.1. "Young people outside of an Accra nightclub, early 1950s." Source: Ghana Information Services. http://purl.dlib.indiana.edu/iudl/em/Plageman/910102

PURL 4.2. "Ghana Freedom Highlife." Source: E. T. Mensah and the Tempos Dance Band. http://purl.dlib.indiana.edu/iudl/em/Plageman/910142

PURL 4.3. "Finalists and winner (seated, middle) of the 1959 'Miss Ghana' pageant." Source: Ghana Information Services. http://purl.dlib.indiana.edu/iudl/em/Plageman/910103

PURL 4.4. *"Agbadza"* [an Ewe recreational music]. Source: Professional Uhuru Dance Band. http://purl.dlib.indiana.edu/iudl/em/Plageman/910145

PURL 5.1. "Julie Okine and Agnes Ayitey perform onstage with the Tempos, 1950s." Source: Isaac Hudson Bruce Vanderpuije, Deo Gratias Studio, Accra. http://purl.dlib.indiana.edu/iudl/em/Plageman/910104

PURL 5.2. "The Red Spots perform at the 1959 National Dance Band Competition in Accra." Source: Ghana Information Services. http://purl.dlib.indiana.edu/iudl/em/Plageman/910105

PURL 5.3. *"Weeya Weya"* [a prostitute] Source: E. T. Mensah and the Tempos Dance Band. http://purl.dlib.indiana.edu/iudl/em/Plageman/910151

PURL 5.4. *"Ewuraba Artificial"* (Artificial Lady). Source: Ramblers Dance Band. http://purl.dlib.indiana.edu/iudl/em/Plageman/910134

PURL 5.5. *"Afotusɛm"* (Advice). Source: Ramblers Dance Band. http://purl.dlib.indiana.edu/iudl/em/Plageman/910158

PURL 5.6. *"Nkatie"* (Groundnuts). Source: E. T. Mensah and the Tempos Dance Band. http://purl.dlib.indiana.edu/iudl/em/Plageman/910136

PURL 6.1. "The Remnants of the Seaview hotel and nightclub, June 2011." Source: Photograph by the author. http://purl.dlib.indiana.edu/iudl/em/Plageman/910095

PURL 6.2. "Members of MUSIGA march through Accra, May 21, 1979." Source: Bookor African Popular Music Archives Foundation. http://purl.dlib.indiana.edu/iudl/em/Plageman/910098

Introduction: The Historical Significance of Urban Ghana's Saturday Nights

Everybody likes Saturday night, at least here in Ghana.

—*DAILY GRAPHIC*, January 31, 1959

There used to be a song, "Everybody Likes Saturday Night."
It was one of the very early highlife songs. In fact, it was
one of the very popular songs of the time.

—KWADWO DONKOH, September 16, 2005

Shortly after the sun set on March 2, 1957, men and women throughout the West African colony of the Gold Coast changed into a set of fashionable clothes, left their homes, and met up with their friends for an evening out on the town. After all, it was a Saturday night. At roughly eight o' clock, cities throughout the colony came alive with the sounds of dance band highlife, the urban Gold Coast's most prominent form of popular music. For the next five to six hours, eager crowds made their way to a nearby nightclub, bar, hotel, or community center, where they claimed a table, purchased refreshments, and reveled in the sounds of one of their favorite dance bands. Patrons of various ages, occupations, and ethnicities spent parts of the evening engrossed in conversation or relaxing with a drink in hand, but nearly everyone spent as much time as possible on the dance floor, where they moved, either alone or with a partner, to the band's unique blend of local rhythms, jazz influences, ballroom standards, and calypso flair.

Yet this was no ordinary Saturday night. In a few short days, at midnight on March 6, the Gold Coast would become Ghana, sub-Saharan Africa's first European colony to gain political sovereignty and national independence. Since this was the last weekend evening before that monumental transfer, the assembled audiences were particularly large and especially jubilant. For those lucky enough to get inside their venue of choice, the palpable energy made it easy to forget that tables were hard to come

FIGURE 0.1. Men and women enjoy a Saturday night of music and dancing at the Weekend-in-Havana nightclub, Accra, 1957. *Photo courtesy of Ghana Information Services Department Photograph Library.*

by or that the dance floor was a bit too crowded to really showcase one's well-rehearsed moves. As nightclubs filled to capacity and overwhelmed doormen brought admission queues to a standstill, the fanfare spilled out into the street, where opportunistic men and women outlined a makeshift dance floor, found a partner, and frolicked to their satisfaction. Through-out the Gold Coast, from Accra to Cape Coast, Takoradi to Tamale, and Keta to Kumasi, it was a Saturday night to remember (see Figure 0.1).[1]

Fifty years later, the music, activities, and memories of that Saturday night experienced a rebirth of sorts. In March 2007, Ghanaians gathered together to commemorate their fiftieth anniversary of national independence. Throughout the month, the government sponsored an impressive lineup of events, including lectures, festivals, television specials, sporting events, parades, fashion shows, and musical concerts, which memorialized the country's inception, showcased past and present achievements, and championed the broader arena of "African excellence." And though dance band highlife had nearly disappeared from Ghana's contemporary musical scene, the scheduled fanfare catapulted the style back into a momentary position of prominence. Highlife made notable appearances in the anniversary's month-long National Brass Band Competition, the Miss Ghana@50 Gala Ball, the President's Show (an entertainment gala held at the Kwame Nkrumah Mausoleum), and the "From Highlife to Hiplife" concert, a twelve-hour extravaganza that celebrated the nation's musical heritage and honored its most prominent artists. For those too young to remember the Saturday nights of old, the music's resurgence may have seemed somewhat overstated, dramatically nostalgic, or even a bit odd. But few seemed to question the celebrations' patriotic insistence that highlife was an authentically Ghanaian music that had allowed earlier generations to set aside their differences, foster a cooperative spirit, and pull together as a nation.[2]

This book, like the 2007 anniversary celebrations, engages the history, significance, and meaning of dance band highlife and, to a significant extent, the broader realm of Ghanaian popular music. Highlife was a vital part of urban life from 1890 to 1970—the time frame that witnessed the music's emergence and gradual decline—and it deserves inclusion within the standard narrative of Ghana's recent past. At the same time, the music cannot be simply inserted into a nationalist storyline that emphasizes countrywide cooperation and collective harmony. Throughout the colonial and immediate postcolonial periods, highlife was a highly contested realm. While many men and women used the music as a means to relax, have fun, and enjoy an evening out on the town, many others employed it to mediate relationships, articulate understandings of similarity and difference, and generate consensus and conflict with those around them. Like its popular musical counterparts in other parts of Africa, highlife was a medium in which participants, patrons, and performers experienced personal and public transformations fundamental to their daily lives.[3] As a result, the music provides us with unique insights not into how urban Ghanaians came together, but into how they negotiated the diverse array of historical transformations that marked the late nineteenth and twentieth centuries.[4]

The following pages capture the relationship between urban Ghana's popular music scene and the larger domain of social history by taking a hard look at "Saturday Nights," the time—both real and figurative—when musicians picked up their instruments and enthusiastic audiences left their homes and jobs to relax, socialize, and dance.[5] For generations of urban Ghanaians, Saturday Night was an exciting occasion. It was the highlight of the week: a moment that offered reprieve from more burdensome tasks, the thrill of novel discovery, and the opportunity to meet new acquaintances or catch up with old friends. A Saturday Night spent among

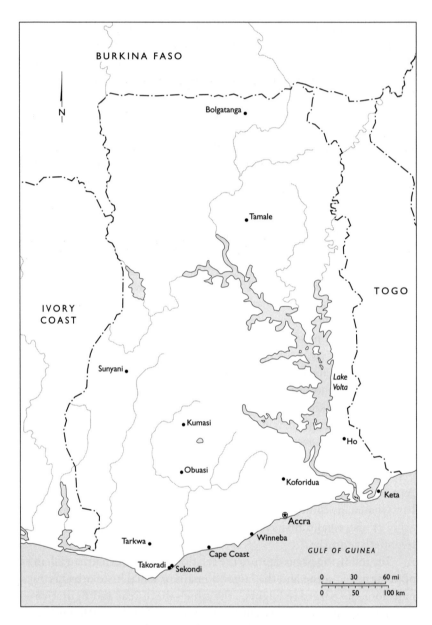

MAP 0.1. Contemporary Ghana. *Produced by Bill Nelson.*

highlife's sights and sounds was particularly electrifying. Few places were as current, fashionable, or memorable as those that featured the music into the early hours of the morning. As Felicia Kudiah explained, highlife also attracted large and consistent crowds because "the music mattered."[6] Over the course of my research, I came to learn that highlife, as well as the broader domain of Saturday Nights, mattered because they accorded participants, patrons, and band members much more than opportunities for enjoyment and fun. When men and women left their homes for an evening of music and dance, they did so not to escape the realities that marked the remainder of the week, but in order to address them, unmake them, and reconfigure them in ways they best saw fit.

In many ways, dance band highlife's history as a source of conflict and medium of social change is part of a larger story about the dynamics of urban life in colonial and early postcolonial Ghana. Throughout the period examined in this book, the country, and the African continent more broadly, witnessed an impressive wave of urbanization. Actual rates of urban growth varied considerably, but many African cities that had populations in the tens of thousands in 1900 counted their residents in the hundreds of thousands fifty or sixty years later. Much of this increase was the result of rural–urban migration, in which young men and women left their home communities in search of new economic, educational, and personal prospects. From 1920 to 1960, migration fueled a continent-wide demographic shift, raising the percentage of Africans who lived in cities from 4.8 to 14.2 percent. In Ghana, these migrants usually made their way to Accra, Kumasi, or Sekondi-Takoradi as well as smaller towns such as Tarkwa, Obuasi, Koforidua, and Cape Coast. Accra, the capital city and economic center of both the colonial Gold Coast and independent Ghana, witnessed particularly explosive growth over this same period, when its population increased from 38,049 to 337,828 residents (see Map 0.1).[7]

Unsurprisingly, this demographic expansion had considerable ramifications for the social, economic, and political make-up of Ghana's principal towns. Throughout the twentieth century, cities like Accra, Kumasi, and Sekondi-Takoradi became important loci of administrative control. During the period of British rule, they housed the offices of colonial authorities, served as depots for soldiers and police, and were home to courtrooms, government buildings, and headquarters of various state agencies. At independence, the new Ghanaian government, led by Kwame Nkrumah's Convention People's Party (CPP), employed these and newly built structures as concentrated centers of the nascent state's power. At the same time, Accra and other towns continued to be places where elders, chiefs, and traditional authorities sought to levy their own measure of control over particular spaces and populations. Since many Ghanaian cities had well-established histories prior to the initiation of British colonialism and national independence, they featured preexisting social and political hierarchies that continued to operate both in accordance with and against the wishes of the state.[8]

Of course, political authorities were not the only ones who shaped Africa's rapidly growing urban areas. The ongoing act of what Frederick Cooper notably called the "struggle for the city" involved individuals of remarkably diverse backgrounds, ages, education, and occupation. This was particularly true in Ghana, where city residents rarely experienced the highly coercive measures of segregation, pass laws, and forced removals common in the settler colonies of eastern and southern Africa.[9] In fact, most men and women regarded Ghanaian towns as places where they could exercise new levels of individual freedom, social mobility, and economic accumulation. Cities, particularly those along the coast, next to railroads, or proximate to mineral reserves, offered opportunities in wage labor as well as the services that facilitated it. They also offered access to schooling and, for successful graduates, white-collar positions with attractive pay.[10] For the migrants who pursued these prospects, cities were simultaneously places of new social formulation and modes of interaction. Separated from lineage structures and free from elders' control, they fashioned new social networks based on shared experiences, common aspirations, or mutual benefit. Oftentimes, they created and recreated these communities around new forms of leisure and popular culture. Popular music and theater, games and sports, reading and debate, stylish dress, and social drinking were all activities that allowed urban residents to engage in fun and gaiety, articulate emergent forms of consciousness, and take part in larger struggles over space, resources, and the allocation of power.[11] In Ghanaian towns, one major source of merriment was dance band highlife, a music that attracted several groups of people. As these various patrons employed the music to articulate distinct, and often different, forms of community, highlife became a central force in cities' wider trajectories of social change.

GENDER, GENERATION, AND POWER IN URBAN GHANA

The dynamics of urban Ghana's popular musical scene varied considerably from 1890 to 1970, but Ghanaian men and women generally approached it as a place in which they could engage three vital, and closely intertwined, components of differentiation. The first was gender: the socially constructed, and thereby fluid, ideas about the roles, behaviors, and actions of men and women. While Western communities often perceive gender as the set of characteristics that distinguish men from women, communities in late-nineteenth- and early-twentieth-century Ghana saw gender as a means of situating men and women into smaller, and much more specific, categories. Most Ghanaian communities recognized a complex web of masculinities and femininities that governed relationships among and between men and women and placed individuals within a hierarchical system of rank and privilege. Among the Akan, the pinnacle gendered position belonged to senior men (*mmpanyinfoɔ*) and women (*mmerewa*), titles reserved exclusively for highly respected individuals who had successfully navigated the life-cycle, managed familial affairs, and retained healthy relationships with the other members of their *abusua* (matrilineage). These *mmpanyinfoɔ* and *mmerewa* did not hold institutionalized positions of leadership similar to chiefs (*ahene*) and affiliated officials, but they did wield moral authority in local affairs.[12] The *mmpanyinfoɔ*, moreover, claimed status as patriarchal figures and worked alongside chiefs to regulate the activities of local men as well as women.

Although the "status of elderhood [was] the desired goal of all" men and women, most upheld different, and less-privileged, notions of masculinity and femininity. The vast majority of older people claimed status as *mmarima* (adult men) and *mmaa* (adult women): people who had married, accumulated property, borne children, and upheld a particular set of gendered expectations. As Stephan Miescher demonstrates, an adult man was expected to provide for his wife, look after and discipline his children, and fulfill obligations toward his *abusua*. Those who successfully met these responsibilities through hard work and conscientious behavior gained recognition and eligibility as possible *mmpanyinfoɔ* in their *abusua* and wider community. Adult women, meanwhile, were expected to conceive and raise their children, manage domestic affairs, and pursue their own means of economic accumulation. Although adult men and women remained subject to the directives of the *mmpanyinfoɔ* and *mmerewa*, they exercised considerable control over the actions of younger members of the lineage and, to a certain degree, the community at large. Young men (*mmeranteɛ*) and young women (*mmabawa*)—"junior" people who were no longer children (*mmofra*), but had not married or started their own households—remained subject to the demands of parents and lineage elders, who exploited their labor, oversaw their daily activities, and insisted that they emulate basic expectations surrounding male and female behavior.[13] Since most *mmerantee* and *mmabawa* eventually gained recognition as *mmarima* and *mmaa* as they progressed through the life-cycle, this system of gendered relations enjoyed relative stability throughout the southern and central regions of the Gold Coast.

Importantly, these understandings of gender also worked, alongside the axes of age, occupation, wealth, and lineage, to uphold a community's basic social organization and hierarchical structure. Throughout the period examined in this book, parents, elders, and traditional authorities continued to endorse the masculinities and femininities outlined above in order to preserve their hold over younger generations of men and women. By the early twentieth century, however, their efforts met considerable challenges, particularly in Ghana's rapidly growing towns. In part, the gendered status quo came under duress at the hands of the British colonial government and independent Ghanaian state. In the late nineteenth and early twentieth centuries, British officials, missionaries, and schoolteachers made expansive efforts to expose Gold Coast men and women to new gendered models that upheld the basic tenets of European "civilization." Schools, workplaces, churches, and courtrooms were places where individuals associated with colonialism attempted to instill new values, refashion relationships and family structures, and promote gendered ideals such as Christian monogamy, female domesticity, and a male ethic of responsible industrial labor. In many cases, these efforts targeted communities' young men and women; people who might be willing to trade their subordinate position for one of advantage and promise within the new social order that the colonial state hoped to erect.[14]

The state promotion of specific gendered models was not, however, a distinctly colonial phenomenon. In the period following Ghana's independence, Kwame Nkrumah's CPP government attempted to outline and enforce its own set of expectations on Ghanaian men and women. It asked them to embrace hard work—in either their occupational or domestic spheres—and to commit themselves to official plans of economic development and modernization. Although it implemented these efforts as part of its larger efforts at nation-building, the CPP also hoped to transform young people into new gendered actors so that they would comply with rather than challenge its expanding political control.[15]

Challenges to Ghana's gendered landscape also came from below. As family, local, and governmental authorities promoted understandings of masculinity and femininity that befit their own interests, ordinary people upheld and undermined them in a variety of ways. Young men and women, in particular, attempted to manipulate their community's plurality of genders in ways that could grant them greater opportunities for personal autonomy and material accumulation. This was especially true of the many migrants who flocked to Accra and other towns. Once free of the confines of kinship and community expectations, these individuals took part in formerly forbidden practices that shocked elders, chiefs, and government officials. They embraced individualism, purchased imported material items, openly initiated nonmarital sexual relationships, favored new forms of dress, and engaged in acts—such as social drinking—that were previously reserved for elders. These actions sparked considerable outcry among authorities concerned with gendered "chaos" and moral "crisis," but growing numbers of young men and women began to uphold them as well-plotted and valid efforts to navigate a rapidly changing world.[16]

In many ways, the gendered contestations that gripped Ghanaian towns also revolved around shifting ideas about age and generation. Generally speaking, Ghanaian societies, similar to those in Africa more broadly, were gerontocracies that honored age, valued experience, and empowered elders at the expense of youth. Many Ghanaian communities were also sites of ongoing intergenerational conflict. Throughout the late nineteenth and early twentieth centuries, the boundaries that separated youth from adulthood were a source of considerable tension and negotiation. Since youth was a social category of people marked by their lack of maturity and incomplete personal development rather than biological age, it was a life stage that had no clear-cut or consistent end. Lineage and community elders insisted that *mmerantɛ* and *mmabawa* became adults only when they deemed them ready for the challenges of independent work and responsibilities of marriage. Individuals who disobeyed instructions and violated social and gendered norms remained unable to marry, accumulate land or property, or participate in community affairs into their late twenties and thirties. Over the course of the twentieth century, however, growing numbers of compliant young men began to argue that their maturation, not just that of their "irresponsible" peers, was being unnecessarily and unjustifiably delayed. This was especially true in urban areas, where young people became consistent targets for officials worried about the preservation of their own authority. At different points in time, chiefs, colonial officials, and members of the CPP-led Ghanaian government all attempted to curb various aspects of a perpetual youth "problem"—including wayward behaviors, juvenile delinquency, and eroding discipline—by controlling young urbanites' actions and guiding their development into proper adults.[17]

Young men and women resented efforts to stymie their ascendancy out of what they perceived to be an ever-lengthening period of subordination. Unconvinced that elders, chiefs, and state officials could control their maturation, many set out to prove that their ever-changing, and often unprecedented, experiences sufficiently prepared them for life as full adults and citizens. In many towns, in Ghana and elsewhere, brazen young male and female migrants took advantage of the changing cash economy. They used the income from their wage labor or illicit work to purchase property and material items, initiate romantic relationships and marry, and start their own households without the assistance of family or lineage members. Such acts, they insisted, demonstrated that they were not the disadvantaged, vulnerable, or marginal persons that authorities perceived them to be. Young men proved especially vigilant in their efforts to shun the trappings of youth. In fact, the "young men's challenge" that erupted throughout the Gold Coast from the 1930s to the 1950s demonstrates that many so-called junior persons had become convinced that their economic prosperity and burgeoning education entitled them to elevated positions within local hierarchies of age, gender, and status.[18]

To a large degree, these contestations over the intertwined axes of gender and generation were also struggles about the changing nature of social and political power in urban settings. By "power," I refer not simply to the disciplinary force monopolized by coercive or governmental institutions, but to a culturally constructed resource that is available to large numbers of a particular community. I define "power" as the ability to produce change within a physical and human environment and, like others who have engaged Foucault's concepts, approach it as an attribute that is grounded in social relations and forms of action.[19] While Ghana's overall culture of power was a complex terrain comprised of both human and supernatural entities, most scholars have examined how power operated within the formal framework of governance, particularly in regards to Asante and the Akan forest states and the post-1957 independent Ghanaian state.[20] The expansive, and undoubtedly important, literature on Ghana's political history uncovers much about how the contestations between political authorities shaped the period of colonial rule, the emergence of Ghanaian nationalism, and the rise of an independent government led by Kwame Nkrumah's CPP. At the same time, it sheds relatively little light on how the ordinary men and women who actively engaged the gendered and generational contours of their urban environment also sought to shape the allocation of power outside formal political realms.[21]

Over the course of the time period addressed in this study, power became an increasingly diffuse resource in Ghana's urban areas. In the early and middle decades of the nineteenth century, most communities allocated power according to the generational and gendered structures outlined above. Power's status as a preserve of chiefs and elders often found further resonance in their ability to direct ritual activities that connected them to gods and ancestors. Male elders' monopoly on many rites and sacred objects further cemented their ability to control the actions of other men and women.[22] From the late nineteenth century onward, the transformations associated with the onset of a market economy and growing British presence upset elders' firm grip and enabled growing numbers of people to claim power via trade, wealth, and new access to once-scarce commodities of prestige. The expansion of wage-labor opportunities, especially in towns, gave young people ways to garner new experiences and gratify individual rather than communal desires.[23] Once-stable hierarchies of power also fell victim to the expanding British state. The colonial government's efforts to lay direct claim to natural resources—through a combination of legislative and military might—left the vast majority of present-day Ghana in British hands by 1902. Many of the new colonial government's early actions, including the abolition of slavery, arrest of prominent chiefs such as the *asantehene* Agyeman Prempeh I, and imposition of taxes designed to pull people into a cash economy, further convinced Gold Coasters that established hierarchies and relationships were now open to subtle, even drastic, revisions.[24]

Importantly, such transformations inspired many urban residents to view the colonial years as a time of possibility, newfound autonomy, and self-empowerment. In cities across the continent residents used various components of their changing world—material goods, forms of education, religious doctrines, avenues of work, and various forms of leisure— to access power at the expense of traditional and colonial authorities. Accra, Kumasi, and Sekondi were just a few of the cities in which established chiefs and colonial officials struggled to convincingly control populations growing in size and assertiveness.[25] Even the independent Ghanaian government, a product of demands to eradicate an illegitimate authority, had trouble managing urban populations who had come to see themselves as arbiters of social and political change. In the months following independence, the CPP faced considerable unrest from unemployed youth who publicly exclaimed that they and other Accra residents were "being despoiled by strangers."[26] In addition to demonstrating just how widely dispersed power had become in many Ghanaian cities, such protests reveal that romanticized notions of the new nation's collective consensus fail to consider important, and often tense, contestations that accompanied the transition to self-rule.

This book uses dance band highlife as a means to further understand the complex dynamics that characterized urban Ghana's fluid landscape of gender, generation, and power during the colonial and immediate postcolonial periods. It argues that the various components of highlife performance—song lyrics, dance, dress, and sociability—were mediums that a vast array of people, including migrants, youth, middle-class individuals, chiefs, colonial officials, and members of the CPP government, used to inculcate social change. In the last several decades, scholars have approached the notion of performance in a number of ways. Many frame performance as an essentially verbal art that privileges language over nonverbal messages or movements.[27] Others theorize it through a theatrical, rather than linguistic, prism. For these scholars, including Victor Turner and Erving Goffman, performance is best understood as a form of "social drama" in which individuals adopt roles rooted in the "rules and regulations" of real life.[28] This book differs from these works because it uses the concept of performance to highlight the agency, intentional strategies, and deliberate actions that musicians, patrons, and participants employed to meet nonrecreational aims. Following the frameworks offered by Johannes Fabian and Kelly Askew, I approach performance as an active process of communication and creation; a means through which individuals can construct—not merely reflect—social realities. When men and women engaged highlife, they often defied established conventions, reconfigured preexisting relationships, and produced new forms of consciousness. In the process, they initiated personal and public transformations within their urban communities, effectively using Saturday Nights to alter and impact the remainder of the week.[29]

Charting dance band highlife recreation as a contested process does more than complicate the notion that it was a national music. From a historical vantage point, it enables us to see the late nineteenth and twentieth centuries as a time of openings and closures not easily recognized in chronologies centered on colonialism and independence. On the one hand, focusing on Saturday Nights allows us to identify particular moments when otherwise marginalized groups renegotiated their subordinate status within existing hierarchies of gender, generation, and power. In the 1910s–1920s as well as the 1950s–1960s, urban youth used popular musical performance to vault themselves into new generational and gendered positions, claim an enhanced set of personal freedoms, and upset the social status quo. On the other, adopting a musical lens also demonstrates how and why these efforts to reallocate power often failed. In both the 1920s and 1960s established authorities laid claim to Saturday Nights as a way to eradicate young peoples' efforts and entrench their own influence over urban affairs. As other people, including educated men and highlife musicians, attempted to exploit the music for their own aims, they helped erect a set of hierarchical structures that remained rather durable amidst the wider transformations of the late nineteenth and twentieth centuries.

In the end, this is a book about the history of a specific genre of popular music as well as the social transformations that engulfed Ghanaian towns from 1890 to 1970. By charting the history of dance band highlife, it captures many of the sights, sounds, and settings instrumental to urban life.[30] Following city residents' Saturday Nights takes us into a number of oft-overlooked spaces of social interaction, including public squares, private venues, and commercial nightclubs. More importantly, it enables us to see how Ghana's conveniently named colonial, national, and post-colonial periods were marked by more subtle, but no less important, struggles. As generations of Ghanaians explored highlife's possibilities and limitations as a vehicle of social change, they actively attempted to shape, rather than passively experience, decades of tumultuous change and worked to create futures that were similar to and different from those that came into being.

APPROACHING GHANAIAN POPULAR MUSIC

While sitting at a table inside of the Accra Arts Centre, Kwadwo Donkoh, a prominent composer and producer, informed me that people often asked him what makes highlife music "highlife." "When I think about highlife," he explained, "I try to identify it by the rhythm."[31] His deceivingly simple statement is important because it reveals some fundamental truths about the fluid character and enduring importance of urban Ghana's Saturday Nights. At a quick glance, one could assume that the term "highlife" reflects a single, coherent musical style (i.e., "highlife music") that gained great currency throughout West Africa in the 1950s and 1960s and, more recently, in the ever-expanding world music branch of the commercial record industry.[32] In actuality, highlife is a much more slippery term. Since the term's first recorded usage in the 1920s,[33] Ghanaians have used it to refer to an ever-changing array of musical products replete with diverse instruments, melodic elements, and stylistic innovations. Today, the word "highlife" denotes a considerable range of interrelated yet distinct musical styles, including dance band highlife, guitar band highlife, brass band highlife, burgher highlife, reggae highlife, calypso highlife, gospel highlife, and hiplife, a recent incarnation that draws heavily from hip hop's influences and elements.[34] As these names suggest, the musical styles referred to as highlife can, and did, sound remarkably different from one another. Such variance has also led scholars to describe the music in a number of ways. Over the last fifty years, studies have characterized highlife as "a creative response to the modern world";[35] a neo-folk music and source of tradition;[36] an urban phenomenon;[37] a "musical hybrid resulting from the acculturative impact of . . . the colonial period";[38] and a quintessential form of African popular culture.[39] Highlife, in other words, has been a lot of things to a lot of people.

During the course of my research, I looked for additional answers to this question—"what is highlife?"—from several elderly men and women, friends, neighbors, musicians, and studio producers. I did so with the hope that their answers would explain how highlife could retain salience as a concrete musical product despite its multifaceted and ever-changing face. Although I was initially discouraged by the varied responses my inquiry invoked, I gradually came to understand and appreciate the music's open-ended, even ambiguous, quality. Musicians, in particular, suggested that highlife was not a "music" per se, but a simple rhythm that can be continuously modified, adapted, and overlain. Jerry Hansen, the leader of the well-known Ramblers Dance Band, described highlife as a basic pattern of three successive offbeats that, when repeated, provide the foundation for more complex rhythmic and melodic structures: "Originally, highlife was one basic thing. It was based on three knocks, 1–2–3; 1–2–3. This is the entire superstructure, this is the rhythm. 1–2–3; 1–2–3; nothing more. You see, it never changes. You can adapt this rhythm, turn it into so many things, but the basic form is always there."[40] Kwadwo Donkoh corroborated Hansen's description: "Highlife began as a rhythm that comes just before the first beat, 'ka, ka, ka; ka, ka, ka.' Rhythm-wise, it can be identified—any music that has this rhythm is a highlife. The rhythm marks it. . . . We usually add a variety of rhythms on top of this, but as long as you have the basic ingredient, you have highlife."[41] The assertion that highlife is little more than a distinct rhythm (perhaps akin to bossa nova or samba) uncovers how highlife dance bands could continually refashion their sound and attract such diverse audiences over the course of the twentieth century.[42]

To gain a better appreciation for highlife's eclectic nature now would be a good time to go to the accompanying website and listen to a few highlife songs. Begin with the Professional Uhuru Dance Band's "*Betu Me Ho Awow*" (Come and keep me warm) and tune your ears into how the triple offbeat rhythm discussed by Hansen and Donkoh underlines the song (PURL 0.1). You can try the same thing by listening to the band's "*Medzi Me Sigya*" (I prefer to be a bachelor) (PURL 0.2). Next, get a sense of dance bands' diverse repertoires by listening to some of the Ramblers Dance Band's regular offerings from the 1960s. To appreciate how the band fostered its own combination of local and foreign elements, listen to "*Alome*" (Death will come in your sleep) (PURL 0.3) and "*Ama Bonsu*" [a woman's name] (PURL 0.4).[43] Then check out two tunes that exemplify the Ramblers' expansive stylistic range: "Knock on Wood," a cover of Eddie Floyd's 1966 soul hit (PURL 0.5), and "*Awusa Dzi Mi*" (I am an orphan), a song that employs an unmistakable reggae beat (PURL 0.6). As you step away from these pages, give your eyes a rest, activate your ears, and allow yourself to submit to the urge to tap your foot or even get up and dance: it will bring you a bit closer to the dynamics that characterized urban Ghana's Saturday Nights.

If this attention to highlife's rhythmic platform clarifies the music's diverse quality, it also sheds light on the music's emergence and complex early history. The popular musical genre that came to be known as highlife materialized in Ghana's coastal communities during the late nineteenth and early twentieth centuries. According to John Collins, it did so as three interrelated yet distinguishable musical streams, all of which were performed by men. The first, brass band highlife, was styled on the music and instruments played by the drum and fife ensembles and marching bands associated with European missionaries, the British military, and the colonial state. By the 1920s, many communities had their own brass bands that featured horned instruments, bells, and a large bass drum. These brass bands did not simply play imported styles, but combined local and foreign musical elements in order to create novel forms centered on a triple offbeat rhythm. Such groups remained popular in many communities for decades and can, to some degree, still be found today.[44]

A second strand, guitar band highlife, emerged at the hands of sailors, dockhands, and urban wage laborers: workers who held a visible, yet marginal, presence in Ghana's coastal towns during the 1910s and 1920s. Similar to their brass band counterparts, these men employed a distinct set of imported instruments, including the guitar, banjo, accordion, and concertina, along with local drums, portable percussive instruments, and the *apremprensemna* (a large hand-piano from the Akan region) to create a new musical style called "palm wine" or guitar band music. Palm wine groups originally formed to meet the recreational needs of their constituent communities, but around 1930 a new generation of musicians such as Kwesi Pepera, Jacob Sam, and Kwaa Mensah acquired great acclaim for their innovative two-finger guitar technique, associated "mainline" and "dagomba" patterns, and use of hymnlike harmonic progressions. The most prominent of these early guitar bands was the Kumasi Trio, which made recordings with the British Zonophone Company in 1928.[45] Though numerically small, record sales of the Kumasi Trio and other guitar bands prompted further innovations in the music's stable tripartite base rhythm. In the 1930s and 1940s, a few guitar bands started to infuse short comedic skits and costumed acting into their repertoire, creating a new performance genre—the concert party theater—that flourished throughout Ghana during the 1950s and 1960s.[46]

The final stream, and primary focus of this work, was dance band highlife. Though cued in part by the above mediums as well as the popular musical exploits of wage laborers and youth, dance band highlife originated as the music of a small and affluent urban cohort. In the first few decades of the twentieth century, educated male clerks, teachers, and accountants—groups that had no real precedent in most towns— formed their own musical ensembles intentionally similar to small-scale European orchestras. In the early 1920s, these bands featured imported stringed, brass, wind, and percussive instruments and performed ballroom music, ragtime, and local rhythms for the enjoyment of rather exclusive audiences. Since these ensembles performed in private spaces for audiences of high status, communities began to use the term "highlife" to distinguish their musical offerings from those of other bands. Over time, these orchestras gained popularity outside elite circles, and by the late 1930s wide urban constituencies patronized the music on Saturday Nights. In the 1950s, an amended version of dance band highlife flourished in nightclubs and other commercialized venues, where men and women of various ages, employment, and aspirations embraced it with considerable frequency and fervor.

While highlife originated and developed within these three separate streams, its various musical forms were never static or isolated from wider cultural currents.[47] Throughout the twentieth century, musicians of each form of highlife exchanged ideas, experimented with new instruments, and willingly transgressed the lines that separated "traditional" or local musical styles from their more "modern" or international counterparts. Dance band highlife proved particularly pliable. While the dance bands of the 1920s and 1930s performed highlife alongside orchestral ballads, ballroom standards, and a few early jazz numbers, successive groups added new musical styles into their expanding repertoires. By the late 1950s, most dance bands were fluent in a diverse range of foreign genres, including swing, jazz, calypso, Afro-Caribbean rhythms, and rock 'n' roll. A few years later, many others had started to incorporate an expanded range of local rhythms and traditional musical forms into their public performances. In part, dance bands' continual efforts at experimentation stemmed from their needs to compete with one another for attention and performance opportunities. But these efforts were also a product of audiences' and authorities' demands. After all, most participants and patrons engaged highlife not as a passive medium of recreation, but as a way to promote particular agendas and actively inculcate social change.

POPULAR MUSIC AS A MEDIUM OF SOCIAL CHANGE

To better understand how dance band highlife could hold such an important position within urban Ghana's landscape of gender, generation, and power, we need to uncover its prospects and limitations as a medium of social change. We also need to confront how the events that took place on Saturday Night could spill over into and shape the other moments of the week. In the last thirty years, dance band highlife has received growing scholarly attention. A number of historians, ethnomusicologists, linguists, and anthropologists have examined the music's form, ongoing transformations, innovators, and lyrical components. With a few exceptions, this scholarship focuses much more on the music's content and messages than its performance culture, dances, venues, or associated activities. As a result, we know much more about the music itself than about the diverse body of urban residents who catapulted it into a position of recreational and cultural prominence.[48] Since, as Christopher Waterman reminds, "musics do not have selves; people do," this book moves beyond highlife's aesthetics and structures and interrogates the values, choices, and experiences that ultimately made it matter.[49]

If we extend our gaze beyond highlife and outside Ghana, the benefits of privileging popular music as a domain of human action and interaction become readily clear. In recent years, works on other parts of Africa have uncovered the intimate links that popular music shares with politics, power, and authority. Laura Fair's assertion that "pastimes and politics were not discreet categories of experience" holds true not only in Zanzibar, but in the rest of Tanzania, Angola, the Congo/Zaire, South

18   HIGHLIFE SATURDAY NIGHT

Africa, Nigeria, Zimbabwe, and Kenya.⁵⁰ The porous boundary between
musical merriment and social change is equally apparent in non-African
contexts. In the United States, popular music has long been a place where
audiences and authorities have negotiated the social aspects that are or
are not open to change. While particular musical styles, such as the blues,
jazz, and rock 'n' roll, have emerged as part of distinct subcultures, they
have also served as tools for wide groups of people to challenge existing
"boundaries of propriety, gender relations, social hierarchies, and the very
meanings of national identity."⁵¹ Similar patterns hold true in the Caribbean and Latin America, where musicians, participants, and governments
approached the many facets of popular musical performance as instruments of politics and mediums of power.⁵²

To unveil how Ghanaians employed highlife to both alter and uphold the realities of their urban confines, this book explores many of the
components—venues, lyrics, and forms of visible display—that characterized Saturday Nights. For starters, it attends to the diverse venues that
featured popular music from 1890 to 1970. Over the course of its history,
highlife music could be found in the street, open spaces on the outskirts
of town, private closed dancehalls, commercialized nightclubs, political rallies, government-sponsored community centers, and national and
international stages. Practically speaking, these musical locales mattered
because they dictated who could or could not take part in the performance. Exclusive settings, particularly those managed by middle-class
patrons or government authorities, tended to preserve existing lines of
differentiation, while their less restrictive counterparts were places where
a certain leveling could take place.⁵³ Yet location also mattered because it
helped determine who witnessed, or did not witness, particular musical
practices. The choice of musical environment was most salient for those
who hoped to use the music to alter, rather than perpetuate, existing hierarchies of age and gender. Initially, young men and women elected to
confine their musical activities to spaces that escaped the attention of parents, authorities, or public at large. They did so to maintain their ability to
have fun, make illicit statements, and partake in unsanctioned behaviors
without fear of repercussion. Over time, many looked to transform these
fleeting benefits into ones that were more consistent and permanent in nature. To legitimize these brazen behaviors as markers of acceptable practice, they had to perform them in public and much more visible realms.
These open efforts to break convention, antagonize existing authorities,
and produce social change were risky endeavors that could result in the
retrenchment, rather than revision, of the status quo.

Popular music's status as conduit of both continuity and change stems from the many performance elements it offered to those who attempted to use it for their own aims. One such tool was song lyrics. Throughout the twentieth century, dance band musicians consistently composed songs that spoke to the realities that characterized life in rapidly growing towns. They wrote songs that addressed family matters, romantic love, money and financial hardship, religious and spiritual beliefs, and conflict resolution, but they also wrote ones that reflected a range of attitudes about these topics.[54] At times, highlife lyrics attempted to undermine the authority of elders, the colonial government, and the independent state.[55] In the early decades of the twentieth century, British officials were often concerned with the supposed defamatory nature of popular musical songs, a phenomenon amplified by their need to have others translate and explain their meaning. Years later, the independent Ghanaian government also approached highlife with a cautious and, at times, censoring hand. As Kwesi Yankah's detailed analysis of Nana Ampadu and the African Brothers' 1967 song *"Ebi Te Yie"* (Some are favorably positioned) demonstrates, highlife songs sometimes offered audiences extensive commentary about social injustice, the limits of power, and the misgivings of government officials.[56] At the same time, other popular musicians wrote songs that accorded open praise to figures of authority. This practice, which was unsurprisingly encouraged by those in power, allowed musicians to claim a position of privilege vis-à-vis their urban counterparts.[57] At the same time, the meaning of specific highlife songs was rarely fixed or absolute. Oftentimes, disempowered people appropriated tunes that discussed the gendered, generational, and social fabric of Ghanaian towns in ways that enabled them, rather than musicians or authorities, to mediate the evolving terrain of urban social relations.[58]

Saturday Nights were also rich moments of visual, physical, and nonverbal display. Many men and women remembered such evenings as moments of energetic dance. Apart from its distinct rhythmic foundation, one of dance band highlife's enduring characteristics was its corresponding style of dance (also called highlife) that was performed predominantly (but not exclusively) by male and female couples. Highlife dance, like the music, was a remarkably flexible medium of self-expression.[59] The paucity of reliable sources limits our understanding of the origins of highlife dancing, but it likely emerged as a fusion of ballroom steps and local dancing movements. In the 1920s, the highlife dancing that took place in affluent circles featured male and female couples who stood face-to-face, clasped one another at the hands, hips, or shoulders,

FIGURE 0.2. A couple dancing highlife, 1963. *Photo courtesy of Ghana Information Services Department Photograph Library.*

and moved together in a simple side-to-side pattern. Despite the music's upbeat tempo, dancers employed small strides, maintained a relatively rigid posture and focused gaze, and incorporated subtle arm and torso movements into their base movements. Outside the confines of the formal ballroom, less affluent dancers unburdened with concerns about respectability practiced a more vibrant form of highlife dancing. Instead of organizing into pairs, dancers congregated together into a large circle that moved in a counterclockwise direction. As participants shuffled together to the dance's basic steps, individuals took turns moving into the vacant middle space and erupting into brief escapades of quick movements, exaggerated hip and torso rotations, and athletic skill. Despite such variations, highlife remained distinct from local styles on account of its emphasis on physical contact—whether sustained or intermittent—between male and female participants. In the 1950s and 1960s, audiences continued to dance highlife in pairs (see Figure 0.2), but they also approached it as an "open" dance that left considerable room for self-expression and creative skill.[60]

While privileging dance pays credence to participants' insistent claims that one could not really enjoy highlife without heading to the dance floor and strutting one's stuff, it also reveals that people used their bodily movements to do more than simply express delight. Dance bands frequently supplemented their highlife offerings by playing musical styles that invoked learned, and much more rigid, dancing patterns. Some of the most enduring were ballroom styles, including the waltz, quickstep, and foxtrot, which remained popular on Saturday Nights from the 1920s into the 1960s. Over the span of these decades, a large number of people upheld the ability to competently dance such forms as a means of flaunting their privileged gendered and social status. Others dismissed ballroom's restrictive air of etiquette and grace as a form of self-presentation. These people, often youth, supplemented their Saturday Nights with alternative dancing styles, such as *konkoma* and rock 'n' roll, that featured fast-paced and athletic movements. While many highlife patrons used dance as a means of expressing "sociocultural status aspiration, acceptance, or defiance," others employed it as a powerful means of courtship.[61] For junior people unable to marry on account of their subordinate gendered and generational standing, dance was a way to meet possible partners, initiate otherwise impossible romances, and experiment with adulthood. Particularly keen movers exploited dance for such personal benefits, but they also employed their bodies as a means of presenting and legitimizing public behaviors that their peers could replicate and adopt.[62]

The larger task of (re)drawing lines of inclusion and exclusion also extended into the realm of personal style, adornment, and dress. Phyllis Martin's concise statement that "clothing matters and dress is political" captures many recent scholarly assertions about the communicative power of fashion, but it also echoes men's and women's vivid recollections about what they and others wore on Saturday Nights.[63] Like their counterparts in Lagos, Luanda, Brazzaville, and Kinshasa, patrons of popular music went to great lengths to don forms of dress that conveyed their wider ambitions.[64] During the colonial period, urban residents marked their popular musical exploits with imported forms of attire and adornment that could distinguish them from others. Many people insisted that in the mid-1950s, one could walk into a nightclub and size up others in attendance simply by looking at what they wore. Middle-class and elite persons donned Western suits and formal evening gowns; workers wore

long-sleeved collared shirts and pants, and dresses, blouses, and skirts
made from imported fabrics and local *ntama* (cloth); and rabble-rousing
youth wore short-sleeved shirts, jeans or slacks, and shorter, tighter-fitting
skirts. Enigmatically, they also recalled that it was possible to wear clothes
to mask one's true age and status and gain new levels of personal freedom.
Experiments with fashion, along with the anonymity that dress could offer, provided people with unique opportunities to skirt otherwise stable
conventions, but it also allowed the state, particularly Kwame Nkrumah's
CPP government, to identify those who were not "proper Ghanaians" in
the years following independence.[65]

In examining the many elements of urban Ghana's Saturday Nights,
this book does not portray highlife recreation as a boundless arena of
agency or surefire means of enacting social change. Nor does it seek to
perpetuate the hegemony-resistance framework that underlines many
works on popular musical practice. Instead, it interrogates the music's
possibilities and limitations from 1890 to 1970 in order to understand how
urban Ghana's current landscape of gender, generation, and power is a
product of complex, multifaceted, and contentious interactions. Looking
at Saturday Nights enables us to better appreciate how rapidly growing
towns were places in which age was not unassailable, gender was far from
fixed, and state power never absolute. Importantly, it also helps us see
the nation's recent past "not as an embryo of the present," but as a period
marked by a range of struggles, unfulfilled aspirations, and moments of
considerable fun.[66]

SOURCES AND EVIDENCE

This book relies on a wide array of source materials collected in Ghana
(2002, 2003, 2005, and 2009) and the United Kingdom (2005). Over the
course of my research, I consulted a range of archival documents, newspapers, government reports, photographs, and other published materials, conducted 110 oral interviews, and collected musical recordings on
a range of media, including 7-inch 45 rpm vinyl records, cassettes, and
compact discs. Though drastically different in form, content, and perspective, each proved important to my efforts to understand the historical
significance of urban Ghana's Saturday Nights.

The bulk of the consulted written evidence consists of documents
housed in the Accra, Cape Coast, Sekondi, and Kumasi depositories
of Ghana's Public Records and Archives Administration Department
(PRAAD), as well as those available in the Public Records Office (PRO)

in London. Though ultimately productive, my initial forays into these collections proved rather fruitless and frustrating. Since archival catalogue systems—at both PRAAD and the PRO—offer few headings of obvious relevance to highlife music or Saturday Nights, I cast a rather wide net. My extensive combing of diverse files, sometimes to the bewilderment of archival staff, brought its share of disappointments (a file entitled "Gold Coast Regiment Bugle Competition, 1906," for example, focused not on music, but on a marksmanship competition), but it also led to many pleasant surprises. After some time, I began to find that documents concerned with political and social disputes offered unexpectedly rich snippets about the actions and intentions of popular musical participants. This was especially true for the colonial period, when British officials struggled to consolidate their control over Ghanaian cities. Although they had little interest in popular music itself, they spent a great deal of energy investigating and documenting the reported links between music, political protest, and social chaos. These scattered records unmistakably privileged the perspectives of colonial officials, missionaries, and the occasional chief, but they helped me understand the structures and struggles at play in urban areas. Such findings shed much more light on popular music's male participants than their female counterparts, but they, along with a few oral interviews and newspaper accounts, comprise the evidentiary base for chapter 1.

Fortunately, colonial officials were not the only keepers of written records during the period of colonial rule. By the 1920s, southern Ghana had a rather sizable population of educated, affluent urban men who formed literary and social clubs, exclusive all-male societies that had a distinct organizational structure, promoted education and self-help, and sponsored a number of social activities. These clubs also kept meticulous records. They compiled minutes of their meetings, produced reports that documented their events, and maintained regular correspondence with other organizations, influential persons, and the colonial state. Today, incomplete files of many literary and social clubs can be found in the Cape Coast and Kumasi depositories of PRAAD, but Sekondi houses a particularly rich assortment of records and correspondence for the Optimism Club, one of the colony's most active from 1925 to 1947. Although few historians have examined these sources,[67] they provide invaluable information about the practices, perspectives, and aspirations of a small but influential segment of urban Gold Coast society. Since club records were compiled by men, they give relatively little insight into the perspectives and actions of women, but they, in addition to other archival records, newspapers, and a small number of oral interviews, comprise the evidentiary base of chapter 2.

Documentary sources that address Saturday Nights and social change expand considerably for the years following the Second World War. These middle decades of the twentieth century, which are the temporal focus of chapters 3, 4 and 5, constitute a particularly well-researched period of Ghana's recent past. Over the span of a few decades, Ghanaians experienced the dissolution of British colonial rule, the movement toward and achievement of political independence, and the process of articulating and creating a new national ethos. Documents produced by state authorities and organizations, both British and Ghanaian, detail the music and musical activities of these decades, but they do so in a way that focuses on official ideals and concerns. Additional written sources, including those found in private and state-owned newspapers, periodicals, and other publications, largely echo government assertions.[68] While PRAAD houses a collection of various newspapers, I also consulted those available at the Balme Library and Institute of African Studies Library at the University of Ghana, the George Padmore Library in Accra, and the School of Oriental and African Studies Library in London.

My archival and library research produced a significant corpus of written materials, but I continually sought out additional sources that could complement their contents and provide alternative perspectives. Once I left the archives, my daily life offered constant reminders that written documents could never give me a full appreciation for the aspirations, feelings, and lived experiences of those who took part in highlife's many offerings. For portions of my research, I lived in various parts of Accra, including Osu, Legon, and Adenta. In 2005, I lived primarily in Madina, a suburban area of Accra, where I shared a home with a group of friends and became part of a neighborhood community. Most days, I left Madina and journeyed into central Accra, where I met elderly men and women, musicians, and a diverse array of musical enthusiasts. I also made a point to attend musical events to hear related popular styles, observe patrons' gestures and movements, and facilitate my efforts to consider the multifaceted process of musical performance. Lastly, I pursued, without much success, a wide range of visual, audio, and video source materials at the Ghana Broadcasting Corporation, the Graphic Corporation, TV 3, and the Gramophone and Records Museum and Research Centre of Ghana in Cape Coast.[69]

During the course of my fieldwork, I collected approximately 150 photographs of highlife musicians, nightclubs and dances, musical competitions, dancing schools, and other components of Saturday Nights. These images illuminate a great deal about popular music's performance environments, highlight the importance of dress, style, and self-presentation, and draw attention to the primacy of dance. Many appear within this book or on the accompanying website. I located most at the Information Services Department Photograph Library, a vastly underused repository connected to Ghana's Ministry of Information offices in Accra. The library's impressive collection houses the work of government-hired photographers, who may have focused their lens according to received instructions or official ideas.[70] I procured additional images from the Basel Mission Image Archive (www.bmpix.org), Bailey's African History Archive (www.baha.co.za), the Bookor African Popular Musical Archives Foundation (BAPMAF) in Accra (www.bapmaf.com), the Deo Gratias Studio in James Town, Accra, and various individuals I met in 2005 and 2009.

This book is largely a product of oral interviews. Without the insights of the musicians, patrons, and participants who shaped urban Ghana's Saturday Nights, it likely would have been impossible. It was these oral interviews, rather than documentary or visual sources, that spoke to the agency and perspectives of those who shaped the contours of popular music and social change. Though oral interviews were dismissed in the 1960s as a means of garnering unreliable information, historians of Africa have come to endorse them as a way to give voice to ordinary people as well as a means of understanding how they reconciled "the private, the personal, and the political" throughout the course of their lives.[71] When used in conjunction with other sources, oral interviews do much to enrich our historical understandings of the subjectivity that often underlines particular events and time periods. Over the course of 2005 and 2009, I conducted 110 oral interviews in Accra, Cape Coast, Sekondi-Takoradi, and other towns.[72] Each interview lasted between one and two hours, and most took place in English, Twi, or a mixture of the two. Interviews in Twi, as well as those in Ewe and Ga, were conducted with the help of Apetsi Amenumey. I recorded the bulk of these interviews and later translated and transcribed them, frequently with Apetsi's assistance.

When I arrived in Accra to commence the bulk of my research in 2005, I immediately set out to renew established contacts and to identify individuals who could discuss their experiences with highlife music, Saturday Nights, and the larger context of urban life. Locating individuals who could reliably speak about the period of highlife's prominence (the 1930s–1960s) was not an easy task. For weeks, I worked with Apetsi,

friends, and colleagues to locate elderly men and women who were willing to entertain my questions. Interviews began among a small cadre of
musical enthusiasts in Accra New Town, a residential area immediately
north of the city center. These men and women gracefully shared their
recollections, but they also directed me to friends, neighbors, and long-
lost peers who could also speak to the dynamics we discussed. With both
a car and a cell phone at our disposal, Apetsi and I were able to follow up
on these leads, move throughout the city, and eventually interview people
of various ages, ethnicities, backgrounds, and experience.

Contacting and interviewing dance band highlife musicians posed
additional challenges. Although musicians were reified as cultural pioneers and public icons throughout the 1950s and 1960s, most have found
the recent past to be far less kind. The decline of highlife and urban nightlife during the 1970s and early 1980s put many musicians out of work. In
2005, the well-known musicians of the past were advanced in age and
relatively few in number, while less prominent bandsmen carried out
lives marked by economic hardship and relative obscurity.[73] My efforts
to locate and meet highlife musicians benefited greatly from the generous
assistance of John Collins, a professor in the Music Department at the
University of Ghana, Legon, and director of BAPMAF, who has done an
enormous amount to document and promote Ghanaian popular music.

After meeting with people and building rapport over food or drink,
I often opened my interviews by asking a set of questions that had nothing to do with music. I asked men and women to tell me about their up-
bringing, their schooling, their household, their work, their marriages,
and their day-to-day lives. When our conversations turned to Saturday
Nights, people discussed music, but they also recalled old friendships
and camaraderie, their acquisition of new clothes, budding romances, the
learning of dance styles and forays on the nightclub floor, and the other
sights and sounds that colored the evening. In this way, our conversations
usually arrived at topics related to the gendered, generational, and social
concerns that enveloped popular musical recreation. To enable readers
to fully appreciate the intimate connection that men and women had,
and still have, to the Saturday Nights of old, I have attempted to use their
own voices and recollections as much as possible, especially in chapters
3, 4, and 5.

These conversations also encouraged me to pursue another source
of historical inquiry: songs and song lyrics. Oftentimes, the men and
women I spoke with enhanced our conversations by recounting their
favorite songs, singing a much-loved number, or humming a particularly

memorable tune. Amazed that such songs continued to make enduring impressions fifty years after their composition, I became convinced that I needed to further appreciate lyrics' importance. Over the course of 2005, I worked to identify, transcribe, and translate over one hundred highlife songs, particularly those that discussed the wider tensions illuminated by written and oral sources. My efforts to collect relevant songs benefited tremendously from the assistance of Francis Akotua, who spent many hours listening to whatever recordings I could get my hands on. After listening to songs, Francis and I discussed their lyrics, contemplated their meaning, and identified those that best captured the dynamics highlighted in written and oral sources. Although we ended up with over ninety songs, similar interactions with Judith Botchway, the librarian at the International Center for African Music and Dance (ICAMD) Audio Visual Library at the University of Ghana, Legon, revealed an additional seventeen. A complete listing of these songs, as well as some of the recordings I consulted, may be found in the discography at the end of this book.

After amassing this corpus of songs, I worked with members of the Department of Linguistics and Language Center at the University of Ghana to transcribe and translate each. Several months later, this lengthy, and rather tedious, endeavor gave me direct access to 115 new texts related to Saturday Nights. Although excited about this prospect, I remained wary of interpreting their contents by myself. First, these songs had been removed—both physically and temporally—from their original context. Despite my research efforts, I remained unfamiliar with the dynamics that informed their composition, made them popular, or gave them enduring meaning or significance. Second, while such songs undoubtedly contained credos, commentaries, and advice, their messages were frequently ambiguous, unclear, or open to interpretation.[74] Finally, my decision to collect such songs had stemmed from my desire to understand their continued importance to the elderly men and women I spoke with. To that end, I selected particular songs and set out to discuss their contents and significance with their original audiences and, when possible, their composers and performers. After several of these discussions, it became clear that song lyrics had not, like the other aspects of highlife recreation, been a domain of collective agreement or social harmony. Instead of passively receiving song messages, audiences had debated them, shaped them, and employed them as proof of the concerns and convictions that fueled their Saturday Nights. A few of these song lyrics appear—in part or in full—within this book or on the accompanying website. I encourage readers to examine their contents and join in on the conversations that revolved around their meanings and significance.

ORGANIZATION AND LAYOUT

The remainder of this book consists of five chapters and a brief epilogue and proceeds in a chronological as well as thematic fashion. The first two chapters place popular musical recreation at the center of the social, cultural, and political transformations that marked Ghana's colonial period. Instead of providing a comprehensive overview of the colonial years, they unveil how various urban residents, including wage laborers, urban migrants, educated elites, chiefs and elders, and British officials, approached the realm of popular musical recreation. Chapter 1, "Popular Music, Political Authority, and Social Possibilities in the Southern Gold Coast, 1890–1940" places popular music at the center of wider struggles about the social and political structure of colonial rule. Specifically, it examines how groups of young men and women used "proto-highlife" musical styles to challenge the hierarchies of race, age, and gender favored by colonial and traditional authorities. After outlining the concerns that these oft-labeled "rebellious" youth forwarded through music, it demonstrates how authorities criminalized new forms of song and dance in order to preserve and extend their own authority. Set in the same temporal period, chapter 2, "The Making of a Middle Class: Urban Social Clubs and the Evolution of Highlife Music, 1915–1940" examines how another group of urban residents, educated men, also used popular music to renegotiate their position within colonial society. These young, prosperous, and ambitious men, often called intermediaries or middle figures, created their own popular musical style—highlife—which they used to establish broader communities, interact with women, and garner power and influence. Unlike its more "dangerous" counterparts, highlife garnered approval among members of the colonial state, who provided clubs with financial, moral, and legal support. In the 1930s this middle class used highlife as a way to socialize large numbers of young men and women into its ranks, a project that expanded its social influence yet undermined its ability to control the music's future.

The remaining three chapters address the 1940s through the 1960s, the decades that spanned the late colonial period, the movement toward independence, and the first decade of self-rule under Kwame Nkrumah and the CPP. Although each tackles a different component of Saturday Nights, they collectively reconstruct how highlife musicians, audiences, and government officials employed the music for purposes that were more specific and contentious than those of national unity. Chapter 3, "The Friction on the Floor: Negotiating Nightlife in Accra, 1940–1960," documents how diverse urban groups capitalized on highlife's expanding popularity and accessibility in the period after the Second World War. In the capital city men and women gathered in dance band highlife's new setting—the urban nightclub—to negotiate the gendered, generational, and social fabric of their soon to be independent nation. Older and middle-class people used Saturday Nights to reinforce past hierarchies and ensure that the end of colonial rule did little to diminish their existing influence. Many others, especially young men and women, used such occasions to claim new levels of personal freedom that could complement and complete the impending political transfer. By reconstructing how city residents used highlife to fulfill these contrasting sets of aims, the chapter demonstrates that the end of colonial rule was a process marked by many negotiations that took place outside the official political domain.

The political climate of the independence period takes center stage in chapter 4, "'The Highlife Was Born in Ghana': Politics, Culture, and the Making of a National Music, 1950–1965." This chapter focuses on how the principal political party of the independence years, the CPP, attempted to transform highlife recreation into a "national" music and medium of collective, rather than individual, identity. Although it argues that the party relied heavily on highlife in order to translate official rhetoric about what it meant to be "Ghanaian" to local and international audiences, it demonstrates that it too approached the music in varied, inconsistent ways. In the early 1950s, the CPP first approached highlife as a medium of social and moral danger, particularly for susceptible youth. It tried, without much success, to control the music and to reform its problematic participants. Once it realized that it lacked the legitimacy to effectively regulate Saturday Nights, it reversed its stance and embraced the music as an open medium of political mobilization and nascent national cultural form. In the aftermath of Ghana's 1957 independence the CPP resumed its interventionist approach. Eager to carry out its program of nation-building and translate official ideas about culture, citizenship, and the "African Personality" into tangible forms of action, it took several actions intended to reshape how urban residents, particularly women and youth, engaged dance band highlife and spent their Saturday Nights.

Chapter 5, "'We Were the Ones Who Composed the Songs': The Promises and Pitfalls of Being a Bandsman, 1945–1970," takes a closer look at highlife's most central figures: its artists and musicians. While one could easily assume that these cultural pioneers were well positioned to control and capitalize on their musical creation, the chapter demonstrates that they were actually ensnared in a complex web of professional and personal constraints. It draws on extensive interviews, reminiscences, and stories to document the promises and pitfalls of being a musician during highlife's period of prominence. Combating the notion that bandsmen were affluent celebrities and national stars, it argues that most struggled to procure a stable income, enduring professional stature, or reputation as successful adult men. Following these artists' actions and strategies over time demonstrates that the musical spotlight was, like other arenas of Saturday Nights, full of shifting possibilities and limitations.

The book concludes with a brief epilogue that outlines dance band highlife's decline in the 1970s and 1980s and revisits its overall importance to Ghana's recent past.

Throughout the book as well as accompanying content on the Ethnomusicology Multimedia website, all song titles appear as offered on their original formats. Where necessary, grammatical changes have been made in transcriptions to clarify their content and meaning.

ONE

Popular Music, Political Authority, and Social Possibilities in the Southern Gold Coast, 1890–1940

In January 1909, W. C. Robertson, the Gold Coast's secretary for native affairs, wrote a letter to Taki Obili, Accra's recently appointed Ga *mantse*,[1] regarding two dances that had become popular among the city's young men and women. The letter insisted that the styles in question, *osibisaaba* and *ashiko,* were immoral and dangerous because they "produce[d] an excitement" that threatened the city's fragile semblance of civil and political order. Robertson urged Obili to ban these objectionable dances and to introduce severe punitive measures that would discourage their performance. Two years later, Obili rallied the city's *mantsemei* and drafted a series of bylaws that responded to the secretary's concerns. The laws, which constituted one of Obili's initial assertions of official authority, read:

1. The dances known as ASHIKO and SIBI SABA or any other dances of a similar nature are hereby suppressed, and whoever takes part or induces any other person to take part in any of the said dances shall be liable to a fine not exceeding five pounds and two sheep.
2. The ashiko and sibi saba songs or any other obscene songs are hereby suppressed, and whoever contravenes this bye-law shall be liable to a fine not exceeding five pounds and two sheep.
3. The foregoing bye-laws shall apply to the whole of the Accra Division, and all proceedings in respect of any breach of the same shall be taken in the Court of the Head Chief.[2]

Trivial as these laws may seem, they provide great insight into the social and political fabric of many Gold Coast towns. A few decades prior, in
1877, the British had claimed Accra as the capital of their nascent Crown
Colony, an act that prompted their fledgling government to transform
the long autonomous Ga polity into the principal seat of their own administrative power. For the next many years, British officials worked to
subsume city authorities', particularly chiefs' and elders', political, economic, and judicial clout. By the time of Robertson's letter, however, these
traditional authorities retained influence alongside, not simply under,
their colonial counterparts. In the decades that followed Obili's bylaws,
Accra and many other towns in the southern parts of the colony did not
simply become dominions of a dominant British state. On the contrary
they remained, in the words of John Parker, "volatile arena[s] of cultural
innovation and political competition."[3]

Though excluded from the tug-of-war taking place among chiefs and
their British counterparts, less prominent people also worked to increase
their leverage within their rapidly changing confines. One measure that
they used to participate in and shape urban areas' allocation of power
was popular musical recreation. In fact, many of the musical styles that
emerged in the years surrounding Robertson's and Obili's exchange were
ones that young men and women used to express their frustration about
their continued marginalization and lack of political voice. Such forms—
broadly referred to here as "proto-highlifes" for their fusion of local and
foreign musical elements, employment of a triple offbeat base rhythm,
and importance as forerunners to the style that will be discussed in the
next chapter—provided urban residents with a way to audibly and visibly express their concerns. As these proto-highlifes became increasingly
prevalent, both local and British authorities came to view them as serious
obstacles to their own efforts at effective governance. Their joint effort to
criminalize and eliminate proto-highlife musical practice was neither a
trivial act nor a symbolic flexing of colonial and chiefly muscle: it was a
way to expand their authority into spaces and onto populations operating
beyond their effective control.

Yet the tensions surrounding new popular musics were not simply
administrative or political in nature. For most proto-highlife propo-
nents, song and dance were ways to congregate with others of similar
age, employment, and circumstance, blow off steam, and have some fun.
In several towns, participants also approached these musical styles as
mediums that could alter their gendered and generational standing. For
many young men and women, the transformations of the early colonial

period—including urbanization, the expansion of education, and the emergence of a cash economy—offered opportunities to escape their marginal position and established junior status. Aspirant and ambitious youth who moved to cities to find work and generate an income used popular music to give meaning to their relatively novel experiences, redefine their political rights, and claim social mobility. While chiefs, elders, and disapproving onlookers quickly decried young popular musical enthusiasts as "rebellious" and "dangerous," a closer look at their musical activities uncovers their true intentions as well as their self-perception as creative agents of social change.[4]

Although the innovative proposals presented within proto-highlife recreation were eventually subsumed by established authorities such as Robertson and Obili, the confines of music and dance were important realms in which various urban residents negotiated the possibilities and limitations that marked the period of colonial rule. This chapter first reconstructs the hierarchal structures that organized Gold Coast communities in the period leading up to the establishment of British colonial rule, summarizes the importance that communities accorded to the axes of age, gender, and lineage, and charts how musical activities overwhelmingly reinforced existing lines of rank. It then outlines the aims and intentions of the early colonial state, examining how it used music to legitimize and extend its own claims to political power. From there, the chapter considers the popular musical styles that emerged in many southern towns, with particular attention to the ways in which young men and women used musical recreation to inculcate wider patterns of gendered and generational change. Finally, the chapter examines how established authorities moved to criminalize these new domains of song and dance and explains why young people remained unable to usurp their relatively marginal positions in urban contexts.

POLITICAL AND SOCIAL HIERARCHIES
IN THE SOUTHERN GOLD COAST

When the British created the Gold Coast Colony in 1874, they claimed prominence over a number of political entities and social conglomerations. Though relatively small in size, the Gold Coast encompassed numerous ethnic groups, including the Fante, Ga, Krobo, Akyem, and Akuapem, who had distinct languages, cultures, and histories. To the north lay Asante, a formidable and highly centralized kingdom that, following its origins in the mid-seventeenth century, became the region's

most dominant political and economic force. Over the course of the eigh-
teenth and nineteenth centuries, Asante expanded into a sizable empire
that exerted influence over other hinterland societies as well as those to
its south. Asante's power also enabled it to successfully repel the growing
British presence emerging along the coast, but its autonomy came to an
end in 1896, when British forces entered the capital of Kumasi, arrested
the *asantehene* (king) Agyeman Prempeh I, and declared Asante a Crown
protectorate. Five years later, the British annexed the Ashanti territory, a
move that brought it, like the areas to its south, into a period of significant
social and political change.[5]

Though distinct, the societies located under the expanding arm of
the Crown had a long history of economic and cultural exchange. An
ongoing tide of trading partnerships, political alliances, war, and geographical proximity endowed regional communities with a basic set of
shared characteristics.[6] Most, for example, were highly stratified and allocated individuals status according to a range of factors including age,
family and lineage, work or profession, wealth, spiritual power, and social
clout. These arrangements were especially apparent among the Asante,
where the position of *ɔhene* (chief), a community's pinnacle political position, was open only to a few distinct lineages that fiercely guarded their
privileged status. Below the *ɔhene* and his royal court stood commoners, slaves, and a small but influential group of bureaucrats and wealthy
traders who preserved their status through heredity and intermarriage.[7]
Among the Ewe, Fante, and Ga, each of whom lived along the southern
coast, similar hierarchies governed day-to-day affairs. Each had recognized chiefs who worked alongside lineage elders to supervise local affairs
and administer political, judicial, and economic policies.[8]

Lineages—extended family groups that were comprised of several
households and spanned generations—often worked to uphold a community's political and social structure. While they sought to ensure the
well-being of their individual members, lineages also situated them into a
gerontocratic order that honored descent, age, and life experience. As a result, families had considerable control over young men (*mmerantee*) and
women (*mmabawa*), whom they expected to abide by elders' directives
and work on behalf of their households and relatives. Over time, young
people became full-fledged adults, but they did so according to their family's circumstances, elders' wishes, and individual achievements instead
of a collective initiation or age-set promotion. In fact, young men and
women could not complete the necessary requirements for adulthood,
including marriage, employment, and accumulation of property, without

the consent and cooperation of their lineage. Most Gold Coast communities considered marriage to be a family, rather than individual, affair and went to great lengths to ensure that their young men and women had fully matured prior to their courtship and union.[9] While the length of a person's maturation varied, the general correspondence between age and status ensured that most individuals married, became adults, and achieved some mobility throughout the course of their lifetime. Outside of the lineage, however, only the most successful men and women came to hold positions of status. In Asante, these individuals (known as the *mmpanyinfoɔ* and *mmerewa*) were renowned as persons of respect and authority who had earned their distinction through a proven track record of wisdom, reputation, conflict mediation, and mastery of proverbial speech.[10]

By the time of Robertson and Obili's exchange, individuals in various towns had begun to pursue social and political mobility through additional means. A few people gained sociopolitical status through entrepreneurial risk and the successful accumulation of wealth. During the nineteenth century, an era in which Europeans looked to replace the slave trade with a more "legitimate" pattern of commerce based on the exportation of raw materials in exchange for imported manufactured goods, economic accumulation became a viable means of garnering a favorable position vis-à-vis other community members. This was especially true along the southern coast, where an emergent mercantile class employed their trade-based wealth to purchase property, acquire dependents, and garner prestige. By the late nineteenth century, a small number of individuals had begun to flaunt personal riches as a means of securing enduring positions of social status and political rank. A few male traders used their financial and material resources to take up positions as chiefs: acts that directly challenged established systems based on heredity and lineage. Others used their wealth to forge an "alternative status index" based around private accumulation, Western education, and a disdain for manual labor. These individuals—to whom we will return in much greater detail in the next chapter—claimed positions of prominence by actively embracing imported goods, developing their own strata of membership, and taking up positions as intermediaries who could bridge local and colonial structures.[11]

In the hinterland areas of Asante, structures of age and lineage proved rather durable well into the mid-nineteenth century. There, restrictions on trade left the ability to garner individual wealth as the exclusive license of the *ɔbirɛmpɔn* ("big man"; pl. *abirɛmpɔn*), a position of distinction and appeal bestowed by the state. Becoming an ɔbirɛmpɔn was a lengthy process reserved only for those who had accumulated considerable economic capital and proved consistently loyal to chiefs and political figures. Aspirant big men claimed the title over a series of years, culminating in public ceremonies marked by tremendous pageantry and elaborate displays of generosity. After their ascension, most abirɛmpɔn lived a "lifestyle that meshed well with the male ideology which underpinned gerontocracy, patriarchy, and the state," meaning that they did little to threaten the established social and political order that the asantehene and other chiefs endeavored to maintain.[12]

The hierarchical structure of Gold Coast communities found further resonance in the expectations that governed understandings of gender. Throughout the colony, communities upheld a complex web of gender identities that did not simply distinguish men from women, but governed relationships between them. In the nineteenth century, Akan societies recognized multiple notions of masculinity and femininity that worked, alongside lineage, profession, and age, to provide individuals with a sense of rank.[13] Since one's gender was fluid, individual men and women usually achieved some gendered mobility throughout the course of their lives. One accessible symbol of male status in the nineteenth century was gun ownership. Because most Gold Coast societies emphasized war as a male domain, the men who came to possess a gun and used it to demonstrate bravery and achieve military success earned status and praise from lineage and community members.[14] A more fundamental component of becoming an adult man, as well as an adult woman, was marriage. For young men, marriage was an essential step in usurping their junior status within their lineage; for women it was a means to bear children, acquire long-term security, and enhance their spiritual and economic standing.[15] Once married, men and women obtained a defined set of rights and expectations that regulated their relationships with their spouse, children, and extended family. Though married persons claimed enhanced status as adults, they remained under the control of patriarchal elders whose positions as mmpanyinfoɔ and abirɛmpɔn endowed them with a senior masculinity highly regarded in local affairs.

The above distinctions between social groups, relationships between rank and privilege, and allure of positions of distinction (particularly those of the ɔhene and the ɔbirɛmpɔn) were maintained through a closely guarded allotment of behaviors, symbols, and material items. Most Gold Coast communities mandated that particular commodities and forms of dress were the exclusive property of select persons of status and importance. As Emmanuel Akyeampong has shown, alcohol was a fluid reserved for individuals of power and wealth; so too were cash, imported manufactures, and many luxury items.[16] The correspondence between a community's established sociopolitical hierarchy and public modes of presentation and display found further resonance in the domain of musical performance. Instead of providing individuals with a means of upsetting the status quo, many forms of song, dance, and music-making were mediums in which "community values [were] displayed, remembered, and reinforced."[17] Occasional forms of music—those linked to community rites and ceremonies—were especially rigid domains that paid public recognition to chiefs, elders, and local authorities. Many of these styles, such as the Akan *kete, fɔntɔnfrɔm,* and *apirede,* the Ga *atumpan* and *obonu,* and Ewe *tumpane* and *bomba,* were the preserve of high-ranking officials, who had exclusive claim to the possession of drums, trumpets, and other instruments integral to their performance. Such styles also obligated participants to adhere to a standardized repertoire of movement, song, and observation, according them little opportunity for individual self-expression or creative output.[18]

While incidental music (informal styles affiliated with occupational tasks) and recreational music (forms of entertainment not bound to the conventions of ritual or ceremony) offered fewer restrictions, they usually catered to specific professional, gendered, or generational subsets instead of the community at large. The Asante *nnwonkorɔ* and Ga *adaawe,* for example, were musical forms that predominately catered to women, while other styles such as *aboɔfoɔ, adɛwu,* and *asafo* remained the domain of male hunters and soldiers.[19] These musical forms linked participants together by emphasizing shared experiences and collective conditions, but did little to accommodate or incorporate members of the wider community. One exception to this pattern was what J. H. Kwabena Nketia has called "popular bands": informal ensembles open to individuals of different resources, professions, and talents. Most popular bands were organized and operated by youth who used local instruments and a regional pool of rhythmic, harmonic, and melodic elements to create new musical styles, garner public attention, and voice their sentiments. These popular bands offered participants a realm of creativity, but they were not immune from local supervision or authorities' directives. Most communities allowed these bands to rehearse and perform only once they had obtained the consent of chiefs and elders; a requirement that usually ensured that they maintained, rather than challenged, established conventions.[20]

At the end of nineteenth century the dynamics outlined here—concerning social relationships, the allocation of authority, and patterns of musical performance—came under growing duress. They did so largely at the hands of an expanding, and rather ambitious, British colonial state. As it embarked on its effort to subsume existing authorities and claim control over local affairs, the colonial government did much to impact the social and political structures operating in many towns. By the beginning of the twentieth century, it had contributed, intentionally and unintentionally, to the erosion of once stable hierarchies of gender, generation, and power. One of the tools that it used to communicate and carry out its agenda was music. Unlike traditional authorities, however, the British proved unable to maintain a strict monopoly over the instruments and styles they upheld as markers of their own superiority. In fact, their musical activities provided marginalized groups with resources they used to promote an alternative agenda of sociopolitical change.

THE PRESENTATION OF BRITISH AUTHORITY
AND EARLY COLONIAL RULE

For British officials, the inauguration of the Crown Colony in 1874 was a dramatic turning point in their efforts to wield political, economic, and judicial influence over local and regional affairs. No longer encumbered with the burden of enacting treaties with individual polities, a tactic they had long employed along the West African coast, the British set out to seize political authority, impose English common law, and pursue their purported agenda of replacing the stubborn remnants of the slave trade with civilization and legitimate commerce. In 1896, a British expedition to Asante entered Kumasi, arrested the *asantehene,* and moved, through military might, to bring the region into the colony in 1901. The area north of Asante was annexed as the Northern Territories, and by 1902 the British had claimed jurisdiction over the totality of the Gold Coast. The state initiated its economic aims by exploiting the exportation of timber, palm oil, gold, and other mineral resources, an act that gave it growing control over large tracts of recently claimed land. By 1911, the colony's gold exports were valued at over £1 million, giving the government much needed revenue to create a new infrastructure of road and railroad transport. The colony's economic prospects also boomed with the rapid expansion of its cocoa industry. Although the Gold Coast exported a mere £4 worth of cocoa in 1891, twenty years later the colony exported more than £6 million of the crop. In the wake of such developments, the colonial state secured the money it needed to carry out its wider aims.[21]

Despite a string of military and economic successes, the newly erected British state often struggled to consolidate its control over social and political affairs. One of the most formidable obstacles in its expansion was established chiefs and elders. In the mind of many Crown officials, diminishing chiefs' political influence was crucial to their efforts to erect a new government that could claim oversight over local affairs. At the same time, other British officials argued that chiefs could be useful allies who could help supplement their numerically small and politically weak presence within the colony.[22] To facilitate the implementation of a new government and healthy partnership with local authorities, the government proposed the Native Jurisdiction Ordinance of 1878, a resolution that attempted to outline the boundaries of elders', chiefs', and British officials' political and judicial domains. Although the ordinance was not immediately enacted, it reflects the state's realization that military might alone could never fully cement or legitimize its newly claimed power.[23]

As British officials stationed in Accra and other towns used legislative and judicial means to expand their authority, they also set out to create a façade of dominance that could mask their weaknesses and dramatically unveil their intentions to the Gold Coast public.[24] In government minds, one of the most potent means of presenting state power was musical performance. The colonial administration's confidence in music stemmed from a number of factors. In the Gold Coast and elsewhere, officials opined that since Africans were "obsessed" with song and dance, the state could use them to capture local imaginations and effectively communicate its intentions. Others noted that since local musical styles were little more than raucous rhythms or heathen noise, people would naturally lean toward European forms that were superior in composition and character. In the Gold Coast, colonial officials also insisted that music had a proven history as a means of imposing British might. During the early and middle decades of the nineteenth century, colonial armed forces employed music to announce their presence, intimidate opponents, and eventually "pacify" several communities. Following its formal intrusion into the Gold Coast in 1821, the Crown used drum and fife bands—often comprised of African recruits—to organize regiments, provide messages during battle, and maintain morale. In the aftermath of military conquest, such ensembles, which played military marches, patriotic tunes, and European melodies, became a central means of imparting social values, including what Terence Ranger has insightfully called "the necessities of industrial time," on subjected populations.[25]

Over time, colonial bands comprised of African conscripts, including the Gold Coast Regimental Band, Gold Coast Police Band, Northern Territories Constabulary Band, and smaller ensembles organized at the local level, most clearly made their mark on special occasions established and observed by the new state. Official holidays such as Armistice Day, Empire Day, and the King's Birthday were certainly important moments for the British to honor their connection to the metropole, but they were also opportunities to convince subjected people that they were now part of a larger empire. For the first several decades of the twentieth century, the secretary for native affairs emphasized such occasions by composing day-long programs intended to display the dignity, importance, and strength of the colonial state. In the weeks leading up to such events, his office provided regional administrators with three-to-four-page circulars that outlined an exhaustive schedule of events, lists of possible attendants, and schematic maps that spatially separated spectators, participants, and guests of honor. Empire Day was a particularly festive occasion. On May 24 of each year, the residents of Accra, Kumasi, and other principal towns gathered to watch an assortment of parades, athletic competitions, police and military marches, demonstrations by Boy Scouts and Girl Guides, and musical activities honoring the British Empire. Most Empire Day activities were created in order to attract and impress Gold Coast youth. In 1915, the secretary asked the colony's school headmasters to celebrate the occasion by directing their students to write essays on the topic of "obedience." In subsequent years, young people spent Empire Day watching military bands perform regimental pieces and British anthems such as "God Save the Queen." When coupled with inspections of school uniforms, the giving of public addresses, and the hoisting of the Union Jack, such events made clear statements about the aspirations and aims of colonial rule.[26]

Though less extravagant than public holidays and ceremonies, government-sponsored social events also worked to expand the power and prestige of the nascent British government. For colonial agents, after-work gatherings were opportunities to relax, socialize, and cement their position as a new ruling class. One of the most common engagements was the garden party, an outdoor function held at a private residence, commercial structure, or public institution. Though initiated as segregated affairs that allowed European residents to convene, relax, and converse in an intimate environment, the gradual inclusion of local guests, principally chiefs and elders, made garden parties rather blunt showcases of colonialism's new pecking order. British residents, who attended such functions in formal suits or military uniforms, often belittled the "uncivilized" attire that Gold Coast guests donned to such events. Music and dance provided further avenues of purported colonial superiority. Most garden parties featured ballroom musical styles that were familiar to Europeans, but made their Gold Coast counterparts, who rarely had the requisite knowledge needed correctly dance such numbers, into passive spectators. Africans' marginalization found further resonance amidst an almost continual shortage of chairs, food, and drink; commodities that were reserved first and foremost for British attendants and distinguished guests of honor. As these participants sat at tables and dined on imported delicacies, the shortchanged parties, who often included elders and members of chiefly retinues, had "to sit apart on the grass" and observe the festivities from a distance.[27]

Members of the British government also incorporated recreation into their arsenal of invented traditions and self-presentation.[28] In the mind of many officials, sports such as tennis and golf were essential means of guaranteeing one's mental and physical well-being. More importantly, however, such activities allowed participants to display their status as proper British gentlemen. In the Gold Coast and elsewhere, the axis of gender, along with those of race and class, was a fundamental pillar of British identity and supposed superiority over colonized peoples.[29] In Accra and other towns, British gentlemen celebrated their prowess within private clubs: organizations that sponsored sporting activities, formal banquets, musical performances, and other decidedly masculine entertainments. Armed with the moral and financial support of the colonial government, clubs such as Sekondi's Central Club and European Club, Accra's Gold Coast Dinner Club and Accra Club, the Kumasi European Club, and the Cape Coast Hill Club, endeavored to distinguish their European members from local men, women, and gendered models. Most refused to admit African men into their fold. In 1933, members of the Cape Coast Hill Club repelled a proposed amendment that would have allowed prosperous Gold Coasters temporary memberships and access to club facilities. The Accra Club, meanwhile, did not admit local members until the period immediately prior to the colony's 1957 independence.[30]

From the 1910s to the 1930s, British government agents invested considerable energy in their official and unofficial self-presentations. They used recreation, ceremony, and musical events to offset the displays of chiefly power communicated in the performance of occasional musical styles such as *kete* and *apirede*. Yet Gold Coast communities did little to facilitate such efforts. Instead of passively observing state-sponsored pageants and recreational activities, men and women scrutinized their contents, selected potent symbols, and began to put them to new uses. In the early decades of the twentieth century, the residents of Accra, Kumasi, Cape Coast, and Sekondi-Takoradi joined those of other cities throughout the continent in incorporating imported cultural elements into their own novel forms of popular culture and entertainment. They created new types of music, novel forms of theater and art, and engaged in forms of dress and socialization to have fun, amplify the importance of their lived experiences, and articulate emergent forms of consciousness. Importantly, such activities also enabled them to mediate changing realities and take part in what Heather Sharkey has called colonialism's "day-to-day performance of power."[31]

Cities' status as vibrant centers of cultural production also stemmed from two important and interrelated processes: migration and the introduction of wage labor. In the early decades of the twentieth century, many junior persons—men and women who were not yet empowered through marriage or property ownership—turned to wage labor as an important means of garnering an independent income. Work gave them access to cash, enabled them to sidestep past economic restrictions, and allowed them to invest in various avenues of enjoyment and relaxation. Work was easily obtained in southern towns, where merchants and trading firms endeavored to profit from the colony's expanding exportation of natural resources and agricultural goods. Many trading houses owed their success to the agricultural boom in cocoa. By 1911, the year in which the Gold Coast became the world's leading producer of cocoa, its southern cities had become home to a booming export sector, sizable wage-labor economy, and bustling road and railroad infrastructure.[32] A decade later, large numbers of migrants from various parts of the colony and, to some degree, the surrounding West African region, had flocked to southern towns such as Cape Coast, Sekondi-Takoradi, and Accra. Others found their way to cities in the colony's interior, particularly Kumasi, Tarkwa, and Obuasi, which became centers of a bustling trade in timber, gold, and other minerals.[33]

The most common destinations for young migrants were Accra and Sekondi-Takoradi, each of which proved to be a prominent site in the emerging colonial economy. In the early 1920s, Accra was the colony's economic hub, linked by railroad to Kumasi and by road to Ouagadougou in French West Africa. These trading routes as well as the creation of jobs oriented around the export of cocoa, palm oil, rubber, and gold and other minerals transformed what had once been a modest Ga urban settlement into a relatively prosperous and ethnically diverse urban center.[34] With the building of a new harbor (opened in 1928) as well as an expanded railroad network connecting it to interior towns such as Tarkwa, Obuasi, and Kumasi, the dual cities of Sekondi-Takoradi became another promising entrepôt of economic activity. Like Accra, these adjoining towns experienced rapid growth, becoming increasingly multiethnic, youthful, and disproportionately male. From 1901 to 1931, Accra's population increased from 17,892 to 61,558, while Sekondi-Takoradi grew at a rate of over 6 percent from 1921 to 1931, giving it a population of 26,041.[35] As they moved to consolidate their control over these two important centers of trade, British officials found that they had to govern large numbers of men and women who were unmarried, detached from their home communities, and becoming relatively well-to-do. This autonomy was especially common for young men who, much more than women, were able to obtain a reliable income through unskilled labor jobs or, with education and training, skilled positions such as clerks, teachers, and civil servants.[36] In 1920, male laborers in Accra made up to two shillings per day, while the city's drivers, painters, and carpenters earned between four and five shillings. The relative abundance of work also gave most young wage-earners considerable control over their daily and weekly schedule. They could, much to the ire of government and commercial interests, move from job to job in search of a higher rate of pay or cease their employment when they had accumulated a satisfactory amount of money.[37]

In the Gold Coast and elsewhere, young people's accumulation of money had social as well as economic impacts. By working hard and accruing a sum of cash, young people found they could purchase land, obtain property, and accumulate material resources without the assistance and supervision of family and lineage elders.[38] When young migrants made these purchases on their own, they effectively sidestepped some of the conventions that marked their junior status. For particularly prosperous young people, money became a means of usurping and transforming social relations oriented along the axes of age, sex, and lineage.[39] Unsurprisingly, family and community elders viewed this development with great concern. Many, in fact, insisted that young migrants had become a formidable threat to established systems of gerontocratic privilege and sociopolitical order.

These unfolding tensions between subordinate youth and anxious authorities found further amplification in the recreational practices that many wage laborers began to favor in hours after they had finished work.

Saturday Nights were particularly vibrant occasions for leisure, social gaiety, and the consumption of alcohol. In the early decades of the twentieth century, growing numbers of young men and women gathered together in drinking circles or bars to relax, socialize, and blow off steam. Oftentimes, such establishments also featured new popular musical styles that fused local and foreign musical resources, displayed free and open forms of dance, and articulated new forms of social and class consciousness. These gregarious, and rather assertive, recreational activities quickly became sources of concern among already anxious chiefs and elders. Throughout the 1910s and 1920s, these authorities looked for ways to curb such practices and reclaim leverage over those young people who were becoming increasingly defiant and difficult to control.[40]

How these young migrants conceptualized their sojourns to southern cities, however, is less clear. While most moved to towns with the short-term objectives of securing some economic and social mobility, we know relatively little about how they understood their unprecedented arenas of work and play. Did they, as elders and chiefs adamantly claimed, hope to use such activities to undermine political structures and cultivate social chaos? Or did they endeavor to place more subtle demands on their emerging colonial world? To engage these questions, and to move beyond the charges of youthful insubordination that dominate officials' allegations, we can turn to the popular musical forms that young people inculcated in their new urban environments. These proto-highlifes reveal the aspirations and ideals that migrants came to hold during their residencies in rapidly growing towns. Importantly, they also shed light on the possibilities and limitations that marked their ability to successfully navigate the political and social climate of early colonial rule.

THE POSSIBILITIES OF PROTO-HIGHLIFE MUSICS

The young migrants discussed above found several sources of inspiration for their efforts to create new forms of popular music. One was the relatively small groups of Gold Coasters who gained access to European musics and instruments during the nineteenth century. The most dynamic, and visible, were those affiliated with the colonial military. By the mid-nineteenth century, the rank-and-file who comprised the bulk of the Gold Coast's armed forces also served as the musicians in its drum and fife units and castle bands. The membership of these ensembles was quite eclectic, including men from the interior regions of the Gold Coast and Nigeria as well as recruits from the British West Indies. The drum

FIGURE 1.1. Gold Coast: African band of the English military, December 31, 1895. © *Basel Mission Archives/Basel Mission German Branch, QW 30.011.0053.*

and fife units provided drill and ceremonial music for military purposes; castle bands were small groups that performed European recreational styles, such as waltzes, polkas, and quadrilles, in order to entertain their relatively isolated superiors.[41] Band members' access to European instruments enabled them to learn a variety of musical forms without the advantages of musical literacy, written scores, or proper notation. More importantly, their successful mastery of imported instruments, appearance in European dress, and displays of military organization set an important precedent for growing cadres of young urbanites (see Figure 1.1).[42]

Outside of the military, European instruments first found their way into the hands of another specific subset of coastal society: male individuals of mixed parentage, the children of European men and local women. In Cape Coast, long a site of European-African interaction, these individuals lived in their own residential district and upheld a unique sense of community. They, like residents of other urban quarters, formed their own *asafo* company—an all-male regiment designed to help defend the town and maintain communal order—known as the *akrampa*. Threats to the town notwithstanding, these *asafo* companies were competitive entities that marshaled instruments, flags, and other markers of identity

to engage in colorful displays of self-presentation.[43] In the second half of
the nineteenth century, the members of the *akrampa* company fused the
musical and visual elements of colonial military bands into their public
exhibitions. They started to don military uniforms, employ a European
side drum to call members, and compile ensembles closely modeled on
the drum and fife bands affiliated with the British state. The *akrampa*
retained exclusive possession of these elements until the last few decades
of the nineteenth century, when the colonial government began to supply
drums, bugles, and other instruments to the *asafo* who complied with
their directives.[44] By the turn of the century, most of Cape Coast's companies had incorporated some type of European instrumentation, dress, and
melody into their performance repertoires, meaning that once-scarce musical resources had become further diffused into the community at large.

As growing numbers of urban residents gained access to imported
instruments and European musical influences, they created their own
drum and fife and brass bands that prioritized local, rather than foreign,
rhythms and aesthetics. A paucity of reliable source materials keeps us
from knowing much about the formation of these ensembles, but they
likely found inspiration in the actions of the West Indian bandsmen who
arrived at Cape Coast Castle during the mid-nineteenth century. Though
required to play the tunes favored by British officers, these West Indian
bandsmen periodically used their imported instruments to perform calypsos and other recreational styles they had forged back in the Caribbean. Within a few decades, these localized drum and fife and brass bands
had become immensely popular sources of urban entertainment. In 1880,
the towns of Elmina and Cape Coast had several local brass bands, including the Lions Soldiers and the Edu Magicians Band, which performed
European and local musics for festivals, celebrations, and holidays.[45]

These ensembles' first prominent form of musical fusion was *adaha*
("dance here"), a vibrant combination of drum and fife music, military
mime, and local rhythmic elements. In 1900, Cape Coast had between
five and ten bands that performed *adaha*, demonstrating that it, much
like the *beni ngoma* of East Africa, quickly became a popular form of entertainment for a wide range of urban inhabitants.[46] *Adaha* found further
prominence among Cape Coast's *asafo* companies, who played the music
to attract attention, gain public favor, and enhance their public image.[47]
Outside of the confines of *asafo* performances, *adaha* became especially
popular with young men and women eager to convene, relax, and engage
with their peers away from the watchful eyes of city authorities. Their
adaha outings were primarily impromptu affairs that commenced when

a group of participants gathered at an open space on the town's outskirts. Once enough musicians had congregated together, they settled into a performance of undetermined length, prompting young men and women to display dance styles that combined local movements, European ballroom steps, and personal flair.[48] As a source of informal recreation and fun, *adaha* gave individuals relief from the regulations of their work environment, reprieve from the direct supervision of family elders, and an opportunity to demonstrate individual skill. For young people in Cape Coast and neighboring towns, the music also became a means to cultivate new communities immune from the directives of local and colonial authorities.

After taking hold in the towns dotting the coast, *adaha* began to spread into the interior, where expanding cocoa wealth created growing demands for new leisure activities. In these smaller, and often more intimate, settings, young people struggled to replicate the autonomous gatherings favored by their coastal counterparts. Since they were further removed from a sizable European presence or wide diffusion of imported goods, they found it difficult to acquire the musical instruments and attire needed to effectively form a brass band ensemble or engage in *adaha* performance. Here, *adaha* spread at the hands of older and more established men who could afford to purchase a set of imported instruments, hire instructors to train a set of local musicians, and administer musical activities. In Swedru and Koforidua, traditional authorities—the *ɔhene* and *asakwahene* ("horn-blower" or principal court musician) respectively—formed and funded brass bands in order to heighten their reputation and prestige. In other towns, wealthy merchants, farmers, and aspirant big men also formed such ensembles in order to claim status as modern day *abirɛmpɔn*.[49] As a result of these efforts, *adaha* became a form of hinterland recreation that upheld, rather than challenged, established social hierarchies. For young men and women hoping to usurp or amend such structures, the music held relatively little promise or popular appeal.

Within a few years, this patron-client model of *adaha* recreation had spread back to coastal communities, where prominent people looked to replicate the actions of their interior counterparts. In Cape Coast, William Zacheus Coker, an educated elite and candidate for the position of *tufuhene,* funded his own brass band as a way to display his wealth and garner support for his political aspirations. In the 1920s, many prominent trading firms, such as those of the Acquah and Yamoah families in Winneba, also set up brass bands and used them to signify their wealth and advertise their businesses. The *ɔhene* of Ampeni even received special visibility in the eyes of the colonial state in 1917, when the commissioner of the Central Province requested to hire his brass band for an upcoming dance in the Cape Coast Castle.[50]

As *adaha*, as well as the brass bands that played it, became overrun by established chiefs, ambitious businessmen, and other privileged individuals, young and less affluent urban residents created alternative forms that could better fulfill their recreational and social needs. Although they varied from community to community, these proto-highlife musics shared a number of important characteristics. First, they abandoned costly brass band instruments in favor of less expensive and more readily available alternatives. Like their popular band precursors, they employed a range of local drums and percussive instruments, featured complex staggered and syncopated cross-rhythms layered over a persistent triple offbeat pattern, and encouraged participant engagement through song and dance. Unlike traditional forms of music, however, these styles made use of foreign instruments, especially the guitar, accordion, harmonica, and bugle: affordable implements that had gained regional prominence among the sailors and dockworkers of West African ports.[51] Second, these proto-highlifes abandoned the military air of brass band music and replaced it with a less regimented environment that accorded participants considerable avenues for individual movement and creative self-expression. Finally, the practitioners of these forms took great strides to ensure that their musical activities were autonomous domains in which their participants could openly violate the regulations that governed most local music-making.[52] By parading such styles in informal, but public, realms such as drinking bars and the street, participants attempted to attract onlookers, draw public attention, and spark social change.

One of the most prominent of these proto-highlife forms was *osibisaaba*, a recreational style that first emerged at the hands of young men and women in the colony's Central Region. Musically, *osibisaaba* fused local percussive forms (including the *osibi* music of Fante communities) with the guitar, accordion, and harmonies popular among local seamen. By 1910, *osibisaaba* had gained prevalence in several coastal towns where young people of various backgrounds and ethnicities performed it in on the Saturday Nights that had come to demarcate leisure time.[53] Structurally, the music provided participants with an autonomous recreational environment as well as occasions for public display. *Osibisaaba* outings began in the town center, where revelers organized together, formed a small mobile caravan, and paraded through town in order to attract additional participants. Eventually, the gathered group settled in an open space on the town periphery where musicians played with unabated en-

FIGURE 1.2. "Obscene dance (Sipisapa)" (*osibisaaba*), c. 1900–1910.
Photo courtesy of Wilhelm Erhardt. © *Basel Mission Archives, D-30.23.027.*

ergy and dancers organized into a ring that moved in a counterclockwise direction (see Figure 1.2). The evening's merriment usually included conversation and social drinking, but its most central activity was a style of dance performed by men and women organized into a large circle that moved in a counterclockwise direction. As dancers maintained this circular pattern, especially eager performers took turns entering its center and offering flashy improvised movements. Eventually, these individual exhibitions gave way to male-female pairs who engaged in sensuous displays purposefully choreographed in order to delight other dancers and the assembled crowd.[54]

As *osibisaaba* gained prominence within the towns along the central coast, another proto-highlife form, *ashiko,* became popular in Accra and the towns to its north. Like *osibisaaba, ashiko* featured the guitar, the accordion, small percussive instruments, male and female singers, and vibrant dancing. Although it likely originated in Liberia or Sierra Leone, the music became especially popular in Accra and surrounding towns, where it spread at the hands of the *akwantufoɔ;* young men, and to some degree women, who had traveled to the capital, accumulated some measure of wealth and urban experience, and returned to their home communities. There, these young men touted *ashiko* not simply as a form of recreation, but as a means of showcasing their newfound status, urban experiences, and access to cash and imported items. By 1920, *ashiko* had gained repute as a musical marker of a new social and political force: young people with money who eagerly displayed their fortune and independence through dress, adornment, or other material items of prestige.[55]

As *ashiko* spread to towns north of Accra, a generation of male migrants in towns further west developed their own musical style called *ikonikoma* (later *konkoma* or "something which has not existed before").[56] *Konkoma*, which emerged in the late 1920s, nearly a decade after *osibisaaba*'s prominence, was a poor-man's brass band popular among young men who had shared the experiences of migration, wage labor, and life in larger towns.[57] As *konkoma* performers used choral singing and percussive instruments to flaunt their participants' experiences, they attracted interest from wider cohorts of young men between the ages of eighteen and thirty, including many who had not yet moved to urban areas or acquired any degree of autonomous wealth. These aspirants could gain membership to a *konkoma* ensemble, but they had to make a financial contribution to the group's operation and attend rehearsals, where they learned rhythms on the castanets, *pati* side drum (a small cylindrical drum roughly ten inches in diameter), and frame drum, rehearsed songs and lyrics, and gradually improved their dancing skills. Many *konkoma* ensembles also required their members to wear specific costumes during their recreational outings and public performances. These uniforms, which were comprised of white shirts with pockets on the chest, white shorts, white socks, white canvas shoes, white handkerchiefs, and a white hat, displayed the young members' disposable wealth, but they also made them readily identifiable to communities at large.[58] By the late 1930s, *konkoma* had become common in coastal towns around Accra and in places as far east as Togo and Western Nigeria.

The considerable popularity of these proto-highlife forms among young people of diverse backgrounds and various geographical locales was a remarkable, and rather unprecedented, phenomenon. In years prior, the ceremonial and occasional musical forms administered by state authorities enjoyed wide resonance, but most recreational musics appealed to far smaller populations of a specific location, age, ethnicity, or profession. What made *osibisaaba*, *ashiko*, and *konkoma* so popular was their ability to attract varied groups of young people and provide them with shared occasions of fun and interaction. For disempowered groups, their lack of strict requirements and encouraging air of creative self-expression was an especially attractive means of communicating their desires and taking advantage of the social offerings of their new urban environment.

At the same time, the wide resonance of these proto-highlife musics demonstrates that they were much more than simple realms of recreation. When situated alongside the rigid, and much more regulated, domains of home and work, such forms stand out as exceptional spaces of social freedom and experimentation. Young, and largely subordinate, people found proto-highlife music and dance exciting because it allowed them to exercise autonomy, flaunt their achievements, and pursue additional desires. Unsurprisingly, many participants used such mediums to challenge their continued marginalization as gendered and generational subordinates. As young men and women danced, flirted, and enjoyed one another's company, they exposed what they saw as the fundamental shortcomings of established social hierarchies as well as those proposed by the colonial state. Eager to claim an enhanced position within their rapidly changing world, they flocked to proto-highlifes not simply to have fun, but to exploit possibilities that would accord them greater positions of social stature and rank.

One of these musics' most attractive possibilities was that they allowed migrants to articulate the trials and triumphs of the new colonial economy. The young men and women who left their homes to go to southern cities in search of work risked much in their efforts to procure a new financial future. Some found success in their new urban confines, but many more experienced considerable toil, loneliness, and poverty. For successful migrants, the open domain of proto-highlife performance was an ideal means of flaunting their financial mobility and legitimizing wage labor as a viable economic pursuit. In fact, such displays were central components of *konkoma* sessions. Although it first gained popularity in Accra and other towns, the music acquired special significance when fortunate migrants returned to their communities of origin after an extended absence and stint of work. Since young men viewed these homecomings as important moments of personal transition, they were usually plotted and strategic affairs. Migrants frequently returned home during the night, when they could reach their family house without attracting the attention of neighbors and other residents. On the morning after their arrival, migrants used *konkoma* to boldly announce their reappearance. Adorned in new clothing—which they frequently changed throughout the course of their performance—and armed with an array of material objects, including umbrellas, handkerchiefs, hats, and goggles, migrants paraded through their community for most of the day, playing their innovative musical style and publicly unveiling their newly acquired affluence. These young men also used *konkoma* to brazenly display elements of style and town ways. During their musical escapades, they frequently brandished cigarettes and openly consumed alcohol, a liquid that had become a focal point of wider contestations between young men and their older counterparts. By the afternoon, the headstrong, and rather intoxicated, performers engaged in carnivalesque behaviors and the singing of bold songs, such as *"Meyε abrentsie a me sogya si naano"* (I am a guy, I smoke), that celebrated their exceptional achievements.[59]

At the same time, *konkoma* was not a mere vehicle for the romanticization of the wage-labor economy. As much as they endeavored to impress older residents with their exploits, *konkoma* performers also made it a point to emphasize the hardships, obstacles, and limitations they had overcome during their absence. They did so primarily through song. After opening their parading ventures with numbers such as *"Adāni, Adani, Asa ni, Ikonikoma"* (The drumming, the singing, and the dancing have not existed before) and *"Konkoma amrana yaateew, ɔman nyinaa wɔ mbɔ mbε, sε Nyame pε a, yebedzi kunyim"* (We have now formed *konkoma*, come and see it for yourself, if it is God's wish, we shall succeed), returnees performed songs that reflected the very mixed realities of the migration experience. Many songs, such as "Bravery," extolled the virtues they had displayed in their sojourns; others, including "It Has Lured Me," warned other young men to think carefully about the prospects and pitfalls of particular lines of work:

SOLO:	It has lured me
CHORUS:	Into tedious work
SOLO:	It has lured me
CHORUS:	Into tedious work
	It has lured me
	Military uniform has lured me
	Into dangerous and tedious work[60]

After highlighting the successes and failures that had characterized their excursions, returning migrants made a further pronouncement: that their demanding endeavors had prepared them for and entitled them to claim newfound rights and responsibilities. One of their most visible demands concerned courtship and marriage, processes that remained under the supervision of family and lineage elders. Oftentimes, proto-highlife

performances were occasions in which young men and women freely in-
termixed, identified prospective partners, and initiated romantic relationships.[61] Dance styles that favored coupled pairs, such as those that characterized *osibisaaba* and *ashiko*, provided especially intimate opportunities
for interaction, as did the public acts of praise and gift-giving that rewarded
exceptional dancers.[62] In addition to enabling young couples to flirt away
from eyes of family and elders back home, dance allowed them to levy
public critiques about the shortcomings of accepted marriage patterns.
One of migrants' most pressing concerns was the geographical distance
that separated them from both their families and potential hometown
partners. Since migrants could make few inroads with either group during their sojourns in town, they asserted that their decisions to carry out
autonomous unions entitled them to recognition as adult members of the
community rather than disapproval or scorn. Claiming that family elders
had little knowledge about the realities of urban life, young migrants also
insisted that they were best positioned to dictate the contours of their own
conjugal prospects. In fact, many popular songs from the period extolled
not established marital forms arranged by lineages, but the prospects of
more open-ended, casual affairs centered upon individual interests and
romantic love. In the Kumasi Trio's 1927 pioneering guitar highlife "*Yaa
Amponsah*" [a woman's name], the singer pleaded with a beautiful woman
to seek divorce so that they could carry out an illicit partnership.[63] A decade later, the Osu Selected Union's "*Homowo Ese*" (Homowo is here)
openly discussed the viabilities of casual relationships in spite of parental
expectations and disdain (PURL 1.1):

WOMAN:　*Be nô beni kpokuai eyimô yâ ntsitsi, no mli â ânyâ kâ ntsâ sumôô
　　　　　nsane tamô tami.*
　　　　　In those days when my breasts were filled on my chest, my
　　　　　mother and father loved me more than sweet berries.

MAN:　　*Shi nô ni hewô ni amâshweô bo â benâ osubaâ etsake yâ amâhiâ.*
　　　　　But the reason why they are sacking you is that your behavior has
　　　　　changed.

WOMAN:　*Ku â jeee bo ofite mi? Obaatao mi toohe.*
　　　　　Were you not the one who spoilt me? You have to compensate me.

MAN:　　*Matao bo toohe kɔ. Bô fââ bô ni eji, akâ mi ni misumôô bo â matao
　　　　　bo toohe kɔ.*
　　　　　I'll surely compensate you. By all means, since I loved you I'll
　　　　　compensate you.

Migrants' proposed possibilities about courtship and marriage were
particularly apparent in *konkoma*. Although the music was predominately

the preserve of young men, its practitioners focused a great deal of their energy toward attracting young women and celebrating established romances. Once their scandalous displays of song, drink, and spectacle had drawn a group of young female spectators, *konkoma* dancers attempted to display skill and strength by knocking their colleagues to the ground: an act of masculine bravado that an admiring woman acknowledged by placing a piece of cloth upon his shoulders. In the context of the homecoming, young men who had established girlfriends or had either initiated or completed marriage payments also utilized *konkoma* outings to make brash statements about their conjugal rights. Particularly daring men led the parading ensemble to the homes of their female partner, where they issued her a rather public invitation:

> Come lover
> Come tonight for colorful conversation
> Come tonight for colorful conversation
> Come lover
> Come lover and converse with me tonight
> Come tonight for colorful conversation[64]

Together, enthusiasts' efforts to legitimize their economic importance and lay claim to courtship were components of an even greater possibility: the modification of the established gendered and generational order. Although the young patrons of proto-highlifes aspired to become adults and elders, they were simultaneously eager to redraw the boundaries that separated youth from adulthood in their communities. Too impatient to abide by established norms that did little to recognize their newly acquired experiences, they sought to amend the requirements for adulthood in ways that accorded them recognition and mobility. Young migrants' calls for respect appeared in a 1939 guitar highlife *"Nkyrinna"* (This generation) recorded by the B. E. Sackey Band (PURL 1.2):

Nkyirmba a yɛaba	We the present generation of youth
Yɛn enyiwa yɛ dzen ae	We are daring
Nkyirmba a yɛaba	We the present generation of youth
Yɛn enyiwa yɛ dzen ae	We are daring
Kweku Adaakwa, yɛn enyiwa yɛ dzen ae	Kweku Adarkwa, we are daring
Kwadwo Buronyi ayɛ edwuma	Kwadwo Buronyi well done

The patrons of proto-highlife forms were, as elders charged, dissatisfied with the gendered and generational order that regulated Gold Coast communities. But instead of plotting its destruction, they wanted to modify it in a way that recognized their risks, rewarded their successes, and distinguished their lived realities from those of previous generations.

For young men, *osibisaaba*, *ashiko*, and *konkoma* were also potent forms for the creation of a new model of masculinity. By unabashedly presenting themselves as "guys," male migrants outlined a category of male behavior that fell somewhere in between those of established adolescent young men (*mmerantee*) and recognized male adults (*mmarima*). Various components of *konkoma*, including songs such as "*Meyɛ abrentsie a me sogya si naano*" (I am a guy, I smoke),[65] dancing styles that frequently consisted of vigorous pelvic thrusts, as well as the public consumption of alcohol and cigarettes, emphasized the importance that these self-proclaimed guys placed on their successful sojourns to urban areas.[66] Although such outings were not a means of fully becoming adult men, they allowed young migrant laborers to outline the contours of a new masculine model, initiate their peers into its purview, and insist that it find inclusion within the existing group of masculinities that gave men status in colonial society.

While available records shed very little light on popular music's young female participants, they also used its recreational confines to claim an enhanced position within the social, generational, and gendered order of Gold Coast towns. Like young men, women used popular music to gain autonomy and to pronounce themselves as assertive, not passive, players in a climate of considerable change. They used dance, song, and dress to obtain heightened visibility and assert their own budding wealth. And while the colonial era did much to disempower women in their relationships with men, popular music provided them with a means of maintaining leverage and agency within their budding romances. As guys proclaimed open romances as a central component of their unique status, young women used the contours of popular music to remind them that courtship was a two-way street and that they too had needs and aspirations.[67]

URBAN AUTHORITIES' EFFORTS TO CRIMINALIZE POPULAR MUSIC

As the young patrons of proto-highlifes gathered together and proposed their visions for social change, urban authorities grew increasingly anxious and alarmed. Chiefs and elders immediately declared the need to reestablish their hold over unruly urban populations, but church and government officials were also quick to express concern about the "un-

FIGURE 1.3. Secondary School Brass Band in Christiansborg (Accra), 1901. © *Basel Mission Archives, D-30-03-043.*

civilized" nature of cities' new Saturday Nights. The first critics to put their worries in writing were Protestant and Anglican missionaries: figures who had once used music to spread their own ideas of discipline and morality. In late nineteenth and early twentieth centuries, leaders from each church endorsed hymns, choirs, and brass bands as reformist tools that could attract new converts and help guide them into patterns of proper behavior. They sold imported instruments such as bugles and drums, provided instruction on their usage, and openly supported the formation of brass bands among students and churchgoers (see Figure 1.3).[68] In addition to pulling people into the church, such bands provided missionaries with tangible evidence that they could use to display their accomplishments to audiences back in Europe. After all, images of Gold Coast men donning European clothes and playing European instruments made lasting impressions on home congregations, who often provided missionaries with much-needed financial support.

Despite their initial endorsement of music and musical ensembles, many church officials reversed their stance in the early 1900s. Seeing that their efforts to provide city residents with European instruments had actually facilitated popular, rather than religious, music-making, several missionaries spoke with great horror about how possible converts often combined procured instruments and musical knowledge with degrading forms of dancing, smoking, and drinking. Concerned that young people had started to "think more of sardines and cigarettes than their souls," missionaries decided to take a firm stance against the spread of problematic proto-highlifes.[69] Around 1910, the Wesleyan Methodist Missionary Society went so far as to ban Christian converts from participating in any musical activities, including those that employed European instruments outside of the sanctioned environment of the church.[70]

One prominent factor in this dramatic about-face was missionaries' mounting anxieties about how urban residents might best fill their newly acquired leisure time. In many evangelical minds, recreation was an important and recognizable need, but it was also one that necessitated caution so that it would not devolve into the excessive exploits characteristic of sin. Individual missionaries drew different conclusions about what constituted proper fun,[71] but few doubted that proto-highlife recreation did not fit the bill. In the early 1900s, church correspondence framed these new musical styles as breeding grounds for an impressive string of moral problems. Some decried popular music as an arena of financial recklessness that encouraged participants to spend their hard-earned savings not on marriage, education, or the accumulation of property, but on instruments, dances, and frivolous merriment. In the colony's interior, missionaries encouraged the church not only to discourage such efforts, but to implement restrictions that would prohibit Gold Coasters from purchasing imported instruments altogether. Others criticized popular music as an unnecessary arena of distraction that was detrimental to an emerging wage-labor economy based on punctuality and precision. Music and dance, they argued, monopolized wage laborers' imaginations, corrupted their sense of time, and rendered them unfit for work.[72] Most, however, agreed that popular music's greatest danger was that it accorded unmarried men and women space for unsupervised interactions. A few insistent missionaries claimed that *osibisaaba*, for example, was an immoral dance that bluntly celebrated sexual deviance, illicit romances, and "doing it slowly or the bed will break."[73]

As missionaries put their concerns into writing, colonial officials also became convinced that emerging popular musics had spawned a number of disgusting practices.[74] In 1904, the British government outlawed *dedewa*, a dance that purportedly induced young men in Akropong to sexually abuse young women. Four years later, the commissioner of the Eastern Province encouraged the secretary for native affairs to completely outlaw *ashiko* and *osibisaaba* on the grounds that each made it "customary that when a woman has consented to be a man's partner for the dance, she stays with him for the night." To bolster this claim, the commissioner insisted that these musical styles had prompted rising instances of adultery and sexual promiscuity in Kwawu.[75] Although Taki Obili's decree did not officially criminalize *osibisaaba* in Accra until 1911, neighboring towns moved quickly to ban the music and prosecute its problematic practitioners. In July 1909, two men in Nsawam were jailed for six months for playing the music, being intoxicated, and physically assaulting police officers, a crime that local officials upheld as a potent example of the music's dangerous influences.[76]

After receiving a number of similar complaints about *adaha*, the district commissioner of the Central Region passed a series of regulations aimed at regulating its performance in Cape Coast. The resulting legislation, passed in 1908 and quoted below, did not outlaw the music, but it went to great lengths to confine it to particular geographical and temporal settings:

– No band shall be allowed to play except between the hours of 4 PM and 9 PM on Mondays, Tuesdays, Wednesdays, Thursdays, and Fridays and 1 PM and 9 PM on Saturdays.
– No band shall be allowed to play on Sundays.
– Only one band shall be allowed to play at a time on Mondays, Tuesdays, Wednesdays, Thursdays and Fridays and no more than two at a time on Saturdays.
– All applications for passes to play must be made by the bandmaster and will be granted as near as possible in rotation.
– On Saturdays, if two bands are playing at the same time they shall not be allowed to play in the same part of the town.
– In case of any annoyance or disturbance being caused the band causing same will be liable to have their passes to play suspended.
– The Band Masters will be held responsible for the Good Conduct of their bands.
– The above rules may be altered or varied at the discretion of the District Commissioner.
– No "objectionable" native tunes or airs are allowed to be played at any time.[77]

By prohibiting *adaha* during the work day, eliminating competing or concurrent performances, targeting objectionable tunes, and requiring bands to obtain a "pass" (a police-issued document) to play music in public domains, the commissioner hoped to facilitate city authorities' efforts to maintain political and social order. But on the ground, such measures seem to have had little impact. Archival records contain no trace of *adaha* offenses, and since the music was largely an impromptu form, the above laws would have been difficult to enforce. More importantly, however, by the time of the legislation, many urban youth had begun to abandon *adaha* in favor of alternative musical styles not covered by the above decrees.

What prompted Robertson to make his request to Taki Obili in 1909 was the British state's growing realization that popular musical recreation was a realm that lay beyond the confines of their effective control. The rapid expansion of *osibisaaba, ashiko,* and other styles demonstrated that the colonial government could neither supervise the distribution of imported instruments nor direct the activities of the young people flocking to Accra and other towns. Robertson had also come to comprehend that he and his staff knew relatively little about what was actually happening in the "dangerous" realm of proto-highlife recreation. In the first decade of the twentieth century, the government proved rather inept in its efforts to garner reliable information about the musical styles missionaries vehemently denounced. A 1907 circular asking district officers to provide information about the evils of *osibisaaba* informed them that Gold Coasters referred to the music by a number of names, including *patsinkyrren* (or "*patsintering*"), ɔdɔ ("love"), and *antekodiwo.* Warning that local residents had a penchant for providing incorrect information about the music's content, the circular also encouraged local administrators to find a reliable source capable of accurately describing its participants' actions and exploits.[78] This lack of knowledge also hampered efforts to arrest and prosecute *osibisaaba* practitioners. In the months following the above circular, many district commissioners confessed that their limited understanding, lack of resources, and inability to provide police officers with firm instructions rendered them powerless against the music's spread.[79]

When Robertson wrote to Obili in 1909, he did so from an office that had become increasingly concerned about the limits of its administrative reach. And since his government could do little to force Obili to create or enforce the proposed bylaws criminalizing *osibisaaba* and *ashiko,* he was fortunate that the *mantse* had his own set of worries about the dangers of proto-highlife musics. As these emerging recreational styles continued to spread at an alarming rate, many traditional authorities grew nervous about the withering of their own political power. Of particular concern was their conviction that the old regulations governing music-making had started to disappear. Wealthy traders and aspirant big men had long sponsored musical ensembles in order to expand their prestige, but by the second decade of the twentieth century a few had become so brazen as to attempt to approve the performance of musical styles customarily reserved for chiefs. In 1909 a local mining contractor in Tarkwa attempted to sponsor a performance of "native drums" in honor of King Edward VII's passing, an act that the local chief saw as a direct challenge to his office and power.[80] Many other authorities found concern in the musical activities of young migrants flocking to southern towns. During the first few decades of the twentieth century, many proto-highlife practitioners denounced chiefs as unaccountable and irresponsible leaders; others formed companies (often referred to in colonial records as *asafo*) that issued their own set of laws and openly criticized local officeholders.[81]

After receiving and considering Robertson's request, Obili and his fellow *mantsemei* concluded that criminalizing *osibisaaba* and *ashiko* not only would strike a blow to the aspirations of unruly youth, it also would provide them with a viable means of reinstating their rightful authority alongside colonial officials.[82] By responding to the secretary's concerns, Obili demonstrated that local chiefs could be profitable partners for a British administration eager to put its own stamp of order on southern towns. In the months leading up to the *mantse's* declaration, many in government circles had concluded that chiefs were too intimidated to take effective action against popular musical protagonists. For those in the Native Affairs Department, chiefs' lack of action was particularly troubling. Months earlier, they had promised their British colleagues that chiefs would use the Native Jurisdiction Ordinance of 1910—an act that recognized the jurisdiction of traditional courts and laws—to reclaim control over problematic populations. In the aftermath of Obili's action, they insisted that chiefs simply needed a bit of prompting to "realize that they had the support of the government" regarding the suppression of undesirable musical practices. Over the next year the department encouraged many chiefs, including those in Eastern Akim, Eastern and Western Krobo, Akuapem, Ada, and Akuse, to enact legislation against musical styles that were "mischievous or demoralizing."[83]

By 1920, the shared desire to criminalize popular music had become a central component of the unfolding partnership between local and colonial officials. Over the course of the next decade, the expansion of indirect rule—a cost-effective system of British colonial control that allocated chiefs considerable political and judicial authority within their home communities—allowed these authorities to take further measures to advance their power. Since the system of indirect rule gave chiefs and elders the power to use precolonial conventions and "customary law" to maintain order within their communities, many found that they had license to ban any objectionable or undesirable musical activities.[84] The implementation of indirect rule was an uneven process that aroused considerable opposition, particularly in communities where chiefs abused their power or ignored long-standing checks and balances that regulated their influence, but it found relatively smooth application in the arena of popular music. Since chiefs and elders adamantly claimed that proto-highlifes had no precedence in precolonial society, British officials found little reason to doubt that their unruly practitioners were violating colonial as well as traditional laws. In June of 1924, Taki Yaoboi, Accra's new Ga *mantse*, requested colonial police to stop young men and women from engaging in a "most obscene" dance that encouraged men and women to behave in a way that threatened Accra's civic harmony and long-standing system of generational and gendered order.[85] That same year, the authorities of the Manya Krobo Division outlawed the dancing and singing of *atsai* and *kasakpe*, claiming that each musical form encouraged a number of unruly behaviors that violated long-standing expectations of morality and obedience: "The songs attached to these dances are quite impious and rather abominable and lead both sexes into cultivation of bad habits. These dances are usually played in the night, and . . . react on [their participants] the possibility of bringing them into the state of disobedience and laziness. Lastly . . . the dancers went so far to inaugurate songs of reproach against their chiefs and headmen."[86]

These distinctions between customary order and popular musical mischief became even more clear in a few of the many cases of destool-ment—the process of removing a chief from office—that gripped the colony in the 1910s and 1920s. In 1914, the secretary for native affairs alerted government officials that established chiefs were facing a growing tide of oppositional movements within their communities. Ten years later, his office confirmed that seventy-nine chiefs had been removed from power.[87] The charges propelling such cases are too numerous to recount here, but several instances demonstrate that popular musical recreation had become a reliable means of tarnishing the reputation of unpopular authorities. In 1927, elders destooled the *tufuhene* of Winneba because of his habitual drunkenness and persistent displays of disrespect "towards his family and the State."[88] Years earlier, the chiefs and elders of Bekwai also destooled their *ɔhene*, Kwame Poku, for his deteriorating behavior. Poku, they claimed, had abused local elders verbally as "fools, beasts, good for nothings, blockheads, nincompoops and various other names" and had taken part in musical exploits more akin to a youthful culture of immorality than one of traditional authority: "He has been in the habit of fighting in the streets, and besides roaming throughout the streets all over the town in European clothes absolutely intoxicated; with a guitar in his hands, playing and singing. Going from place to place to the educated classes 'CADGING' for drinks. A disgraceful habit for an *Omanhene*."[89]

For a colonial government that had agreed to throw its weight behind traditional authorities, the rising discord about chiefs, custom, and popular music was extremely concerning, especially when such tensions erupted in instances of rioting and violence. In December of 1920, fighting broke out between Tantum and Legu, neighboring coastal towns located in the colony's Central Region. The end results were astonishing: as young men from Tantum invaded Legu, they burned 168 houses and destroyed twenty-two canoes, large quantities of fishing nets, clothing, crops, and animals, and various objects of state paraphernalia. Sixteen men and women from Legu died in the siege, along with nine men from the invading Tantum. State officials arrived too late to interfere in the carnage, but they promptly arrested twenty-one men on charges that ranged from the possession of offensive instruments to acts of murder and arson. In the weeks that followed, the government conducted an extensive investigation of the riot, which it hoped to use as a case study to understand the causes of regional unrest as well as measures the state could take in order to ensure future peace. When their investigation closed, officials pinpointed a range of factors responsible for inciting the violence. Parts of their report put great emphasis on the ethnic and cultural differences between the two towns. Legu, they noted, was home to Goma people, while Tantum was inhabited by the Ekumafie: two communities that purportedly had irreconcilable differences, including a long-standing boundary dispute and a well-established history of quarreling over fishing waters.[90] But the real spark for the riot, the report claimed, was music. In his testimony to a British court, Legu's Eduafu II, an ɔhene who had a European education and was "acquainted with native custom," claimed that the conflict started when some members of Tantum's No. 1 Company (*asafo*) marched to Legu, rang bells, and sang songs insulting his constituents:

> A shady tree we blow (belch) on you
> We shit upon you, Legu we don't like
> We want Mumford people.

The colonial court was particularly struck with Eduafu's description of what followed:

> When I got near them and heard the song I knew that it was Tantum people.
> ... They were men who were singing. They were going through my town in
> the direction of Mumford. I saw that some of these Tantum people had spears

and cutlasses. . . . I was surprised when I saw these Tantum people going through my town ringing their bell and blowing their bugle with cutlasses and spears. It is not in accordance with native custom. I am acquainted with native custom. It would be contrary to native custom for people from another town to pass through in this way by night without first obtaining permission. These people had not obtained permission from me to pass through. Such passing through with bells and bugle and arms would, if made without permission by strangers to a town, lead to fighting.[91]

In its final verdict, the court agreed that the main culprits of chaos were the young men from Tantum who had entered Legu to play music and sing songs in a way that clearly violated established convention. Had these individuals followed traditional protocol and respected chiefly authority, the court asserted, the riot would never have taken place. To the Native Affairs Department, the case revealed that the dangers of popular music were more volatile than they had previously imagined. In the years that followed, the secretary of native affairs encouraged officials in various districts to distinguish between the "ceremonial, customary and social dances" important to precolonial society and popular musical styles that were "dangerous to public morals" so that it could target the latter for elimination.[92]

Throughout the 1920s, traditional and colonial authorities used a variety of administrative and legal measures to dismantle proto-highlifes as a realm of recreation and social change. Chiefs and elders targeted such styles under the auspices of the Native Jurisdiction Ordinance and the expanding system of indirect rule, while a 1925 amendment to the colony's Criminal Code allowed the governor to restrict Gold Coasters' rights to assemble, meet, and parade in common places in the name of public safety.[93] By the 1930s, officials in many communities required all musical performers to obtain a "pass" or "permit": a document that held them legally liable for any disturbances that might occur as a result of their merriment. Because these passes had to be obtained from either a local chief or the police department before the performance took place, they became an effective means of expanding state control into a previously autonomous confine.[94]

Official concern about the dangers of proto-highlifes also extended to the realm of recorded music. In 1930, administrators in the colony's Central and Western regions became concerned with a collection of locally made and marketed gramophone records that allegedly contained a direct reference to the Tantum-Legu riot of a decade earlier. Fearing that these songs might "arouse the anger of the Legu people and lead to a recrudescence of their old dispute with Tantum," officials worked to translate their presumed defamatory lyrics as a precautionary measure to control "the importation of undesirable records" into the colony:

> Aye! Is this your way of fighting? Aye! Is this your way of fighting?
> Aye Safuhene [sic]; is this all your fighting?
> Aye! Is this your way of fighting? Aye Kwesi! Is this your way of fighting?
> Aye is this all your fighting?
> Safuhene [sic] has failed to fight
> O! Fighting is bravery[95]

After receiving the lyrics that levied insults to a *safohene* (a divisional captain of an *asafo* company), the commissioner of the Central Province insisted that they were highly provocative and might easily be used "in any town in which there is disaffection between [*asafo*] companies." Seeing no good reason to allow such records to be sold, he recommended that their sale be prohibited throughout the colony.[96] The following year, after riots in Apam and Cape Coast, additional towns in the colony's Central Region, the commissioner's investigation once again identified "singing of annoying songs" by the town's *asafo* companies as the trigger for acts of violence. The incident, in addition to previous reports, suggested a pattern all too clear to the Native Affairs Department: "The temperament of the uneducated African is such that he is too easily carried away by the joyous ecstasies of the dance amid the drumming and singing—aided as a rule by quite an appreciable amount of gin—and it only requires a word or a gesture against another company to set the place ablaze. The riot at Appam [sic] is an instance."[97]

By 1930, proto-highlife forms had not disappeared from Gold Coast towns, but the possibilities that had characterized, even fueled, their emergence had become greatly subsumed under the expanding arm of local and colonial authorities. To a large degree, chiefs and government agents had turned the tables, transforming what had once been a creative realm immune from their supervision into a place where they could reclaim control over young men and women, prohibit particular modes of behavior, and reinforce the axes of race, age, and gender essential to their desired social order. Legislating popular music not only allowed those in positions of political power to come together, but did so in a way that closed off wider possibilities that had been unintentionally engendered by urbanization, the expansion of the capitalist economy, and the presentation of British racial supremacy.

For young men and women, authorities' legal actions and rhetorical assertions did much more than prohibit a vibrant arena of enjoyment and fun. As popular musical enthusiasts suffered repute as rascals, drunkards, and deviants, the domains of music and dance worked to threaten, rather than enhance, their social reputation and standing. This was especially true in the intimate realms of domestic and family life. From the 1930s into the 1960s, many Gold Coast families explicitly prohibited their young men and women from learning imported instruments or taking part in popular musical recreation. Peter Manuh recalled that his parents distanced him from music altogether in order to ensure that he became a "respectable person."[98] Such attitudes even prevailed within families with close ties to musicians of established repute. In the 1940s, a young Kofi Lindsay started to study the guitar under the tutelage of his uncle, the prodigious Jacob Sam. Despite Sam's notoriety as one of the colony's first artists to record with the British Zonophone label, Lindsay's father adamantly refused to allow his son to set foot upon what he considered to be a path to social vice and hooliganism:

> When I was a small boy, my uncle Sam used to play [the guitar]. I liked the sound, so I got a guitar and started learning it. One time my father came and saw me playing it. [He said] "Yeeeaaah! What the hell? What the hell? Playing a guitar? Do you want to be a drunkard? If you want to play that you've got to get out of my house immediately." So that was the end of [my efforts to learn the guitar].[99]

The negative stereotypes surrounding popular music proved even more restrictive to young women. In the years following the mounting legislation against proto-highlife forms, women found it increasingly difficult to observe, much less participate in, popular musical performances. As we will see in future chapters, wider concerns about moral degradation and gendered chaos branded female music enthusiasts as loose women or prostitutes. Growing numbers of families made it a point to carefully supervise their female members, in part so that they could prohibit them from accessing popular musical spheres.[100] By 1940, young women had become nearly invisible within the confines of popular musical recreation. Their removal from the creative process of song and dance not only divorced them from what had been a prosperous realm of possibility; it helped confine them to domestic and labor spheres that accorded elders considerable leverage over their day-to-day affairs.

CONCLUSION

Despite their gradual marginalization by local and colonial officials, popular musical forms such as *ashiko, osibisaaba,* and *konkoma* left an indubitable mark on the sociopolitical climate of southern colonial towns. For young people, most of whom held subordinate positions in local hierarchies, they were exciting domains of possibility and social change. At a basic level, these musical forms constituted a novel domain of urban pleasure, a means for young men and women to exercise creative agency and communicate their unprecedented experiences. For those who had left their rural homes in search of new prosperity, song and dance were ways to comment on the shifting allocation of authority, evaluate forms of work, and give advice to their peers. Importantly, such activities also allowed young people to renegotiate their gendered, generational, and social standing. Through *osibisaaba, ashiko,* and *konkoma,* urban migrants distinguished themselves from previous generations of juniors, claimed economic clout and sexual autonomy, and outlined the basis for new gendered models that could complement those already in existence. By attending to such possibilities, we can see beyond the official charge that proto-highlife participants were simply rebellious youth who wanted to defy authorities and inculcate disorder. They were, like traditional and colonial authorities, active progenitors of transition and change.

If popular music allows us to see the colonial years as an era of contestation, multivocal negotiations, and opportunistic partnerships, it also allows us to appreciate the restrictions, limitations, and continuities that marked life in southern towns. In the later colonial period, popular music was a place of opening, but it was also one of closure and official control. As proto-highlife recreation became increasingly a contested domain, it became a place where influential persons, rather than marginalized youth, actually gained leverage over the allocation of power in urban contexts. In the 1920s, officials' legal edicts, invocation of tradition, and repeated condemnation of popular musical dangers branded successful migrants and autonomous youth as ruffians and criminals whose sole intention was illicit pleasure and self-gratifying debauchery. These cooperative efforts did not completely eliminate proto-highlifes from the sphere of urban life, but they allowed chiefs and elders to expand their control in a way that upheld, even expanded, preexisting modes of generational and gendered authority. At the same time, the targeting of proto-highlife recreation enabled the colonial state to extend its authority into intimate, and previously inaccessible, spheres. By 1940, many urban publics looked upon popular musical practice with considerable disfavor, a practice that reinforced young persons' subordination in the wider realms of urban life.

TWO

The Making of a Middle Class: Urban Social Clubs and the Evolution of Highlife Music, 1915–1940

In January 1916, Joseph William de Graft-Johnson, a prominent Cape Coast citizen and school headmaster, contacted the commissioner of the Central Province about a group of educated men's recent effort to "try and raise a public subscription band." The band, de Graft-Johnson explained, had the backing of Reverend Kowfi at Richmond College and with the commissioner's kind support and patronage could initiate rehearsals and be ready to stage performances by Easter of that year. The commissioner, however, was hardly enthusiastic about the idea:

> I do not understand your proposal. Supposing you collect sufficient funds to purchase band instruments who is going to be responsible for the main-tenance of the instruments and the payment of the members of the band? Organized bodies, such as a Regiment of Soldiers, Theatrical Companies and the like have bands which form part of their organizations, but I do not quite appreciate how the band you speak of is to be maintained or for what purpose it is to be formed. If you will be good enough to enlighten me on these points, I will be pleased to further consider your letter.[1]

In his response, de Graft-Johnson did his best to address the commis-sioner's stated, as well as unstated, concerns. He went to great lengths to emphasize that the proposed group would be drastically different from the so-called bands that played proto-highlife styles such as *ashiko* and *osibisaaba*. First, the ensemble would be attached to a city club comprised of reputable Cape Coast citizens who would oversee and maintain its function. Second, it would be "a good and properly organized band" that resembled a European orchestra, trained its members how to read sheet music, and performed classical pieces and ballroom numbers. Finally, the group would serve as a "source of pleasure and education" for club members and the wider Cape Coast community.[2] In short, the band would work to uphold, rather than challenge, the colonial state's ideas of order and civilization.

Despite these lengthy pleas, the district commissioner remained convinced that the proposed band would likely "die an early death." Given the administration's mounting assault on popular musical activities, his decision to lend this band neither financial nor moral support was not necessarily surprising. But the commissioner had additional reasons for his caution. One of the most pressing was the rather tense relationship the colonial government shared with the colony's cohort of educated urban men. In the 1910s, these men—who had acquired a British education and secured employment as merchants, clerks, schoolteachers, registrars, and civil servants in the expanding colonial economy—occupied a complex niche in colonial towns. Their education, salaried jobs, and noticeable financial resources set them apart from other Gold Coasters, as did their proximity to the colonial administration and familiarity with European cultural and legal categories.[3] But in the eyes of their peers, elders, and chiefs, they were figures not of admiration, but of suspicion and general distrust. While local communities did not welcome these men with open arms, neither did British government officials. For them, educated men's avid embrace of European cultural mores constituted a threat to their own fragile claims to power. Many, in fact, argued that these men's vainglorious air and diminishing regard for authority made them a troublesome cohort not all that different from unruly youth.[4]

In the years surrounding the above exchange, these educated men came to occupy what a growing number of scholars have called an intermediary or middle position in Gold Coast towns. Their professional occupations and relative financial affluence, which set them in better financial straits than most farmers and wage laborers, but in less comfortable ones than the colony's mercantile elite and prominent chiefs, made them a small but influential economic group. But while these men's middle economic standing provided them with financial advantages, it did little to bolster their cultural position or social standing. Since most were young in age and unmarried, they could not claim distinction in local hierarchies predicated on age, gender, and lineage. Their shared experiences, interests, and sense of destiny often isolated them from other urban residents, including wage laborers, chiefs and elders, and members of the colonial state. Lastly, these men constituted a rather ambiguous political group. Stuck in-between the British colonial government and chiefs reinvigorated by indirect rule, this middle class had few readily accessible avenues of claiming power. All in all, they were an unprecedented subset of Gold Coast society who, like their migrant wage-laboring counterparts, had to find novel ways to redefine their identity, cultivate new relationships, and assume greater sociopolitical influence.[5]

De Graft-Johnson's written communiqué to the district commissioner underscores several components of the collective strategy that this middle class initiated to transform its precarious middle position into one of advantage and prosperity. In cities like Cape Coast, Sekondi, Accra, and Kumasi, they formed literary and social clubs: pan-ethnic organizations that maintained an environment of education, social integration, and material affluence. These clubs were also sites of cultural creativity and novel self-expression. Within club confines, educated men adopted cosmopolitan styles of dress, embraced specific patterns of consumption and exchange, celebrated English-language writing and literacy, and took up an array of particular pastimes. A key ingredient of their self-advancement was music. Like their wage-laboring counterparts and colonial supervisors, these men used musical performance to communicate and achieve their aspirations. By the mid-1920s, they had centered their Saturday Nights around the ball dance: a private recreational event that featured elaborate dress, coupled male-female dancing, strict standards of etiquette, and a distinct form of popular music known as highlife. Like the other popular musics of the period, highlife garnered considerable interest among the many people struggling to stake a claim over Gold Coast towns. Unlike its many counterparts, however, highlife came to enjoy an advantaged place in urban areas' social and political landscape. While the British colonial state initially targeted highlife as a source of danger or unrest, it gradually endorsed the music as a means of inculcating order and civilization. By the 1930s, highlife had a virtual monopoly on urban areas' Saturday Nights: a development that made it a widely attractive conduit of enjoyment as well as social change.

This chapter charts how a small group of educated men used highlife to gain power in their urban environments from 1915 to 1940, a period when they held considerable control over the music's form and meaning. Music and dance, much like the more studied realms of the classroom, office, and courtroom, were central to their gendered, generational, and social ascension. The chapter first provides a brief examination of the origins, aspirations, and early operation of this middle class. From there, it details the principal organization of that these men used to claim influence: the literary and social club, with particular attention to the musical exploits of these clubs, the birth of highlife, and the music's mounting importance as a centerpiece of an emerging middle-class culture. Next is the crux of de Graft-Johnson's exchange with the commissioner: the relationship between educated African men and the British state. Through their fluid interactions, highlife came to gain official favor as a protected, rather than besieged, site of popular musical performance. The chapter ends with an examination of how these men used highlife to socialize young people into their middle-class culture. Opening highlife to wider audiences enabled these men to claim further prestige and influence within colonial society, but such efforts caused them to lose control over the music's meaning and significance.

THE ORIGINS AND EMERGENCE OF THE *AKRAKYEFOƆ*

The middle-class men behind de Graft-Johnson's proposed band and city club owed their origins to the expansion of Western education within the southern Gold Coast, a process initially fueled by missionaries rather than the colonial state. In the 1840s, the Wesleyan Methodist Missionary Society sponsored nine schools in the colony, most of which were located in towns such as Accra, Winneba, Anomabu, and Cape Coast.[6] For decades, these schools attracted a small number of pupils, most of whom came from elite merchant families eager to secure their children's prospects for trade, employment, and economic prominence. While the act of going to school set these children apart from other urban residents, it also endowed them with a unique set of social practices and cultural tastes. In the late nineteenth century, school graduates built homes of distinct architectural styles, embraced English and other European languages, frequently converted to Christianity, and worked hard to secure imported material goods. A few, including the members of the Aborigines' Rights Protection Society, also used education as a means of securing a place in the colony's political landscape.[7]

In the late nineteenth and early twentieth centuries, the colonial government took greater charge of the colony's system of Western education. Armed with a growing sense of purpose and the provisions of education ordinances passed in 1852, 1882, and 1887, the British erected new schools, offered curriculum-based grants to nongovernment institutions, and moved to attract growing numbers of Gold Coast children. Over time, their efforts met with considerable success. In the 1880s, the colony's total school enrollment was less than 3,000 students, but in 1902 it stood at 12,136. This trend toward expansion continued over the course of the next few decades. In 1919, total enrollment was 27,318; in 1928 it jumped to 34,446. By that time, the colony had a sizable group of educated Gold Coasters, overwhelmingly young men, who had gone on to secure positions of employment in Accra, Kumasi, Sekondi-Takoradi, or another of the colony's principal towns. Unlike their wage-laboring counterparts, these men remained separated from their families and community members for lengthy periods of time, or even permanently. Isolated from home and immersed in a new physical and cultural environment, they began to adopt values, role models, and ideals rather different from those who did not share their plight. By the time that they finished school and started work, many had come to hold day-to-day expectations and long-term aspirations that were quite distinct from those of their wage-laboring or uneducated peers.[8]

One of the primary markers of this first generation of school graduates was their occupation. Although very few of them ascended to the ranks of lawyers or doctors, many secured positions as teachers, clerks, and civil servants: desk-work occupations that offered attractive salaries and close proximity to the mechanics of the colonial state. In fact, C. C. Reindorf's 1895 observation that graduates had "no difficulty in obtaining an apprenticeship in a mercantile business or in the Government office" held true for the next twenty-five years.[9] In 1911, clerks living in the colony's main towns numbered 2,349. Ten years later this number had grown to 12,273, making them one of the colony's largest occupational groups. Although the pace of this growth slowed, the need for additional clerks continued throughout the 1920s. After the completion of the Takoradi harbor and railway lines connecting the area to the mining and cocoa areas of the interior, the colonial government hired a large number of school graduates. By the mid-1930s it alone employed a clerical staff of over 500 men.[10]

Once gainfully employed, these school graduates looked to capitalize on their earnings by avidly consuming imported goods and luxury items. Salaried men set out to acquire material items, such as furniture, clothing, books, paper, and magazines, which reflected occupational needs and provided them with an air of authority and prestige.[11] Over time, these lavish epicurean ventures left lasting, albeit different, impressions on groups of urban residents. While many Gold Coasters came to see schooling as a surefire means of material wealth, colonial officials began to view graduates as overly enthusiastic purveyors of imported goods:

"I remember vividly the hats, tail coats, walking sticks, parasols, cloth goods, electrical goods, and bicycle accessories that used to be delivered at my bungalow for the staff and their friends. . . . Gamages, Liberty's and Dallas's of Glasgow are names I remember most in connection with my term on the Gold Coast."[12] While this caricature is certainly an embellished account of clerks' commercial appetites, it captures the importance that they accorded to dress and appearance.[13] Although they held various lines of work and degrees of wealth, nearly all school graduates came to value particular articles of clothing, such as a black dinner jacket, tie, and matching shoes, as essential possessions.[14] Such items were also more than markers of education and wealth. As Stephan Miescher's admirable use of life histories demonstrates, these men envisioned themselves to be a unique social and gendered subset of Gold Coast society. In Akan areas, they became known as the akrakyefoɔ (sing. krakye), a Twi term that was derived from the English world "clerk" and implied their status as educated scholars and gentlemen.[15]

To a large degree, the public recognition of these men as akrakyefoɔ was the gradual culmination of their collective efforts to cultivate a shared identity and set of social practices outside the domains of school and work. Their most prominent forums of communal interaction were urban literary and social clubs: organizations that brought individuals of various ages and ethnicities together to celebrate their shared interests and desires for continued self-improvement. These clubs were not, however, an initiative unique to the akrakyefoɔ. As we have seen, British colonial officials had their own social clubs that provided various amenities, excluded Africans entirely, and served to solidify the structure of early colonial rule. Akrakyefoɔ clubs consciously invoked this form of colonial organization, but they also found inspiration in the fraternities and organizations created by elite Gold Coast residents in the mid-nineteenth century. By the 1860s, Cape Coast's lawyers, doctors, and wealthy merchants had formed a number of bodies, including the Self-Improvement Society, a Freemason Lodge, and the Philanthropic Society. In the decades that followed, many West African cities, including Freetown, Lagos, Sekondi, and Accra, became home to similar clubs.[16] While many akrakyefoɔ aspired to join these elite organizations, the membership fees put them far beyond their reach. In 1915, membership in the Cape Coast's Freemasons cost £11 9s. (shillings), an inconceivable amount for a clerk who earned an average annual salary of £36.[17]

Excluded from organizations that belonged to those of different racial and economic strata, school graduates decided to form establishments

FIGURE 2.1. Accra's Optimist Club, late 1930s. *Photo by J. K. Bruce Vander-puije, courtesy of Isaac Hudson Bruce Vanderpuije, Deo Gratias Studio, Accra.*

that would provide them with additional legitimacy and self-empower-ment. These clubs proved immensely popular among educated men of various geographical regions. Roughly twenty years after the formation of the first club in 1915, there were over fifty operating in the colony's major towns. Cape Coast, for example, had the Eureka Club and Literary and Social Club; Sekondi had the Optimism Club and Literary Circle; Accra had the Social and Literary Club, Young People's Literary Club, Cosmo Club, and Optimist Club (see Figure 2.1); and Kumasi had the Eureka Club and Literary and Social Unity Club.[18] As their names suggest, these clubs were spaces of intellectual collegiality that enabled members to come together, debate contemporary issues, and perfect their use of the English language. But they were also spaces in which like-minded men mingled, relaxed, and shared news and insights. Clubs made explicit ef-forts to maintain a cohesive environment that celebrated their education, occupations, and shared status as middle-class men instead of established markers of identification such as age, lineage, and ethnicity. They made no effort to admit women into their ranks and, like their more exclusive

counterparts, had rigorous qualification standards. An aspirant member
of Sekondi's Optimism Club, for example, had to be a fully employed
school graduate, but he also had to obtain a letter of invitation, pay a subscription fee, and deliver a lecture in English in front of the club before he
was elected as a member—an honor bestowed only on those of a favorable
character and reputation. Both clubs and candidates took such requirements seriously. Clubs expected all new members to attend regular club
meetings, uphold the club's chartered constitution, and abide by its rules.
Applicants who were denied admission, meanwhile, faced social slander,
loss of status, and even exclusion by their social and economic peers.[19]

The exclusive, pan-ethnic, and rather domineering nature of these
clubs has earned them various characterizations, from organizations of
emulation that spread Western habits to crucial networks of support that
facilitated members' efforts to adapt to new realities and urban life.[20] But
for their members, these clubs were places to address their unique needs
and transform their middle position into one of enablement and mediation. Clubs were, in Stephanie Newel's insightful estimation, paracolonial
networks that permitted members to translate cosmopolitan symbols
and behaviors into powerful markers of their social and gendered status.[21] Clubs sponsored events that demarcated an ideology of educational
and occupational distinction, emphasized the present and future rather
than the past, and allowed their members to claim influence over women,
within local communities, and alongside the colonial government.[22] To
fully appreciate clubs' efficacy as vehicles of social mobility and political
empowerment, we must take a closer look at one of their central accomplishments: the creation of highlife music.

THE REGULATED RECREATION OF URBAN GENTLEMEN

To understand the intentions that underlay literary and social club activities, one needs only to follow the paper trail these organizations accumulated from 1915 to 1940.[23] Relatively few historians have examined
such sources, but clubs' letters, minutes, speeches, and event programs
document their formation, operation, and aspirations in considerable
detail. Two of the colony's most prominent social clubs, the Cape Coast
Literary and Social Club and the Optimism Club of Sekondi, emerged in
1914–1915. The Cape Coast Literary and Social Club's founding patrons
included a number of the city's notable male residents, including William
Zacheus Coker, E. J. P. Brown, and E. H. Brew. Because the club owed its
emergence to a rather influential male cohort, it quickly attracted a sizable

membership of recent graduates living in Cape Coast and neighboring towns. The club's stated purpose was "the improvement of its members in debating and public speaking and the furtherance of their intellectual, social and moral advancement," but it sponsored a wide array of activities during its first decade of operation. Members attended regular weekly meetings, read and discussed foreign literary works such as Shakespeare's *Merchant of Venice,* debated topics such as the status of "education in the Gold Coast," and patronized lectures such as "What Aims Should a Club in This Country Pursue?" By 1927, the Cape Coast Literary and Social Club had proved so successful that it formed affiliate branches in other towns, including Half-Assini, Sekondi, Kumasi, and Accra.[24]

In Sekondi, club life originated with the Optimism Club, an organization founded by C. W. Techie-Menson and five other energetic young men in 1915. Though initiated as a forum for Sekondi's literary aspirants and social enthusiasts, the Optimism Club became a popular refuge for local desk workers eager to socialize with a like-minded community of peers. By 1925 it had acquired a tract of land, established a permanent clubhouse that it surrounded with a high wall (effectively symbolizing its status as an exclusive preserve), and secured the support of eight affluent urban patrons.[25] Like the Cape Coast Literary and Social Club, the Optimism Club held weekly meetings and engaged members in English-language debates, literary discussions, and readings, but it also sponsored sporting activities and recreational nights that featured musical concerts and social dancing.[26]

The most immediately visible events sponsored by these clubs were the ball dances they staged on Saturday Nights. For many *akrakyefoɔ,* who were among the first Gold Coasters to abide by the European work week and weekend schedule that demarcated clear times for labor and play, Saturday Nights constituted the most opportune occasions for fun. Clubs, moreover, sought to ensure that their members had fun in ways that could uphold, even expand, their collective interests. In December 1915, shortly after its founding, the Cape Coast Literary and Social Club gave a Christmas concert and ball party; a few months later it staged a Grand Soiree of music and dance. Other clubs followed suit. The Native Club held a dance in the Court Hall of the Cape Coast Castle in 1917, and the Eureka Club held a ball dance with live music in December of the same year.[27] As their names suggest, these events featured musical forms quite different from those favored by wage laborers, migrant workers, or traditional elites. Ball dances featured an array of imported styles of music and dance, but they originally revolved largely around the performance of ballroom numbers such as the waltz, foxtrot, and quickstep. Most clubs went to great lengths to secure bands that could perform these styles at the appropriate tempo and with audible grace. For the first few years of their operation, this meant hiring bands that had been founded and directed by the colonial state. In 1919, the Cape Coast Literary and Social Club invited the Gold Coast Regimental Band to perform at one of its dances; three years later the Optimism Club hired the band for a Grand Ball held at the Cape Coast Castle.[28]

Ballroom dancing—complete with its male-female couples, learned sequences of steps, short duration, and established culture of precision and etiquette—lay at the center of early *akrakyefoɔ* musical events. At one level, the appropriation of ballroom dances was an intentional display of their intimacy with the contours of European culture and civilization. Learning ballroom's movements, variations, and culture of propriety allowed the *akrakyefoɔ* not to mimic the British, but to showcase their attention to detail and intrude on a domain of musical practice long affiliated with the colonial state. It enabled them to, in the words of Thomas Turino, emphasize their cultural position as "cosmopolitan" persons distinct from other urban residents.[29] Since relatively few Gold Coasters had learned more than a few basic ballroom steps, the *akrakyefoɔ*'s fluency in several styles marked them as a unique subset of urban society.

To many local eyes, ballroom also distinguished the *akrakyefoɔ* as gendered actors who engaged in rather immodest male-female interactions. Few local musical forms, including those that featured paired dancing, enabled men and women to publicly maintain physical contact or hold one another around the waist or shoulders. Even nefarious proto-highlife musics did not allow men and women to hold one another throughout the duration of individual songs. For chiefs and elders already sensitive to the links between musical activities and gendered and generational chaos, the *akrakyefoɔ*'s embrace of ballroom and its intimate means of male-female interaction came dangerously close to replicating the acts of their less affluent, and far more controversial, urban counterparts. Unlike proto-highlife enthusiasts, however, these men took a number of measures to place their musical exploits within a wider climate of honor and respectability. Such efforts, as we will see, allowed them to eschew public criticism and convince authorities—particularly those affiliated with the colonial state—that their efforts would have positive impacts on their urban environs.[30]

As ball dances became increasingly important to middle-class culture, a new kind of musical ensemble began to form in the colony's principal towns. These groups, locally known as dance orchestras, first emerged in the second decade of the twentieth century, largely at the prompting and initiative of the *akrakyefoɔ*. In 1914, members of an early Accra literary club formed the Accra Excelsior Orchestra, an ensemble that employed a vast array of costly imported instruments, including violins, violas, cellos, sousaphones, flutes, trumpets, trombones, and a Western drum set and upright bass, to perform well-rehearsed ballroom and orchestral numbers (PURL 2.1). In 1923, the philharmonic members of Sekondi's Optimism Club gathered their rather expensive instruments and collective musical knowledge—which they likely acquired through their connections to missionary schools or churches—to form an orchestra that could play at club events. Within a few years, the group had become an essential component of club activities as well as regional *akrakyefoɔ* social life. The Optimism Club orchestra performed at ball dances, contracted out to private parties, and staged public performances in Sekondi, Takoradi, and the nearby towns of Shama and Tarkwa.[31] By 1930, a number of these dance orchestras performed ballroom numbers, ragtimes, sambas, and other cosmopolitan styles in major Gold Coast towns, while similar ensembles flourished in cities such as Freetown and Lagos. In each of these settings, dance orchestras became associated with educated men who saw themselves as members of a unique community of taste and mounting status.[32]

In the Gold Coast, the *akrakyefoɔ*'s embrace of ballroom did not prevent them from experimenting with the larger prospects of musical creativity taking place in their urban communities. While their colleagues in Sierra Leone and Nigeria continued to place ballroom and classical musical forms at the center of their recreational ventures and self-presentations, social clubs in Accra and other towns took a cue from proto-highlife practitioners and incorporated local musical elements into their Saturday Nights.[33] By 1920, *akrakyefoɔ* dance orchestras had used their familiarity with a wide range of instruments, European chord sequences, and local rhythmic patterns to concoct a new musical form that employed a $\frac{4}{4}$ time structure, heptatonic scales, and the triple rhythmic effect common to proto-highlife styles. The music's flexible format found further resonance in its corresponding style of dance, which featured male-female couples who moved together in a basic pattern of side-to-side steps interspersed with periodic hip rotations and circular movements. Unlike ballroom styles, this music gave its participants considerable room for improvisation, self-expression, and personal flair.[34] In time, this combination of local and cosmopolitan elements garnered a name that reflected its association with the colony's ambitious middle class:

This particular fusion with three successive beats became the favorite of the people of the "high life," the high living people; you might say the relatively well-to-do. And these people used to dance waltzes and such, but when the highlife came on they all flocked to the floor because the indigenous thing was inside. And the people who gathered together to watch these people said, "Ah, that is the music of the people who live the high life; the 'high life' people." So that is how this type of music got that name [highlife].[35]

The exact moment or location of highlife's emergence remains unknown, but printed programs of ball dances from the 1920s demonstrate that the music quickly became a central feature of *akrakyefoɔ* recreation. In 1920, the Excelsior Orchestra gave a program at the Old Wesley School in James Town, Accra, where it played a variety of foreign songs such as "Pat O'Hara," "Arizona," "Banjo Duet," "The Jazz Craze," "That Mellow Melody," and "Stars of the Summer Night." In addition, the group played a tune entitled "Look Trouble," composed in pidgin English: a coastal lingua franca that blended English words with grammatical elements common to Akan languages. Since the lyrical component of "Look Trouble" was itself a translation of local and foreign influences, the song was likely an early highlife.[36] Two years later, the Cape Coast Literary and Social Club sponsored a rather exclusive Grand Ball at the town's West African College. On that evening, club members danced to a wide range of musical styles, including ballroom forms such as the waltz, one step, and lu lu foxtrot, the jazz roll, quadrille, Boston polka, tango valse, and rag. Importantly, the evening's program also delineated space for a few highlife numbers, suggesting that the music had then become known by that name (PURL 2.2).[37] Three years later, highlife played an even more prominent role at the club's 11th Anniversary Celebration, an elaborate affair that featured a wide array of speeches, toasts, theatrical performances, and coupled dancing.[38]

Although highlife did not immediately supersede ballroom's importance to *akrakyefoɔ* recreation, it did much to enhance these men's efforts to refashion their middle position into one of agency and aptitude. When a highlife aired and club members hit the dance floor, they problematized the neat dichotomies—European/African, traditional/modern, and civilized/uncivilized—that had come to mark the social, political, and cultural climate of many Gold Coast towns. Ball dances enabled the *akrakyefoɔ* to carve out their own position alongside and beyond local and colonial hierarchies, often in front of a gathered and curious crowd. Clubs placed strict restrictions on who could enter the ballroom—a privilege reserved only for male members, their female guests, and the occasional European official—but they did little to prohibit members of the wider urban public from gathering outside and observing the evening's fanfare. In fact, most clubs proved eager to exploit their ball dances as moments of public spectacle. To enhance their visible impact, many organizations required male members to appear dressed in suits, ties, shoes, and even top hats and canes: costly, but striking, implements of their economic and gendered influence. By the 1930s, the importance of dress to *akrakyefoɔ* recreational culture was so widely acknowledged that storekeepers endeavored to enhance their stock in the weeks leading up to such events.[39]

One of highlife recreation's most important components was its strict culture of social etiquette. Though eager to attract the eye of the larger urban public, clubs went to great lengths to ensure that their Saturday Nights remained free of any of the degrading elements that characterized their proto-highlife counterparts. Most mandated that their members follow a strict set of behavioral expectations throughout the evening. They delegated considerable authority to the master of ceremonies (M.C.), a high-ranking club member who had the task of administering the strict schedule of dancing, socializing, and dining outlined in the preprinted program distributed to attendants as they walked in the door. In addition to abiding by the M.C.'s directives, clubs asked members to assiduously avoid any form of boisterous behavior. Because individuals who consumed too much alcohol, used inappropriate language, or engaged in other deplorable acts threatened the reputation of the entire club, such organizations regularly imposed fines, probation from club activities, and even expulsion on those who failed to maintain a gentlemanly standard.[40] The reification of proper *akrakyefoɔ* behavior even entered the domain of highlife music itself. The Mexico Rhythm Band's *"Nana Kwesi Wade Kwahu"* (Nana Kwesi what have you done for me), is one example of a song that endowed praise on an educated young man who moved to Sekondi and became a proper *krakye* (PURL 2.3):

Nana e, yɛma wo ayekoo	Nana, accept our congratulations
Nana Kwasi Wadeɛ yɛma wo ayekoo	Nana Kwasi Wadeɛ accept our congratulations
Osiandɛ ayɛ amama-a	Because you have become a distinguished man
Nipa a ɔfiri Kwawuman	He is a man who hails from Kwahu
Wayɛ amama wɔ Sekondiman yi mu	And has become a distinguished man at Sekondi
Wayɛ amama wɔ Sekondiman yi mu	And has become a distinguished man at Sekondi
Nana Kwasi Wadeɛ yɛ amama	Nana Kwasi Wadeɛ is a distinguished man

Clubs' regulation of ball dances also ensured that they provided their male members with an environment of gendered and generational mobility. Although most clubs unapologetically excluded women from their membership ranks, ball dances' emphasis on coupled dancing made them crucial attendants at such affairs. Without a female partner, a club member could not hit the dance floor, fully emphasize his genteel nature, or exemplify his growing gendered stature. For young and unmarried *akrakyefoɔ*, ball dances were also important moments of conversation, courtship, and budding romance. Like other Gold Coast men, they longed to marry, acquire dependents, and have children: processes that, as we have seen, came to be quite contentious in the early decades of the twentieth century. At the same time, these men were particularly keen on attracting the interest of a certain female subset of urban society: the *nwuraanom* ("ladies"; sing. *awuraa*). An *awuraa* was a woman of reputable background, some education, and a distinguished character. Unfortunately for the *akrakyefoɔ*, she was also a woman of relatively short supply. In most Gold Coast towns, education remained a male preserve, and elite families socialized and married within their established enclaves. Discontented with the relative lack of available *nwuraanom* who could provide their members with suitable marital prospects, clubs used ball dances to attract young women, introduce them to the basics of middle-class culture, and mold them into proper ladies.[41]

During the late 1920s and early 1930s, social clubs attempted to transform scores of young women into *nwuraanom* by socializing them into their regulated environment of decorum, respectability, and highlife recreation. Since ball dances remained open only to women who received formal invitations, clubs had considerable control over the female demographic who attended such affairs. Most reserved this honor for club members' wives or unmarried women who had received some level of schooling and could reasonably afford to arrive wearing a formal evening gown, jewelry, white gloves, and other fashionable articles.[42] Once they arrived at the evening's venue, clubs ensured that these prospective *nwuraanom* became objects of considerable attention and courtesy. Clubs insisted that a gentleman bow to a lady when asking her to dance, provide her with refreshments throughout the evening, and introduce her to other club members and guests. The Optimism Club even asked that those bringing a female guest to a dance arrive with a chair so that they could guarantee her access to a seat during periods allotted for relaxation and conversation.[43]

In the minds of many club members, these efforts to make *nwuraanom* were a resounding success. In May 1934, Sylvanus Wartemburg delivered a speech to Sekondi's Optimism Club in which he summarized the club's history as well as some of the important benefits it had bestowed on the community at large. He recalled how the club had established a local printing press, built a clubhouse that added to the amenities of the town, and provided numerous social occasions that had improved town life. But one of the club's most glowing achievements, Wartemburg insisted, was that it had increased "the number of ladies" residing in Sekondi. In particular, he credited the club's dances and social events as instrumental in increasing local women's interests in social affairs, literature, and other activities of importance to middle-class culture. By successfully bringing many of Sekondi's young women into the idealized lifestyle of the *nwuraanom,* Wartemburg noted, the club had not only enhanced the romantic prospects of its young members, it had also helped establish the *akrakyefoɔ*'s status as people of social and gendered importance.[44]

As social clubs became increasingly self-assured about the potency of their highlife performances, they made ball dances more frequent and elaborate affairs. In 1924, the Optimism Club held an average of one dance a month. A few years later, when the club had acquired land, built a clubhouse suitable for dances and garden parties, and established its own orchestra, it held dances on a weekly basis. This increased provision of ball dances made the club immensely popular amongst the city's *akrakyefoɔ* and prompted members of less-established clubs to request permission to attend such events.[45] In other towns, nascent social clubs organized dances in order to attract attention, increase their membership, and legitimize their status. In 1926, a group of Cape Coast clerks, typists, and storekeepers decided to inaugurate their Starlite Club by way of a maiden dance, an event they pitched to the city's *akrakyefoɔ,* prospective *nwuraanom,* and resident government officials including the commissioner of the Central Province.[46]

This expansion of ball dances was further facilitated by the emergence of several new dance orchestras in the colony's major towns. Although capable ensembles had been a limited commodity when de Graft-Johnson presented the proposed club band in 1916, fifteen years later the colony had a large number of reputable dance orchestras that specialized in highlife, ballroom, and other styles favored by the *akrakyefoɔ.* Sekondi-Takoradi had the National Jazz Orchestra, Optimism Club Orchestra, and Nanshamaq Orchestra; Cape Coast had the Rag-a-jazzbo Orchestra, Professor Graves' Orchestra, and Cape Coast Light Orchestra; Winneba had the Winneba Orchestra (see Figure 2.2); Kumasi had Warrab's Orchestra and the Ashanti Nkramo Band; and Accra had the Excelsior

FIGURE 2.2. The Winneba Orchestra, c. 1920. *Photo courtesy of
Bookor African Popular Music Archives Foundation.*

Orchestra, Teacher Lamptey's Accra Orchestra, the Jazz Kings, and the
Accra Rhythmic Orchestra. Since the members of these ensembles frequently belonged to social clubs, they made it a point to cater to highlife's
emerging culture of middle-class prestige. Bandsmen performed in suits,
coats, and ties, learned how to read sheet music, rehearsed a number of
musical forms, and took great pride in obtaining a polished reputation
among their community of peers.[47]

By 1930, urban literary and social clubs had transformed their popular
musical creation into a central component of *akrakyefoɔ* culture, public identity, and middle-class empowerment. As ball dances came to be
regular features of the colony's Saturday Nights, they garnered their participants growing visibility and public recognition. When curious community members gathered to catch a glimpse of the fanfare and proceedings, they saw a select group of men and women who donned elaborate
dress, abided by code of social decorum, and took to the dance floor in
order to move together in a refined and dignified fashion. They saw, in
other words, an intricate display of economic affluence, social influence,
and gendered privilege. Over time, ball dances also caught the eye of the
British colonial state. And while many officials, like the commissioner

who rejected de Graft-Johnson's proposal, initially viewed these events as additional arenas of popular musical danger, they gradually reversed this attitude. In fact, many came to see highlife not as a threatening music, but as an ideal vehicle through which to reform urban areas' more problematic populations.

THE COLONIAL STATE'S SHIFTING
APPROACH TO HIGHLIFE RECREATION

To understand the rationale behind the colonial government's discordant views of highlife, we must return to the wider sphere of British-*akrakyefoɔ* relations. From the 1890s to the 1910s, the primary determinant of these dynamics concerned the latter group's financial prospects and prosperity. As we have seen, this early generation of school graduates found it relatively easy to secure positions of employment in southern towns. Since most of these men came to enjoy a relatively prosperous economic position shortly after the end of their schooling, they could fashion themselves as *akrakyefoɔ* with relative ease. Over the course of subsequent decades, these neat links between school, employment, and elevated status steadily deteriorated. As the numbers of graduating students grew, immediate employment became a much more competitive, and far less secure, prospect. The shortage of desk-work positions increased further as a result of the colonial state's effort to recruit larger numbers of British men into entry-level bureaucratic positions.[48] By the early 1920s, a sizable group of graduates found that they were no longer able to obtain employment as clerks, teachers, or accountants, but instead faced the prospects of manual labor, a possible return to their communities of origin, or, at best, an apprenticeship that offered little mobility or remuneration. Even those fortunate enough to land entry-level clerical positions found cause for concern. In 1896, government clerks earned £36 a year, an enviable sum that allowed them to cover essential expenses. By 1919, these employees had gone twenty-three years without a raise in pay. Years of inflation and the doubling in the price of many imported goods meant that even fully employed graduates had problems obtaining the goods and services central to *akrakyefoɔ* life.[49]

Graduates' efforts to appeal to the state for greater remuneration, however, garnered much more animosity than sympathy. In the late 1910s, many British officials exclaimed that they had grown tired of graduates' consistent calls for raises in pay. Some argued that clerks and other low-level bureaucrats were becoming a thorn in the side of the colonial state;

others insisted that their requests for higher pay were sparked only by their desires to imitate a European lifestyle. By such logic, raising salaries was a detrimental act that would only compromise "the moral character of many young teachers and Government clerks." Although a 1914 colonial committee estimated that the lowest possible cost of living for a clerk was actually £45 per year—£9 more than their current rates of pay—the government refused to raise their salaries until the 1920s, a decision it justified on the premise that a spell of financial hardship would develop such men's integrity, work ethic, and sense of financial responsibility.[50]

To many British officials, one of the most obvious examples of *akrakye-foͻ* fiscal waste was the lavish ball dances becoming popular in southern towns. In the early 1920s, most Europeans considered these musical galas to be little more than upscale versions of dangerous musical exploits, sources of "discomfort and unbroken rest," or laughable attempts at mimicking European civilization. In a formal complaint lodged with the commissioner of the Central Province, one resident presented a ball dance held in the Cape Coast Castle as an embodiment of all of these stereotypes:

> Shortly after 2 AM I was disturbed by shouting and unseemly noises caused by the striking of a woman outside the upper Castle Gate in the street (between the Castle and the Lighterage). The cries were those of a woman in great pain; further, I heard excited people shouting. Half-an-hour had elapsed when I heard the sentry stationed at the lower Castle Gate (Customs) challenging certain persons. The voices answering the challenge were those of women. They were asking the sentry to allow them to return to the District Commissioner's Court House for clothing they had left there.[51]

In the wake of such reports, individual members of the colonial government started to keep a watchful eye on club-sponsored musical events. Although he allowed clubs in Cape Coast to sponsor ball dances, the commissioner of the Central Province, Colin Harding, regularly dispatched police officers to supervise such events in the name of security and order. Many of Harding's contemporaries, as well as his successor, J. L. Atterbury, approached club activities with a similar level of suspicion and distrust. Most regularly declined invitations to ball dances and adamantly refused to provide their sponsors with any logistical assistance. In accordance with the times, a few even commissioned investigations into the character and personalities of local social clubs and dance orchestras. And while these inquiries asked officials to scrutinize individuals who often worked behind desks adjacent to their own, they showed little restraint in branding them as glorified ruffians and potential criminals. One report on the Rag-a-Jazzbo Orchestra informed Commissioner Atterbury that the group was an untalented musical outfit "composed of young men of no importance in the community."[52] The newly formed Starlite Club received similar treatment in 1926, when a member of Atterbury's office modified the group's member list with a cutting evaluation of individuals' lowly rank in the government bureaucracy:

> Mr. E. A. Garr-M.C. (*3rd class warden*) Clerk, prison department
> Mr. R. K. Fenin (*2nd level clerk*) Clerk, Posts & Telegraphs
> Mr. C. W. B. Aggaine (*2nd section storekeeper*) Clerk, A&E.T.C. Ltd
> Mr. J. B. G. Arthur (*Temporary clerk Pt.Dept*) Clerk, Posts & Telegraphs[53]

Official opinions and relationships with the colony's *akrakyefoɔ* improved dramatically under the administration of Sir Gordon Guggisberg, who served as the governor of the Gold Coast from 1919 to 1927. Shortly after his arrival in Accra, Guggisberg initiated an ambitious development program that sought to advance the colony's education system, enhance its road, rail, and harbor transport networks, and expand local trade and economic output. To facilitate these projects, Guggisberg also looked to polish up the state's soured relations with local desk workers. He began by announcing plans for the "Africanization" of the state's low-level bureaucracy, a process that would create a number of new professional posts for recent school graduates, remove racial favoritism, and increase existing employees' salaries. Guggisberg also threw his weight behind the colony's expanding educational system. In his first few years at the helm, the government increased the number of schools in the colony's Central and Western provinces, opened the Prince of Wales College at Achimota, and raised teachers' rates of pay. By heeding the *akrakyefoɔ*'s economic and educational concerns, Guggisberg did much to improve their efforts at self-presentation and social mobility.[54]

For his Africanization program to succeed, the governor also worked to patch up *akrakyefoɔ*-British social relations. He initiated this project by extending an olive branch to many of the colony's literary and social clubs. Although he later took issue with their ardent embrace of English and failure to promote vernacular education, Guggisberg saw these clubs as a way to showcase the merits of literacy, model the development of good character, and encourage wider groups of urban residents to adapt markers of European civilization.[55] While improving state-club relations required little more than a public pronouncement that their members were respectable gentlemen rather than dangerous ruffians, his government also gave many clubs logistical and financial support. Few clubs benefited more from this new-found favor than Sekondi's Optimism Club. In 1923, the club leased a tract of government land for the nominal rent of one shilling per year. A few years later, the state gave it money for the construction of a new clubhouse, a building officials opined would be "good for the community as a whole."[56] But Guggisberg did more than offer the club a small portion of the colonial coffers. In 1925, he gave the inaugural speech in the organization's new clubhouse, paid £3 3s. to become a subscribing member, and promised to make a £120 contribution toward the building of a tennis court. When the club requested an additional tract of land to provide it with a yard suitable for garden parties Guggisberg not only agreed, but also directed the commissioner of the Western Province to outfit it with flora from the Government Garden in Tarkwa.[57] In rather dramatic fashion, the Optimism Club could rightly proclaim that its facilities were on par with those of any other organization in the colony.

What accounts for the colonial government's sudden push to establish cordial relations with urban social clubs? What, exactly, did the British have to gain from this rather abrupt about-face? Part of the answer certainly lies with Guggisberg's desires to promote the *akrakyefoɔ* as a viable model for dissemination of civilization in Gold Coast towns. Club members' embrace of reading, writing, and oral debate gave the state readily identifiable proof that they could use to tout the benefits of government education and hard work. For urban authorities, clubs' emphasis on punctuality, morality, and polite cooperation was also a greatly welcomed alternative to the undisciplined and chaotic behaviors of young migrants and wage laborers. If clubs were allowed to flourish, many British officials argued, the colonial state would acquire a new ally in its efforts to curb the spread of dangerous behaviors and instill its own vision of social order and cultural progress.[58]

The government's convictions about the positive benefits that *akrakyefoɔ* recreation and highlife ball dances could have on urban publics also found reinforcement from the Colonial Office. In the late 1920s and early 1930s, officials in London endorsed Western music and media technology as tools that could help various colonial administrations enlighten, modernize, and reform African peoples. Throughout British Africa, officials experimented with various communicative mediums, including films, recorded dramas and music, and live bands, as ways to convince illiterate persons that they needed to alter their economic, social, and cultural practices.[59] In the Gold Coast, authorities first embraced live music as an educational tool within the confines of the Gold Coast Regiment and colonial police force, bodies that sponsored bands to instill discipline,

FIGURE 2.3. The Gold Coast Regimental Band during World War I.
Photo courtesy of Bookor African Popular Music Archives Foundation.

invoke morale, and impose standards of time on their young, nonliterate African recruits. In the second decade of the twentieth century, the colonial government set out to enhance such ensembles' impact and reach. It first sent members of the Gold Coast Regimental Band to London's Royal Military School of Music (Kneller Hall), where they received training in technique, composition, and various musical styles. Shortly after their return, the band began to perform military, orchestral, and ballroom musics at government ceremonies, private parties, and public events in many towns (see Figure 2.3).[60] In 1917, the government in Accra purchased a full set of brass band instruments in order to form a Gold Coast Police Band. The band took a few years to get off the ground, but it too held public concerts that aimed to expose urban audiences to the merits of proper musical recreation. In 1927, Governor Guggisberg was so convinced about the band's educational potential that he proposed sending two of its musicians to Kneller Hall so that they could receive extensive training, return to the group, and transform it into a fully developed colonial band.[61]

Although Guggisberg's proposal ultimately fell on deaf ears, the colonial government made great efforts to promote the Gold Coast Regimental and Police Bands as a means of swaying urban audiences away from objectionable popular musical styles. During the 1920s and 1930s, it directed these ensembles to give free public concerts, broadcast live performances via the radio, and carry out extensive tours throughout the colony. To attract larger audiences in Accra, Sekondi, and other towns, the government also initiated the construction of public bandstands that would provide a suitable environment for the appreciation of civilized music.[62] They enacted additional efforts to target young men and women. The Police Band performed at many community schools, so that it could "shape the minds of the [colony's] youth" and endow them with appropriate musical sensibilities.[63] Even the need to slash expenditures following the onset of the Great Depression did little to squash officials' enthusiasm to fund these efforts at musical outreach. Few voiced their conviction about the transformative power of European music more directly than Governor Sir Arnold Hodson, who endorsed a 1936 Police Band concert as a surefire means of spreading civilization: "[The upcoming Police Band performance] is a matter of importance and will be very excellent from the propaganda point of view—'Music hath power to soothe the savage!'"[64]

Despite the state's lofty intentions, these efforts had rather uneven impacts on urban audiences. Reports reveal that well-advertised and free Police Band concerts attracted scanty crowds consisting of small children, "one or two loungers," and others "with nothing better to do."[65] In fact, official correspondence suggests that the only residents who exhibited sustained interest in state-sponsored musical activities were the akrakyefoɔ. Unlike their urban counterparts, many middle-class residents made regular appearances at free concerts, expressed enthusiasm for the completion of public bandstands, and tuned in to special radio broadcasts. Some social clubs even hired the Regimental and Police Bands to perform at their lavish ball dances. Such bookings had a cost—the Regimental Band opportunistically charged African audiences a higher rate than it charged Europeans—but they further cemented clubs' cozy relations with government officials.[66]

Musically speaking, one important result of these shifting attitudes— about the akrakyefoɔ as well as the educational value of European musical forms—was that the colonial state came to view highlife and social club ball dances as attractive, cost-effective ways of promoting its own project of cultural development. Clubs' embrace of ballroom forms, strict etiquette, and cosmopolitan conventions embodied many government ideals. Even highlife, many opined, was a close-enough approximation of the refined types of music and dance colonial officials hoped to impart on Gold Coast people.[67] Clubs' public denunciation of proto-highlife styles further convinced government officials that they could be effective tools for disseminating order and respect for British authority. Many officials noted how clubs in Accra, Cape Coast, and Sekondi explicitly prohibited their members from patronizing *osibisaaba* and *konkoma*; others, meanwhile, refused to rent their premises to any groups that played these or other proto-highlife styles.[68] Pleased by such developments, growing numbers of British townspeople began to attend ball dances, where they mingled with ladies and gentlemen and gradually learned to dance to highlife tunes. Others offered to help clubs prohibit unwanted roughs from interfering with their Saturday Nights. In Sekondi, the director of police dispatched officers to patrol the Optimism Club grounds to prevent noisy disturbances and deter ill-intentioned hooligans from spoiling such affairs.[69]

By 1930, highlife had come to hold a position of distinction within many towns' climate of musical recreation. It was the colony's only popular musical style immune from official oversight and legislation and came to enjoy a highly visible and audible presence on Saturday Nights. As clubs gained a growing monopoly on the colony's recreational music, they took considerable strides in their efforts to transform their ambiguous middle position into one of considerable political, social, and gendered clout. In order to claim further influence over other city residents, many clubs set out to make highlife available to wider, and much more diverse, audiences. Such efforts allowed clubs to entrench the music's popularity, but also caused them to lose their exclusive hold over its meaning and significance.

THE EXPANSION OF HIGHLIFE RECREATION IN THE 1930S

In many ways, the 1930s was an odd time for a small group of clerks, teachers, and low-level civil servants to claim a greater role in urban affairs. In much of the Gold Coast, the decade following the onset of the Great Depression was one of considerable financial hardship. The rapid decline in cocoa prices, which dropped over 30 percent from 1927 to 1930, struck a considerable blow to the local economy. Rising costs of living, including a 200 percent increase in food prices, dramatically reduced most people's purchasing power, forced employers to cut wages and salaries, and obliged the government to shelve many of Guggisberg's ambitious development plans. Alexander Ransford Slater, who succeeded Guggisberg as the Gold Coast's acting governor, attempted to minimize the colony's economic woes by introducing an income tax and forcing cocoa farmers to sell their crops in spite of shrinking prices. In the end, these measures became sources of political discontentment rather than economic aid. Price hikes, lowered incomes, and shortages of economic goods increased many people's frustration with the colonial government, wealthy merchants, and local chiefs. Politically speaking, the 1930s launched the colony into an era of animosity and tension that would culminate in the formalized anticolonial movement that erupted shortly after the end of the Second World War.[70]

For the *akrakyefoɔ*, the 1930s were also a period of challenge and transition. Salary reductions, import hikes, and renewed hostilities with their colonial employers threatened to upend educated men's recent economic, political, and social gains. At the same time, many of them were well positioned to weather the Depression-era storm. During the early 1930s, clerks, teachers, and low-level bureaucrats' real wages and salaries left them in a position of affluence vis-à-vis other urban residents. In 1930, skilled laborers and entry-level clerical staff employed by the government's Public Works and Railways Departments earned from 3 s. to 7s. 6d. (pence) per day, more than twice the amount given to their unskilled counterparts. Similar disparities continued in the private sector, where skilled workers and clerks earned from 3 to 10 shillings per day and often received pensions or other benefits. Since middle-class people's Depression-era standards of living continued to accord them some allowance for social and recreational pursuits, literary and social clubs continued to prosper.[71] Throughout the 1930s, the membership rolls of new and established bodies grew considerably. The vitality of club life meant that ball dances enjoyed ever-growing acclaim as sites of intrigue, public discussion, and popular renown. In fact, highlife's increasing appeal in an otherwise adverse environment gave birth to the expression "ɔkɔɔ ball" (He attended a ball dance), a phrase used to single out those who patronized the music on Saturday Nights.[72]

For established clubs, a growing demand for highlife recreation—from members, colonial officials, and the general public—was a cause for both celebration and concern. Many clubs viewed highlife's expansion as a potentially difficult endeavor. Economically speaking, ball dances had always been rather expensive affairs. To hold a successful dance, clubs had to pay a band, secure refreshments, print out invitations and programs, hire bartenders, servers, and police protection, and foot an electric bill for keeping the grounds illuminated until the wee hours of the morning. In the 1920s, clubs covered these costs through the sale of refreshments and a general allowance from their annual budget. But as they began to hold dances on a more regular basis, these organizations asked members to help pay for a growing list of unmet costs. During the belt-tightening years of the 1930s, this solution proved untenable, and many *akrakyefoɔ* encouraged their organizations to find an alternative means of financing these important events.

In the end, most clubs adopted a policy that enabled them to hold regular ball dances and welcome growing numbers of urban residents into their culture of middle-class prestige: they began to sell tickets. Initially, clubs sold a rather limited number of tickets to their musical affairs, but they quickly made ticket sales a central component of their planning and preparation. In the weeks leading up to a dance, clubs printed handbills and small posters, and placed announcements in newspapers promoting the evening's program, its starting time and location, the M.C., the band in attendance, special guests and happenings, and the price of admission. These promotional means likely had limited reach among illiterate or less-affluent residents, but clubs insisted that they were the best way to garner appropriate interest in their offerings. Though eager to attract larger audiences to their ball dances, many club members remained wary about the prospects of attracting unrefined persons who might drink, misbehave, or bring other disruptive elements into their highly regulated Saturday Nights.

To limit such risks, clubs offered the sale of three types of tickets. First-class tickets, which were also issued to club members, their invited ladies, and honored guests, accorded holders the best seats, unobstructed access to the dance floor and bar, and extensive opportunities to mingle with those in attendance. Since these tickets were both expensive— roughly four shillings—and in relatively short supply, clubs also offered second-class tickets that gave holders assigned seats further from the dance floor and center of activities. The least expensive tickets went to spectators; individuals who could enter the dance for a modest one or two shillings, but were barred from claiming a seat or heading out onto the dance floor. Spectators, as their ticket title suggests, had to stand by and passively observe the evening's events.[73]

Many clubs considered their offering of tickets to be a resounding success. From a financial standpoint, it allowed them to cover existing expenses and, from time to time, make a small profit that could be used to improve club facilities, purchase materials, or sponsor future events.[74] More importantly, the sale of tickets gave established *akrakyefoɔ* a means to cement their growing prominence within their communities. The sale of tickets stratified gathered parties into readily identifiable categories and enabled club members to display their fancy dress, exhibit their refined behaviors, and unveil their well-rehearsed dance moves to wide groups of people. Many clubs augmented their ticket-dances with new attractions that thrust their members into the evening's limelight. One of the most popular was the dance competition, a preannounced event that allowed skilled participants to showcase their mastery of a specific style of dance—say waltz or foxtrot—in front of a panel of judges and the assembled crowd. These competitions proceeded in a series of elimination stages and ended when the final couples took the floor for a championship round. For those already proficient in ballroom and highlife movements, such contests were potent occasions to showcase their mastery and refined skills. Another common attraction was the dress competition, an event that gave ladies and gentlemen a chance to celebrate their knack for fashion and cosmopolitan style. Contest winners received notoriety as well as prizes, often cash or an item donated from a commercial trading company, for their physical beauty and exhibition of proper *akrakyefoɔ/ nwuraanom* attire.[75]

For nonmembers, guests, and curious spectators, ticket-dances held an alternative set of intriguing possibilities. Many recent graduates and aspirant club members paid admission rates as a way to gain entry into their city's social club scene. For a young clerk newly arrived in Accra, Sekondi, or another town, attending a ticket-dance was an excellent way to meet local personalities, explore a club's offerings, and solicit the possibility of earning an invitation to apply for membership. It was, moreover, a way to obtain a degree of fluency with *akrakyefoɔ* expectations. Dress and dance competitions allowed onlookers to study the movements and etiquette that underpinned ball dance affairs. Outside of Saturday Nights, these young people found further inspiration in the new speaking engagements that clubs started offering to members of the public. Lectures, with blunt titles such as the "Evils of Alcohol" and "What Is a Lady and Gentleman" offered telling insights into the basic tenets of middle-class culture. Club debates provided aspirant members with practical advice, some of it intentionally geared toward them, such as "You are standing in front of an audience of young men just starting life as clerks. Warn them of the evils ahead of them and give them something to copy," and "You are asked by a group of enthusiastic young men to inform them about how to become a member of your club."[76]

Local newspaper articles covering ball dances also promoted highlife as a prominent means of enjoyment and social mobility. During the 1930s, publications such as the *Gold Coast Times, West African Times,* and *Gold Coast Independent* regularly praised ball dances as prominent occasions that deserved widespread notice. They did so largely on account of their

strong ties to urban social clubs and interests in *akrakyefoɔ* empowerment. The founder of the *Gold Coast Leader*, one of the colony's first local
newspapers, was E. J. P. Brown, who also helped create the Cape Coast
Literary and Social Club. Alfred Ocansey, a wealthy Accra merchant
who regularly attended the city's ball dances, founded another prominent newspaper, the *Gold Coast Spectator*.[77] Unsurprisingly, most articles
covering ball dances accorded them elaborate acclaim. Take, for example,
the *West African Times'* presentation of a dance held by Accra's Yaccas
Club in 1931:

> The Palladium came into its own yesterday with the first dance of the
> Easter season given by the Yaccas Club, of which His Excellency the Acting
> Governor was announced to be the distinguished guest of honor. . . . The
> dance was one of the most brilliant shows witnessed in Accra for a long time
> and the Yaccas excelled themselves in the perfection of their organization.
> Almost everybody who counts attended the dance.
>
> The general standard of dress among the ladies was high. The long dance
> frock predominated, and the bright young set had some dashing styles to lead
> off the season. There was a dance competition in which a fairly good number
> took part. Miss Edwards of the Printing Office, and Mr. H.L. Mingle, also
> of the Printing Office, won the cup which was presented to them by Miss
> Mary Evans. The Police Band rendered excellent music and many extras were
> provided. The function was brought to a close soon after two o'clock this
> morning.[78]

The fundamental message of this and other newspaper pieces was clear:
ball dances were must-see moments in which urban residents could access a budding community of power and prominence. Since articles often
listed the names, employment, and credentials of those in attendance, we
know that many of the colony's most prominent political figures, including J. Kitson Mills, T. Hutton-Mills, and E. C. Quist, made regular appearances at ball dances, where they socialized with other attendants and
hit the dance floor to highlife tunes. For recent graduates and other urban
residents who read these publications, highlife became much more than
another style of urban popular music: it became a medium of possibility
in an era characterized by hardship and constraint.[79]

As highlife gained a vaunted position in and outside of the confines
of urban Saturday Nights, growing numbers of young men, and to some
degree women, set out to access the music. Since most of them lacked the
credentials or resources needed to become a club member or regularly
purchase dance tickets, they had to do so by other means. One possible
method, at least for men, was to learn an instrument or join a dance orchestra. Throughout the 1930s, southern towns became home to a grow-

FIGURE 2.4. The Accra Orchestra, 1930s. *Photo courtesy of*
Bookor African Popular Music Archives Foundation.

ing number of dance orchestras, which were usually comprised of ten
to twenty musicians. Starting a reputable band, however, was a rather
difficult venture. Bandleaders had to attract musicians, procure necessary equipment, and ensure that members reached a level of proficiency
needed to entertain demanding *akrakyefoɔ* audiences. To that end, they
unequivocally preferred to draw the interest of those who owned instruments or had some degree of musical knowledge. Since trained musicians
were in short supply, most dance orchestras relied on those who could be
"trusted to keep a gentleman's band going" or were simply "determined
to give their best."[80] The vast majority of novice bandsmen were young
men whose lack of responsibility gave them the time and energy needed
to learn an instrument, attend regular rehearsals, and follow instructions.
In the early 1930s, Joe Lamptey, a teacher at a government school in James
Town, Accra, conscripted a number of his male students to transform the
school's drum and fife band into a fully fledged dance orchestra. His band,
which became known as the Accra Orchestra, used school instruments, secured assistance from musicians in the Gold Coast Police and Regimental
Bands, and gradually became proficient in highlife and the ballroom styles
essential to middle-class events (see Figure 2.4). Within a few short years,
the Accra Orchestra was one of the colony's most respected highlife outfits
on account of its regular appearances at ball dances and private parties.[81]

For young men, the benefits of joining one of these ensembles extended beyond the confines of Saturday Nights. Since dance orchestras charged for their services, their members occasionally earned small but welcome amounts of pay. Frequent appearances at notable events and well-attended performances also accorded them new levels of visibility and recognition.[82] When prominent dance orchestras, such as the Cape Coast Light Orchestra (also known as the Cape Coast Sugar Babies), the Sekondi Nanshamaq, and the Accra Orchestra gave public performances in Gold Coast towns, they attracted much larger audiences than their state-sponsored counterparts did. The Cape Coast Light Orchestra, a well-organized outfit that had a professional structure, solid reputation, and even personalized letterhead, garnered considerable fanfare. Jerry Hansen recalled that people would travel thirty to forty miles to see the group perform in the 1930s, an assertion that long-time Cape Coast resident Kofi Lindsay adamantly echoed: "When I was young, the Sugar Babies—now that was an orchestra. The Sugar Babies, ah! It was a wonderful group. When they performed they played ballroom numbers and early highlife. And they were all neatly dressed in white. Neatly dressed! They played at top places."[83] The orchestra's mastery of middle-class musics allowed it to travel to Nigeria in 1934–1935 and again in 1937, excursions that accorded band members novel experiences unavailable to many of their peers (PURL 2.4).[84]

For those uninterested in joining or unable to join a dance orchestra, another way to harness highlife's performative power was to master its various modes of dance. While clubs eagerly flaunted the ability to dance ballroom styles as an exclusive marker of their close-knit *akrakyefoɔ* community, the sale of tickets and increased frequency of dance demonstrations gave nonmembers ways to learn basic movements and standard sequences. During the 1930s, growing numbers of young men and women set out to learn ballroom forms so that they could participate in, rather than observe, such dances. In larger towns, they formed new organizations committed solely to the study of ballroom movements and etiquette. In Tarkwa, dance-oriented clubs included the A'koon Shining Star Club, the Tarkwa Moonlight Dancing Club, and the Tarkwa Octette.[85] In Cape Coast, several low-level clerks, teachers, and unemployed graduates formed the Half-Moon Club, a body dedicated to social dancing and theatrical plays. Similar clubs emerged in many of the colony's smaller towns. The Kwakwaduam Sunlight Dancing Club formed in Akropong in 1931, while Nkwakwa's Optimism Dancing Club became an authority in "high class dancing" and standards of dress in the Akuapim region.[86]

As they grew in size and stature, these clubs even sponsored ball dances pitched not at an established middle class, but at enthusiastic novices. In 1935, Sekondi's Ga Youngsters Club held an evening dress dance that was open to all members of the public and featured the Gold Coast Regimental Band performing all of the "latest highlife hits."[87]

The final way that young graduates, desk workers, and other urban residents gained access to highlife recreation was by attending one of the new commercialized entertainment venues sprouting up in the colony's major towns. In Accra, the first spots dedicated solely to leisure were cinema halls such as the Merry Villas (founded in 1913), the Cinema Theatre at Azuma, and the Accra Palladium, which was established in the early 1920s by Alfred Ocansey. In 1924, the Palladium branched beyond film to feature an array of nightly entertainments, including variety shows, theatrical concerts, and various types of music and dance. The venue's offering of stratified tickets attracted a range of customers, from affluent audiences to the less well-to-do but curious.[88] In the 1930s, other venues followed the Palladium's model, particularly in regard to popular musical recreation. Tommy's Club, an Accra dancehall and bar, became an especially popular venue for young *akrakyefoɔ*, recent graduates, and skilled workers eager for a "fine night out somewhere select." Like social clubs, Tommy's hired prominent bands, offered both dance demonstrations and competitions, and only admitted ladies who had been invited to attend the event. Unlike social clubs or the Palladium, however, Tommy's charged a flat admission rate that gave all ticket holders equal access to the evening's affairs. For the modest price of two shillings—the rate of a spectator ticket at most ball dances—a Tommy's patron enjoyed unfettered access to dance floor as well as a complimentary drink.

While its low admission rates made Tommy's popular among a range of urbanites, the venue also earned the endorsement of the city's established middle class. In 1932, many of the colony's newspapers promoted the venue as a place where readers could enjoy a proper night out on the town:

> A very enjoyable time was spent at Tommy's Club on Saturday night last. . . . Everything went on smoothly and orderly and this speaks well for the management. It is just the place where one should go to enjoy himself on Saturday night after all the toils and worries of a busy week. This, no doubt, inspired all to sing and dance so merrily to the tune played by the Orchestra entitled "Everybody Likes Saturday Night." A very lively time is promised all who would attend tonight and it is hoped that all who are desirous to have a real reaping time will turn up in full force.[89]

As Tommy's took Accra by storm, other venues, such as the Merry Villas and the Gold Coast Bar (later renamed Van's), began to sponsor highlife dances on weekend, and sometimes weekday, evenings. By the mid-1930s, highlife had become the recreational medium of choice for large numbers of city residents, particularly those who were eager to enhance their social, gendered, and generational standing.[90]

As it became increasingly popular, highlife attracted audiences who looked to use the music to fulfill a set of concerns that were not entirely in line with those of the middle class. The *akrakyefoɔ* had long touted ball dances as important spheres of male-female interaction and courtship, but growing numbers of young people soon approached them as avenues of amorous autonomy and flirtatious fun. The torrid financial climate of the 1930s levied a considerable shock to young peoples' romantic prospects, regardless of their class position or relations with family and community elders. The price of marriage rose steadily throughout the decade, leaving many families unable to assist their young male members' entrance into the realm of adulthood. Those who wanted to marry without the financial or logistical support of their lineage—an established practice of migrant wage laborers as well as educated desk workers—found that these costs made the process extraordinarily difficult. Even fully employed *akrakye-foɔ* suffered diminishing marriage prospects. The price of conducting an ordinance marriage, a monogamous union legally recognized by the colonial state, performed by a church official, and valued as a marker of social affluence, made marrying an accepted *awuraa* a nearly impossible venture. Trapped by escalating costs and the expectation that they wed a woman whom they could "display at social gatherings" and rely on to share similar interests and concerns, many *akrakyefoɔ*, like their less-affluent counterparts, become stuck in a state of perpetual bachelorhood.[91]

In the early 1930s, the state of affairs surrounding marriage became so tenuous that city authorities discussed its scope as well as possible solutions. In 1934, members of the Optimism Club sponsored a series of discussions centered on finding a solution to the problem of exorbitantly priced unions. A few years later, staff at Achimota College performed an extensive analysis of thirty-four recent middle-class marriages. Their investigation revealed that they were shockingly expensive affairs. Fifteen of the thirty-four men studied had spent more than a year's salary on their wedding, half had borrowed money for the event, and over one-third remained in debt for two or more years. As a growing number of organizations, as well as the colonial state, voiced concern about the plummeting prospects of proper marriages, young clerks, teachers, and civil servants began to look for other ways to alleviate their concerns and to make in-roads into acquiring some gendered and generational mobility.[92]

Many young men turned to highlife. Given the sex-segregated nature of many urban spheres, including those of education and work, it was often difficult for young men to meet young women, converse, and evaluate their relational prospects. In fact, because of cities' wider climate of gendered chaos and generational rebellion, highlife was one of the few means by which junior men and women could publicly and acceptably interact throughout the 1930s. Since ball dances were protected events that had the favor of affluent residents as well as the colonial state, the young men and women who attended them could socialize, flirt, and forget about the more tenuous landscape of marriage without fear of repercussion.[93] On the dance floor, highlife's continued emphasis on coupled dancing, often in close proximity, allowed young people to catch one another's eye, chat, and launch possible partnerships. Such opportunities did not necessarily alleviate the hardships affiliated with marriage, but they convinced young people that they could use music to make some progress toward becoming full-fledged adults.[94]

CONCLUSION

By the end of the 1930s, the *akrakyefoɔ* had come to occupy a position of distinction and influence within the sociopolitical landscape of the urban Gold Coast. Over the course of several decades, they transformed their middle position from one of relative ambiguity and isolation into one of public recognition, tangible privilege, and wide appeal. Their successful rise was due to a variety of factors, including their education, positions of employment, and access to various modes of knowledge, but it owed much to their impressive organization and cooperative engagement. The prospects of many *akrakyefoɔ* improved considerably following the creation of urban social clubs: collective pan-ethnic bodies that enabled these men to demarcate an autonomous environment of interaction, celebrate their shared achievements, and cultivate a clear social and political agenda. In many senses, clubs were places where the various components of their middle-class culture—the consumption of imported goods, particular understandings and expectations of gender, and importance of embracing both local and cosmopolitan practices—coalesced into a readily identifiable package.

Clubs' most powerful communicative medium throughout the early decades of the twentieth century was popular musical recreation. Their creation of a new musical style, highlife, as well as appropriation of ball-room dances, elaborate dress, and a strict culture of etiquette allowed club members to distinguish themselves, in sight, sound, and practice, from the colony's other urban residents. Importantly, it also enabled them to reconfigure their position vis-à-vis traditional authorities, the wider public, and the British state. It gave individual *akrakyefoɔ* a means of elevating themselves above their less affluent peers, claiming influence over real and imagined *nwuraanom,* and garnering the approval of a co-lonial administration eager to spread order and civilization among urban communities. In the process, highlife enabled the middle class to situate themselves alongside British authorities, where they could capitalize on colonialism, work within the confines of the state, and bypass local hier-archies that accorded power to chiefs and elders.

After using Saturday Nights to carve out a unique niche in colonial society, the *akrakyefoɔ* set out to popularize their music and expand their newfound power. They invited wider groups of people to take part in and watch their ball dances and endeavored to socialize them into the nuances of middle-class life. Their sale of tickets and expanded program of activi-ties aimed specifically at non–club members certainly helped the music flourish. At the same time, however, such actions enabled the young men and women who had lost access to other forms of popular music to pur-sue their own set of gendered, generational, and social possibilities. As young men, and to some degree women, accessed highlife outside of the regulated confines of urban social clubs, the *akrakyefoɔ* lost their control over its meanings and significance. By the mid-1930s, it was possible for a young man to learn how to dance highlife and ballroom outside the gaze of middle-class older people and, as the attention to the tumultuous state of courtship and marriage suggests, put the music to slightly different uses. In the decades that followed, highlife became further enmeshed in urban areas' complex, and rather contentious, landscape of social rela-tions and personal power.

THREE

The Friction on the Floor: Negotiating Nightlife in Accra, 1940–1960

On Saturday Nights in the mid-1950s, a young Alex Moffatt would sneak out of his family house so that he could go to the Tip-Toe, Seaview, or another of Accra's many nightclubs. To prepare for these excursions, Moffatt would raid his uncle's closet, select a suit, tie, and pair of black shoes, and inform the other members of his family that he was retiring to bed. When it was clear that everyone else had fallen asleep, Moffatt got up, changed clothes, and quietly made his exit. When he returned home hours later, he took extreme care to open the front door, replace the borrowed items, and enter his room without alerting his unsuspecting parents, uncle, or grandmother. On Sunday morning, Moffatt awoke to a household that had no idea that he had ever left. For the next few years, Moffatt and his equally devious peers used these secretive methods to gain access to one of the city's most exciting spheres of musical recreation. At that time, many city residents upheld nightclubs as *the* place to go on Saturday Nights. Within their walls, large crowds gathered to enjoy the offerings of a new generation of highlife dance bands, such as Accra's Rhythm Aces, the Black Beats, and E. T. Mensah and the Tempos, that had taken the colony by storm. But nightclubs offered patrons more than an evening of music and dance. Like many other residents, Moffatt and his friends sought out these venues not simply to revel in highlife's vibrant sound; they did so in order to actively participate in a wider struggle concerning the colony's social and cultural future.[1]

While certain components of Moffatt's musical outings mirrored the popular musical exploits of earlier generations, they were distinctly postwar phenomena characterized by different venues, musical influences, and audiences. Unlike their predecessors, Moffatt and his peers did not take part in an impromptu musical performance or an elaborate ball dance catered by a large dance orchestra. Instead, they sought out a new kind of dance band: a small combo that performed a revised form of highlife alongside a variety of imported musical styles including ballroom, jazz, calypso, Afro-Caribbean rhythms, and rock 'n' roll. His destination, the nightclub, was also new. Unlike private social clubs, these were commercialized spaces open to a wide swath of city residents. Established elites, desk workers, and other middle-class people now attended such venues, but so did manual laborers, apprentice workers, youth and students, and newly arrived migrants from other rural and urban areas. From time to time, even members of the colony's crumbling colonial administration and rising crop of nationalist leaders entered their gates, where they rubbed shoulders and shared the dance floor with the rest of the assembled crowd.

As nightclubs were diverse environments of recreation and exchange, they also became spaces of formidable friction. In the years following the Second World War, Accra was a city of considerable, and often intense, political and social transformations.[2] The most obvious concerned the fate of British colonial rule. Throughout the late 1940s and 1950s, large numbers of people voiced adamant calls for self-government and political independence. While the emerging movement for decolonization was spearheaded by public protest and the rise of Kwame Nkrumah's Convention People's Party (CPP), the city became so politicized that relatively few spaces, including nightclubs, remained exempt from the movement's reach. Outside of party politics, many residents embraced popular music as a means of inculcating and celebrating the prospects of independence. The links between the music and the political transfer were particularly salient on March 6, 1957, when thousands of men and women marked the official birth of a sovereign Ghana by congregating together and dancing to highlife's jubilant sounds.

At the same time, men and women flocked to nightclubs in order to negotiate more subtle, but no less important, transformations. Throughout the 1950s, individuals hit the dance floor to contest the continuities and changes that would accompany the abolition of colonial rule. For those who held positions atop the city's existing hierarchies—including members of the middle class and older residents of gendered and generational standing—the ousting of the British was an opportunity to retrench, even expand, their influence. On Saturday Nights, they perpetuated highlife's prewar form in order to communicate their intentions. They donned elaborate attire, favored learned forms of dance, and insisted on the maintenance of formal etiquette. But for others, the postwar years were a time to set aside past arrangements in favor of something new. Encouraged by an environment of "wide horizons and exciting possibilities," less-empowered residents set out to reject the contours of the past, improve their daily lives, and embrace new practices that could complement and enhance the impending political transfer.[3] This was especially true of city youth, who went to nightclubs in order to challenge their marginal status and unhinge hierarchies that they associated with British colonial rule. For them, Saturday Night was a time to embrace new musics such as rock 'n' roll, arbitrate between the local and the international, and mediate between their personal liberation and that of the nation at large. By the time that Ghana gained its independence, the nightclub had become a site of tremendous friction, a place where city residents gathered not to come together as a unified community, but to actively negotiate individual realities, collective concerns, and the fabric of the nation's future.[4]

This chapter opens with an examination of the major transformations that characterized the period's Saturday Nights, including the cultural impacts of the Second World War, the rapid expansion of commercialized leisure, and the evolving form of dance band highlife music. By the late 1940s, these changes had sparked a new era of popular musical recreation fueled by small dance combos who performed jazz and other foreign musics in nightclubs rather than private and exclusive social clubs. These early nightclubs preserved many aspects of highlife's prewar culture and middle-class distinction, but they also attracted new audiences who introduced subtle, but important, changes into their midst. Many young men and women, including Alex Moffatt, attended nightclubs in order to challenge their subordinate position, claim personal freedoms, and initiate otherwise impossible relationships. By the end of the 1950s, another set of youth used a new genre of popular music, rock 'n' roll, to express their visions for the city's postcolonial future. As rock 'n' rollers invaded city nightclubs, they did more than transform its Saturday Nights: they prompted vigorous debates about the gendered, generational, and social fabric of the city and newly independent nation.

THE GROWTH OF COMMERCIALIZED
LEISURE IN ACCRA

The predominant catalyst for dance band highlife's transformation—from a regulated medium of middle-class influence to one of open contestation—was the Second World War. The war had an especially noteworthy imprint on Accra, which became the headquarters of the Allied West African military operations in 1942. Over the next several years, American and European military personnel made visible impacts on the city, particularly in the areas adjacent to the harbor, airport, and their two bases of operation and residence, Giffard Camp and Burma Camp. The presence of thousands of foreign soldiers as well as their requisite military equipment placed new demands on the city's roads, ports, and communication facilities, but it also sparked a new era of infrastructural expansion. The gradual implementation of the Colonial Development and Welfare Acts of 1940 and 1945 helped fund the construction of new residential areas, schools, and commercial enterprises as well as improvements to the city's radio and communication infrastructure. The founding of the Gold Coast Information Department in 1939 and subsequent diffusion of the colony's radio broadcasts through publicly erected loudspeakers gave Accra's residents ready access to new information about current events in and outside of the colony.[5]

Importantly, the war also helped reinvigorate the prospects of wage labor in Accra and other towns. In the early 1940s, the coastal cities of Accra and Takoradi continued to attract large scores of migrants eager to find work at a trading company, the railways, or city harbors. The presence of Allied troops, modernization of urban airfields, and use of the Gold Coast as a depot for provisions heading to North Africa and the Middle East made each city an important center for manual labor. While many migrants flocked to these cities in pursuit of such opportunities, others reached them in an effort to escape rural areas beset by growing hardships. Throughout the duration of the war, many rural communities bore the brunt of government-directed food drives, import shortages, and chiefs' efforts to conscript needed military recruits. To avoid such circumstances, many young people flocked to cities, even if they had little hope of immediate employment. By 1948, Accra had 133,192 residents, more than twice its 1931 population of 61,550. And while the city had a relatively equal share of men and women, over half of the population fell in between the ages of 16 and 45.[6]

FIGURE 3.1. The Accra Palladium c. 1945. Although erected as a cinema house in 1924, the Palladium became one of Accra's first commercial spaces to feature highlife music and ballroom dancing. *Photo courtesy of Bookor African Popular Music Archives Foundation.*

Like their predecessors of earlier decades, these migrants came to the city in search of something more than work. In the early 1940s, many of them approached Accra as a place of modern intrigue and social excitement. Once settled, most proved eager to take advantage of the city's entertainment scene, especially during the evening and weekend hours, when they were free from the burdens of work. Many first stopped at one of the city's established venues of musical recreation. Although places such as Accra's Merry Villas, the Gold Coast Bar, the Palladium, and Tommy's Club continued to cater to middle-class patrons, they attracted a steady, and ever-growing, stream of people of various ethnicities and social backgrounds (see Figure 3.1). As demand for musical leisure grew, additional

commercialized venues purposefully catering to wide and diverse clienteles sprouted up in the city's center. One the most prominent was the
Hotel Metropole, which opened in 1936. Though originally conceived as
a hotel for European visitors, the Metropole gained prominence as a place
of open frivolity and lively entertainment. Its location in James Town—
an established commercial and residential area that the colony's medi-
cal officer dubbed as "primitive," "badly congested," and "most unpleas-
ant"—made it proximate to the harbor, railway station, and other spheres
important to young male wage laborers.[7] Following the outbreak of the
war, many British, American, and West African soldiers also flocked to the
Metropole in search of drink, conversation, and other forms of leisure.[8]

By embracing its new clientele, the Metropole became one of the
city's most prominent spots for popular musical recreation. In 1946, the
venue abandoned its reliance on recorded music and started featuring live
bands that could perform dance band highlife and other musical styles
in front of fervent crowds.[9] The Metropole claimed distinction as the
city's first nightclub, but other establishments quickly followed suit. The
Gold Coast Bar, a nightspot in the Kardiri Zongo area of Accra, became
popular among affluent urbanites, seamen and dockworkers, and local
and foreign soldiers. As they came together to drink, socialize, and enjoy
bands' offerings of highlife, ragtime, and European ballroom tunes, this
diverse clientele spawned a recreational culture quite different from the
private social clubs or commercialized settings of a decade earlier.[10] Many
of these new patrons proved quite willing to transgress the music's prewar
culture of middle-class etiquette. The most egregious were the city's foreign servicemen, who had deep pocketbooks and a penchant for making
heavy drinking, commercial sex, and illicit activities regular components
of their Saturday Nights. Troops' brazen behavior, blatant disregard for
middle-class expectations, and apparent immunity from consequence left
lasting impressions on city residents:

> The Americans . . . usually came to town with wads of money, [would] count
> so much of it and buy about two or three bottles of beer. When you wanted
> to give them the balance they would say "keep the rubbish." The whites,
> especially the Americans, often left their camps to patronize the local bars.
> Bars began to spring up during the war so that any small corner there was a
> kiosk selling beer. They didn't mind sitting down and talking and listening
> to jazz and swing on the gramophone.[11]

In addition to funding the emergence of new recreational establishments,
foreign servicemen also spawned an expansion of prostitution, particu-

larly in places associated with popular music and dance.[12] Several venues made efforts to prohibit the open solicitation of sex—an act that would have been inconceivable in highlife's prewar settings—but most had a hard time ousting "pilot boys": young male residents who connected interested clients to enterprising women. Although these pilot boys commanded up to 40 percent of a prostitute's earnings for their services, they became popular among servicemen who patronized musical venues such as Takoradi's Akropolis Hotel and Accra's Chicago Bar. There, these men drank, gambled, and acquired a notorious reputation.[13]

Servicemen's insatiable demand for drink, dance, and indulgence garnered considerable disfavor from many realms, but it held appeal for young men and, to some degree, women, who were eager to find greater freedom in the colony's regulated recreational scene. Many found particular promise in the musical styles these buoyant visitors favored and demanded on Saturday Nights. Many young men became avid consumers of swing, Dixieland jazz, and Caribbean styles such as the rumba, mambo, and calypso favored by African American troops. By the end of the decade they openly endorsed these musics as forms of modern intrigue and novel fun. Others found inspiration in the American films that screened in the city's cinema houses, particularly those such as *Cabin in the Sky, Orchestra Wives,* and *Angels with Dirty Faces* that featured jazz bands, new urban fashions, and potent dancing displays.[14] Dedicated enthusiasts purchased imported jazz records at department stores such as the Union Trading Company (UTC) and Kingsway, the flagship store of the United African Company (UAC), so that they could listen to the exciting music on a more regular basis. Less affluent but equally enterprising youth bought jazz recordings from visiting troops; others became avid patrons of the colony's radio station, Z.O.Y., which aired jazz numbers throughout the duration of the war.[15]

For young men, the appeal of jazz, swing, and other foreign musics stemmed not simply from their rhythmic quality or danceable sound, but from the liberating possibilities they appeared to engender in American audiences of a similar age range. In the 1940s, growing numbers emulated the dress and mannerisms of carefree GIs living within the city's confines. They donned blue jeans, smoked cigarettes, and incorporated phrases such as "O.K. Babe" and "How' yer Toots?" into their everyday speech.[16] By adopting this new range of behaviors, they also shunned the "higher-than-thee" atmosphere that had long characterized highlife events. Disenchanted with the supposedly superior conventions favored by the British state and established middle class, young and increasingly mobile residents began to see the city's popular music scene as a place of open merriment and self-expression.[17]

Accra's wartime climate of leisure also left strong impressions on local musicians. In the early 1940s, two of the colony's most respected highlife ensembles, the Accra Orchestra and the Accra Rhythmic Orchestra, incorporated jazz and swing tunes into their existing repertoires. To facilitate their performance, these groups eliminated their large, and increasingly irrelevant, string sections and focused exclusively on brass and horned instruments, the bass and guitar, and percussive elements such as the claves and "jazz" (Western drum kit). These downsized orchestras—more accurately called dance bands—continued to perform at private events and ball dances, but they also solicited new engagements in front of well-funded audiences of foreign troops. To prepare for such outings, they mastered American jazz standards, including Count Basie's "One O' Clock Jump" and Glen Miller's "American Patrol," which they played alongside highlife and ballroom numbers.[18] Following the war, some young musicians continued to perform jazz and swing numbers in front of enthusiastic local crowds. Guy Warren and Joe Kelly, members of the Accra Rhythmic Orchestra and Accra Orchestra respectively, capitalized on jazz music's prominence by forming a new band, the Fire-works Four, which gave frequent "tosses" at various city venues.[19]

Few musicians fueled highlife's shifting culture more than E. T. Mensah, an innovative artist who later earned recognition as the "King of Highlife." Mensah began his musical career in 1933, when he joined the Accra Orchestra at the age of fourteen. Over the next several years, he performed with the ensemble, became proficient on the flute, and gained intimate knowledge about highlife's importance to middle-class culture. In 1940, Mensah met Jack Leopard, a former professional saxophonist who was in Accra as a member of the British military. Upon learning of Mensah's musical exploits, Leopard invited him to join his Leopard and His Black and White Spots, a jazz band comprised of British soldiers and local musicians. Under Leopard's tutelage, Mensah and his compatriots enhanced their training in jazz phrasing, refined their technique, and experimented with the prospects of adding new elements into highlife's flexible triple offbeat rhythmic structure. They found further encouragement at the hands of foreign troops, whose lucrative endorsement of their music convinced them that the city's popular musical scene was ripe for revolutionary change:

> [During the war] we played from one army camp to another in the Accra district. Each of us got a pound after each engagement. Boy, oh, boy, that

FIGURE 3.2. The Tempos, 1952/3, with E. T. Mensah seated at center.
At ten members, the Tempos were much smaller in size than the
dance orchestras that had previously fueled dance band highlife.
Photo courtesy of Bookor African Popular Music Archives Foundation.

> pound seemed a fortune to us in those days. For some years we had been
> playing in one of the other of the three orchestras in town, the Accra,
> Rhythmic and City. . . . In these we used to get about two shillings for every
> engagement.[20]

Although the end of the war prompted the departure of military audiences as well as the demise of Leopard's band, Mensah took a number
of steps to ensure that it did not bring a halt to the city's changing music
scene. He promptly joined the Tempos, a small dance band comprised entirely of Gold Coast musicians that specialized in jazz, calypso, highlife,
and ballroom numbers. In 1949, shortly after his ascension as the Tempos'
bandleader, Mensah arranged for the group to take residence at the Weekend-in-Havana, one of Accra's newest and largest nightclubs. The financial security of weekly engagements enabled the group to compensate its
members, hold regular rehearsals, purchase instruments and sheet music,
and bring further innovations into the city's postwar Saturday Nights.
While the group's fluency in jazz and calypsos garnered it considerable

FIGURE 3.3. E. T. Mensah's Tempos give an outdoor performance in 1950s Accra. While affluent patrons retained their privileged place within the musical proceedings, such performances also attracted new, and rather young, audience members. *Photo courtesy of Bookor African Popular Music Archives Foundation.*

acclaim, it was their infusion of Afro-Caribbean rhythms into highlife's established structure that earned them legions of fans throughout the city, colony, and West African region (PURL 3.1).[21] In the early 1950s, the Tempos' vibrant and danceable sound brought them numerous engagements, including a string of successful tours to Nigeria, and enabled them to become the Gold Coast's first fully professional dance band. As other groups rushed to duplicate their novel sound, dance band highlife entered a new, and incredibly inclusive, era of prosperity that would captivate urban audiences for the next twenty years (see Figures 3.2 and 3.3).[22]

In the wake of the Tempos' meteoric rise, Accra became home to several combo-sized dance bands that fused highlife, calypso, jazz, and ballroom forms into lengthy musical sets that lasted three or more hours. In the early 1950s, Gold Coast towns contained a great number of reputable highlife dance bands, including the Black Beats (led by King Bruce), the Red Spots (led by Tommy Gripman) (PURL 3.2), Joe Kelly's Band, the Rhythm Aces (led by Spike Anyankor) (PURL 3.3), the Stargazers (led by Eddie Quansah), as well as the Modernaires, the Rakers, the Hot

Shots, the Downbeats, the Top Spotters, the Havana Delta Dandies, the Springbok Dance Band, and the Shambros Dance Band.[23] As the number of capable bands grew, so did the number of nightclubs. Major cities such as Accra, Kumasi, and Takoradi soon housed several of these venues, as did smaller towns eager to attract dance bands into their midst. The revitalization of His Master's Voice (HMV), Decca, and other European recording agencies enabled bands to produce seven-inch 45 rpm records that audiences could play in private and public settings. Together, this potent combination of small mobile bands, commercialized nightclubs, and expanding musical outlets transformed a once middle-class music into one that appealed to individuals of various occupations, ages, and backgrounds.[24]

While new audiences embraced highlife's transformations with considerable enthusiasm, the city's vanguard of established patrons struggled to reconcile its new audiences, influences, and venues with their well-established aims. Concerned about their inability to control either highlife's form or function, many middle-class people complained that a once respectable and civilized music had begun to spiral out of control. Using the same newspaper outlets they had employed to praise club ball dances, they framed newly erected bars and nightclubs as domains of vice and social problems. Others insisted, in rhetoric strikingly similar to that invoked by the missionaries and traditional authorities of earlier decades, that the sexual deviancy, gross materialism, and uncontrolled social gaiety of prostitutes, pilot boys, and "Americanized" social degenerates posed a significant threat to the colony's social and moral order.[25] A few went so far as to appeal to the British government, whom they implored to regulate and supervise the city's changing popular musical scene.[26]

To a certain degree, these vocal critics had the state's ear. In the midst of the war years government officials expressed growing alarm with the capital city's growing number of "juvenile delinquents": young men and women under the age of eighteen whose repeated dabbles in illegal acts such as gambling, petty thievery, and prostitution threatened the colony's welfare and social development.[27] Delinquents' criminal acts, idle behaviors, and presumed destiny as "beggars" and "loafers" also left a readily identifiable blemish in the state's promotion of hard work, "civilization," and stable family life. Throughout the early 1940s, British authorities advised that the best way to combat juvenile delinquency was to target and prosecute the unruly residents who set a bad example for city youth. Their first, and most obvious, scapegoat was women. In 1944, the government passed a set of anti-prostitution laws that intended to remove "immoral" women from the capital and other major towns. Over the next several years, Accra police carried out these regulations to great success, resulting in a 30 percent increase in juvenile convictions (largely pilot boys), a 16 percent increase in female arrests, and the deportation of more than seventy Nigerian women accused of polluting the city's environs.[28]

While established middle-class audiences applauded such actions, they were also hesitant about maintaining a cordial and codependent relationship with the British state. In the years following the Second World War, numerous *akrakyefoɔ* were among the many Gold Coasters questioning the legitimacy and longevity of colonial rule.[29] Wartime improvements in communications, infrastructure, and technology enabled them to extend their gaze, imagine new political possibilities, and directly confront the authority and operation of the colonial state.[30] In 1947, a group of urban businessmen and lawyers led by J. B. Danquah, R. S. Blay, and George Grant formed the United Gold Coast Convention (UGCC), a political movement that asked for the immediate incorporation of educated men into the structures of the colonial government as well as the gradual achievement of self-rule.[31] Although the UGCC failed to garner widespread support for its demands, the plight of returning ex-servicemen, postwar tensions over the colony's economic picture, and the onset of swollen shoot disease—a pathogenic virus that crippled the colony's export sector—fanned the flames of political discontentment among the wider public.[32] In 1947–1948, a wave of strikes, boycotts, and riots crippled British confidence and thrust the colony onto the path toward political independence.

For middle-class people, this expanding climate of anticolonial indignation was also a sign that their future prospects hinged on their relationships with their countrymen and countrywomen rather than British officials. In the aftermath of the creation of the UGCC, many *akrakyefoɔ* looked for other ways to convince other urban residents that they were well positioned to inherit authority over the city's affairs. On Saturday Nights, they attempted to do so not by decrying the character of highlife's new venues or audiences, but by modeling "healthy" recreational habits that others could emulate. In August, 1944, the Railway African Club of Sekondi invited city residents to take part in a public forum on highlife's changing face. Although the forum's title, "Wanted: A Minimum Code of Behavior," likely reflected the concerns of many established *akrakyefoɔ*, the chair, Joe S. Annan, encouraged attendants to "revolutionise and purify" highlife so that it could reclaim its status as a respectable realm of musical recreation.[33] Similar efforts followed in several Gold Coast towns. In Cape Coast, middle-class residents offered public demonstrations on how to properly dance various styles, dress up, and behave during nights out on the town.[34]

At the same time, many *akrakyefoɔ* came to realize that the colony's postwar Saturday Nights could not merely replicate those from a decade earlier. The main catalyst for this admission was the decline of the literary and social club. Amidst the war years' advances in communications, commercialized leisure, and political organizations, once-illustrious clubs such as the Cape Coast Literary and Social Club and the Sekondi Optimism Club started to experience an irreversible decline. The clubs' fall began at the hands of new generations of school graduates, who came to view them as outdated organizations better equipped for earlier years. As they failed to attract new members, most clubs became smaller in size, older in composition, and diminished in reputation and influence.[35] In the mid-1940s, clubs also lost the financial and logistical support of the colonial state, which saw commercialized entertainment venues as more useful spots in which to influence urban populations. By 1947, club memberships had shrunk so far the *Gold Coast Observer* reluctantly declared these once-prominent organizations to be "a matter of history."[36] Robbed of their long-standing forum of social influence, established middle-class residents had little choice but to attempt to carry out their aims within Saturday Nights' new setting: the commercialized nightclub.

THE CONTOURS OF NIGHTLIFE IN EARLY 1950S ACCRA

Dance band highlife's meteoric rise as Accra's most dominant form of popular musical recreation stemmed largely from the rapid growth and expansion of the city's nightclub scene. In the early part of the 1950s the city boasted dozens of nightclubs; less than twenty years later, it had over sixty, giving it roughly one per five thousand residents.[37] The sheer abundance of these venues made them one of Accra's most vibrant spaces of social interaction. By day, nightclubs unassumingly blended into their surroundings near the harbor, main business district, and city center. They opened their doors in the afternoon, enabling workers bound for home to stop by for a bit of relaxed conversation, to sip a drink over quiet radio or gramophone music, or scope out the lineup for an upcoming evening's events. Shortly after dark, however, these venues transformed central Accra into a hotbed of popular musical activity. James Town came alive to sounds ushering forth from the Seaview, Metropole, and Weekend-in-Havana; Adabraka from sites like the Kit Kat, Tip-Toe Gardens

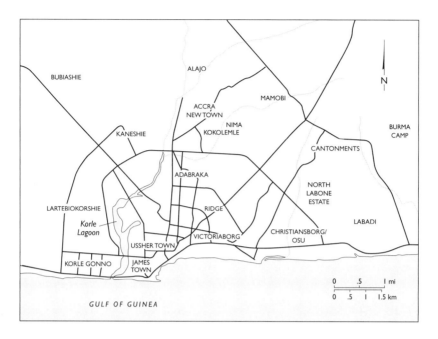

MAP 3.1. Accra, 1950s. *Produced by Bill Nelson.*

and the Lido; Osu from the Red Rose and Kalamazoo; and Victoriaborg from the Paramount, Town Hall, and the Ambassador Hotel (see Map 3.1).[38] For residents of these well-established areas, Saturday Nights soon became synonymous with highlife's sights and sounds.

Though concentrated in the city's central areas, nightclubs regularly attracted audiences who lived in more suburban and outlying areas. During the course of the 1950s Accra's population continued to grow, creating an escalating demand for housing and necessitating the creation of new residential areas beyond the established outskirts of Kaneshie, New Town, and Nima.[39] Suburban construction, coupled with the infrastructural developments of the wartime period, also spawned a considerable expansion in the city's transportation network. Private taxis offered well-to-do residents a way to quickly reach their destination, while tro-tros—lorry buses that traveled a fixed point-to-point route for a small fare—linked most residents to their destinations.[40] In 1950, Adbul Rahim and Ahmed Tettey Dixon lived in Alajo, roughly four miles from the bustling city center. Although Alajo was rather quiet on Saturday Nights, the brothers found that getting to a nightclub was a relatively cheap and simple venture. They often took tro-tros destined for places like James Town, Adabraka, and Osu and finished with a short walk to their venue of choice. Occasionally, they opted to join with friends and pile into a private taxi, a small splurge that took them directly to their destination for less than two shillings per person.[41]

A more pressing challenge was deciding when and where one wanted to access the emerging postwar music scene. By the mid-1950s, Accra's musical enthusiasts could access highlife recreation every day of the week. Budget-conscious patrons preferred going to nightclubs on week-day evenings or Sunday afternoons. Although these occasions usually featured less-prominent bands and attracted small crowds, they also offered discounted admission rates and rather intimate settings of music and dance. Unsurprisingly, most venues reserved their best offerings for Friday and Saturday nights. On these evenings, reputable bands took the stage around eight o'clock, played two or three lengthy sets, and closed at one or two in the morning. These six-hour spells enabled patrons either to enjoy an extended stint at the hands of a particular band or to move from venue to venue in order to get a taste of the evening's offerings. To plan their night on the town, many people enlisted the help of the colony's newspapers. The classified ads section of the Daily Graphic, the colony's most prominent daily, contained numerous advertisements that listed nightclubs' featured bands, admission rates, and special offerings. Nightclubs posted large signboards outside their front door to alert passersby about upcoming shows; members of the public who did not read relied on the radio or word of mouth.[42] Since patrons tended to plan their outings according to the evening's scheduled fanfare, most nightclubs attracted a rotating clientele comprised of individuals of various ethnicities, occupations, and backgrounds. Dance bands attempted to reach these broad audiences by performing songs in a variety of languages, including English, Twi, Ga, Fante, and, from time to time, Ewe and Hausa.[43]

While nightclubs attracted large and diverse crowds, not all urban residents took part in Accra's Saturday Nights. Throughout the 1950s, two salient factors mediated who attended the city's nightclubs. The first was age. Despite the liberal environment of the war years, most 1950s nightclubs operated as adult spaces and, at the encouragement of city authorities concerned about the susceptibility of youth, barred individuals under the age of eighteen.[44] Since few city residents had any form of identification, venues could not completely or consistently omit youth, but most posted doormen who turned away any individual who looked underage.[45] The second principal requirement for admission was the ability to pay a

FIGURE 3.4. An Easter Dance at the Seaview hotel and nightclub, March 28, 1959. On holidays nightclubs often filled to their capacity, forcing patrons to find a spot near the band performing on stage (background), on the dance floor (middle), or at a table that lined the venue's periphery. *Photo courtesy of Ghana Information Services Department Photograph Library.*

modest gate fee. These fees varied slightly from venue to venue and evening to evening, but they were usually between two and five shillings for a single admission and four to eight shillings per couple. For established middle-class audiences who had paid two shillings for a spectator ticket in the 1930s, such rates were easily affordable. Admission rates certainly made a larger dent in the pockets of less-affluent individuals, but many insisted that a Saturday Night spent at a nightclub was an affordable indulgence, particularly on an intermittent basis or on special occasions and holidays (see Figure 3.4).[46] Avid fans, including those who were workers and students, insisted that gate fees were neither a deterrent nor an exorbitant expenditure: they simply made a budget that allowed them to attend a nightclub every weekend and, if possible, during the week.[47]

Economic data from the 1950s corroborates these claims. For many Gold Coasters, the decade was one of considerable economic growth, prosperity, and rising standards of living. This was especially true in the booming enclave of Accra, which continued to offer various opportunities for skilled or semiskilled work, manual labor, and self-employment. Given the wide availability of jobs, many residents enjoyed some level of disposable income that they could allot to the general realm of recreation and leisure.[48] In 1953, a government survey of Accra household budgets found that the average family dedicated 6.1 percent of its expenditures toward the broad category of drink and tobacco. Although this category does not include the expenditures they dedicated toward nightlife or highlife recreation, its position behind only food and clothing as an average monthly expenditure demonstrates the potential income that urban residents could, and often did, dedicate to such pursuits.[49]

Most nightclub patrons insisted that the financial costs of the gate fee, necessary transportation, and an evening's refreshments were a small price to pay for what was usually a joyous and memorable outing. Throughout the early 1950s, nightclub advertisements confidently guaranteed their patrons an environment of relaxation, prolific urban amusement, and first-rate music and dance. Most lived up to this promise. Without exception, men and women recalled their evenings at such venues with pronounced enthusiasm. As Diana Oboshilay recalled, dressing up, meeting friends, purchasing refreshments, and dancing into the early morning hours were things that made people extremely happy:

> When we went out, we really enjoyed ourselves. We would wear our finest clothes—those days formal dresses weren't too expensive—go to a nightclub and find a place to sit. If the band was special, we would go early to sit and wait. We'd sit and talk until the band started playing. Then I would dance the entire night. It made me happy! Maybe around 11 or 11:30 the band would stop for a break. Then people would be chatting, sitting, or drinking. When the band came on, back to the dance floor![50]

In addition to their provision of unrivaled fun, nightclubs held appeal as one of the city's most modern postwar arenas. They were places where people of various ethnicities and backgrounds could congregate together, see the city's latest styles, mingle with others, and catch a glimpse of future trends. In 1953, a journalist proudly proclaimed that "nightlife" had become a "household word" within the city: an assertion that certainly held true for those eager to take part in a novel realm of interaction and intrigue.[51]

If nightclubs epitomized the modern nature of postwar Accra, they simultaneously reflected many of the established conventions that had long characterized highlife's past. Following the end of the war, as well as the departure of the numerous foreign servicemen, nightclub owners had to find ways to make a sound profit while catering to local, and much more frugal, audiences. In an effort to secure steady earnings, many catered to the city's established middle class: a subset that had a track record of allocating their disposable income toward Saturday Nights. To ensure that such people entered their venue's gates, owners consciously endeavored to recreate a recreational environment similar to that endorsed by the urban social clubs and *akrakyefoɔ* of earlier years. They mandated that all patrons wear suits and ankle-length evening gowns: strict dress standards that matched the preferred attire of established ladies and gentlemen. J. J. Sarpong, a doorman at the Seaview nightclub, recalled that he and his counterparts at other venues had firm instructions to turn away patrons who failed to appear in respectable clothing.[52] As Josephine Ayitey recalled, these policies found further enforcement within nightclub walls, where well-dressed persons openly mocked those who donned overly casual apparel: "If you went out [to a nightclub], you had to make sure that the outfit you were wearing would let you feel happy. If you knew that something would make people talk about you, you wouldn't wear it . . . people would shout on you! You'd be ashamed."[53]

While the need to dress up likely discouraged some Accra residents from venturing out to the city's nightclubs, the men and women I spoke with insisted that the favorable economic conditions of the early 1950s enabled them to purchase new clothing articles, experiment with formal styles of dress, and don garments that exceeded their actual economic standing. Grershon Gaba purchased his first suit while working as an apprentice photographer in the early 1950s, an ensemble he proudly purchased to wear during his evening excursions. Over the next few years, he purchased several additional suits as well as collared shirts, ties, and a pair of black leather shoes. Many working men came to acquire a least one such outfit by patronizing either a city department store or one of the many smaller shops and trading stalls dotting city markets. Others made a trip to a local tailor, where they could peruse scores of mail-order catalogues from Britain and the United States, admire a range of innovative fashions, and select a style of their choice.[54] Women also enjoyed shopping for Saturday Nights. Like men, they eagerly pored over the selection of evening gowns, shoes, and other accoutrements offered at commercial stores and market stalls, always on the lookout for something distinctive or unique. Others purchased cloth and set out to design, sew, or tailor their own customized garments that could cut costs and provide them with greater individualized style.[55] In the end, many men and women insisted that one did not have to own a set of fancy clothes to enjoy an evening of nightclub recreation. Students or unemployed patrons—including Alex Moffatt—skirted such expenses by borrowing or temporarily pilfering clothing from friends or family members.[56]

The desire to attract a reliable base of middle-class patrons also led many nightclub owners to enforce behavioral prescriptions similar to those that regulated highlife recreation in the years prior to the war. In the early 1950s, these venues expected patrons to behave in a calm and disciplined manner. They strictly prohibited verbal disagreements, physical confrontations, and intoxication. To enforce these measures, venues employed doormen and security, and occasionally asked city police to help remove unwanted ruffians.[57] Few of the men and women who attended nightclubs in the early 1950s recalled witnessing a serious breach of club protocol, but most admitted that they strove to blend into, rather than challenge, this respectable environment. In fact, they closely monitored their behavior, especially in regards to the consumption of alcohol, for fear that any undue excess would bring shame to themselves, partner, or peers: "[Nightclubs] would ensure discipline at the dance. If you went there and misbehaved, you disgraced yourself. [Security] would walk you out and everyone would wonder what kind of person you were."[58]

Women faced even more restrictive behavioral codes and prohibitions. As a result of escalating concerns about postwar female mobility and prostitution, many venues admitted only partnered women: those who arrived at the club in the company of a man. Although venues tacitly encouraged this practice by offering a discounted couple's entrance fee—which was less expensive than two single admission tickets—they frequently refused to admit women who came without a male partner or large group of friends. Women devised ways to bypass these restrictions, by soliciting a "partner" outside the venue, entering with a friend, or cajoling the doorman, but admitted that single women usually attracted undesirable attention inside of the nightclub gate. As James Allotey summarized, city audiences frequently, and scornfully, assumed that such women were prostitutes: "I do not know elsewhere, but in this Accra here, a woman alone was not expected at a nightclub. When people saw you alone at a nightclub, they did not respect you. [Women] had to be there with a partner; [they] had to be there with somebody."[59]

If nightclubs' emphasis on partnered couples, elaborate dress, and respectful behavior helped placate middle-class audiences, so did their emphasis on ballroom dancing. Although many dance bands' booming popularity was the result of their growing proficiency in jazz and Afro-

Caribbean styles, nightclubs asked that they play mainly ballroom numbers throughout the course of their performances. As a result, many new patrons found that knowing how to dance the foxtrot, waltz, and other ballroom styles was essential to enjoying Saturday Nights. Although nightlife novices attended nightclubs in order to dance, not sit, most admitted that initially they vacated the dance floor when such numbers aired. This was especially true during their first few outings, when many men and women were afraid that any missteps would make them look foolish or out of place. J. O. Mills explained:

> [Before you go to a nightclub] it was good if you had learned polished dances; it was good to have learned them well. The M.C. [started each dance] by announcing that the floor was going to open for a certain number—maybe waltz—and then the band would start. Maybe I came with my partner and she didn't know how to dance that number. If so, we couldn't go [out on the dance floor]. People would laugh at you! . . . You would have paid all that money just to sit down and wait for highlife. You would sit a lot! Then you would think "if I can't dance anything then why should I be at a dance"?[60]

The continued proliferation of ballroom forms prompted Mills and others eager to remain on the dance floor to seek instruction at one of the city's many dance schools: formal institutions that offered lessons on how to dance the waltz, foxtrot, quickstep, and other styles. In the early 1950s, Accra had at least seventeen dancing schools, which ranged from small, intimate institutions to large-scale outfits that enrolled hundreds of students. By 1960, the city had thirty-five dancing schools, and other cities, such as Kumasi, Cape Coast, and Takoradi, had many of their own.[61] Interested pupils selected a school for a number of reasons, including its physical location, the type and number of classes it offered, and the reputation of affiliated instructors.[62] Ultimately, a student's choice of school stemmed from his or her desired proficiency in ballroom's culture of dance and etiquette. Those interested in gaining a quick and basic familiarity with particular styles usually attended one of the city's large dancing schools: institutions that offered a number of daily classes, charged a small fee per lesson, and enabled students of all abilities to acquire an enhanced level of confidence in the dance of their choice. Many large schools also held classes within nightclubs themselves, allowing students to gain familiarity with their layout and spatial confines. While most people attended these large schools for a quick lesson, a few dedicated students also used them to perfect their skills in numerous dances. Harry Amenumey attended a dancing school at the Lido nightclub every day for about three months, while Charity Agbenyega went to the Seaview nightclub three times a week for a four-month period. At the conclusion of their respective training, each received a certificate confirming that they had met teachers' expectations and could now hit the floor with proficiency and confidence.[63]

Other students elected to attend smaller, and more private, schools of instruction. Like the dancing clubs of the 1930s and 1940s, these schools had organized positions of leadership, including a president, vice president, treasurer, and a few secretaries, and offered students a complete education about ballroom movements and etiquette. Interested students joined these schools by paying a modest membership fee of a few shillings per month, which was used to compensate instructors, rent practice space, and purchase gramophones needed to perfect various dance styles. James Allotey, who attended the Charles Lee Dancing School in James Town, and Margaret Acolatse, who joined the Rhythm and Sounds Dancing School in Adabraka (PURL 3.4), recalled that their schools offered an intimate means of learning how to navigate the dance floor, elude potential embarrassment, and refine their mannerisms and self-presentations. Many staged general dances, formal practice sessions that provided students with real-life opportunities to put their budding skills to the test.[64] Oftentimes, private schools also provided students with lessons that had little to do with dance steps. Benny Amakudzie, who taught at a number of small dancing schools throughout the 1950s, offered his students extensive instruction in ballroom etiquette and proper nightclub behavior. He taught his male students how to "behave like a gentleman," "dress well," and carry on an air of "politeness" (see Figure 3.5). Grershon Gaba recalled one such lesson: "If you want to dance with a woman you go, 'Excuse me, lady.' And then you carry on. If she is also having a partner, you ask the partner, the gentleman, 'Excuse me, your lady.' And then he will allow you before the lady will stand."[65] Women received similar lessons. Josephine Ayitey recalled how her dancing school encouraged its female students to uphold a concrete set of "respectful" behaviors not only on the dance floor but in the everyday spheres of home and work: "Sometimes if we went [to the school], we did not do any dancing. They would sit us down and talk about how to respect an elderly person; how to talk to our parents, how to do housework. They taught us all those things!"[66]

As they instructed their pupils about the correct approach on and off the dance floor, these middle-class dancing school instructors declared that long-standing hierarchies of age, class, and gender would continue to

FIGURE 3.5. A young man asks a young woman to dance to a ballroom number, Accra, 1961. © *Bailey's African History Archives.*

operate in the postwar period. Like nightclubs, schools framed highlife recreation as a tranquil domain that needed to mirror, rather than challenge, the city's existing order.[67] Most refused to accept students under the age of twenty, an act that validated nightclub policy as well as government concerns about the susceptibility of youth. The National Association of Teachers of Dancing, an organization comprised of established middle-class experts on highlife and ballroom dancing, supplemented these efforts by sponsoring a number of lectures, teaching demonstrations, and dances aimed at educating new audiences about the basic standards of Saturday Nights. The *Sunday Mirror,* the major weekend correlate of the *Daily Graphic,* also featured columns that offered beginners step-by-step instructions on a number of basic ballroom techniques, including "the hold of the lady," "poise," and "contrary body movement," as well as easy variations that more advanced dancers could take to the floor.[68] A few writers even offered guidance to the colony's dance bands, encouraging them to play ballroom numbers at their appropriate pace and tempo: "I reproduce here the statistical figures as regards the time for the four standard dances: Waltz $\frac{3}{4}$ Time, Tempo 32–36 bars per minute; Quick Steps, $\frac{4}{4}$ Time, Tempo 48–52 bars per minute; Slow Foxtrot $\frac{4}{4}$ Time, 31–33 bars per minute; and Tango $\frac{2}{4}$ Time, Tempo 32–36 bars per minute."[69] Together, these actions worked to keep novices in their place, curb their wider ambitions, and suggest that the seismic shifts gripping the colony's political sphere would make little headway into the city's more intimate structures of authority and control.

Many of highlife's new audiences never got the message. Rather than simply following such directives, growing crowds of curious workers, eager students and fun-loving residents engaged highlife recreation in ways that helped them meet their own needs rather than those of middle-class experts. Some men and women approached dressing up, finding a partner, and engaging with a life of "formalities and respect" as little more than a particular form of fun. For them, studying dances, purchasing elaborate clothing items, and learning the nuances of ballroom etiquette were enjoyable and unencumbered acts. More aspirant people engaged middle-class directives as way to make a claim to their own budding stature as ladies, gentlemen, and empowered adults. Justina and Edna Fugar, sisters who began attending nightclubs in their early twenties, upheld these standards because they saw them as a validation that they had made their entrance into an established and respected community of privilege. For them, such venues were sites of opportunity, places where they could feel an enhanced sense of importance and obtain a level of personal mobility.[70]

Others chose to undercut such measures by injecting alternative elements into their Saturday Nights. This was especially true for the city's young men, who continued to find appeal in the jazz, swing, and care-free lifestyles displayed by recently departed foreign troops. When they went out on Saturday Nights, these individuals met nightclubs' dress requirements by donning zoot suits: flashy attire that enabled them to enter venues, display an enthusiasm for dressing up, and distinguish themselves from older, and more established, gentlemen.[71] Other young men chose to lean on more subtle marks of individual style and modern flair. Grershon Gaba, who enthusiastically purchased suits to take part

FIGURE 3.6. A young Grershon Gaba (left) and a friend dressed and ready for an evening of dancing. Components of the photo—including the crossing of their legs and Gaba's holding of a curled Ghanaian banknote—constitute clear attempts to evoke urban style. *Photo courtesy of Grershon Gaba.*

FIGURE 3.7. Men and women seated at a dance at Accra's Seaview nightclub, 1958. The man's donning of sunglasses (left) is a subtle, yet striking, addition to nightclubs' established codes for evening attire. *Photo courtesy of Ghana Information Services Department Photograph Library.*

in the city's Saturday Nights, recalled that he and his peers accentuated their appearance by purchasing colorful ties, crossing their legs while sitting, or occasionally brandishing cash in ways intended to catch the public eye (see Figure 3.6). Some young men also openly consumed alcohol, though not to the point of intoxication, attended nightclubs in large groups, and flaunted material possessions such as wallets, shoes, and sunglasses (see Figure 3.7). By supplementing their outings with these touches of personal style, these young men announced their desire to be active, rather than passive, players in the city's postwar environment of popular musical recreation and social change.[72] In the mid-1950s, such actions became increasingly common amongst a generation of highlife enthusiasts eager to engage highlife's future rather than its time-honored past. City youth, in particular, began to approach nightclubs not as spaces of continuity, but as locales of change, expanded freedoms, and personal liberation.

NIGHTCLUBS, PERSONAL FREEDOM, AND "STARTING LIFE"

The generation of men and women who first attended a nightclub in their late teens and early twenties consistently described the outing as the moment in which they "started life."[73] At one level, this English phrase, which was repeatedly invoked during conversations in several languages, captures the considerable excitement they found in their evening ventures. Many remembered attending a nightclub as their official entrance into a realm of tremendous enjoyment and fun, one that continued to invoke vivid nostalgia many decades later. At the same time, they insisted that the real essence of starting life lay in more serious, and certainly more weighty, realities and concerns. Most recalled this first outing as a transformative experience of liberation and empowerment. Taking part in Saturday Nights' offerings of song, dance, and sociability convinced young people that their personal coming of age was closely linked to the city's abandonment of its colonial past and embrace of a new independent future. When they returned home from their first night out on the town, they did so confident that it was time to abandon their marginal status and take a more active place in city affairs.

To fully appreciate how nightclubs enabled youth to start life, we must look back at the city's established gendered, generational, and social hierarchies. Like their predecessors of earlier decades, Accra's young people who had not become adults via marriage, stable employment, or the accumulation of property remained subject to a relatively stable system of generational rankings and gendered mores. In the mid-1950s, most young men and women, including some who had entered their late twenties and early thirties, were confined to a perpetual state of what Mamadou Diouf has called "life on hold."[74] As long as they remained unmarried, partially employed, or under the watchful eyes of lineage and neighborhood elders, they could not fully participate in the wider domains of urban life. This was especially true for those who continued to live in their family house.[75] Nii Armah lived with his mother and father until the age of twenty-five, when he finished his apprenticeship, began to work as a paid mechanic, and successfully rented his own accommodations. Until that moment, Armah confessed, he had lived a rather constrained life. He had to inform his parents of his daily activities, abide by their authority, and even obtain their approval before leaving the house at night.[76] Most Accra youth faced similar conditions and behavioral expectations. In many

households, even communal activities such as eating meals followed a set
of protocol that inculcated gerontocratic privilege and parental respect:

> Eh! They [youth] respected them [elders]! Serious! You feared to not respect
> someone who had grown past you. I remember that my senior brothers, if
> my father was eating, they had to take cloth and tie it on his neck, put their
> hands back, and stand behind him until he finished eating. They would stand
> there until he finished. If he had a visitor, they had to wait until both finished
> before taking food. Those days you couldn't even use the same plate or cup
> that your elder used. You had to wait, pack the plates, wash them, and give
> them water to wash their hands before you could eat. . . . The younger ones
> used to respect their elders![77]

Parental restrictions proved equally stringent for actions and activities that took place outside of the family house. Although most young men
and women—especially those who had to attend either school or work—
could freely move about the city during the day, few had the license to
leave their family compounds at night. Those who did not have any gainful work or had not finished their schooling faced extensive restrictions,
meaning that their prospects for attending a nightclub were extremely
slim. As Elizabeth Amonoo explained, most household authorities, middle class or not, upheld nightclubs to be adult spaces off-limits to junior
persons: "We had discipline at that time—people were under serious
control! If your parents would not allow you to go [to a nightclub], it was
very difficult for you to go. You couldn't go! Maybe from the house you
can hear the music or see it, so you can get something. Those that have
matured will go and see them, but you could not. Have you seen?"[78]

Young men and women resented these nocturnal limitations for a
number of reasons. First, they, like other city residents, wanted firsthand
access to the city's Saturday Nights. Dance band highlife's proliferation
in newspaper articles and on local radio stations exacerbated their feeling
that what their parents framed as a forbidden realm was actually a place
of considerable excitement and modern intrigue. Over the course of the
late 1940s and early 1950s, the Gold Coast Broadcasting Company transformed its small subscription service into a mass medium of information and entertainment. In 1941, the colony had only four thousand radio
subscribers, most of whom were educated elites, government employees,
and places of business. Shortly after the Second World War, however,
the colony expanded its radio infrastructure and offered an expanded
number of programs designed to cater to the interests of large and diverse
audiences. In addition to the creation of news and music programs in
several languages, including Twi, Fante, Ga, Hausa, and Ewe, the local

airwaves carried the Voice of America program, which featured news from abroad as well as a generous offering of American and Caribbean musical styles.[79] From 1951 to 1960, the colony's radio audiences jumped from forty-five thousand people to over one million, and many of these new listeners were urban youth.[80] As they huddled around speakers and listened to local bands and popular numbers, , scores of Accra youth became increasingly anxious to thwart their families' wishes and set foot inside one of the city's nightclubs.

For most youth, the desire to leave their homes was also a product of highlife's budding ties to the colony's larger climate of political change. Perhaps more than any other period in the twentieth century, the transitory years between the end of colonial rule and the obtainment of independence enabled young people to see themselves as arbiters of their community's future.[81] In the Gold Coast, youths' newfound confidence stemmed in part from the rhetorical exploits of Kwame Nkrumah's Convention People's Party (CPP). Unlike the UGGC, a conservative political body that mobilized the colony's educated and affluent residents to confront the British, the CPP fashioned itself as a mass party that encouraged diverse groups of Gold Coasters to demand "self-government now." Many ardent CPP supporters were those who had long been marginalized under the auspices of colonial and traditional authorities. In Accra, which served as the epicenter of the party's activities, young people were one of the many constituencies that flocked to its events and echoed its calls for political reform. The CPP's string of political successes, including a victory in colony-wide elections in 1951 and the achievement of internal self-government under Kwame Nkrumah in 1954, convinced many young men and women that they were no longer junior persons, but powerful agents of sociopolitical change.[82]

The inclusive air of the CPP also gave many city youth their first direct access to highlife performances. During the 1950s, the party incorporated various forms of music—including *oge* drumming, church tunes, pro-emancipation anthems from the American Civil War, and rural brass band songs—into their political gatherings, largely as a way to attract and spread messages among devotees. In Accra, its most prominent source of musical mobilization was highlife. As we will see in the next chapter, CPP rallies often featured prominent highlife musicians who helped entertain and excite the assembled crowd. In this setting of what Thomas Turino has called "musical nationalism," where highlife stood as a symbol of the colony's future rather than its past, growing numbers of young people decided that they could no longer stay at home on Saturday Nights.[83] By the mid-1950s, many had mustered up the courage to defy parental authority and to venture out into the city's nightclub scene.

To actually get to the dance floor, young men and women had to overcome a series of obstacles. First, they had to carry out carefully planned excursions that escaped the attention of parents and neighborhood elders. Alex Moffatt, whose covert outings opened this chapter, noted that his parents would have never allowed him to openly leave the house on a Saturday Night, despite the music's growing stature as a symbol of political change:

> They didn't know that we were going out to those places. They wouldn't have liked it at all—AT ALLLL (*shouting*)! They would have never liked it. To let us go out there to dance? No way. They would have never allowed us to go. If they had known that we had gone to those places even just to watch what was happening it would have been a problem for us—a big, big problem for us.[84]

Moffatt's predicament was hardly unique. Although they risked great peril, including eviction from their family house and long-standing disfavor among parents and elders, many young people found ways to leave their homes, enter nightclubs, and effectively start life. Rebecca Torshie Adja, who began her Saturday Nights in 1956 at the age of eighteen, would prepare for these outings by hiding one of her church dresses outside of her family compound. After sneaking out of bed and leaving the house, she would change clothes, only to do the same when she returned late at night: a strategy that ensured that even alerted family members would never see her in her nightlife attire.[85] Georgina Okanee Acei and Happy Gaba escaped such restrictions by going to live with their senior sisters, recognized adults who encouraged, rather than prohibited, their heading out to enjoy the city's nightlife offerings.[86]

Leaving the house undetected was not the evening's only hurdle. To really access highlife's performative power, young men and women had to get inside a nightclub, where they could see the band, meet other people, and hit the dance floor. For those of questionable age or little income, getting past the gate was not an easy task. Most spent their first few excursions outside the venue's walls, where they listened to the music, chatted with friends, and eagerly observed the evening's events. From time to time, more experienced onlookers blocked off part of the street to make room for a makeshift dance floor, allowing novices to watch couples dance or experiment with their own movements to various songs. Others gained knowledge about nightclub culture through different means. Young men recalled jumping up on a venue's wall so that they could catch a glimpse of particular bands or finely dressed dancers. Others made excursions to such venues during the afternoon, when they could meet the musicians, help them carry and arrange their equipment, and obtain a complimentary admission to the evening's show.[87]

As they gained confidence and familiarity with the physical layout of the city's nightclubs, young enthusiasts found ways to slip past the security guards who manned the gates. Young men scaled venue walls at strategic points, especially in the bathroom, or entered via a back door or service entrance. Friends frequently concocted schemes together. Vincent Mensah noted that he and his friends pooled their money so that they could purchase a ticket for a single admission. When their ticket holder entered the club, security took his receipt and stamped his wrist as proof of admission. Before the ink had time to dry, he would exit the door, rejoin his friends, and rub their wrists against his own: effectively "stamping" them for reentry. Young women developed their own strategies. Rebecca Torshie Adja got to know the doorman at the Kyekyeku nightclub in Osu, who allowed her to enter without paying the gate fee or having an accompanying man. Margaret Acolatse also recalled that she knew the security of various nightclubs "very well" and that they would allow her to enter for free.[88]

For their first several ventures inside a nightclub, young people made few efforts to draw undue attention or rush out into the gathered crowd. Fearful that a neighbor or family friend might be among those dancing and having fun, they paid close attention to their surroundings and made it a point to head to the exit if they saw someone who could report their exploits. Many, such as James Matthew Thompson, took up inconspicuous positions away from the dance floor, bandstand, and bar so that they could observe the evening's events without garnering undue attention:

> We used to see a lot of older people at nightclubs; those were who the pleasures were for! So we used to go as underdogs, we used to hide ourselves. We wouldn't go bare-chested like this. But the older men, they would be around doing as they liked. We would be there, but we would dodge them. Sometimes, if an elderly man was there who knew your father you had to leave the place.[89]

These stints in hiding also allowed young patrons to carefully study the nuances of the city's nightlife scene. Since they were barred from dancing schools, friends worked together to scrutinize others' appearance and study the movements of master dancers, whom they gathered together to emulate in their spare time. Though sporadic so as to not garner the attention of parents or neighborhood elders, these practice sessions enabled many young people to learn the basic steps to many dances and acquire the courage to venture out onto the nightclub dance floor.[90]

While most men and women remembered their first forays onto the dance floor as moments of shy hesitation and nervous concentration, they also insisted that they wasted little time making it into a place of personal freedom, self-expression, and competitive fun.[91] Young men recalled trying to out-dance their friends, joking about errant missteps, and aiming to catch the eye of young women. Alex Moffatt and James Allotey remembered the dance floor as a site of a youthful bravado that, when coupled with the consumption of alcohol, the use of "guy names" (nicknames), and access to young women, enabled them and their peers to claim status before a public that had yet to recognize their mounting needs or influence.[92]

Others employed the dance floor in different ways. Avid dancers made it a point to patronize venues that offered dance competitions, organized contests that became increasingly common throughout the 1950s and 1960s. Like their prewar predecessors, these competitions enabled participants to make their way through a series of elimination rounds. When the number of participants had sufficiently dwindled, a handful of finalists squared off for the title of contest champions. These competitions were serious affairs that attracted well-practiced entrants as well as expansive crowds of onlookers eager to cheer on their friends and see first-rate dancing. Victorious couples enjoyed great fanfare, tremendous pride, and enduring empowerment. Margaret Acolatse won her first dancing competition in Akuse, but following her move to Accra she and her partner won competitions in quickstep, waltz, and highlife. Charity Agbenyega won a highlife competition at the Lido in 1956; Harry Amenumey and his future wife took first place in a quickstep competition at the Kit-Kat nightclub in the mid-1950s. Each recalled these events as transformative moments that awarded them public prominence, an enhanced reputation, and recognition as individuals who had indeed started life. Victory also came with more tangible benefits, including trophies, prizes such as money or drinks, and if they were lucky, a picture in the *Daily Graphic* or another of the colony's newspapers (see Figure 3.8). After his victory Amenumey shared his prize, a crate of beer, with the friends who had supported his efforts and encouraged his public coming of age.[93]

In the late 1950s and early 1960s, dancing competitions were regional, and in some cases national, events. The Star Brewery promoted its highlife competition as a country-wide contest aimed at identifying, and rewarding, the country's best dancers. Opening rounds took place at the

FIGURE 3.8. Mrs. Akiwumi presents the silver cup and bottle of champagne to the winning couple of the 1958 National Highlife Competition held at the Lido nightclub. A similar picture of the couple appeared in the March 10, 1958, edition of the *Daily Graphic,* announcing their achievement to a wide readership. *Photo courtesy of Ghana Information Services Department Photograph Library.*

local level, where residents gathered in a principal town to face off to the sounds of an area band. The top couples from each locale moved onto the regional and national finals, where they competed for the title of "national champion." For finalists, the championship round was a life-changing event, an opportunity to strut one's stuff in front of a panel of experts, members of the press, and prominent big men and political leaders. Successful contestants gained renown, initiated new trends, and collected a range of rewards and prizes. After winning the Star Highlife Competition in 1968, Mama Adjoa was one of many champions who obtained an invitation to travel to Europe, where she carried out a long career as part of a professional dancing troupe.[94]

For young people, the dance floor's principal attraction was that it provided them with opportunities for courtship and male-female interaction. Nearly all young men considered nightclubs as ideal spaces in which to meet young women and, if fortunate, to start a budding romance.[95] In part, such attitudes stemmed from dance bands themselves, who offered audiences countless tales of love and physical attraction. Songs such as the Tempos' "205" (PURL 3.5) and "Odo Anigyina" (Love sickness) (PURL 3.6), the Black Beats' "Medaho Mao" (I am there for you) (PURL 3.7) and "Nibii Bibii Babaoo" (Many small things), and the Ramblers' "Auntie Christie" [a woman's name] celebrated romantic relationships as sources of considerable happiness and personal fulfillment. In "Odo Anigyina," for example, the singer framed love as an essential component of his daily life and future plot:

San bra o, ɔdɔ	Come back, oh my darling
Bra o, bra o, ahoɔfɛ	Come back, oh come back my beautiful one
San bra o, onua	Come back, oh come back my sister
Bra na bɛgye m'ani	Come and make me happy
San bra o, ɔdɔ	Come back, oh my darling
Bra o, bra o, ahoɔfɛ	Come back, oh come back my beautiful one
San bra o, onua	Come back, oh come back my sister
Bra na bɛgye m'ani	Come and make me happy
ɔdɔ regya me hɔ akɔ	My lover has abandoned me
Meka ho asɛm a, ɛnka	There is nothing I can say about it
Me nna nyinaa ayɛ me atiben	Life is now a headache for me
Ma me nna mpo agyigya	I cannot have a sound sleep
Enti san bra o, ɔdɔ	Therefore, come back, oh my darling
Bra o, bra o, ahoɔfɛ	Come back, come back my beautiful one
San bra o, onua	Come back, oh come back my sister
Bra na bɛgye m'ani	Come and make me happy

"Auntie Christie" offered a more lighthearted, but no less impressionable, endorsement of romantic relationships (PURL 3.8):

Auntie Christie	Auntie Christie
W'enyiwa mba yi, edze rokum me o	Oh, you lure me with your eyeballs
Ewuraba Christie	The lady Christie
W'anantsew yi, edze rehaw me o	Oh, you entice me with your footsteps
Mewu e, Christie e	Em! Christie I am calling you, I am crazy
Fa wo nsa bɔ to me kɔn mu	Put your hand around my neck
Nna w'ekyir yi dze, edze rokum me paapa bi	You make me so crazy with your behind
Mewu e, sister e	Em, my sister, I am crazy

Fa wo nsa bɔ to me kɔn mu	Put your hand around my neck
Nna w'ekyir yi dze, edze rokum	You make me so crazy with your behind
me paapa bi	

The dance floor was not, however, a level playing field of courtship. Good dancers—those who could claim proficiency in learned and improvised styles of dance—stood out as particularly lucrative and appealing partners. Benny Amakudzie recalled the dance floor as a place where he and other skilled men could garner the attention of women and initiate otherwise impossible romantic relationships. Although he was a modest technician by trade, Amakudzie attracted the interest of many well-to-do young women, some of whom offered to take him out for an evening of first-rate dancing. A few even invited him to travel with them outside of Accra to a town such as Takoradi, Koforidua, and Keta "just to dance and come back." According to Amakudzie, these outings offered him extraordinary opportunities, usually at little dent to his own shallow pockets:

> Because the woman knew that I could dance very well, she would sponsor me, pay for my transport, and even pay the gate fee. Yes, and then drinks and all that. But rather, she would give me money to put in my pocket because a woman could not be buying drinks for a man at a bar. So she would give me the money, and then I'd be calling for the beer.[96]

As he and his partner enjoyed a lavish evening and proceeded to "condemn" others on the dance floor, Amakudzie took on the appearance of the modern "big man," a figure whose money, romantic prospects, and power was the subject of the Black Beats' popular song *"Agodzi"* (Money) (PURL 3.9):

Agodzi, baby nara trust	Money, the lady herself trusts me
Agodzi baby nara trust dɛ	Money, the lady herself trusts me
ɔda mo ho oo	I have it in abundance
Entsi m'ewuraba ee, mm ɛnsuro oo-oo	Therefore, my lady, don't be afraid
Agodzi ɔda mo ho oo	I have money in abundance
ɔda mo ho oo-oo	I really have it
Entsi m'ewuraba ee, mm ɛnsuro oo-oo	Therefore, my lady, don't be afraid
Agodzi ɔda mo ho oo-oo	For I have money in abundance[97]

Dance allowed Amakudzie to enjoy romantic prospects unavailable to his less-agile male counterparts, eclipse social and economic limitations, and experiment with courtship in ways usually reserved for those with more money or established social status.

Of course, the benefits of splendid dancing were not the sole preserve of men. The women who accompanied Amakudzie did so because his proficient movements accorded them more than an evening of fun. His bravado attracted onlookers' eyes and wrapped the couple in a veil of grandeur and desirability. Since men were consistently on the lookout for women of corporeal style and grace, skilled female dancers also enjoyed considerable attention on Saturday Nights. Diana Oboshilay remembered that she and her friends, all of whom were adroit movers, made conscious attempts to entice male suitors during their evening outings. Shortly after their arrival at a nightclub, the group took the dance floor en masse, showcased their moves for a particular song, and nonchalantly returned to their table to wait. Before long, most had secured one or more invitations from men eager to accompany them on the floor. Margaret Acolatse echoed Oboshilay's insistence that skilled female dancers were tremendously popular: "Men were always looking for the women that could dance well. . . . If you were not good, no man would invite you onto the floor. When I went to the club, everyone would want to dance with me. If you hadn't seen me dance before, you would come and want to dance with me!"[98]

For the young men and women who were new to the city's Saturday Nights, the dance floor's promise of intimacy and courtship was an extremely exciting marker of their personal liberation and coming of age. In fact, most recalled that the opportunity to publicly interact with members of the opposite sex was the central factor that made their secretive ventures worth the energy and repeated risk. As they entered their twenties, many youth considered their inability to publicly chat with a member of the opposite sex, flirt, or pursue any form of romantic relationship without the explicit consent of their parents to be one of the most frustrating components of their "life on hold."[99] A few initiated secret romances that they carefully concealed from family elders, but as Abdul Rahim Dixon recalled, such partnerships had little prospect for long-term success:

> [My father] wouldn't allow me to bring a girl to our house. No! To do that, you had to reach a certain age and you had to be working. Before that, to bring a girl in front of my father? Never! If I did, he would sack me from the house. Just like that, you see? So this is why I had to go out [of the house], because of my father. At this time I was twenty-something years of age, but when my father said "sit here" I would do it. If I went out with my girl it was a secret.[100]

Gloria Ocloo lived with her parents until she was twenty-seven years old. Though she was advanced in age and fully employed as a seamstress, her father would not allow her to go out in the evenings, fraternize with young men, or have a boyfriend. Convinced that she had fulfilled many of the requirements important to becoming a full-fledged adult, Ocloo defied her father's wishes. She left the house, found a boyfriend, and carried out a relationship under an elaborate veil of secrecy:

> Do you know what I did? It is a funny thing (*laughs*) . . . In 1955, I had a boy-friend. My brother was aware, my mother was aware. But my father was not aware. . . . I was a full seamstress, working on my own. In the evening, when I had finished my housework, I had to dress as if I was not going any place at all. I had a housecoat, a big one with long sleeves which I put on over my evening gown. I didn't powder my face, I didn't put on shoes. For my shoes, I would either hide them somewhere outside of the house or would give them to my friends. So my father would see me wearing sandals and the housecoat and would think that I was staying in the house. When he went to bed, I left! All of the sudden I was on my way! Away! I had an appointment (date)—I had to go![101]

Throughout the mid-1950s, growing numbers of young men and women, including James Allotey, came to view strict parental supervision as a "colonial" imposition incompatible with the city's transition toward independence.[102] They valued nightclubs as spaces where they could carry out romantic relationships and flaunt their not yet recognized maturity. Once again, Allotey and his like-minded peers found encouragement in the context of popular highlife songs. The Black Beats' *"Misomo Bo Tamo She"* (I love you like sugarcane), a tale of a heartbroken youth who remained resolutely in love despite the interference of family elders, reso-nated with many junior persons (PURL 3.10):

Akââ åkâ bo akakpe dôåå	They say I should not meet with you again
Akââ wôkpa nâkâ nyiâmô nââ nôåå	They say we should stop this relationship
Aagba n' naa kâ osane sôåå	They are worrying me about your matter
Akââ kâ n' na bo lâ åkwâ bo yâ shôåå	They say when I see you I should look at you from a distance
Akââ åkâ bo akawie hu	They also say I should not talk with you
Ni wôteå sane lâ mfo mli kpu	And should break off our relationship completely
Kâji n' na nô ko yâ Osu	If I see something at Osu
Mibô môdåå ni åyatsô Kôle Bu	I should try and pass through Korle Bu
Akââ åkaåma bo wolo dôåå	They say I should not write to you again
Åkatswao telephone hu dôåå	I should not give you a telephone call again
Akââ åkajwåå ohe po	They say I should not even think about you

FIGURE 3.9. A young couple at an Accra nightclub, c. 1960.
Photo courtesy of Aeshitu Zinabo.

Ni kâji miwô lâ mikala bo po.	And even when I am asleep I should not dream of you
Shi moå, miitao makââ bo akâ	But I want to tell you that
No ji, misumôô bo tamô she.	Really, I love you like sugarcane
Ni kâji akâ bo wo jata bu mli po	And if you are put in even a lion's den
Mikâ bo baakpe ke.	I'll surely meet with you again[103]

Another Black Beats song, *"Enya Wo Do Fo"* (You have got your lover),
sympathized with young peoples' plight by explicitly encouraging a young
woman to announce her secret romance to her family (PURL 3.11):

ɔbaa Lizzy ee, ɔbaa homatseaa	Lady Lizzy, the slender lady
ɔbaa Lizzy ee, ɔbaa homatseaa	Lady Lizzy, the slender lady
Ka kyerɛ wo nkorɔfo dɛ	Tell your relatives that
Afei enya wo dɔfo	You have now got your lover
Ka kyerɛ wo nkorɔfo dɛ	Tell your relatives that
Afei enya wo dɔfo	You have now got your lover

In the mid-1950s, many young men and women used Saturday Nights
to momentarily abandon their status as generational and gendered subordinates. Insisting that dressing up, dancing, and blending into large
crowds accorded them a considerable level of anonymity, they often car-

FIGURE 3.10. Grershon Gaba (right), his male friends, and their female partners enjoy a dance, c. 1960. *Photo courtesy of Grershon Gaba.*

ried out acts that would warrant repercussion in the other spheres of home and work. Young men made it a point to show off their finely dressed girlfriends, cover an evening's financial expenses, and dabble in other restricted acts such as the consumption of alcohol: activities that they remembered as key components of their efforts to start life (see Figures 3.9 and 3.10). Young women also recalled such outings as key components of their burgeoning maturity and mobility. The opportunity to experience courtship with young men or even interact with doctors, lawyers, and other more established men made them feel not like marginalized "girls," but like empowered and desirable women.[104]

As growing numbers of young people ventured out of nightclubs' peripheral spaces to openly dance, flirt, and socialize over alcohol, older patrons did in fact take note. By 1957, the year in which the Gold Coast gained independence as the nation of Ghana, established city residents had grown increasingly concerned about the city's crumbling façade of so-cial, gendered, and generational order. Their concern was not completely unfounded. A few months earlier, a group of city youth had embraced a new set of aesthetics and styles in order to place another set of demands on the city's popular musical scene. They had turned to rock 'n' roll.

YOUTH, ROCK 'N' ROLL, AND
ENVISIONING THE FUTURE

On September 18, 1956, the CPP-led internal government announced
that the Gold Coast had ended its struggle against British colonialism
and that it would assume its independence in less than six months. For
Accra's youth, this announcement was a cause for great joy, but it also
cemented their impression that it was a perfect time to reconfigure their
place within their urban environs. Demographically speaking, the capital
city had become dominated by young people. From 1948–1960, the city's
population more than doubled in size, increasing from 133,192 to 337,828
residents. To a great degree, this growth was due to a large influx of young
migrants, who abandoned their rural homes in search of economic opportunity and a glimpse of modern life. At the end of the 1950s, 61 percent of
Accra's population was under the age of twenty-four; a development that
convinced many young people that established patterns of gerontocratic
authority and middle-class privilege had become outdated and needed
to give way.[105]

     This rapid population growth also made the city, especially its outly-
ing areas, a site of constant construction and physical expansion. Because
central Accra was densely populated and bounded by the sea, most young
migrants had to settle in the newer, and more spacious, suburban areas
sprouting up to the north of Kaneshie, New Town, and Nima. A number
of infrastructural developments, such as the construction of the Accra
airport, the University of Ghana at Legon, and a new network of roads,
ensured that these emerging areas were not completely severed from the
city center, but their youthful residents remained convinced that they
were not yet targets of official concern. Throughout the 1950s, government
authorities, urban planners, and affluent residents consistently prioritized
development projects designed to enhance the city's economic growth,
approve its public appearance, and ensure its existing political order over
those that would benefit the residential needs of newly arrived immigrants.[106] In fact, many middle-class residents, including local journalists,
suggested that the government needed to do more to eradicate Accra's
informal settlements, dilapidated buildings, and unsanitary spaces so that
the city could take its place among the world's modern capital cities.[107]

     Youths' growing marginalization was also apparent in the contrasting
realms of education and employment. During the 1950s, school enroll-
ments in the colony increased considerably, giving many young men and
women access to a primary education. By the early 1960s, nearly half of

Accra's working people had received enough schooling to accord them proficiency in English, advanced literary and written skills, and considerable knowledge about the outside world. Like previous generations of graduates, they also left school with aspirations for gainful employment and financial success. Unfortunately, most found that they were unable to secure employment befitting their education or experience. In 1960, only 16 percent of Accra's population held desk-work positions, meaning that many educated young people had to make a living through less prestigious means, including trading, shopkeeping, or unskilled labor. Others had a difficult time securing any form of employment at all. In 1961, a report by the Ministry of Labor claimed that nearly 10 percent of Accra's total population, over thirty-one thousand individuals, was unemployed, a figure that included large numbers of educated as well as uneducated youth.[108]

When young people juxtaposed their hardships with the city's wider climate of prosperity and political promise, they became increasingly concerned about their individual prospects under independence and CPP rule. They insisted that instead of working to dismantle the hierarchies that characterized the colonial period and marginalized the "ordinary man," many state-sponsored development projects actually worked to reinforce them. A few disenfranchised youth channeled such frustrations into newly created political bodies, such as the Ga Shifimo Kpee (Ga Steadfast Organization), which publicly challenged government failures. Many more, however, elected to eschew party politics and use cultural and recreational mediums as a means of claiming individual freedoms and altering their urban environs.[109]

Those who had become avid participants in Accra's Saturday Nights initiated such efforts by confronting the elements of the city's nightlife scene that they considered outdated or incompatible with their own advancement. One of the youths' first targets was ballroom forms, a set of learned musical styles that they saw as the antiquated amusements of a small elite. Denouncing ballroom dances as dull, boring, or ultimately uninteresting, many youth, including Gloria Ocloo, refused to take the dance floor when such numbers aired: "We [young people] didn't enjoy ballroom like the couples. The husband and wife, they would enjoy it, but we didn't enjoy it. So when they were playing it we would sit somewhere and enjoy our drink."[110] Ocloo and others further cemented this disfavor by turning their full attention to the unstructured highlife or by embracing new foreign dances that allowed for innovation, flashy exuberance, and active physical movements.

The vast majority of Accra's youth favored rock 'n' roll. While the music became immensely popular in various parts of the world in the 1950s, it first appeared in Accra via American films that aired in local cinema houses. In the months immediately preceding Ghana's independence, many youth flocked to see films such as *Rock around the Clock* and *Shake, Rattle, and Rock,* which showcased the vibrant music and accompanying forms of athletic dance.[111] For young viewers frustrated with ballroom's outdated airs and nightclubs' rudiments of age, dress, and respectful gaiety, rock 'n' roll's modern and flashy aura was immediately attractive. Many city youth, including Vincent Mensah, saw rock 'n' roll as the perfect vehicle for announcing their frustration with the city's continued maintenance of gendered mores and gendered conventions:

> The gentlemen, they went in for quick-quick-slow, but we, we didn't go in for that one. Mostly, we went for the highlife and rock 'n' roll. . . . The ballroom dances, we didn't want to do them. They were boring! The way you did them calmly, the way you held the woman; no. We wanted to move! Rock 'n' roll, those dances made you sweat! When you were dancing you knew it! They were very nice.[112]

Convinced that rock 'n' roll could facilitate their efforts to claim a greater voice in city affairs, many youth adopted the music as their recreational medium of choice. They did so first within the confines of rock 'n' roll clubs, organizations explicitly dedicated to accessing the music and offering instruction in its vibrant dance movements. Vincent Mensah and Frankie Laine took part in the Black Eagle Rock 'n' Roll Club, an organization formed in 1958 by youth impressed by *Rock around the Clock.* Based at the Park Cinema in Adabraka, which it rented out for meetings and practice sessions, the club became considerably popular among the area's students, recent graduates, and young workers in their late teens and early twenties. Within a few years, the city had several other rock 'n' roll clubs that attracted enthusiasts within a particular neighborhood or district. New clubs included the Black Stars, the Island Club, the Tokyo Joes, Rodger's Group, the Rockin' Aces, the Big Yanks Rock 'n' Roll Club, and Billy's Group (see Figure 3.11). By 1960, most city youth had easy access to one of these clubs, which they joined in order to meet people, learn dances, and celebrate their shared enthusiasm.[113]

Youth found rock 'n' roll clubs appealing not simply for their musical offerings, but for their organizational power, promotion of shared values, and modern worldview. Most were highly coordinated outfits that held regular meetings, elected officers, established rules, and issued membership cards.[114] Although such measures invoked strategies employed by

FIGURE 3.11. Members of the Tokyo Joes Rock 'n' Roll Club, Accra, enjoy a practice dance, 1959. © *Bailey's African History Archives.*

the middle-class social clubs and dancing schools that rock 'n' rollers despised, many youth insisted that they facilitated the creation of a close-knit cooperative community. Several club members recalled that, aside from providing lessons in rock 'n' roll dances, such organizations were places where young people could get to know one another and foster an intimate sense of camaraderie. As Nii Adgin Tettey explained, most clubs saw their open environment and protection of individual expression as a key component of a new youth culture:

> We the young ones went to the beach to practice rock 'n' roll. We would learn the dances there, but we wouldn't accuse each other. We didn't talk about who knew what; you did what you liked. Highlife and rock 'n' roll, they were open dances based on how you felt. There wasn't right or wrong! In the Ga language we have a proverb, "However I dance, it's a dance." . . . Whether you dance rough or you dance smooth, the ground will not die. It doesn't kill the land. . . . We would use that phrase to encourage everybody.[115]

For those disheartened with their continued marginalization at the hands of elders, elites, and political authorities, rock 'n' roll clubs' atmosphere of respect, collegiality, and vibrant self-expression made them an attractive, and considerably potent, means of promoting their interests and intentions to the city at large.

Once they had solidified a stable membership and accumulated some level of fluency in rock 'n' roll music and dance, clubs ventured out to take charge of Accra's Saturday Nights. On a given evening, members gathered together at a particular nightclub, where they unveiled their rehearsed movements and athletic skill. Such outings were a source of great excitement. Frankie Laine recalled that he and his fellow club members took Saturday Nights by storm, when they referred to one another by American names, wore handkerchiefs in their pant pockets, and loudly exclaimed "I'm ready, I'm willing, and I may go dance rock 'n' roll all night!" Bob Biney claimed that rock 'n' roll outings "opened his eyes," allowing him and his peers to publicly announce their coming of age and international purview: "When dancing rock 'n' roll I felt joy. I felt joy because it was a new life. I wore trousers at that time, my first time wearing trousers, and a good shirt and went out. And we used to behave like Yankees you know? . . . I felt proud, that wisdom was taking place, that I was different than others."[116] By dancing rock 'n' roll, embracing American slang, and behaving like a "Yankee"—a phrase that Biney used in direct reference to the carefree attitudes projected in American films—young city residents demanded that they be seen, heard, and recognized as citizens important to the nation's future. A few even demanded that dance bands and nightclubs "decolonize" by eradicating ballroom altogether:

> There reached a time, if you went to the nightclubs, the young ones liked rock 'n' roll. . . . Sometimes, you wouldn't hear ballroom or highlife too much. And if you heard it, then the youth would yell "Old timers! Old timers!"—like they wanted to come and spoil the dance for them. [Young people] wanted their own music, and they made the nightclubs not like the way they were before.[117]

Coincidentally, many dance bands and nightclub proprietors complied with young peoples' demands. Several of the city's most prominent ensembles started to incorporate foreign rock 'n' roll numbers into their existing repertoires of ballroom, calypsos, and highlifes. The Ramblers Dance Band, a group formed by Jerry Hansen in 1961, often performed rock 'n' roll numbers at nightclubs, as did the Red Spots, Jazz Kings, Tempos, and Black Beats. Francis Laryea, a trumpeter for the Tempos No. 2 Band and later Red Spots, was one of many young highlife musicians who also played at rock 'n' roll dances sponsored by the Black Eagle Club (see Fig-

FIGURE 3.12. A young Francis Laryea plays trumpet at a rock 'n' roll dance
sponsored by the Black Eagle Club, c. 1960. *Photo courtesy of Francis Laryea.*

ure 3.12).[118] Certain venues, such as the Metropole, Lido, and Paradiso,
held "jamborees": dances that featured rock 'n' roll and gave the city's
"ballroom people" little chance to strut their stuff. Other establishments
reached out to young patrons by sponsoring rock 'n' roll dancing competitions alongside those in highlife and ballroom forms. These competitions,
which included both group and individual categories, were immensely
popular among city youth. Clubs trained hard to defeat rival outfits, win
prizes, and obtain recognition as an authority of the city's new musical
scene. As Vincent Mensah recalled, rock 'n' roll clubs took such competitions very seriously:

> They had panels who would sit by the stage side and judge. Rock 'n' roll had
> so many styles, so they judged you on the styles that you used and what you
> did to be admired. As for rock 'n' roll it was very nice, but it was not easy. Not
> everyone could dance it. If you were not smart, you couldn't do it. You had
> to practice! If the man held you like this, you knew that you were going this
> way. If you did this move, another would follow. If I turned you like this, you

knew what was happening. You couldn't just take any girl and do it; it took practice. It wasn't a joke. We would train hard and practice many hours for the competitions.[119]

Individuals, meanwhile, found competitions to be occasions when they could garner an enviable reputation and growing self-esteem. Frankie Laine, who won several rock 'n' roll competitions in the late 1950s and early 1960s, noted that such events made him "feel like somebody." Extolling the maxim, "to dance rock 'n' roll you have to be young and you have to be smart," young people upheld Laine and other champions as ambassadors for their wider platform of social change.[120]

Individual rock 'n' rollers also claimed clout through dress. Rejecting nightclubs' standard apparel and refusing to wear the heavy suits and elaborate evening gowns favored by older and more affluent patrons, they turned to alternative decorum that celebrated their emerging assertiveness and embrace of modern international cultural elements. Young men donned dungarees, short-sleeved shirts (often T-shirts), caps, and white shoes; young women sported an ever-changing array of shorter, tighter-fitting skirts. This apparel was better suited to athletic movements and steps, but it also allowed young men and women to visibly challenge existing links between self-presentation, gender, and social status. James Allotey, who became an adamant young rock 'n' roller in spite of his earlier Saturday Nights, invested heavily in new forms of dress. His new clothing—consisting of short-sleeved collared shirts, less-formal trousers, and brown shoes—filled him with pride, in part from his peers' approval and in part because it elicited a mixture of admiration and bewilderment from his father, who still considered him to be a junior person.[121] Rock 'n' roll dress did, however, have its limitations, particularly outside of Saturday Nights. Although they took great joy in displaying new styles of clothing at nightclubs and in the company of friends, young women rarely risked donning them in front of their parents or elders, for fear that they would voice disapproval, reprimand them, or confine them to the house. Grace Yawa Aye proudly wore rock 'n' roll attire out on the town, but did so covertly when in or near her home: "I didn't just wear [short dresses] anywhere. I would wear a long dress over the top, and when I reached the nightclub, I would remove it!"[122]

By 1960, rock 'n' roll's proliferation had aroused considerable opposition from established city residents, including political authorities, members of the press, and household elders. Many middle-class people and ballroom enthusiasts decried rock 'n' roll as a dance that one could do "anyhow" and argued that its adherents openly violated long-standing conventions and modes of respectful recreation. Others denounced the music for more personal reasons. Benny Amakudzie—the man who employed dance as a vehicle for initiating romantic relationships—claimed that rock 'n' roll undermined, even destroyed, his own Saturday Nights:

> Changes occurred when different dances came in, like cha-cha-cha, rock 'n' roll, Madison: some funny, funny dances. These things liquidated ballroom dancing. It reached a time where classicals (ballroom numbers) couldn't come on again, it was only highlife and these new dances. [Nightlife] changed. It became a place of ruffians . . . an eyesore.[123]

Outside of nightclubs, critics insisted that the music's growing presence constituted more grave threats, including a shift toward individualism, a growing disdain for authority, and an increase in public indecency. Rock 'n' roll invoked tensions in many contexts,[124] but those expressed in Ghana revolved around the significance and meaning of the nation's independence. For rock 'n' roll adherents, the music was a fresh and exciting form that emanated an international aesthetic, alleviated daily hardship, contributed to the city's cultural modernity, and linked its participants to cohorts of young people beyond Ghana's borders.[125] It was a means by which they could arbitrate between the local and international, reconcile the past and present, and mediate between their personal liberation and that of the nation at large. For their older counterparts, however, rock 'n' roll was a gross misinterpretation of what the end of colonialism actually signified. In their eyes, independence was a time not to completely break with the past, but to preserve the gendered, generational, and social fabric that had long governed city affairs. A lengthy lament published in the August 7, 1960, edition of the *Sunday Mirror* insisted that established authorities, rather than ambitious youth, needed to control the city's recreational environments:

> Come with me to a typical dance hall. The bills outside advertise an evening dress dance. But what do we see inside? A FRENZIED CROWD OF YOUTHFUL DANCERS SHUFFLING AND GYRATING HELTER-SKELTER AND JOSTLING INTO EACH OTHER WHILE WEARING AN ASSORTMENT OF CLOTHES . . . This is not what things used to be in the "good old days" of our ballrooms. In the "twenties" when dancing schools did not exist, dance enthusiasts behaved themselves—even if they bungled their steps.[126]

Nostalgic for the days when "midnight follies" were "reserved for the old and respectable along with a few young couples who had good-manners and were well-dressed," established residents insisted that the nation's political independence should not be understood as an event that granted all Ghanaians total "freedom of movement, freedom of actions, freedom of drinking, and freedom of enjoyment."[127]

CONCLUSION

In the years surrounding Ghana's 1957 independence, highlife music entrenched its position as one of Accra's most popular domains of leisure and recreation. In a twenty-year period, the music abandoned the exclusive confine of the social club for the much more open nightclub, shunned its orchestral emphasis in favor of jazz, Afro-Caribbean rhythms, and other modern styles, and discarded its prewar affiliations with colonial rule for a place as a cultural marker of a postcolonial and independent future. On Saturday Nights, the music filled the air, captured the imagination, and prompted individuals of various backgrounds to congregate to relax, dance, and socialize.

Despite its growing popularity, highlife never became an arena of postwar harmony, consensus, or collective cultural practice. In fact, when men and women gathered on Saturday Nights, they did so in ways that emphasized difference, privileged individual concerns, and, in some cases, prompted considerable animosity and public outcry. The friction that gripped Accra's dance floors demonstrates that independence was marked by a number of struggles that were connected to, but not defined by, the larger abolition of colonial rule. It also demonstrates that the years surrounding self-rule were a time of gendered and generational strife as well as strident negotiations about the allocation of freedom, responsibility, and power. Saturday Nights were certainly times of fun, merriment, and unrivaled excitement, but they were also occasions that people used to pursue individual aspirations and amend components of their daily lives.

By 1960, the friction on the dance floor had polarized city residents and entangled them in a set of complex conflicts over the city's social, cultural, and recreational future. In the late 1950s and 1960s, however, another player—the new Ghanaian government—launched its own effort to outline the meaning and significance of national independence. In rather ambitious fashion, it also declared its intention to transform highlife into a "national" symbol of which all Ghanaians could be proud. Ironically, its efforts, to which we now turn, upheld neither the interests of the city's ballroom people or its rabble-rousing youth.

FOUR

"The Highlife Was Born in Ghana": Politics, Culture, and the Making of a National Music, 1950–1965

On July 1, 1960, the independent nation of Ghana became a republic, enshrined with a new draft constitution and office of the president, which was assumed by the prime minister and leader of the CPP, Kwame Nkrumah. That same day, his government made two important announcements concerning dance band highlife. The first was that highlife was Ghana's "national" dance music: a pronouncement that many listeners interpreted as either a confirmation of its wide popularity among individuals of different ages, ethnicities, and occupations or recognition of its prominence in the years surrounding the country's independence. The second declaration was that this national form needed to change. More specifically, the government called upon dance band musicians and patrons to relinquish their embrace of international elements and make the music into something that was more "Ghanaian" in composition and character. Nkrumah asked performers to enhance the genre's local meaning by utilizing a regular tempo, by limiting, and over time eliminating, foreign numbers, and by encouraging a standardized set of dance steps that all residents could adopt. He also insisted that the music needed a new name. As an English-language title, "highlife" did not befit a musical genre that was essentially "Ghanaian in character and African in content." Although he ultimately charged the National Association of Teachers of Dancing with the task of selecting a new moniker, Nkrumah proposed rechristening the music *osibi,* an Akan term that made explicit

147

reference to *osibisaaba*, the proto-highlife that had flourished many decades earlier.[1]

Although these proclamations had little immediate impact on dance band highlife's form or character (Nkrumah's proposed name change never took hold), they demonstrate the music's importance to the wider realms of national politics and culture in the years surrounding Ghana's 1957 independence.[2] As many scholars have shown, the new African countries of the 1950s and 1960s were places of nation-building: a project that attempted to privilege local, instead of colonial, elements and inculcate a shared patriotic sentiment among diverse populations. Although nation-building was not a process confined to the formal political sphere, it was one that many newly independent governments hoped to direct and control. In Ghana and elsewhere, optimistic officials used a wide range of cultural forms to foster a shared sense of belonging, allegiance, and cultural unity. By fostering this sense of "we-ness," they hoped to engineer a cohesive nation in which culture and politics were intimately intertwined. Nation-building was not, as Thomas Turino emphasizes, a project concerned with the political aspects of nationalism, but it was a way for newly independent governments to outline and legitimize the scope of their desired political control.[3]

Over the course of its tenure as Ghana's main political force, roughly the period from 1950 to 1965, the CPP leaned especially hard on dance band highlife as a means of outlining and codifying what it meant to be "Ghanaian." At the same time, its efforts to nationalize highlife were often riddled with tensions and inconsistencies. By the time of the proclamations mentioned above, most Ghanaians approached the music as an open arena where they could pursue individual rather than collective aims. The state could easily proclaim highlife to be a national cultural form, but it could not easily refashion or repackage it as a component of communal practice. As a result, Nkrumah's government had to expend a considerable amount of energy attempting to alter how, and why, men and women should hit the dance floor on Saturday Nights. This uphill battle was made all the harder because of the government's own shifting needs, concerns, and future visions. Although CPP officials were consistently eager to consolidate, even extend, their political authority, they approached highlife differently in the years before and after Ghana's independence. In the late 1940s and early 1950s, the CPP engaged highlife as a way to enter an intimate sphere of social interaction, improve its ability to supervise urban populations, and gain increased leverage as a social and moral, rather than simply political, force. Realizing that it was too weak to alter the music's recreational culture, it changed its approach. In the years leading up to 1957, it employed the music to mobilize broad publics and perpetuate its popularity among diverse groups of people. Following independence, a newly empowered CPP rekindled its ambitious approach to highlife. Eager to carry out its own plans for development and modernization, it used dance band highlife to translate official rhetoric about abstract ideas—the nation, citizenship, and the African Personality—into clear domains of individual practice and communal identification. It also rallied the assistance of various state institutions and coercive tactics to force popular musical enthusiasts to abide by its directives. By the mid-1960s, portions of highlife recreation, as well as the larger domain of Saturday Nights, had become what Marissa Moorman has called "state-supported centers of national cultural values."[4]

This chapter examines Nkrumah's government's engagement with highlife in its varied efforts at nation-building in the years surrounding Ghana's independence. Like its counterparts in other parts of the continent, the CPP relied on popular musical performance to entrench its authority outside the formal political realm; highlife, in fact, was central to its larger attempts to bring the nation into being.[5] The first section analyzes the interests and efforts of the Department of Social Welfare and Community Development, a government branch that CPP officials used to outline early ideas about citizenship, civic responsibility, and national practice. After identifying highlife as a problematic and threatening medium, particularly for urban youth, the department attempted, albeit unsuccessfully, to limit the music's prominence and accessibility within urban areas. The next section shows how CPP officials abandoned such efforts and worked instead to assimilate highlife into their wider campaign against British colonialism—specifically, the ways in which they incorporated highlife into an eclectic political repertory designed to mobilize diverse publics and transform them into active party supporters. The third section focuses on government authorities' efforts to use popular musical recreation to translate official rhetoric about the African Personality, citizenship, and gendered practice into readily identifiable modes of social and cultural behavior. The CPP government, not unlike its traditional and colonial predecessors, used the music to marginalize two groups that had been important to its past political successes: women and youth. The last section explores the actions of the Arts Council, a government body that supervised and reformed highlife musicians. Throughout the 1960s, the council employed a number of tactics, including the offering of training courses and issuing of state performances to compliant bands, in order to transform Saturday Nights into highly supervised, and even scripted, celebrations of a top-down version of national culture.

PRE-INDEPENDENCE EFFORTS
TO PURIFY POPULAR MUSIC

The CPP's first attempts to interfere in urban Ghana's postwar climate of Saturday Nights took place within the Department of Social Welfare and Community Development, a multiracial body created in 1943. During its first few years of operation, the department oversaw various tasks affiliated with what John Iliffe has called colonialism's period of "compassionate rule."[6] It launched an ambitious program of community development and mass education that sought to promote "better living for the whole community" as well as active participation in civic affairs. Financial constraints hampered the department's initial efforts to intervene in community life, but the economic and political developments of the early 1950s increased its importance, particularly for the newly appointed internal government that took charge of the colony after elections in 1951. Shortly after the CPP's victory at the polls, Kojo Botsio, the minister of education and social welfare, announced that the party had decided to use the department "to teach people not merely how to read, but how to live." To carry out this ambitious aim, Botsio oversaw the creation of a fifteen-member advisory committee comprised primarily of affluent educated Ghanaian men. He also hired a large number of welfare officers—primarily educated Gold Coasters—who could supervise projects in each of the colony's regions. Over the next several years, these individuals constructed an array of programs designed to assist and reform the colony's marginalized publics. They sponsored literacy campaigns, vocational training sessions, family assistance courses, leadership training classes, and other mass educational efforts. Importantly, such efforts also promoted notions of citizenship and civic responsibility that could complement the CPP's efforts to inculcate anti-British sentiment.[7]

Unsurprisingly, the department's early attempts to delineate a national spirit of hard work, promote patriotism, and enforce collective obligations upheld, rather than challenged, the colony's well-established axes of class, age, and gender. Although the department was no longer encumbered with British concerns about "civilization," it was quite wary about the social and moral threats that had become increasingly common in the years following the Second World War. Among the department's most ardent worries was juvenile delinquency, a phenomenon that endangered its efforts at community development and plans for the colony's future. In the early 1950s, CPP officials, including Botsio, announced that many towns had become sites of a rather serious "youth problem." One of the department's first CPP-era circulars, "Citizens in the Making: A Report on Juvenile Delinquency in the Gold Coast in 1951," outlined the proof that supported Botsio and others' conviction. First, the report insisted that the colony's number of juvenile delinquents was rapidly on the rise. Despite past efforts, which had been directed by the British colonial state, an alarming number of young men were being sent to industrial homes or probationary centers for gambling, theft, and prostitution. More concerning, the report cautioned that the number of "potential delinquents"—a category that included teenagers who had migrated to urban areas, had lost contact with family, or were for some other reason one step away from committing criminal acts—had also reached worrying levels. The report drew attention to the scores of youth who "roamed [city] streets," used foul language, embraced a "cowboy" lifestyle, and abused urban areas' postwar culture of Saturday Nights. After guiding its readers through numerous vignettes of young people who had become pilot boys, taken up prostitution, or adopted other wayward practices, the report encouraged parents, town councils, and government authorities to work together to "face up to the problems of the leisure hours of the young" and improve the colony's social and political prospects.[8]

Although these charges about errant youth were hardly new—they had long concerned chiefs and British officials—they raised considerable alarm among newly elected CPP officials as well as members of the local press. During the 1950s, many writers for the *Daily Graphic*—most of whom were highly educated middle-class men—echoed the department's assertions that Saturday Nights had come to house several dangers that could thwart the proper development of young men and women. A steady stream of articles portrayed nightclubs as places where susceptible minors could fall into sexual immorality, acquire an unhealthy taste for alcohol, and learn to disrespect elders and local authorities. Journalists' frequent warnings about the exploits of "smoking, hard-drinking [and] wriggling" youth resonated with middle-class readers, but they also prompted additional concern in official circles. In the mid-1950s, the CPP government pressured the Department of Social Welfare to make further inquiries into how young people appropriated Saturday Nights as occasions to embrace individualism and vice instead of a broader sense of social responsibility and civic engagement. In 1954, it dispatched a team of undercover welfare officers to visit nightclubs in three of the colony's principal towns: Accra, Kumasi, and Takoradi.[9]

The officers' findings, which were published in *Problem Children of the Gold Coast* and "Juveniles in Drinking Bars and Night Clubs," hardened the internal government's conviction that it needed to do much more to steer young people away from popular musical domains. Each insisted that nightclubs were danger spots where young men and women picked up dishonest practices, earned easy money, and erroneously acquired "a feeling of being important, experienced, and adult." Although they found it difficult to assess the actual ages of assembled patrons, the assigned officers surmised that many problematic patrons—prostitutes, truant students, pilot boys, and young workers who exercised shocking levels of "independence and freedom"—were under the age of eighteen. *Problem Children* confirmed this impression by including photographs depicting urban youth loitering outside nightclub walls (PURL 4.1). From there, the reports recommended that the government take two courses of action to purify highlife recreation and help young people return to their proper gendered and generational positions. First, they insisted that various civic actors, including parents, police officers, and local authorities, become more vigilant in their efforts to prohibit young men and women from taking part in Saturday Nights. Second, they asked that the government allow the department to sponsor a new wave of programs that could facilitate young peoples' development as responsible adults and citizens.[10]

The department's first suggestion found immediate response in Accra, the city that had the majority of the colony's nightclubs as well as potential juvenile delinquents. Shortly after the release of *Problem Children* and "Juvenile Delinquents," the Accra Municipal Council (AMC), a body comprised of twenty-seven elected officials and four traditional representatives, announced that it had decided to take a stand against the city's falling "standards of public morals and behaviors." Noting that it was especially troubled about supposed links between popular musical recreation and the city's growing numbers of wayward youth, the AMC mandated that Accra's drinking bars, nightclubs, and hotels without a C license—a government-issued liquor permit—would have to close their premises at 8 PM on weekday and weekend nights. Although the AMC's declaration garnered considerable enthusiasm from government officials, welfare officers, and members of the press—all of whom upheld the edict as a measure that would protect youth from negative influences and safeguard the city's civic order—it found little support from the wider public.[11] Most highlife enthusiasts, including some of middle-class status, opposed the measure because it truncated their own recreational outings and hampered their efforts at self-expression and social mobility. The city's musicians and nightclub proprietors, meanwhile, insisted that the regulation unfairly targeted their economic well-being. Three months after the law's passage, the AMC had issued C licenses to only five additional establishments, meaning that the vast majority of the city's recreational venues still had to close their doors shortly after dark. For many proprietors, band patrons, and bandsmen, this meant dwindling profits and considerable financial hardship. After a few short months, dissatisfaction with the city's abbreviated Saturday Nights had become so fervent that the AMC reluctantly revoked its ban.[12]

In the wake of the AMC's failure, officials in the Department of Social Welfare decided to dedicate their energies toward the reports' second recommended course of action: enacting new programs that could transform susceptible youth into upstanding citizens. It pursued this aim within the confines of the community center, a government-sponsored venue dedicated to disseminating information, attending to local needs, and bringing residents together for supervised social activities. In the mid-1950s, many of the colony's community centers inserted carefully planned recreational events into their existing schedule of educational and vocational programs. Though initially formed to lure youth away from urban danger spots, such events, which included sporting contests, beauty pageants, and musical performances, were also designed to expose young people to the importance of good citizenship, proper male-female relationships, and civic duty.[13]

Ironically, department records suggest that centers' most popular offerings were those that enabled young people to facilitate their own efforts at starting life. Throughout the mid and late 1950s, many community centers sponsored social dances: events that were held in the early evenings and featured live bands, ballroom and highlife music, and abundant refreshments. Although these dances did not provide the sale of alcohol, tolerate uncouth dress or behavior, or feature objectionable musical styles such as rock 'n' roll, many young people attended them in order to learn from local dancing instructors, meet new people, and simply have fun.[14] Other community centers offered young people practical instruction on how to play a range of instruments, read sheet music, and organize a functioning band. These programs were especially popular among young men. A 1956 course on brass instruments in Ejisu attracted over thirty young men, while a similar course in Axim enrolled ten male students for a five-week term. Unsurprisingly, these attendants also received lessons in an array of nonmusical topics. Several department courses featured sessions on responsibility, literacy, and "the importance of bandsmen in the community": topics that welfare officers extolled as important ingredients in their project of transforming potential delinquents into dedicated citizens who shunned "nightclub ways."[15]

In the end, such efforts had little impact on the recreational practices of young men and women or the Department of Social Welfare's concerns about the colony's future well-being. As colonial rule came to a close, large numbers of youth continued to flock to nightclubs, where they engaged in problematic practices that reflected individual rather than official concerns. Such shortcomings discouraged department officials, but they left a considerable impression within the wider confines of Kwame Nkrumah's CPP. As party officials came to realize that they could not yet control the colony's young urban populace or remake the colony's Saturday Nights, they decided to alter their approach to highlife music and recreation. Over the course of the mid-1950s, the CPP endorsed popular music not as a source of moral danger, but as a tool of mass mobilization and anticolonial action. As we will see, this strategy did much to help the party attract followers, widen its base of support, and outline a platform of collective action that was unmatched in the colony's early playing field of party politics. Eventually, it also put CPP leaders in a position to exercise greater control over highlife's confines, meanings, and significance as a form of national culture.

THE CPP'S USE OF DANCE BAND HIGHLIFE
FOR POLITICAL CHANGE

While historians have yet to fully reconstruct the ways in which individual people engaged the flurry of political activity in the postwar Gold Coast, most agree that the colony's era of party politics emerged along existing social, economic, and cultural fault lines. The colony's first postwar political party, the United Gold Coast Convention (UGCC), which was formed in August 1947, never established itself as a body of mass politics or broad appeal. In fact most men and women viewed the UGCC as an elitist organization concerned with advancing the interest of a small cohort of Gold Coast society. Its early priorities, which included a revision of the 1946 Burns Constitution, the replacement of the Legislative Council's nominated chiefs with elected educated citizens, and the establishment of accessible loans and import licenses, corroborated such views.[16] A few weeks after its formation, a group of disempowered young men, locally known as the *nkwankwaa,* formed the Asante Youth Association, an organization that immediately countered UGCC influence by proclaiming itself the colony's first political organization aimed at fulfilling the needs of the "ordinary man."[17]

Desperate to invigorate its public image and to attract the support of workers, students, and other less-established constituents, the UGCC invited a young anticolonial activist, Kwame Nkrumah, to become the party's secretary in December 1947.[18] While Nkrumah accepted the invitation, he soon distanced himself from the older and more conservative UGCC vanguard. In 1949, he broke away from the UGCC to form his own political organization, which he named the Convention People's Party (CPP). The CPP, which became the colony's first real mass party, openly confronted the UGCC on two fronts. First, it adopted a doctrine of "self-government now" that specifically challenged the UGCC's willingness to work with British officials to gradually transition the colony toward independence. Second, the CPP actively solicited the support of a broad range of residents, including marginalized urban workers, young men who had left school ("school-leavers"), unemployed and homeless youth ("verandah boys"), and market women, to join in its efforts to dismantle colonial rule.[19] Over the course of the 1950s, the CPP morphed from a small oppositional party into an inclusive sociopolitical movement that was vocal and virulent in its demands. The party's "Positive Action" campaign enabled wage laborers to participate in strikes and work stoppages; its newspaper, the *Accra Evening News,* rallied students and educated parties to support its ideological cause; and its Women's Section and Youth League allowed previously marginalized groups an opportunity to hold political rallies and raise much-needed party funds.[20] When the colony held internal elections in 1951, the CPP gained each of the five municipal seats in the new General Assembly, and its leader, Kwame Nkrumah, became the leader of government business (a position similar to that of prime minister). The CPP's electoral success continued in 1954, when the party won 74 of 104 legislative seats, Nkrumah officially became prime minister, and the colony achieved internal self-rule. Three years later, when Nkrumah announced that Ghana had obtained independence from British control, the CPP became its ruling party.[21]

The CPP's success was remarkable, especially since the colony's emerging political arena was in many ways an experimental one. Despite a growing fervor for self-rule, few Gold Coast residents, including those who were educated and economically affluent, had any direct knowledge about the nuances of party politics or government affairs. Throughout the 1950s, literate publics familiarized themselves with the colony's new political environment by reading an array of newspaper articles, with titles such as "Do You Vote for a Party?," that explained the basic mechanics of a parliamentary system.[22] The CPP, meanwhile, addressed such ambiguities by attempting to transform party politics into something that was local, familiar, and easy to understand. In fact, many residents elected to follow the CPP not simply because they agreed with its adamant calls for change, but because they felt comfortable taking part in its activities. Throughout the 1950s, the CPP incorporated an impressive array of local cultural forms—dress, music, theater, prayer, libation, and ritual symbolism—into its political events. This carefully selected repertory of cultural elements allowed it to create confidence in its actions, invoke a distinct sense of historical consciousness, and appeal to sentiments that transcended geographic, generational, and temporal bounds. More simply put, the CPP used culture to bring people together, emphasize collective practices, and encourage them to work together to deliver national independence.[23]

One of the CPP's most important cultural tools was highlife music. Despite their earlier reservations about the music's emerging dangers, many CPP leaders, including Nkrumah, came to see highlife as a perfect means of drawing public interest and extending the party's political reach. It was popular and accessible, and it offered a sonic embodiment of the colony's past, present, and future.[24] By infusing highlife music into party rallies, picnics, and parades, CPP leaders could also take their platform for change into the street, where curious residents could learn about their agenda and interact with ardent supporters.[25] The CPP made explicit use of the music during its mass rallies: events that attracted large crowds and took place outdoors in spacious public settings. Although the party announced these rallies in advance, Elizabeth Amonoo explained that it employed highlife to guide people to the event grounds, provide entertainment, and set a jovial and optimistic air:

> The CPP used highlife music at their rallies. During the campaign, they had to attract people and get them to come out to see what was going on. So they played records to let people know that something was happening. Sometimes they used brass bands or dance bands that people could follow to the rally site, singing and dancing. Once everyone was there they would continue to play. When you got to the rally, you would see the musicians there

playing highlife. They played highlife because everyone liked it and anyone could dance to it. Those songs gave people strength to dance—it didn't make them tired![26]

But highlife did more than create an inclusive environment of excitement and enthusiasm. As George Hagan describes, such rallies were conscious ploys to evoke shared emotions and create collective experiences:

> The rally had its own qualities as a mass gathering. It created close bodily contact and *individual freedom of action was restricted*. Not only was one shoved and pushed in all directions physically, one was also subjected to the emotional currents in the audience. Also the rally had people on their feet, *singing, dancing, joking*. A sitting audience could not do anything but listen—rather passively. And the remarkable feature of the CPP rally was that the platform had not just the elite on it, but also the ordinary man. Any individual member of the audience could be asked to come on stage and make a contribution.[27]

If curious men and women arrived at a CPP rally with little understanding about the party's aims or platform, such activities helped ensure that they left it impressed and willing to actively contribute to its efforts to inculcate political change.

Dance was a particularly effective means of transforming idle spectators into active CPP supporters. As a means of enjoyment and communication, dance enabled its followers to interact, garner shared experiences, and enjoy one another's company. Highlife dancing was an integral component of CPP conferences and social events, each of which helped raise proceeds for other party activities. In rural communities, the CPP employed brass bands so that local supporters could dance to highlife tunes as well as "new songs of liberation." Much of this enthusiasm for dance came from Nkrumah himself. He purportedly once told a group of dancers that they were "dancing their way to independence" and often advocated dance as a form of political action. In Accra, the prime minister's occasional appearances at one of the city's many nightclubs further solidified the music's importance to the broader struggle for national independence (see Figure 4.1).[28]

The CPP's embrace of highlife earned the party the ardent support of many popular musicians, some of whom dedicated their talents to popularizing the party's aims. E. K. Nyame, arguably the colony's most popular guitar band highlife musician, was a committed CPP enthusiast.[29] Nyame composed over forty songs in the party's favor, many of which, including *"Ghanaman"* (The land of Ghana) and *"Mo ma yεmbo mu, na*

FIGURE 4.1. Kwame Nkrumah (seated, middle) enjoys an evening at Accra's Kit-Kat nightclub, mid-1950s. Nkrumah's presence at the venue and his seated position below faded portraits of Queen Elizabeth (left) and the Duke of Edinburgh (right) encapsulate highlife's significance to Ghana's climate of political independence. *Photo courtesy of Isaac Hudson Bruce Vanderpuije, Deo Gratias Studio, Accra.*

yebɛdi nkunim" (Let us unite, for we shall overcome"), issued clear calls for patriotism and civic engagement. Concert parties—traveling troupes of theatrical performances and guitar band highlife music—also urged audiences to join the CPP in an effort to bring the colony its independence. Bob Cole, a prominent concert party theater actor, "began and ended his concert shows with pro-CPP government messages," while other groups performed pieces such as "The Creation of Ghana" and *"Ghanaman momma vensua biako"* (Ghanaian, you learn to become one). By the mid-1950s, many urban residents found that their local nightclubs, stages, and radio airwaves were filled with songs that celebrated CPP aims and achievements.[30]

They were also filled with songs that praised and popularized Kwame Nkrumah as a hero and "Africa's Man of Destiny."[31] E. K. Nyame's *"Kwame Nkrumah Ayɛ"* (Kwame Nkrumah has done it) and *"Onimdifoɔ"*

(Learned one), quoted below, praised Nkrumah and called upon Ghanaians to give him their full support:

Kwame Nkrumah aɛ bi ama	Kwame Nkrumah has done good things
yɛn abibiman yi mu	for us on our African continent
Monyi n'ayɛ monyi n'ayɛ	Give praises to him, praise him
Na ayeyi ne aseda sɛ no o	For he deserves praises and thanksgiving

The Tempos frequently performed their signature pro-Nkrumah tune,
"Nkrumah Highlife," as they traveled throughout the colony during
the mid-1950s. Other highlife songs, such as Kwaa Mensah's *"Kwame
Nkrumah,"* E. K. Nyame's *"Ghanaman"* (The land of Ghana), and the
Fanti Stars' *"Nkrumah kɔ Liberia"* (Nkrumah is going to Liberia), paid
tribute to his leadership style, courage, commitment to his cause, and
international reputation.[32] Such songs became especially prolific in the
months leading up to the colony's March 1957 independence, an event
that propelled Nkrumah as the leader of a transforming African continent. Lord Kitchener, a popular calypso musician from Trinidad and
Tobago, composed "The Sixth of March, 1957," which "placed Nkrumah
as the first among a long line of equals, of nationalist fighters and agita-
tors that the country (and indeed Black Africa) had had in time." E. T.
Mensah's "Ghana Freedom Highlife" paid similar reverence to the CPP
leader (PURL 4.2):

> Ghana—we now have freedom
> Ghana—the land of freedom
> Toils of the brave and the sweat of their labours
> Toils of the brave which have brought results
> Kwame, the star of Ghana
> Nkrumah, the man of destiny
> Toils of the brave and the sweat of their labours
> Toils of the brave which have brought results[33]

Nkrumah reciprocated such support by taking highlife artists, including
E. K. Nyame, with him on his official travels. In 1956, the prime minister
accorded highlife further recognition by publicly declaring that the medium was Ghana's "national" dance music.[34]

The party's embrace of dance band highlife culminated around March
1957, when the British Gold Coast became the independent country of
Ghana. Since Ghana was the first sub-Saharan African nation to shed the
colonial yoke, independence was cause for tremendous celebration. From
March 2nd to March 16th, the newly elected CPP government encouraged its constituents to attend a lineup of parades, durbars (ceremonial

assemblies of chiefs and citizens), sporting contests, and performances that were designed to memorialize the occasion and "show the world the energy and capacity of the people of the Gold Coast for running their own affairs." Unsurprisingly, highlife concerts headlined the festivities at the local, regional, and national levels. As it distributed the £350,000 that it had set aside for celebrations outside of the colony's main cities, the CPP government directed communities to hold one or more independence dances, concerts, or musical competitions.[35]

Many men and women continue to remember March 6, 1957, as an occasion filled with highlife music and dance. Felicia Kudiah, who lived in Asante Mampong, recalled the day as one of singing and dancing:

> When Nkrumah took power and Ghana became independent, people were happy. They went out singing, enjoying, getting together. People were happy that our own person was coming to rule us. They wanted to celebrate! Some people had radios and in the early morning they started playing them. [They started at] maybe 5 or 5:30 in the morning. And when people woke up to hear it, they went out and joined them. For days people didn't sleep, they were out celebrating! Highlife could be heard all around the town.[36]

In the Central Region alone, residents of Assin Apimanim, Assin Atan-daso, Equafo-Abrem, Komenda, Elmina, and Asebu marked the end of British rule by patronizing an impressive number of popular musical con-certs.[37] Planning committees staged similar events in the Greater Accra, Volta, Eastern, Ashanti, Brong-Ahafo, Western, and Northern Regions, as did urban nightclubs, which sought to capitalize on the occasion by offering special independence dances that proudly displayed the new national flag and other symbols (see Figure 4.2). Highlife also marked the occasion for the hundreds of foreign dignitaries and visitors who had come to Accra to witness the event, as both the Police Band and Tempos performed hours of entertainment at the government's lavish Indepen-dence State Ball.[38]

If independence validated Nkrumah's declaration that dance band highlife was Ghana's national music, it also marked a turning point in the CPP's use of the medium as an agent of nation-building. In the years leading up to the monumental transfer, the party had shelved its reform-ist efforts and openly endorsed highlife's eclectic character as a means of cementing its popularity and enhancing its political clout. Embracing, rather than changing, highlife allowed the party to attract and convince marginalized groups, including women and urban youth, that they were important to the nation's future. Yet while the state-sponsored dances

FIGURE 4.2. An unidentified dance band performs at the Weekend-in-Havana nightclub on April 9, 1957, a few weeks after Ghana gained its independence. *Photo courtesy of Ghana Information Services Department Photograph Library.*

that marked independence were publicized as open affairs that would perpetuate the party's inclusive stance, they were actually closely managed extravaganzas that placed considerable restrictions upon gathered crowds. Most required attendants to don specific forms of dress. Men had to wear suits, ties, and collared shirts and women formal evening gowns, clothing styles that many urban residents, especially young people, had abandoned in favor of more liberating attire.[39] Similar restrictions applied to forms of dance. The National Association of Teachers of Dancing adjudicated many of the country's official dance competitions and selected winners not for individual style or innovative flair, but for their correct movements, precision, and general etiquette.[40] Rock 'n' roll was consistently absent from state-sponsored independence celebrations. During its preparations for the event, the government ignored young rock 'n' rollers' proposals to invite prominent bands from the United States so that they could perform alongside local musicians. Officials even mandated that the state airwaves refrain from playing rock 'n' roll during the two-week period dedicated to marking the achievement of national liberation.[41]

Although such actions prevented many constituents from freely expressing their enthusiasm or positioning themselves within the newly born nation, many CPP officials insisted that independence was the perfect moment to set aside an inclusive air and begin to emphasize a more specific understanding of national culture. This conviction was born partly out of their desire to ensure that international audiences there to witness the occasion garnered a proper impression of Ghana and Ghanaians. Since independence would attract thousands of foreign guests into Accra and other towns, CPP leaders wanted to ensure that their program of celebrations was uniform, respectful, and devoid of potential strife. Privileging highlife also gave visitors a tangible look at the cultural contributions the new nation would offer the international public: an act that began with Nkrumah leading the duchess of Kent to a round of highlife dancing at the State Ball.[42] Yet the government had other, and much more enduring, reasons to regulate highlife's venues, audiences, and performers. In the lead-up to Ghana's political independence, CPP officials had promised to transform the colony into a modern and prosperous nation that could play an active role in continental and global affairs. To make good on this declaration, it set out to erect a new framework of citizenship, civic practice, and gendered relations designed to guide the daily behaviors of all men and women. It hoped to do so, moreover, through a reformed version of dance band highlife.

CITIZENSHIP, GENDER, AND POPULAR MUSICAL PRACTICE IN THE NEW GHANA, 1957–1965

In his speech announcing Ghana's independence, Kwame Nkrumah informed Ghanaians that the end of empire was a cultural, as much as a political and economic, phenomenon (see Figure 4.3). True liberation, he insisted, was an act of self-realization: "From now on—today—we must change our attitudes, our minds. We must realize that from now on, we are no more a colonial but a free and independent people! . . . In the assembly just minutes ago I made a point that we are going to create our own African Personality and identity. It's the only way that we can show the world that we are ready for our own battles."[43] By rejecting their past experiences of subjugation and embracing their own merits, values, and principles, Nkrumah declared, Ghanaians could work together to create

FIGURE 4.3. Kwame Nkrumah announces Ghana's Independence, March 6, 1957. During his speech, amidst a variety of state symbols including the black star and the *fugu,* which later he endorsed as national dress, Nkrumah charged Ghanaians to develop an "African Personality." *Photo courtesy of Ghana Information Services Department Photograph Library.*

a glorious future and propel the nation into a position of global promi-nence. The best way that Ghanaians could change their attitudes and minds, moreover, was to return to the conventions of traditional "African" culture.[44] Nkrumah encouraged Ghanaians to make this transition under the guise of the African Personality, a collective persona that embraced both "the cluster of African humanist principles which underline the tra-ditional African society" and "the struggle of the African people . . . to liberate and unify the continent and to build a just society." As a source of cultural pride and self-empowerment, the African Personality would en-able Ghanaians to fully transcend the "artificial barriers erected between them by the colonists," find an independent means of self-expression, and demonstrate their capacity to manage their own affairs. As a source of col-lective identification and communal ethos, it would encourage Ghanaians to embrace hard work and sacrifice, contribute to the nation's economic and social future, and set a precedent for an "African rebirth" that could inspire other colonized peoples to fight for and achieve their own libera-

tion. If it came to underlie all aspects of daily practice, the African Personality would also demonstrate that Ghanaians "never really surrendered to
the British" or lost an appreciation of their own self-worth.[45]

While Nkrumah enthusiastically promoted the African Personality
as a return to a natural African identity, many Ghanaians first approached
the term as a nebulous call for cultural change. Alex Moffatt recalled
Nkrumah's directives as "big words" that intended to emphasize the
need for people to have pride in their own cultural activities. Felicia Kudiah remembered the African Personality as a charge to "do things that
belonged to us," while Elizabeth Amonoo saw it as a call for "all Africans
to come together."[46] Although such interpretations certainly captured
aspects of Nkrumah's grandiose vision, CPP officials remained cautious
about individuals' ability to misinterpret the leader's endorsement of
traditional cultural forms. In spite of the CPP's many political successes,
the party continued to face staunch opposition from established and
emergent political organizations, such as the National Liberation Movement and Ga Shifimo Kpee (Ga Steadfast Organization), which catered
largely to residents of particular geographical regions or members of
particular ethnic groups. If components of tradition were rallied within
these smaller confines, they could be used to subvert the CPP's political
programs, hamper its plans for economic development, and effectively
roadblock its calls for national unity. To ensure that Ghanaians adopted
an appropriate version of the African Personality, Nkrumah's government strategically assembled a national culture that it could endorse,
supervise, and promote.[47]

Compiling this national culture was no easy task. From 1957 to 1965,
Nkrumah's government attempted to outline its tenets within a number
of domains, including education, clothing and dress, and community
organizations.[48] Importantly, it also took up this task within the confines
of the popular arts, a highly visible realm that was open to wide participation and offered a ready means of displaying collective conditions and
values. Since many popular cultural forms, such as theater, music, and
dance, attracted large and enthusiastic audiences, CPP officials upheld
them to be effective platforms for the dissemination of national ideals:
much more so than speeches, public meetings, or illustrated pamphlets.
Their continued emphasis on traditional elements, including allusions
to history and shared spiritual sentiments, befit the African Personality, as did their capacity, in the words of Jay Straker, to help participants
"unlearn and disavow" colonial practices. At the same time, the popular
arts were places where many Ghanaians had already begun to creatively

engage modernity, address current concerns, and outline the contours of the nation-to-be. Since highlife's and other popular cultural forms' novel combinations of the old and new already encapsulated many facets of the African Personality, CPP officials saw them as ideal mediums to encourage people to think of themselves as Ghanaians and commit themselves to national needs.[49]

Musically speaking, highlife was also an ideal means through which to clarify Nkrumah's calls for the African Personality. For starters, it was a readily identifiable recreational form that large numbers of people had come to embrace. Second, as Felicia Kudiah recalled, highlife's status as the most local component of Saturday Nights made it an obvious medium for advancing the government's cultural aims:

> Nkrumah said that highlife belonged to us, that it was a Ghanaian music. And he wanted everyone to think of the music in that way. You see, everyone could dance highlife, it was open. But if you heard a waltz or rock 'n' roll maybe you couldn't dance it. That was because those musics came from the whites. Nkrumah wanted to push highlife so that our music became different from the others: so that it had its own face.[50]

Official interest in highlife also stemmed from long-standing concerns about the music's growing stature as a haven for problematic moral and social practices. By regulating highlife recreation, the government could directly target the undesirable practices of some of the new nation's most dangerous citizens, including prostitutes, pilot boys, and idle youth: individuals whose wasted talents could be remedied only through an avid promotion of productive citizenship and appropriate gendered behavior.[51]

As it embarked on its effort to clarify and enforce its calls for the adoption of the African Personality, Nkrumah's government asked the nation's men and women to uphold particular gendered expectations and responsibilities.[52] It encouraged all men to aspire to the standard of the nation's "new man": an adult male dedicated to the country's prosperity, moral standards, and women and children. In several of his public speeches, Nkrumah went to great lengths to emphasize this new man as a loyal and reliable guardian of Ghana's moral health. He shunned adultery, violence, and social vice, celebrated the importance of literacy and education, and was committed to upholding the obligations of Ghanaian citizenship. He despised laziness, was infused with "the spirit to work hard and learn fast," and worked hard to provide for his family. In short, Ghana's new man was devoted to protecting the nation's culture of civic responsibility, particularly from those who willingly shunned such expectations.[53]

Concurrently, the state promoted its own vision of the nation's "new woman." Initially, these efforts focused largely on regulating women's public appearance and dress. In the late 1950s and early 1960s, various state-owned press outfits published pictures and articles that depicted the dress, hair, and accoutrements that marked "true Ghanaian woman-hood." These pieces encouraged women to reject foreign fashion, mod-ernize local styles of *ntama* or *kente*, and to wear such outfits to work, recreational events, and social gatherings.[54] To further encourage such practices, the state sponsored national beauty pageants, whose winners earned grand titles such as "Miss Cedi" or "Miss Ghana," as well as pub-lic promotion as idols for the nation's female population (PURL 4.3).[55] Though beautiful and image-conscious, a true Ghanaian woman was also committed to the nation's political, economic, and cultural development. She contributed to Ghana's economic growth by bringing her feminine influence into its fields, factories, and offices.[56] More importantly, she was a dedicated wife, mother, and homemaker. She aspired to faithfully marry, bear children, and set a moral example for her family to follow. By pledging to manage her home, tend to her family, and reproduce national values, this new woman agreed to contribute to the betterment of "her country and Africa as a whole."[57]

Outside of the realm of rhetoric and beauty pageants, these calls for men and women to embrace gendered personifications of the African Personality found early emphasis within the domain of Saturday Nights. As it set out to enforce its calls for cultural change as something more than idle talk, Nkrumah's government immediately set its sights on highlife's purported prostitute problem.[58] In the late 1950s and early 1960s, prosti-tutes' brazen dress, elaborate makeup, and ostentatious behaviors, such as drinking alcohol and smoking cigarettes, made them highly visible additions to many urban nightclubs.[59] Many Ghanaians disparaged such women as *ashawo* ("moneychanger" in Yoruba), but government officials moved to aggressively confirm their status as un-Ghanaian persons who grossly violated the African Personality. Shortly after independence, E. R. T. Madjitey, Accra's first Ghanaian superintendent of police, organized a series of raids intended to remove all *ashawo* from the city's nightclubs and public spaces of musical recreation. For the next several years, authorities arrested suspected prostitutes, tried them in city courts, and fined them £2–25 for an array of charges, including loitering and "obstructing the public way." In October 1959, Accra police arrested and detained twenty-four women during one weekend alone. In Takoradi, similar campaigns focused on the city's Nigerian residents, whom police framed as outsiders who threatened to corrupt their young Ghanaian counterparts.[60]

If initially conceived as a way to remove practicing prostitutes from an arena of national culture, these raids became widely used to punish women who publicly defied the African Personality in dress, appearance, or behavior. In the early 1960s, Accra police often arrested women who wore short, tight-fitting skirts, makeup, and wigs—standard nightclub attire for many young women—insisting that they were markers of immorality and promiscuity. J. O. Mills, who served as a police officer in Accra during that time, recalled that he and his colleagues regularly apprehended women on account of their appearance:

> Yes! We arrested them for it. I was a police officer and was assigned to a special task force. We'd come to [Kwame Nkrumah] Circle, we'd see them and we'd arrest them. We took them to the Central Police Station in Accra every night. We would start at 6:30 PM, come to the Police Station, we'd go to Tema and circle around. Other times we'd start at Accra Central and go to Mamprobi. . . . We'd catch the girls, put them inside the car, and take them to criminal court.[61]

Although Mills and his partners occasionally arrested men for drunkenness, violence, or lewd behavior, they focused most of their attention on young women because their supervisors insisted that the women were a more urgent threat to the nation's moral and social fabric. Police action found further support from other official realms. In 1963, Ghana's education minister, A. J. Dowouna-Hammond, publicly condemned a popular tightly shaped, knee-length skirt known as "the fish" as a disfiguration of "Ghanaian Womanhood" and called upon all women to abandon it as a form of public attire. A month later, the *oguaahene,* the paramount chief of the Cape Coast Municipality, advised his constituents that the fish and other short skirts were "alien to our pattern of behavior and incompatible with our cultural background" and urged the municipal council to criminalize them as illegal forms of dress.[62]

Of course prostitutes were not the only Saturday Night participants guilty of violating the African Personality and abusing the confines of the government-declared national music. Another early target of official concern was urban youth, a cohort that had become increasingly lewd, recreationally assertive, and politically volatile. In the months following independence, growing numbers of young people expressed their frustration about mounting rates of unemployment, housing shortages, and their general marginalization within urban affairs. In Accra, a group of unemployed youth who proclaimed themselves the "Tokyo Joes" took to the streets in opposition to the CPP's failures and betrayal of "the common man." The government countered by declaring such protests to be little more than illegitimate uprisings by idlers and delinquents who had embraced "social vices as a substitute for productive pursuits." Others, including Accra police officers, insisted that the young protesters' discontent stemmed not from government shortcomings, but from their unhealthy obsession with rock 'n' roll, an un-Ghanaian music that flew in the face of the African Personality.[63] Over the next few years, various branches of government, including the National Board of Film Censors and state-owned press outlets, launched a vigilant campaign that intended to remove rock 'n' roll and its corrupting influences from public recreational venues.[64]

More importantly, the government set out to create new organizations that could refashion misguided youth into self-respecting citizens who embraced the African Personality. Roughly six months after independence, it created the Workers Brigade (later renamed the Builders Brigade), a collective of work camps that provided young men and women with occupational training, an ethic of hard work, and a sense of patriotic service. The brigade got off to a slow start, but by 1960 it had enlisted over eleven thousand young men and women. Though technically open to Ghanaians between the ages of fifteen and forty-five, the brigade's real focus was providing those under the age of twenty-four with a clear understanding of cultural nationalism, civic pride, and gendered behavior.[65] The organization sought to instill such virtues through a mixture of discipline, education, and hard work. Young men and women each received training in literacy and general sanitation, but women's education focused largely on domestic tasks, such as cooking, sewing, child care, and catering. This curriculum prepared them for tasks completed within the brigade, such as farming, food preservation, and the general maintenance and cleaning of the residential camps, but it also laid the groundwork for their future roles as wives, mothers, and guardians of the domestic sphere. Male education centered upon technical trades such as electrical engineering, vehicle mechanics, tractor operations, and driving. Young men also received hands-on training in the building of new roads, waterworks, schools, drainage systems, and low-cost housing: tasks that gave them various skills they could employ in their occupational and civic environments.[66]

The education of brigade members also extended into the sphere of Saturday Nights. The organization explicitly discouraged its members from embracing rock 'n' roll by instilling a uniformed dress code, lambasting the danger of material indulgence, and offering its members access to more healthy leisurely pursuits.[67] Shortly after its inception, the brigade formed the Builders Brigade Band, a ten-piece dance band that performed highlife music at parades, marches, and other public events. Overtime, the band became one of the CPP's primary vehicles for exposing young people to the merits of Ghana's national music. Band members sported brand-new instruments, wore matching outfits, and performed behind bandstands painted with the black star, Ghana's distinctive national emblem. Spike Anyankor, a professional alto sax player who had been a member of the Tempos and Accra's Rhythm Aces, directed the band, provided members with extensive musical training, and managed its public performances and recording sessions. The band also had a musical director, who carefully comprised the group's repertoire of local musical styles, popular standards, and acceptable modern songs.[68]

In addition to using the band to guide young brigade members into the confines of an officially decreed domain of we-ness, the government set out to establish the group as one of the country's most visible and celebrated dance bands. In 1959, the ensemble was a finalist in the National Dance Band Competition, miraculously (and rather suspiciously) advancing further than many well-established groups, including the Tempos, the Black Beats, and Joe Kelly's Band. Over the next few years, the band made numerous recordings, provided entertainment at government functions, and became a regular feature of Accra's nightlife scene. In the early 1960s, the government established a branch of the Brigade Band in each administrative region, so that wide audiences could witness its carefully screened repertoire of highlife and pro-government tunes.[69] Many nightclubs in Accra and elsewhere booked the group because the government allowed them to rack up shocking levels of debt. A post-Nkrumah report found that Accra's Tip-Toe, for example, owed the government nearly 1,904 cedis for outstanding band performances.[70]

In the years immediately following independence, the CPP government adopted a drastic, and rather reformist, approach to dance band highlife. Instead of using the music to mobilize or entertain the nation's citizenry, it employed it as a way to articulate what it meant to be Ghanaian, outline the African Personality, eliminate unhealthy practices, and punish those, particularly women and youth, who purportedly continued to place their individual aims and well-being over those of the new nation. At times, the CPP government flexed its institutional muscle and employed coercive tactics that many Ghanaians, particularly marginalized groups, associated with chiefs and colonial officials. Additionally, it authorized the creation of organizations that could align young people with its official directives. In the years that followed, the government took further steps to transform the colony's most popular musical form into what G. Thomas Burgess has called a "fairly neat, one-dimensional, top-down assertion of state power."[71] It did so largely under the directives of a new government body charged with supervising and training those most central to highlife music: its bands and musicians.

REGULATING A NATIONAL MUSIC

The CPP government's most ardent effort to reform Saturday Nights took place in the confines of the Arts Council, a national body established to organize and encourage the arts. The council was first formed in 1955 as an interim committee that could outline a cohesive cultural program in the waning years of colonial rule. Archival records provide few details about its early operation, but in the months immediately following independence branches of an enlarged council were active in Accra, Ho, Keta, and other southern towns.[72] The Accra branch, which was comprised of thirteen Ghanaian members and chaired by Philip Gbeho (then an instructor of music at Achimota), dominated its early discussions about Saturday Nights. Like their CPP counterparts, many council members had become concerned that such occasions had become overrun with idle youth. In February 1958, members of the Accra Committee joined with officials from the Ministry of Education, Information Services, and the Broadcasting House to watch *Jaguar Highlife,* a film written and produced by the newly formed Ghana Film Unit. Although the film was a fictional narrative about modern urban life, council members had serious reservations about its depictions of vulgar behaviors, sexual immorality, and gambling. Their conclusion that the film would do little to promote the African Personality, and recommendation that it not be screened either in or outside of Ghana, made a firm pronouncement about their intentions and sense of purpose.[73]

In December 1958, Ghana's Legislative Assembly passed the "Arts Council of Ghana Law" making the Arts Council a permanent government body. The new council, also headquartered in Accra, was comprised of highly educated and distinguished men and women, including Nana Kwabena Nketsia (chair), Dr. Seth Cudjoe (deputy chair), Philip Gbeho, Professor J. H. Kwabena Nketia, Eugue Koranteng, Kofi Antubam, Efua Sutherland, J. C. de Graft, and W. P. Carpenter. Nkrumah himself took up the position as acting president and extended honorary memberships to other established political authorities, including Dr. J. B. Danquah, Sir Arku Korsah, Sir C. W. Techie-Mensah, and all six regional presidents of the House of Chiefs. In effect, the council was a body of prestigious individuals who approached the task of nation-building as an essential prerequisite to the further expansion of state power.[74]

The "Arts Council of Ghana Law" charged this motivated cohort with a variety of highly important tasks. It was entrusted to "foster, preserve, and improve" Ghana's cultural forms, awaken public interest in and appreciation of performance mediums, establish a national theater movement, and arrange for exhibitions of the arts in Ghana and other countries. To accomplish these goals, the council organized its personnel into subcommittees responsible for particular artistic genres. The organizer of music, drumming, and dancing, for example, was responsible for annotating and recording traditional music, training local musical ensembles, and preparing musical "propaganda"—as it was called in private correspondence—that could be distributed to the Ministry of Education, Department of Social Welfare, and the nation's schools and colleges. Each subcommittee was based at the Arts Centre, the council's main Accra office, but most established local committees in the country's regional capitals, an organizational structure that enabled the council to implement programs that could address both local and national needs.[75]

Over the next several years the Arts Council endeavored to foster a coherent sense of Ghanaian national culture in three main ways. First, it looked to support the country's existing performers, theatrical groups, and bands. From its headquarters in Accra, the council deployed a number of scouts to identify talented artists whom the government could promote and hire for official performances.[76] Second, the council took up the task of evaluating how these artists' "objectives, quality, and integrity" matched those endorsed by CPP officials. Throughout the late 1950s and early 1960s, regional officials left their offices, observed artists' work, and compiled detailed reports that described them for their superiors. One such report on the Black Star Troupe, an Accra drumming and dancing ensemble, unveils the rigor council members employed in this process:

> The dances being produced by the Black Star Troupe in projecting African Personality . . . have a different meaning to what I understand. . . . The sort and the type of drumming and dancing produced by the Black Star Troupe is in fact very appalling. I am not in a position to condemn the dances they produced, but as far as my twelve years research to Ghanaian Customs,

FIGURE 4.4. Professional Uhuru Dance Band members wear *fugu* in an effort to reflect Nkrumah's African Personality during a 1963 performance.
Photo courtesy of Ghana Information Services Department Photograph Library.

> Drumming, and Dancing is concerned, I feel their production is not the Ghanaian type. The Leader should be invited with his troupe to put up a show at the Art Centre in the near future ... to verify my findings.[77]

Lastly, the council attempted to train the nation's artists to be proper purveyors of Ghanaian culture. In some instances, these efforts focused on rather innocuous details such as a group's name, costumes, or song titles. But they were usually much more intrusive. More often than not, the council directed groups to censor performance aspects, add or remove group members, or revise significant portions of their existing repertoire. Over time, such efforts made a considerable impact on the nation's artists, the form and content of live performances, and the ways in which audiences could, and did, appropriate various popular cultural forms' meaning.[78]

One of the council's first tasks was to refashion highlife dance bands into outfits that could help promote the spread of national values.[79] After making its initial assessments of dance bands in various regions, the council concluded that most groups remained far too reliant upon foreign influences and imported musical styles. An obvious source of concern was bands' continued embrace of the much beleaguered rock 'n' roll, but many council members voiced equal discouragement about their concurrent performance of ballroom numbers at nightclubs and government events. Since the foreign origins of both of these genres clearly conflicted with the mandates of the African Personality, the council launched an ambitious program designed to reform dance bands' repertoires and modes of self-presentation. Take, for example, the issue of musicians' dress. For years, bandsmen had donned Western suits, but in the early 1960s, the council pressed them to wear national attire, especially on stage. Though a subtle change, musicians' embrace of Ghanaian apparel, often *kente* or the *fugu*, was one that many government officials, including Kwame Nkrumah, publicly applauded (see Figure 4.4).[80]

Next, the council turned its attention to bands' status as purveyors of purely Ghanaian musics. In 1961, it encouraged dance bands to infuse highlife with "traditional rhythms and dancing," a step that would promote the merits of local culture and help eliminate some of the vulgar components of Saturday Nights.[81] That same year, the council unveiled a six-month training course designed to teach dance bands how to perform traditional rhythms, incorporate local dances and dancers into their staged acts, and compose new musical and lyrical arrangements.[82] These courses required bands to attend daily rehearsals at council headquarters and to subject all aspects of their musical and nonmusical activities to revision. Oftentimes, bands that enrolled in these courses experienced personnel changes that operated along gendered lines. The Council insisted that all male bandsmen had to be disciplined, punctual, and willing to conform to the council's standard code of behavior. In addition, it directed many groups to recruit female dancers who were talented, beautiful, and literate: all characteristics of the "Ghanaian woman."[83]

The council's first pupil was the Messengers Dance Band, a group that had acquired an enviable reputation as one of the nation's most prolific highlife ensembles. The band, led by George Lee, had also gained the approval of the CPP government, which awarded it residency at the state-owned Star Hotel, one of Accra's most prominent nightspots. The Messengers performed at the hotel until the summer of 1961, when they elected to take part in a council program designed to improve their familiarity with Ghana's "traditional and folk music." Council reports suggest that the Messengers' training was a resounding success. Within three short months the band had "acquired an almost uncanny prowess in interpreting a wide variety of authentic Ghanaian dances and rhythms." After watching the band perform such numbers, several council members agreed that the outfit had eclipsed its status as a mere dance band and become an ideal instrument for promoting the merits of the African Personality.[84]

From 1962 to 1963, several other dance bands took part in similar council training courses. Takoradi's Broadway Band, later renamed the Professional Uhuru Dance Band, took a six-month course at the Arts Centre in 1962, as did the Globemasters Dance Band, the Builders Brigade Band, and the Ghana Farmers Dance Band. In each instance, enrolled groups learned how to play traditional numbers, acquired female dancers, and procured a repertoire of pro-government songs.[85] While musicians admitted that this training was rigorous and somewhat onerous, it provided bands with several advantages. Council-trained ensembles secured numerous government engagements, lucrative pay, and the possibility of becoming full-time professionals who could abandon their other lines of work.[86] They also received enhanced press coverage in state-owned newspapers, extended play on the national airwaves, and a leg up in government-sponsored band competitions.[87]

Few bands benefited more from their council training than the Professional Uhuru Dance Band, an outfit managed by two CPP ministers, Krobo Edusei and E. K. Dadson. Stan Plange, the guitarist and eventual leader of the band, recalled how he and his fellow bandsmen capitalized upon their council training:

> [In the 1960s] we came for a special traditional course at the Arts Centre because Nkrumah's government decided that all the dance bands should add cultural components to their music. . . . They trained us in *fontomfrom* drumming, *agbadza,* and others so [that] we would incorporate them into our performances. . . . You know, Nkrumah was interested in getting his African Personality into the mainstream of everything. Occasionally we would go to him to perform, especially when foreign ministers were in town. I remember playing for the President of the World Bank. Another time, we performed for the [Assistant] Secretary of State in charge of African Affairs from the United States.[88]

Over time, the Professional Uhuru Dance Band's ability to perform traditional rhythms such as *agbadza* (an Ewe recreational music) made it the government's de facto national band, a designation that came with an enviable reputation, financial security, and state-sponsored bookings in international cities such as Moscow, London, Beirut, Khartoum, Nai-

FIGURE 4.5. The signboard outside the Professional Uhuru Dance Band's
head office in Accra, c. 1963. Its inclusion of "Cabaret Troupe" indicates
that the band could perform traditional music and dancing styles. *Photo
courtesy of Ghana Information Services Department Photograph Library.*

robi, and Kampala (PURL 4.4). The group became so successful that
they established a head office near the Accra Post Office, where nightclub
owners and other interested parties could directly hire it for engagements
(see Figure 4.5).[89]

Although the council rarely matched the favor it lavished on the Professional Uhuru Dance Band, it ensured that highlife ensembles followed
its directives through a mixture of reprimand and reward. It punished
bandsmen who arrived at training sessions late, suspended problematic
members, and prohibited offending groups from participating in government performances and competitions. At the same time, it rewarded
cooperative ensembles by extending endorsements, invitations, and even
opportunities for international travel. In the early 1960s, the council provided the government passport office with firm instructions about which
bands should be allowed to perform outside the nation's boundaries. Its

decision that only bands that had been trained as "musical envoys"—
performers who had been taught to project the African Personality—
proved quite firm. Shortly after independence, council members rejected
a proposal to send E. T. Mensah as a delegate to a conference sponsored
by the Société Africaine de Culture in Paris because he was not "quali-
fied in traditional African culture."[90] The council also investigated the
linguistic and educational background of traveling ensembles so that it
could handpick those who would conduct interviews with members of
the foreign press: an act it took to "protect the reputation of the country
and people of Ghana."[91]

The council's approach to preparing musical envoys was particularly
well documented in regards to the Messengers' month-long visit to West
Germany in 1962. In the months leading up to the band's departure, council officials went to great lengths to oversee the various components of
its trip. It required band members to attend daily rehearsals at both the
Arts Centre and the University of Ghana's new Department of African
Studies, added new members to the group, dictated song choices, and
compiled costumes. When they deemed the group ready, they held a series of trial performances, including shows at Accra's Ambassador Hotel,
the British Council, and the Goethe Institute, so that other government
officials could assess the band's preparations and identify possible areas
of improvement.[92]

The council's most pressing concern was the full-length script it had
prepared specifically for the Messengers' tour. The script (presented
in full below) outlined the exact songs, actions, and dialogue that the
group was to perform in front of German audiences. More importantly,
it was designed to convey a closely managed understanding of the nation's musical heritage, recent history, and wider embrace of the African
Personality:

> **"Messenger's Band Show"**
> (*The stage is set with band already in position with Western instruments.
> Traditional instruments—Akan and Ewe—are arranged respectively at either
> front corner of the stage. Band starts a number, "Deep Purple," and curtain is
> drawn*).
>
> 1. *George: (After "Deep Purple"—2½ minutes, moves to front of Band)* Ladies
>   and Gentlemen, my name is George Lee and I lead the Messengers Dance
>   Band. I have the pleasure of introducing to you my colleagues (*each mem-
>   ber is introduced—playing a phrase on his instrument. The drummer, being
>   the last to be introduced, plays a 'break' bridge to lead in other members for a
>   final ensemble—one chorus only*).

2. *George:* And now Ladies and Gentlemen, I should like to welcome you, on behalf of the Messengers Band of Ghana. We are very pleased that you have come to see our show. Eddie (pointing at him) will welcome you on the traditional talking drums. But before that he will play the customary greeting to the Drums. (*Eddie plays 'Akyeampong Tententen' etc., pausing after each phrase, for the Akan translation to be given by George . . .*).

3. *George:* Eddie has just played the customary traditional greetings on the talking drums, paying tribute to tall Akyeampong, our ancient drummer, and also to the Tweneboa Tree from which traditional drums are carved. He will also mention the various parts that make the drums complete.

Eddie will you now welcome the audience [*Eddie plays—'Ghanaman, Kotoko friaman friaman dom, yema wo akwaba, anyaado, akwaaba aferaw, akwaaba ahenewa'. Or (for abroad) 'Muntie, Okasa kyere!' (Attention please) 'Odomankoma kyerema se' (The ancient drummer says) 'Sokwafe ma mo akwaaba' (The musicians from Ghana welcome you to this show)*].

4. *George:* Traditional Drum language is a language of its own, and is made up of poems, royal titles, orders and commands special occasions. When the talking drum players meet at public functions, they exchange fraternal greetings or rivalry. The talking drums also often play a leading part in traditional dance groups.

5. *George:* The Band will now give you an ever popular Ghanaian High Life. This tune is the most popular amongst people of most parts of Ghana. It is called "*Yaa Amponsah*" and it was composed in 1918 by two young Cocoa Brokers—Asante and Otoo—whose work took them from Akropong-Akwapim to Apedwa near Kibi. These gay and prosperous youngmen [*sic*] mixed a lot with the white people in southern Ghana and they formed the first Dance Club at Apedwa shortly after arriving there. There they discovered a beautiful dark skinned girl called Yaa Amponsah who, though illiterate, had been brought up at Cape Coast where she learnt to cook well, to sew well, and above all to dance the Waltz, Quick Step and the High Life. She spent a lot of time with Asante and Otoo who became so fond of her and her gaiety that they composed this High Life, in which they begged Yaa Amponsah to never marry but stay single and remain with them always in the little club. The High Life is very popular on the West Coast of Africa and we hope that soon it will spread all over the world. The High Life was born in Ghana, and we think that this is how it might have started (*Drums and handclap with vocal—fade*).

The Guitar is perhaps the earliest European made musical instrument that came to Ghana, and because of its traditional counterpart which [was] already in use in the interior of Ghana, it very quickly grew into popular use. Let us now hear what the tune sounds like on the strings (*Guitar and Bass*). The next instrument to be made popular was the Military trumpet which quickly found its way into the Traditional Military (or Asafo) companies.

But it was the Brassband that continued the story of the high life, and in this the most popular instrument was the cornet. Instead of the cornet let the trumpet now play the tune for you (*Trumpet*). Now with the whole band together, it sounds like this.

The high life has changed from year to year. It is now 1962—and the age of progressive jazz and *we* have indeed progressed (*Band in progressive jazz style—guitar still maintains tune in background—then straight chorus—and instruments stop by gradual elimination—fade out on rhythm*).

Did you like it?

But our music is older than this, much older and its dances and rhythms are different from one region to another. We would now like to play for you some of the traditional rhythms of Ghana.

First of all, in Southern Ghana, the music of the Akans (*Akan Drumming*) Now for the Volta Region in the extreme South of our country (*Ewe Drumming*).

(*Band changes to Takai Costumes*) Now we travel 500 miles to the North to hear the music of the xylophone. In the North of Ghana, the Takai is a princely and graceful dance usually performed by about 40 dancers. We will now dance it for you. (*Play and Dance "Takai"...*)

INTERVAL

(*Band returns to stage with Takai Costumes*). Now for a little experiment. Here is an authentic Ewe rhythm called *"Husango"* (*Play*).

And here is a Western tune you may recognize. It is called *"Answer Me"* (*Play*).

Now let us put them together (*Play*)

6. *George:* The High Life comes back again. First the girls will give you a demonstration (*Play and Dancing*).

   Now I want you to meet Comfort Onyina and Edward Addy, our stars of the High Life, winners of the National Competition of 1961.

7. *George:* Before we get through there remains one last thing to do. We now tear apart a high life and turn it into a Cha-Cha (*Play*).

Thank you very much indeed, ladies and gentlemen. You have a very nice audience. We can do greater things, but only with your support and patronage. The floor is now open for dancing, and let us all do some Ghana Dances. (*Band will now play High Life, girls picking partners from audience and teaching them...*).[93]

Convincing or not, the Messengers' scripted show was an obvious effort to clarify and control highlife's status as a national music. Its invocation of traditional musics from the country's various regions, jazz numbers, and other international styles, allowed the council to claim jurisdiction over the breadth of the country's popular musical landscape and to clarify how highlife embodied aspects of each of these diverse forms.[94] Its presentation of highlife's history ignored the music's real origins and contentious past, and instead suggested that it was a timeless manifestation of Ghanaian citizenry and the African Personality. Its depiction of highlife's early founders, "Asante" and "Otoo" (who were hardworking and prosperous young men) and "Yaa Amponsah" (a skilled and beautiful young woman) suggested that Ghana's new men and women were not government impositions, but well-established models of male and female behavior. The Messengers' show was, in other words, not an effort to give German audiences a glimpse into Ghana's Saturday Nights: it was an effort to perform an official version of Ghanaian national culture.

Although the Messengers' show was not designed for Ghanaian audiences, the council made similar efforts to control dance bands' performances on local stages. In the early 1960s, it encouraged dance band musicians to think of themselves as role models who could inspire all citizens to embrace the ethics of hard work, civic responsibility, and national pride. Private and state-owned newspapers assisted this effort. Articles in two different publications presented the Modernaires Dance Band not as a recreational outfit, but as a group of serious professionals who had to follow strict rules, obey bandleaders, and attend daily rehearsals. They also emphasized that band members upheld these responsibilities while carrying out their rightful roles as husbands, fathers, and household heads.[95] The press gave similar acclaim to the Ramblers Dance Band, a semiprofessional outfit whose 1964 song "Work and Happiness" encouraged Ghana's young men and women to envision hard work as a central tenet of citizenship and patriotic duty:

> Work, and happiness, yes I must confess
> All must give their best
> For beautiful Ghana
> United Farmers and Workers of Africa
> God will bless you wherever you are
> Work and happiness, yes I must confess
> We must give our best
> For beautiful Ghana[96]

While numerous articles heaped praise on upstanding bands, others reinforced state directives by demonizing musicians who engaged in offensive conduct or incited riotous behaviors among their listeners.[97]

The council's final means of influencing bands' behavior came from its ability to supervise a lineup of national concerts and musical contests. Throughout the 1960s, it sponsored numerous national highlife competitions, events that usually took place on national holidays and drew heavy crowds. While bands entered these competitions in order to showcase their talents and enhance their prestige, such events were highly regulated affairs that rewarded those which had received council training and abided by official instructions. Council members supervised these contests, determining which bands were eligible to perform, the length of their set, and even which musical styles they were allowed to play onstage.[98] In addition, they asked selected judges to not simply evaluate each band's sound, but to rank individual groups according to their "appearance, showmanship, and general behavior and discipline."[99] Since council-trained bands usually stood on the medal stand, it became increasingly difficult for dance bands to avoid upholding at least some of the government's musical mandates. Audiences felt similar restrictions. In the mid-1960s, various components of the nation's Saturday Nights reflected government aims. Nightclub dance competitions, long an arena of competitive self-expression, were often de facto celebrations of official standards of dancing. In part, this shift was the result of the council, renamed the Institute of Arts and Culture, directing its regional offices to educate young people on how to correctly dance highlife. Although the dance had a long history as an open form of movement and self-expression, the institute outlined a new national standardized sequence of steps that it demonstrated before audiences at public festivals and holiday celebrations.[100] By 1965, Saturday Nights were times when a growing number of Ghanaians had to set aside past practices and personal preferences in favor of those consistent with official directives and a top-down understanding of national culture.

CONCLUSION

In the September 28, 1960, edition of the *Daily Graphic*, Oscar Tsedze wrote an article entitled "The 'Highlife': Did it Originate in Ghana?" In its half-page spread, Tsedze reminded readers of Nkrumah's two announcements that opened this chapter and lauded the music's popularity throughout the country, West Africa, and places as far away as East Africa and parts of Europe. But Tsedze's central assertion was that highlife was not necessarily a Ghanaian music. He claimed that highlife had actually originated in Sierra Leone, where freed slaves had forged a new music to mark their triumphant return to African soil after a painful and forced sojourn across the Atlantic. To reflect their exuberance for their newfound home and freedom, Tsedze stated, these newly liberated people named their musical creation "highlife."[101] A few weeks later, the newspaper published a few of the many responses readers penned to answer Tsedze's claims. Most vehemently disagreed. The music was, they argued, "native to Ghana" where it was "known long before the advent of the white man" and had blossomed at the efforts of the Tempos and other modern bands.[102] It was, in their estimation, a purely Ghanaian music that had begun to emanate out to other West Africans and the rest of the world.

Though light-hearted (and rather historically accurate), readers' adamant opposition to Tsedze's article was in part a product of the music's intimate links to the CPP government and Ghana's newly declared domain of national culture. Over the course of its tenure as the main source of opposition to colonial rule and the leading party of sub-Saharan Africa's newest nation, the CPP worked to refashion highlife into something that was, as the readers claimed, quintessentially Ghanaian. In the years leading up to independence, it employed the music as a tool to guide wayward youth, a conduit of political mobilization, and a medium of anticolonial action. In March 1957, it proclaimed, through words and action, that highlife was Ghana's national dance music—an assertion that different government officials made fifty years later to a less optimistic, but rather accepting, Ghanaian public.

Yet highlife's status as a centerpiece of Ghana's national culture was not an organic or inevitable phenomenon. On the contrary, the music's "national" label was largely a product of the independent CPP government's broader program of nation-building and political legitimization. In the years following the end of British rule, Nkrumah's government struggled to effectively communicate its ambitious arsenal of plans, rhetoric, and official credos to its diverse civilian body. It co-opted highlife and the domain of the performing arts more broadly to solve this problem. In many ways, officials used the music to put their ideas into practice: to define in sound, movement, and aesthetic, what it meant to be Ghanaian, embrace the African Personality, and take up the mantle of civic responsibility. By shunning highlife's foreign influences and promoting the embrace of those linked to a more authentic national past, the government helped transform a highly charged form of popular recreation into a domain of consensus and collective practice.

Nationalizing highlife was no easy task. In many ways, the CPP government's efforts to remake the music hinged upon the punitive measures that its predecessors—chiefs and the colonial state—had used to enforce their own directives and authority. During the party's period of prominence, various state institutions, including the Department of Social Welfare and police, targeted problematic youth and women and enforced their removal from the wider realm of Saturday Nights. Arts Council officials, meanwhile, reformed dance band musicians by rewarding those who embraced traditional elements, altered repertoires, and government supervision and reprimanding those who did not. The employment of these mechanisms and methods of power demonstrates that nation-building in Ghana, as in many other African contexts, was a project that created new forms of both synergy and disconnect between government officials and their constituents. Of course, CPP authorities were not the only people working to remake Saturday Nights. In addition to scores of city residents who continued to use popular music in pursuit of their own aims, another cohort—the nation's highlife musicians— struggled to employ their music in a self-serving manner. It is to their actions that we now turn.

FIVE

"We Were the Ones Who Composed the Songs": The Promises and Pitfalls of Being a Bandsman, 1945–1970

In 1950, a young Charles Kofi Mann left his hometown of Cape Coast for Takoradi, a rapidly growing city that served as the locus of the colony's rail and harbor works. Like a number of young men before and after, he made the move in hopes of finding employment, earning money, and charting a future.[1] Unfortunately, Mann's arrival in Takoradi was marked not by opportunity, but by obstacles and hardship. Without friends or family to lean on, he spent his days searching for work and a place to live. After scouring the city center without much success, Mann descended on the harbor, where he secured a steady stream of odd jobs, found friends, and became immersed in his new urban environs. For the next year he loaded and unloaded cargo, cleaned ship decks, and assisted with various maintenance tasks on and off the docks. One day a British captain impressed with Mann's work ethic and array of skills offered him a position aboard a ship bound for Nigeria. Convinced that he had finally found his lucky break, Mann eagerly accepted the offer and began a four-year stint at sea.

Mann's new work allowed him to overcome adversities, acquire a steady income, and claim status as an independent and autonomous person. After a few years, however, he came to the realization that it would not enable him to secure enduring recognition as a successful adult man. Although his long trips abroad garnered good money, they left him few opportunities to accrue or develop property, reconnect with his family in Cape Coast, or enhance his position in Takoradi's hierarchies of age,

FIGURE 5.1. Sign for C. K. Mann Street (now C. K. Mann Avenue)
in Takoradi, September 2005. Photo by the author.

gender, and social standing. With an eye on his long-term prospects, he
started to consider other possible lines of work. One afternoon, he ventured into a Decca record store, where he heard a recording of a young
highlife guitarist named King Onyina. It was, in Mann's recollection, a
life-changing event. Immediately impressed by Onyina's sound and style,
he decided to purchase a guitar and dedicate his free time to learning
the instrument. A few years later, he abandoned his work at sea, moved
to Tarkwa, and joined Kakaiku's Band as a full-time guitarist.[2] Mann
stayed with the group for several years, but eventually returned to Takoradi and formed his own highlife ensemble. In 1966, his newly named
Carousel Seven Dance Band became the resident band at the city's most
prominent nightclub, effectively launching what would be a long and il-
lustrious career.[3]

　　Over the next several decades, Mann became one of Ghana's most
successful highlife musicians. He recorded numerous albums, won ac-
colades for his energetic performances, and traveled outside of Ghana
to perform in North America and Europe. In rather remarkable fashion,

Mann used popular music to fuel his personal transformation from a marginal youth into a widely recognized figure of stature and authority. In fact, his onstage performances provided him with fame, fortune, and renown as one of Ghana's national icons.[4] The full extent of his success, as a musician and man, became evident during one of our phone conversations in 2005. Eager for our first meeting at his Takoradi home, I called Mann to verify driving directions from Accra. With a hint of prideful laughter, Mann insisted that I would have little trouble finding his house after arriving in Ghana's fourth-largest city. "Anyone in Takoradi can direct you to where I live" he exclaimed, "I live on C. K. Mann Street!" (see Figure 5.1).[5]

In many ways, Mann's rags-to-riches narrative exemplifies the possibilities that made highlife such a popular and contested medium. By mastering the terrain of urban Ghana's Saturday Nights, he found economic security, permanently altered his identity, and became a widely regarded social figure. In the decades surrounding Ghana's independence, several young men pursued similar paths, deciding to become highlife musicians in order to enhance their personal prospects for the immediate and distant future. Very few, however, proved able to replicate Mann's eminence and outcome. Although highlife was extremely well liked by audiences and government officials, it was rarely a kind occupational sphere. Many musicians, in fact, recall highlife's period of prominence—the decades before and after independence—as a time of limited personal gains. They described being a bandsman as a profession marked by intense competition, irregular engagements, and constraining demands. It was also an occupation that made it difficult to uphold the expectations they faced as adult men. In addition to satisfying the requests of audiences and patrons, musicians attempted to achieve less public, but no less important, aims. They looked to purchase homes, start and maintain families, and acquire respect in their communities. Oftentimes, the spotlight and stage did surprisingly little to facilitate or aid these ventures. In fact, most musicians, including those who had gained great acclaim as popular icons and celebrities, found that the years surrounding Ghana's independence were ones not of boundless possibility, but of unexpected hardship, limitations, and unfulfilled hopes.

This chapter examines the lived experiences of highlife's innovators, artists, and performers and charts how they engaged their profession to achieve gendered, generational, and social mobility. Although these musicians were creative cultural pioneers, they faced inconsistent opportunities and challenges over the course of their lives and careers. The chapter first looks at conditions and strategies young musicians embraced during their early professional years. Between the end of World War II and 1965, young men struggled to enter popular music and establish themselves as budding professionals, exceptional talents, and empowered social figures. Personal, familial, and social difficulties marked people's decisions to become highlife musicians, and popular music became dominated by young men because they were best equipped to take on the risks associated with becoming bandsmen. As the first-person testimonies of two artists reveal, many young men were able to use popular music to stretch, and occasionally overcome, the boundaries of age and inexperience. Older and more established bandsmen, meanwhile, often struggled to balance a complex confluence of professional, public, and personal demands. Even those who achieved stardom found that their newfound prominence was a mixed bag rather than surefire means of gaining personal and professional success. The chapter ends with an examination of song lyrics, a realm that musicians used to directly enter the debates surrounding urban Ghana's Saturday Nights. Particular examples demonstrate that while musicians went to great lengths to compose songs that could enhance their own professional and personal stature, audiences could, and often did, imbue them with alternative meanings and significance.

THE CHALLENGES OF ENTERING
POPULAR MUSIC, 1945–1960

To an overwhelming degree, the dance band musicians who rose to prominence in the postwar period were young men of junior status within their urban confines. Like earlier generations of popular music-makers, they picked up instruments in order to have fun, socialize with others, and expand their individual autonomy. Yet the youthful character of Ghana's mid-twentieth-century popular music scene was also a product of the logistical challenges, social attitudes, and prominent stereotypes that prevented other men and women from becoming bandsmen. One of the most basic obstacles to entering popular music was the ability to access and learn dance band instruments. In the late 1940s and 1950s, imported instruments such as trumpets, saxophones, trombones, guitars, and drum kits remained rather expensive, well beyond the reach of most people. Those who could afford their purchase, meanwhile, often lacked the time or knowledge needed to play them at a fluent level. In the decades following the end of the Second World War, however, a large number of urban youths were able to access musical instruments and training at school.

The expansion of government education drew growing numbers of young people into the classroom, but it also led numerous primary and secondary schools to incorporate music into their curriculum. Many schools purchased instruments, hired musical instructors, taught students how to read sheet music, and offered lessons on how to play various musical styles. In larger cities like Accra, Kumasi, Takoradi, and Cape Coast, schools sponsored choirs, brass bands, and dance orchestras that performed at school and community events.[6]

Many prominent dance band musicians credited their education and participation in school ensembles as being fundamental to their later decisions to enter popular music. Oscarmore Ofori became one of Ghana's most prolific highlife composers of the late 1950s and 1960s, but he first cut his musical teeth at the Old Juaben School in Odumase Krobo, where he participated in the choir, played drums, and studied guitar. Desmond Ababio, a longtime musician, learned the flute from the music master of his school band, and Jerry Hansen, the leader of the immensely popular Ramblers Dance Band, became immersed in music as a student at Achimota College, where he took piano lessons, learned how to read sheet music, and studied the compositions of prominent Ghanaian musicians such as Philip Gbeho and Ephraim Amu.[7] Though each admitted that he was drawn to music as a form of fun, they recounted how such experiences gave them the foundational skills and confidence needed to launch their budding careers. As more and more young people acquired some musical education in the decades surrounding independence, larger towns became home to an ever-growing number of highlife ensembles. By the end of the 1960s, Ghana had roughly five hundred popular bands, the vast majority of which were led by and comprised of young men.[8]

The youthful domination of popular music was also a product of the air of suspicion that had long surrounded urban entertainers. As a result of popular music's associations with social upheaval, gendered strife, and generational chaos, many urban communities viewed performing artists as rascals, drunkards, and failed men. Even highlife music's gradual rise as a national medium did little to combat entrenched stereotypes that painted musicians as dangerous rogues who pilfered property, seduced young women, and willingly ignored the directives of elders, chiefs, and political authorities. These supposed links between music and immorality also caused many families to prohibit members from learning musical instruments or taking part in musical activities outside of regulated and supervised social spheres. While some parents proved willing to abandon such concerns for school-sanctioned musical exploits, many urban residents, young and old, remained unable to learn a musical instrument for fear that they would be viewed with suspicion or held in low esteem.[9]

For many older people, becoming a bandsman was a nearly impossible prospect. In part, their inability stemmed from popular music's reputation as an unviable or illegitimate line of work. Although the rise of commercialized leisure, expansion of recording opportunities, and growing possibility of lucrative tours increased popular musicians' financial hopes, few Ghanaians considered it to be a suitable means of making the money needed to support a family or cover household expenditures.[10] Others steered clear of popular music because of the unconventional demands of the profession. Unlike laborers or desk workers, musicians undertook constant travel, experienced long periods away from their families and home communities, and made their living amidst a nighttime environment of drink, dance, and joviality. Popular musicians' itinerant lifestyle was particularly unsettling to residents of Ghana's smaller towns and villages, who showered such figures with ridicule, distrust, and, in some cases, verbal and physical abuse.[11] In the 1950s, such communities often received highlife musicians by publicly warning their residents that "thieves had come to town"; others went so far as to ban artists from performing or sleeping within their midst.[12] For older and more established men, particularly those who had entered adulthood and had families, this mobile lifestyle exposed them to severe consequences and tremendous risk.[13] Stan Plange, the guitarist and leader of the Professional Uhuru Dance Band, noted that musicians could do little to combat the stereotypes that tinted their individual and familial reputations. Although Plange carried himself in a respectable manner on- and offstage, he found that others continued to assume that he, like all musicians, led a life of considerable vice:

> [Musicians] were lower down on the social ladder; we were regarded as those who didn't do well. I didn't smoke, I didn't drink, and I was able to keep it that way. But people were always surprised with me when I told them that I didn't smoke and I didn't drink. When they heard that they came to the conclusion that I was a womanizer! They said that there was no way that I could be in music and not drink, not smoke or not be a womanizer. [In their minds] a musician had to suffer from one of these three evils.[14]

Since established adults who had families, responsibilities, and reputations to protect rarely attempted to pursue a popular musical career, it was a path wide open for younger persons willing to take individual risk and face public scorn. In many ways, urban youth were well positioned to combat stereotypes, because they were unencumbered with expectations or responsibilities that accompanied adulthood.[15] At the same time, the young people who pursued popular music did so with considerable hazard and consequence. Most highlife musicians explained that their early popular musical exploits prompted considerable scorn from family and community members. Oscarmore Ofori's decision to join the Koforidua Orchestra in 1953 brought strong opposition from his father, who did not consider music to be a proper career.[16] When Desmond Ababio was invited to perform with E. T. Mensah's Tempos and King Bruce's Black Beats, two of Ghana's most prominent dance bands in the 1950s, his parents insisted on meeting the respective bandleaders in person. These meetings reassured them that their son was not joining a group of ruffians, but they did little to challenge their assumption that music could never provide him with the means to become a successful adult man:

> They were worried about me being a musician because [they thought] the money was too small to support a wife or family. At that time, there were not many musicians who were successful in life—there were few who owned a house, owned a car, or had a good family. It was the people in government or business who organized their family well. That is what my parents wanted [for me].[17]

Secondary school students and recent graduates found that their decision to become musicians invoked particularly vehement opposition from relatives and family friends. Throughout the 1940s and 1950s, most households regarded schooling as a surefire means of procuring reliable employment, a degree of sophistication, and public repute.[18] Since their friends, families, and neighbors considered leaving school for music to be an act of professional suicide, the few young men who risked this transition attracted significant criticism. Ebo Taylor, one of Ghana's most prominent highlife guitarists of the 1960s, encountered widespread disbelief at his decision to abandon his studies to take up a career in popular music:

> [My choice] to leave school in order to become a musician was serious, especially when I had been getting high grades in school. A musician was nobody in our society in the 1950s. Some people would not even allow musicians in their home! For a musician to gain respect was quite difficult, quite difficult indeed. So my decision was big talk all over the place. Some of my relatives came to me and asked, "Why? You won't go to school anymore?" They were surprised! It was not pleasant. My parents were upset and my mother grieved over it for many years.[19]

FIGURE 5.2. Julie Okine singing vocals for the Tempos, 1950s. Okine was
one of the first female highlife vocalists in the Gold Coast and became
known for the song "Nothing but a Man's Slave." *Photo courtesy of
Isaac Hudson Bruce Vanderpuije, Deo Gratias Studio, Accra.*

Although many young men decided that becoming a bandsman was not
worth their possible expulsion from lineage circles, those who entered the
field often had to do so without the support of their parents, siblings, or
extended family members.[20]

   Negative stereotypes about popular musicians and music-making
also had gendered ramifications. While families, friends, and communities did their best to dissuade young men from pursuing their musical
aspirations, they essentially barred young women from doing the same.
For the most part, such opposition revolved around notions of domesticity, female respectability, and sexual morality. Many families insisted
that a woman who embraced a popular musical lifestyle of travel, nightclubs, and proximity to social vice was not a respectable artist, but a loose
woman or prostitute.[21] To that end, they explicitly prohibited their female

members from learning how to play instruments, participating in school bands, or publicly fraternizing with male musicians. Most nightclub-going men and women insisted that they never witnessed a female artist perform in the 1950s or 1960s, despite the fact that a few women, such as Agnes Ayitey, Julie Okine (each of whom performed with the Tempos), and Charlotte Dada (who joined the Professional Uhuru Dance Band as a vocalist) did take the stage (PURL 5.1). Unsurprisingly, these women experienced considerable scrutiny and disdain. Stan Plange recalled that while Charlotte Dada often wowed audiences with her vocal talent, she had to simultaneously endure public clamor that she was a prostitute and un-Ghanaian woman.[22] Comfort Sarpong, who was a vocalist for the Broadway Band in Takoradi, experienced similar criticism, as did her family members who owned and operated the band: "[Onlookers] would see me going up and down with musicians; [they would] see me at nightclubs all the time. Because of that, they took me as a hopeless person . . . they even thought that my entire family was hopeless."[23]

A paucity of evidence blurs our full understanding of female musicians' lived experiences, but available sources suggest that they were not passive recipients of public scorn.[24] Once onstage, these women directly confronted those who delegitimized their talents or status as respectable figures. Charlotte Dada's prolific stage presence earned her public embrace as "The Girl with the Golden Voice," a title of endearment that deflected and diminished disparagement. Julie Okine, a vocalist with the Tempos Band, was even more direct in her refutation of public accusations and assumptions (see Figure 5.2). In "Nothing but a Man's Slave," a song that she recorded with the Tempos in 1957, Okine remarked that it was young men, not women, who constituted popular music's most problematic personalities:

I went downtown one Saturday night just for a bottle of beer
I met a lovely Cape Coast boy looking so nice and sweet
He stepped into a taxi-cab heading straight for me
We went to a busy nightclub and he asked for a table for two
We went into a private saloon and he asked for gin-and-lime
I searched into my breast pocket nothing was left for me
He wants to know my name, he wishes to know my game
If I died of a man's love, I'm nothing but a man's slave[25]

By portraying her female subject as a victim of an unscrupulous act, Okine rebuked gendered stereotypes about Saturday Nights and demanded that audiences recognize how women could engage popular music as respectable, rather than illicit or wicked, persons.

Unfortunately, Okine and Dada's efforts found little support from their male counterparts. Throughout the 1950s and 1960s, most highlife bands refused to accept women into their ranks. Many claimed that they did so in order to uphold long-standing gendered taboos that governed local musical performance. In the late nineteenth and early twentieth centuries, most Ghanaian communities prohibited women from learning, playing, or even handling prominent musical instruments, including horns and most types of drums.[26] Some highlife bands preserved such standards by allowing women to take up only minor roles as dancers, backup singers, or side percussionists who played simple rhythms on gourds, rattles, or bamboo tubes.[27] Many more refused to admit women at all. A few did so for fear, based on traditional beliefs, that a menstruating woman would, intentionally or not, come into contact with band instruments and render them unplayable.[28] Others refused to incorporate female members because they thought that they would distract male bandsmen, cause trouble, and threaten the group's camaraderie and work ethic. Kofi Lindsay, the manager of Cape Coast's Pelikans Dance Band, refused to admit female musicians because he feared that they would bring "loose" behaviors into the group:

> NP: And [the band members] were all men?
> KL: They were all men. We had some women but they didn't last. . . . You know women. They were not stationary, so we didn't like to take them. Sometimes it would bring troubles within the band, you see? The bandsmen too, everybody would like to monopolize her and bring trouble. So if we were men we were men. That's all.[29]

In the end, the overall social, generational, and gendered climate of postwar urban Ghana rendered popular music a field that was open only to a small number of young urban men who were willing to confront an initial period of hardship and peril. In their first few years of being bandsmen, these young men faced isolation, insult, and inevitable strife. They did so, however, with the hope that they would acquire autonomy, financial success, and eventual renown. As they endured considerable troubles in pursuit of these long-term aims, many young artists found that popular music could offer opportunities for extraordinary social advancement and personal acclaim.

BECOMING MUSICIANS AND MEN, 1950–1965

Many of the young men who elected to pursue a musical path in the decades surrounding independence remembered their early careers as moments of professional promise, conquered obstacles, and personal change. Compared to their nonmusical peers, these young men often enjoyed expanded liberties and other personal benefits. One of the most important was their heightened levels of physical mobility. While parents, elders, and employers continued to confine other junior men to the supervised realms of home, school, and work, young musicians recalled that they had unfettered access to wider realms of urban life.[30] This freedom of movement stemmed largely from their newfound access to cash. While their siblings, friends, and schoolmates rarely had money, young musicians accrued sizable disposable incomes that they could use at their discretion. Most marked their emergence as a bandsman by spending exorbitant amounts of money on material items, including clothing, instruments, and other accessories. By dressing very well, many musicians hoped to be favorably noticed by the public and to demonstrate the financial merits of their budding careers. Stan Plange recalled that such lavish materialism brought a mixture of curiosity and criticism, but insisted that he, and many other young musicians, considered it to be a central marker of their early success:

> When I first started as a musician, I was young and I didn't have much responsibility. [As a result], I wanted to wear the best clothes that came out those days. Any time I got money there was a shop, Bob Joy's shop, where I would buy the latest socks, the latest shirts, leather shoes. I wanted to get all of them. I remember I bought some ballet shoes for seven pounds. I wasn't worried, but I told my friend and he said "Are you crazy? How can you go and buy shoes for seven pounds?" It was a lot of money. Nobody bought shoes for seven pounds and ballet shoes were very expensive, Italian, handwoven shoes. These are the things I then liked to do—I didn't think about savings![31]

In addition to their becoming known as public figures with a propensity for fine clothes, dressing up helped novice artists gain the attention of young women. Female adulation was a central aim of most up-and-coming musicians, who wanted to initiate romantic relationships as a way to announce their unconventional coming-of-age. Unlike the bulk of their peers, young musicians claimed to enjoy considerable romantic autonomy and female interest. Daniel Kinful Sam insisted that he and many of his peers were targets of unrelenting admiration from women: "If you were a bandsman, you were being courted! We didn't have space at all; women were always at our feet. In Ghana here, if you were a musician, you had women!"[32] While they were not the only urban men to make such claims, their musical performances certainly gave them opportunities

to meet and freely interact with potential partners.[33] Elders condemned
such behaviors as proof that musicians were immoral and devious, but
urban youth, male and female, celebrated such acts as proof that they
had managed to transgress the boundaries that blocked their entrance
into adulthood.[34]

Despite the fact that nearly all young musicians experienced this
shared set of advantages and obstacles, individual artists used a variety
of strategies to launch their career, eclipse their junior status, and gain
some measure of personal success. Some, such as George Nanabanyin
Johnson, employed their popular musical talents to develop a flashy persona and claim status as exceptional men. Johnson, who was born into a
relatively prosperous family in Cape Coast, had a rather typical upbring-
ing and early life. Like most of his peers, he spent his late teenage years
living at home and attending a local secondary school. He had no job and
no money, and spent the majority of his time under the watchful eyes of
his mother, teachers, and family elders. While his superiors did much to
restrict Johnson's engagement with wider urban life, they allowed him
to study music. Armed with the encouragement of both his grandfather
and uncle, Johnson joined his school choir, learned how to read music,
and studied the guitar under the tutelage of his school music master. He
proved to be a quick learner, and by the time he was eighteen years old he
could play highlife and a number of related popular musical styles. While
Johnson initially approached music as a form of private recreation, he recalled that it became his ticket to acquire public acclaim, secure financial
resources, and live an otherwise impossible life:

> To make a long story short, things began one evening when I went to a dance
> with a few of my friends. When we got there I saw the band's guitar lying
> fallow. This was in 1959 and I was in Form 4.[35] After I saw the guitar lying
> fallow, I went to the bandstand and asked, "Is there nobody playing?" and
> they said "No, the guitarist is not coming. Can you play?" But they looked
> at me like a small boy,[36] I was very short! I told them I could play and they
> said, "What the hell are you talking about, do you think you can play?" They
> thought I was a child! I told them I could play. So they gave the guitar to me
> to play. They mentioned one song, "Can you play it?" I said I could play it.
> Another, "Can you play?" I told them I could.
>
> The guy who usually played the guitar was a big man in music, but no one
> had heard of me. I lived on the outskirts of Cape Coast and the main dance
> hall was on the opposite side of the town. So I was little known, only my
> classmates knew me. Few people in town knew me at all.
>
> So they said "Can you play?" I said, "I can play." They said, "No, we are
> seeing something else altogether." Most of the songs that they played were

things that I had practiced in the house, things like "Blue Moon."[37] So I showed them that I could play them. Then the band started to wonder where I learned to play the guitar this way. They asked my name and invited me to play with them.

When we finished, the man gave me fifteen shillings. I said "What? Fifteen shillings?" I had never seen this much money in my pocket before! It wasn't small for me! I used the money to buy cigarettes—it was fine! When I went back to school, people gathered around and I told them about the playing and the money. That very term, I used the money to buy a guitar. It was the only time in my life I had ever seen big money before. And I kept playing with that band. After a few more dances, they gave me £1 10s. I used that money to buy some clothes, student carpet, so many things . . . Life became spoiled!

Shortly after, to tell you the truth, the school dropped me because of my playing guitar. I protested and my mother was very upset. But what could I do? I couldn't return to school. Fortunately, the then Commissioner of Police in Cape Coast wanted to form a band for Kwame Nkrumah. I joined the band, the Jazzmen Sunset Band, and we began to rehearse. One day Nkrumah came to Cape Coast to see the band. He liked it, so he told the commissioner to take some of the band members to Accra so that they could join the Ghana Police Dance Band.

When I got to Accra, I got stuck up. There were no rehearsals and I was not a policeman, so there was no work for me to do. But I was staying at the Police Depot, so I had to wait. I waited and waited and waited. One day we heard that the commissioner was coming to the depot and that everyone should be ready to rehearse. The next day I went to the band section and I sat with the bandsmen. They set up their instruments under the supervision of the Inspector. When the commissioner came, he came straight to the band section. He looked at them and asked a few questions. Then he asked who I was. No one thought I was a policeman because of my size and my stature. My friend from Cape Coast told him that I knew how to play music, that I was a guitarist. And he told them that I was not a policeman, I was a school boy!

I had been brought from Cape Coast because the band needed a guitarist, so the commissioner asked if I could play guitar. So I went to play the guitar with the band. The sounds coming out were great. The man was standing there saying "I can't believe it! I can't believe it! You are not going back. If you are a school boy, I will take care of your schooling here!" I was given lodging in the Police Depot and was enrolled in the Accra Academy. From then on, I became known as a guitarist and as the school-boy policeman (*laughing*)![38]

Johnson's testimony offers striking details into how a mixture of hard work, musical talent, and good fortune enabled him to gain favor, enhance his status, and eclipse the limitations of age and inexperience. His opening recollection of his brazen inquiry about the band's missing guitarist demonstrates the widely shared conviction that he was a junior person. In fact, the band's collective dismissal of Johnson as a small boy captures the notion that he was, like the majority of his peers, a disempowered subordinate incapable of occupying a more visible or important position. Once he picked up the guitar, however, things irreversibly changed. The demonstration of his musical ability immediately repudiated the band's assumptions and earned him an invitation to perform with them onstage. In the weeks that followed, music provided Johnson with additional dividends. His talented displays earned him admiration from urban audiences and allowed him to become known within the city at large. Such performances also bolstered Johnson's status at school, where he attracted growing attention from classmates who were smitten with his image as a guitarist. His association with musical recreation led to his dismissal by school officials, but it connected him to other powerful figures who invited him to Accra and secured him lodging, a position in an elite academy, and a regular salary.

In the midst of these important developments, Johnson implemented his own strategy for claiming social and generational mobility. Instead of saving his earnings so that he could fulfill the conventional markers of maturity, he elected to purchase items that could reflect his exceptional status. One of his first purchases was a new guitar, a strategic investment that reflected his conviction that popular music could provide him with a successful life. Next, he invested in items of flashy personal display. He procured cigarettes, an item associated with the urban "guys" who used Saturday Nights to promote personal liberation and cosmopolitan modernity. His other early purchases, including clothing and a carpet for his living quarters, constituted additional investments in style and material extravagance: qualities that many young people, in Ghana and elsewhere, valued as symbols of their maturation and ability to navigate the demands of urban life.[39]

At the same time, Johnson's recollections demonstrate that his ability to capitalize on popular musical performance was possible only because of his standing as a junior person. Unconstrained by the expectations and responsibilities that burdened older adult men, he could afford to take risks, challenge existing hierarchies, and channel his resources in a self-serving manner. Few adult men could have replicated Johnson's actions, especially his impromptu decision to pursue an uncertain opportunity in another city—where he waited for it to come to fruition—because it would have made them objects of ridicule and disbelief.[40] Johnson, meanwhile, faced few familial or relational restraints. His parents chastised him for his removal from school, but they were elated about his subsequent enrollment in the Accra Academy, which was widely regarded as one of the nation's top secondary schools. In Accra, he was also able to enjoy uncommon levels of autonomy while simultaneously enjoying the assistance of prominent patrons who supplied him with accommodation, food, and money. His growing reputation, as both a musician and the "school boy policeman," exemplifies his ability to escape some of the trappings of youth while continuing to enjoy some of its benefits. In the end, Johnson used music to claim status as an exceptional social figure, enjoy renown, and, in his words, go "places that I could have never otherwise gone."[41]

While many young musicians sought to replicate Johnson's carefree endeavors and obtain similar recognition as members of an unprecedented cohort of young men, others directed their talents to meet, rather than stretch, the established conventions of maturity and adulthood. One such artist was Nana Kwame Ampadu, who was born in Obo Kwahu in Ghana's Eastern Region (see Figure 5.3). Like Johnson, Ampadu first learned music at school, where he took part in choir and gained notoriety for his singing ability. Although he went on to become one of Ghana's most renowned highlife guitarists of the 1960s and 1970s, his entrance into the popular musical field was marked by a number of challenges. After moving to Accra to escape an outraged father, Ampadu attempted to shed his status as a young unknown artist and exploit his talents for personal gain. As his recollection suggests, however, Ampadu employed music to concoct a rather unique strategy of success:

> When I was in school, I took delight in music. And I was told that my voice was good. So I was enrolled in the school choir in my hometown. When I came out of school, I wanted to be a musician. But those days, music was not a career that good parents would allow their children to enter. This is because our predecessors, I was told, were trying to create nuisance and introducing vice into the profession; taking alcohol, chasing after women and the like. So when I came out of school and said I wanted to be a musician, it became a brawl between me and my father. He didn't want me to be a musician. But I had a chance to come to Accra and join my relatives and find some job to do. It was at this time that I bought a guitar and I learned how to play. I used a manual book on Spanish guitar. That was the book I used. But before that I had been introduced to one of the old bands, Yamoah's Band.[42] They had enrolled me as a treble singer. My stint with the band didn't last long, because it was an amateur band. The leader had other work and he was transferred to Kumasi. He wanted me to go with him, but I said no, because my relatives would not allow me. I was a kid and I didn't have any relatives there.

After he left, I secured a job with a brother-in-law at a drugstore. And having learned how to play the guitar, I was seeking for a band to join. But I was so smallish, tiny in figure. At that time, young men were not playing music. It was all adults, from twenty-five years and upwards. At this time I was eighteen looking for a band to join. And I had little luck until I met a guy who later became my assistant band manager. One day he called me and said "Small, I have seen you going around with your guitar and I came to watch you play it for some people. Can we form a band? My brother-in-law has got some instruments." He had all the electronics, but he was lacking drums. I had a conga but it was a Ghana-made.[43] So we went to inspect the instruments. Those days, instruments were not many [hard to obtain]. Maybe you got one speaker, one microphone, and you were off.

So we formed a band. We were all young kids at the time. The oldest member, who was incidentally my older brother, was only twenty-two. We started a band and we decided that we needed a name. We charged each member with devising a name, everyone had to think of a name and be ready to defend it. One guy came back and said that he had written "African Brothers Band." So we asked him why. He said, "Because Dr. Kwame Nkrumah is fighting for African unity. I think if we use the title, he might want to use us for African unity." So that was it. It was in 1963.[44]

We started on an amateur basis; all of us bandsmen were working [other jobs]. We met in the evenings to rehearse. At first, we mostly played for Muslim weddings, we call them *sunna*. We played for these weddings because the hotels and nightclubs would see our figure [young age] and we would not be accepted. They would think that we could not do anything. So we relied on those small small[45] parties and weddings.

Before we formed I had written a lot of songs. You see, we didn't have too many recording studios at the time. Rather the white people would come with their machine, record, and leave. Every year they came two or maybe three times.[46] We tried to look for producers to entice them, but they didn't listen to us because they said we were small boys and we didn't have anything to offer. They were concentrating on big groups, those I listened to when I was growing up. I would listen to them on gramophone and I thought they were coming from the machine! You get me? I would examine the machine, thinking they were hiding inside (*laughing*)! So that was the situation. And why would anyone waste time on a small boy? So I had to struggle a lot.

In those days I was working with the United Ghana Farmers Council Corporation. One day when I closed from work I heard some musicians rehearsing with some horns and guitars. I found out it was the Marquee Players Dance Band.[47] I hid somewhere and listened to them. I loved the way they played. It was then that I decided to approach the leader. So the next day, during our break from work, I went to that house. And I found a man there repairing cameras. I introduced myself and told him that I had heard a band playing there yesterday and that I would like to meet the leader. He said, "Small, what is it?" I said that I had some songs and I wanted to give them to the band. They looked at me—they were two—and they started to speak in Ga, which I didn't understand. Later I got to know that they said, "What can this small boy offer?" So the man asked me, "Small, do you have some songs?" And I said, "Yes sir." "Your own songs, you composed them?" he asked. "Yes." "You didn't steal them?" "No sir." "How many?" I said, "Plenty!" "Hmmm, ok, can we hear one?"

So I started singing and he started nodding. He was nodding, enjoying it. When I finished he smiled and said in Ga, "The boy is perfect." So he asked me if I could come in tomorrow to sing for his people.

When I went I sang two songs. Straightaway the band accepted them. And I was asked to teach the musicians how to sing them because the chorus was complicated. They recorded the songs; I gave them to them for free. For free! And I was happy that they did! I was happy that a big band had accepted my work. I felt proud. So I gave them another three numbers.

It was then that I approached this bandleader and I said, "I've got a band. Can you help me to record? Because whenever these people see me they tell me to go because I am a small boy." He said, "You are no longer a small boy. I will tell them that you gave me these beautiful songs." You see all of the songs that I gave him became hits, none of them flopped. So he said he would introduce me to Phillips, a West African recording company. And he kept his word. One day, a man came to see me. He said, "Small, we have to audition you and your band. The Marquee Players said you are good." So we picked a date and the place. I sang fourteen good songs, but the man said he would pick only two. I said, "Oh, Master! Ok, you record a few more and you don't pay me for them, just record them." But he said no. We recorded them at Ghana Films Corporation, 1966, the 14th of November. The first was released six weeks later, 25th December and it became an instant hit. If I was in America, I would say it topped the charts. And because of this, the next time they came, I was the first artist that they looked for.

At that time, the people who didn't know me thought that I was an elder person, like E. K. Nyame, Kakaiku, King Onyina, or K. Gyasi, because my lyrics contained thought provoking philosophical messages, stories, and the like. When people heard them, they got that impression. But when they saw me, they said "Ah, are you the one who composed that song?" [People didn't believe me] so it became a superstition, a rumor, that I had some old people in the house who supplied me with those lyrics. But I wrote them myself!

[Because my songs were popular] the producers started chasing me here and there. Ambassador Records in Kumasi first got a hold of me and recorded my songs. When we were in Kumasi, the producer wanted to sign a contract with me, but I said "No, I want to wait." It was then that an individual producer came down from Accra to Kumasi. He said that he wanted to buy me a set of instruments and that he wanted to give me and the boys a house to live in. This would be in Accra, where we would go and join him. I

said, "Oh, this is a very good offer." So we went to Accra and recorded with
him for ten good years, from 1968–78. After that I left him because I bought
a house and started on my own. But during that time I recorded more than
300 individual songs.

    That is how I got started.[48]

Ampadu's recollections embody many of the challenges young musicians faced as they embarked on their careers. He first learned music in
school, met significant resistance from his father for his decision to enter
the musical profession, and had relatively meager resources at his disposal. His efforts to save money and purchase a guitar, rely on his education to learn the instrument, and garner experience as part of an amateur
band show his resourcefulness, but they also speak to the limitations of
his social position. Since he remained dependent on extended family for
a place to live, he could not follow the Yamoah's Band to Kumasi. Once
he and his peers had formed their own band in Accra, they continued
to suffer on account of their subordinate status as disempowered youth
and unknown musicians. Cut off from two of highlife's most important
realms, the nightclub and the recording studio, and relegated to marginal
opportunities, Ampadu struggled to showcase or capitalize on his musical talent.[49]

    He did not, however, attempt to overcome these obstacles by adopt-
ing the flamboyant dress, material style, or brazen behaviors characteristic of many young artists. He instead alleviated his situation by operating
within the generational, social, and professional hierarchies that marked
him as a junior person. In many instances, Ampadu and his peers willingly catered to the interests and demands of established persons of influence. The group's choice of a name, the African Brothers Band, was a
strategic effort to align the young bandsmen with Kwame Nkrumah and
the CPP, invoke the nation's active political environment, and attract government support. Similar motivations prompted Ampadu's interactions
with the Marquee Players Dance Band. After approaching the group's
leader and surprising him with his lyrical compositions and musical abilities, Ampadu gave several of his compositions to the band for free, an act
that signified his position of dependence, placed him in the leader's good
favor and initiated a patron-client relationship of mutual benefit. Once
the songs proved successful, Ampadu was well positioned to request and
receive the bandleader's assistance in a way that upheld, rather than challenged, his junior status. When the leader agreed to connect Ampadu to
a producer—an act that stemmed from his conviction that the young
artist had readily proved that he was no longer a small boy—the African

FIGURE 5.3. Nana Ampadu
performing at Accra's
Roxy Cinema, 1971. *Photo
courtesy of Ghana Information Services Department
Photograph Library.*

Brothers finally gained access to vital, and previously unavailable, spheres of professional mobility.[50]

After navigating the confines of the recording studio, Ampadu was finally able to claim stature as a widely regarded adult man. His use of thought-provoking messages and lyrical themes appealed to audiences and convinced them that he was not a young novice but a fully fledged musician of similar caliber as some of the nation's most recognized artists. Record sales gave the thirty-three-year-old financial security, a new set of band instruments, accommodations, and the money needed to purchase a home. As rumors abounded about these extraordinary feats, Ampadu renegotiated his professional relationships with record producers—powerful people who now "chased" him—and the other members of his band—who he referred to as "boys." In relatively rapid fashion, he used his musical talent to sidestep the barriers of age and inexperience and claim stature as a respected man and musician.

Together, Johnson's and Ampadu's recollections explain how and why young men endeavored to overcome the challenges that defined becoming a popular musician in the years surrounding Ghana's independence. Despite its formidable risks, starting life as a bandsman could offer young men remarkable opportunities and highly desirable rewards. It was a way for them to trade positions of dependence for ones of self-reliance, abandon invisible realms for those that caught the public eye, and overcome financial limitations by acquiring property and monetary wealth. It also enabled young men to make active inroads toward their own maturation. Some used music to play with the boundaries that blocked their entrance into adulthood, defy convention, and celebrate their rare ability to both claim personal benefits and eschew responsibility. For others, it was a way to permanently eclipse their status as youth and gain recognition as legitimate adult men. As they moved beyond their early careers and settled into more permanent positions on Saturday Nights' stage, highlife artists had to negotiate a more complex web of possibilities and limitations. Their progress through the life course added to these burdens and forced many to make difficult decisions about their status as musicians and men.

ESTABLISHED MUSICIANS' STRUGGLES AND STRATEGIES, 1960–1970

In the years following Ghana's 1957 independence, the general plight of its popular musicians improved markedly. With highlife entrenched as urban Ghana's most prominent form of dance music, artists found that government officials as well as the population at large were much more ready to accept their talents and budding stature. The proliferation of nightclubs gave capable ensembles profits and visibility, and the expansion of the Ghana Broadcasting System's radio and television service (the latter of which was launched in 1965) provided musicians with new ways to reach and impress audiences. Several musicians also found prominence outside of musical realms. During the 1960s, highlife artists frequently graced the pages of Ghanaian newspapers and magazines, a phenomenon that affirmed their growing status as popular cultural icons and national stars. In many ways, highlife musicians were some of the young nation's first celebrities, meaning that they enjoyed levels of exposure and fanfare that earlier generations of artists could have never imagined.[51]

The stardom that came with these developments had many benefits. It gave heightened importance and meaning to musicians' work, eased family tensions and social scrutiny, and provided additional opportunities and engagements. Prominent bands, such as E. T. Mensah's Tempos and Jerry Hansen's Ramblers Dance Band, experienced remarkable suc-

FIGURE 5.4. The Ramblers Dance Band outside the Accra Airport prior to their departure for England, August 1967. *Photo courtesy of Ghana Information Services Department Photograph Library.*

cess. As they gained phenomenal acclaim within Ghana, they received invitations to travel to Europe and North America: opportunities that provided excitement and adventure, lucrative pay, and prestige as "been-tos," individuals who had seen the world, dabbled in cosmopolitanism, and made Ghana proud.[52] Positive publicity could also snowball in less obvious ways. Well-known musicians received gifts and entitlements, an expanding circle of friends and acquaintances, and extensive social capital. A select few even gained entry into elite circles, where they could interact with government officials, international diplomats, and Ghanaian heads-of-state.[53]

At the same time, most musicians insisted that their expanding stardom was a mixed bag. Today, it is far too easy to peruse newspapers or magazines from the early 1960s and come to the conclusion that highlife musicians had secured a prosperous position in Ghanaian society. Photographs of the era corroborate this impression, conveying musicians as a confident and contented bunch. In a 1967 picture taken before their departure for a tour of Great Britain, the members of the Ramblers Dance

Band appear well-dressed, successful, and important (see Figure 5.4). Such photographs highlight the possibilities that came with being a bandsman during the 1960s, but most musicians insisted that they fail to capture the full breadth of their experiences. While some artists, including a few of the Ramblers, became modern big men and national stars, most experienced success in smaller and far less satisfying bites.

As they grew in age and stature, many bandsmen found that "being a musician was hard," a maxim that echoed another common axiom of the period: "to be a man is hard."[54] The similarities between these two statements are not the result of coincidence or chance. In fact, most insisted that being a musician was hard because it required them to do things that countered, rather than facilitated, their efforts to uphold their positions as responsible adult men. While young musicians proved able to readily exploit their profession for personal mobility and individual gain, their older counterparts were saddled with ambitions and concerns that were not easily addressed onstage. Many declared that their professional activities and aims often stood at odds with their personal and family lives. As much as musicians wanted to achieve fame, travel abroad, and exploit the many benefits that came with being a well-known artist, they also wanted to marry, have children, accrue property, build a home, and eventually secure a senior position as *mmpanyinfoɔ*. Over time, many artists found that it was exceedingly difficult to meet all of these divergent goals. Even prominent musicians who enjoyed the fruits of stardom described their line of work as one where successes were relative and failures far more easily found.

One thing that made it hard to be both a successful musician and a respectable man was the overwhelming lack of privacy that most artists experienced on a day-to-day basis. While bands eagerly competed for the spotlight on Saturday Nights, their members came to resent feeling that people were always watching them long after they set down their instruments. Since they could never effectively escape the public gaze, musicians recalled having to "tread carefully" in their everyday affairs. They had to watch what they said, how they behaved, what they wore, and their manner of social interaction so that they did not attract negative attention or errantly damage their personal reputation. In effect, most insisted that they had little room for error on- or offstage, a condition that was stressful and at times quite taxing on their ability to relax, socialize with friends, or carry out such mundane tasks as making routine purchases or moving about the city.[55]

Being a musician was also difficult became it was often an unreliable means of meeting the financial responsibilities most men assumed
as fathers, uncles, and household heads. While young musicians openly
flaunted their earnings in well-publicized acts of self-indulgence, their
older counterparts came to find that they accumulated irregular and all
too often scant amounts of pay. Only a small number of musicians owned
their own instruments; even fewer had formal contracts that outlined
their rights or remuneration schedules as members of a band. Many proficient musicians had trouble procuring a stable twelve-month income.[56]
During the rainy summer months, inclement weather and impassible
roads prevented bands from traveling, performing far outside their hometown, or holding scheduled engagements. Even seemingly lucrative opportunities, such as recording deals and international tours, brought musicians limited financial gain. Band patrons—the financial sponsors who
owned the band equipment, including the instruments, transportation,
and sheet music—often took 40–60 percent of the group's total earnings.
Once the band had used its share to cover necessary expenses, including
promoter's fees, travel costs, and equipment repairs, it had a relatively limited pool of funds to dole out to each individual member. For large dance
bands, some of which had fifteen to eighteen members, these amounts
were minuscule. Since groups received a one-time payment for recording
sessions instead of consistent royalties from the records that came out of
them, releasing a record also did very little to pad musicians' pockets or
provide relief from money difficulties.[57]

What made this financial plight particularly unbearable was the common assumption that highlife musicians earned a lot of money in the
years following independence. Young musicians certainly perpetuated
this idea by spending large sums on otherwise lavish possessions, and
press coverage about highlife bands and their onstage appearance did
much to wrap musicians in a presumed veil of wealth. As a result, very few
Ghanaians, including family members and friends, could comprehend
how a highlife musician could ever fall into economic hardship. As Ebo
Taylor recalled, the predominant assumption that musicians were well-
to-do burdened many with "an empty name":

> [At times] my family expectations were not being met because the sal-
> ary I was taking was too small. Things became very difficult. Sometimes
> your nephew would come to you and say that he had this problem. And he
> thought that because you were his uncle and you were a famous musician
> that you had the money to help him. But I had an empty name! Even my

children, it was hard to let them know that I was famous but did not have money. We [highlife musicians] were pioneers and we became well known, but we were not rich people.[58]

Taylor's experiences encapsulate a common conundrum that underlined popular musicians' personal lives: that while they came to enjoy enviable reputations as national icons or stars, they often struggled to meet the basic expectations incumbent on all adult men. Many readily admitted that it was a difficult, even impossible, situation for others to comprehend. For how could a famous popular musical idol not have the money needed to assist his nephew? How could an artist who had traveled to Europe and performed in front of international dignitaries have problems meeting the everyday needs of his household? Many musicians confessed that the perplexing nature of such questions made them determined to find a way to rectify such shortcomings and improve their professional prosperity. To do so, however, they had to navigate a number of occupational challenges.

In the years following independence, Ghana's popular music scene was tremendously vibrant, but it was also highly competitive and rather cutthroat. Many large towns boasted several nightclubs and performance venues, but they often had an even larger number of dance bands eager to earn concerts, air time, and recording sessions. Collectively, band members emphasized that the best way to get a leg up on their competition was to establish a positive reputation and acquire a strong base of fan support. Most groups used daily rehearsals and regular meetings to not only improve their sound, but to craft a distinct identity. Some artists, such as K. Gyasi and C. K. Mann, emphasized creativity and became known for their efforts to incorporate local musical elements into highlife's flexible rhythmic structure. Others, such as the Ramblers Dance Band, continued to emphasize foreign styles that remained popular among devoted clienteles. A few bands tried to do a bit of everything. Kofi Lindsay forced his Pelikans Dance Band to master sixteen distinct styles of local and international music so that it could satisfy any audience in need of musical entertainment.[59]

Bands also sought to enhance their reputation by offering regular live performances. While moving from venue to venue allowed groups to reach wide and diverse audiences, most hoped to secure a fixed contract and regular set of engagements with a particular nightclub or hotel. These residencies at a single venue decreased travel expenses, ensured regular work, and facilitated the emergence of a "pet crowd": a loyal following who consistently paid to attend their shows. Securing such arrangements, however, was not easy. Most nightclub and hotel owners employed only one resident band; others elected to sponsor and manage their own in-house ensemble as a way to cut operating costs. As a result, most dance bands had to make a living by piecing together individual performances within a particular town or region. Prominent owners could also be shrewd businessmen. Many musicians recalled making sacrifices, such as foregoing a portion of their earnings or giving free performances, in order to win owners' favor and obtain lucrative engagements or contracts. Few bands could afford to do these things on a regular basis, but most maintained that the prospects of landing a long-term agreement were worth the risk. The Ramblers Dance Band's contract at the government-run Star Hotel, for example, brought the band great publicity, official esteem, and a handsome payout of £600–800 per engagement.[60]

While bands employed a number of strategies to bolster their reputation, including taking requests, repeating well-received numbers, and socializing with audiences during intermission or after their show, many agreed that they most effective way to foster success was to take part in and win a dance band competition. Like their dancing counterparts, such competitions pitted multiple bands against one another, required each to perform in front of a large audience and set of judges, and ended with the clear declaration of a winning ensemble. In the 1960s, these competitions were immensely popular in Accra, Kumasi, and other large towns. Sponsors, whether nightclubs, hotels, or the Ghanaian government, went to great lengths to advertise such events and encourage urban audiences to purchase tickets, take to the dance floor, and watch their favorite bands compete. Over the course of the evening, participating bands took turns performing a single musical set that was usually thirty to forty-five minutes in length. Once each band had finished, the judges convened and the M.C. dramatically invited the winning band to accept a trophy or prize, obtain recognition and applause, and give an encore performance that would last into the wee hours of the morning (PURL 5.2).

For dance bands, these competitions were invaluable forums to introduce new songs, showcase their talent, and outshine rival groups. Musicians often recalled such events with great intensity, insisting that they were moments that literally created or destroyed their future prospects.[61] Kofi Lindsay described "jumps," informal contests in which two bands exchanged alternating sets in a battle for audience acclaim, as crucial displays of a group's skill:

I had an uncle who was working in Accra, so I knew that the Accra bands were very pompous. One day my uncle told a band proprietor that his nephew had a band in Cape Coast, and he would like them to come and jump them. And he said, "Ok, come." So we arranged to meet them at a certain place. In a short time, we went. His band played first, they started around 9:00 PM. We came next and it was so nice. The way we were playing, eh! Their band couldn't play again! When we finished, the crowd demanded that we play on. It was time for the other band to play, but the crowd wanted us to continue. The other bandleader, come and see! "Mr. Lindsay, you collapsed my band, you disgraced my band. Mr. Lindsay, stop, stop." So we stopped and left. When we left, the place became empty! The entire crowd followed us outside. . . .

Later we went to another town, Bolga[62] in the Northern Region. I've forgotten the place, but there we met this stubborn band. The minute we set up our instruments the bandleader came and he brought a whole set of people with him. "Hey! The Pelikans, we've heard of you. We'd like to come and jump you." I said "Ok, it's a pleasure, come, come, come." The band was good, so we invited them to come. So by 7:30 PM, they were all around. I asked them if they would like to start, but they said that we should start. My brother, we started (*laughs*). First song, second song, third song, fourth song, fifth—ahhh! Then the place was boiling. The place was boiling, the place was REALLY boiling—BOILING (*shouting*)! Ehhh . . . Then, huh, we had to brief and tell everyone, "It's ok, it's ok. We have our brothers here and we'd like them to come and touch their hands on our instruments. Opus! Opus! Opus!"—they were called Opus, Opus was the name of the group. "Opus? Opus?" They were nowhere to be found. They vanished like thin air. Not a single bandsman was there.

They were scared! They never thought we could play like that. They thought they were coming to walk over us. But they ran away! They ran away! So instead of closing, we played until 4:30, almost getting to 5:00 in the morning! The second day we played there, I think the whole town came. The place was full—shaaa! That day, oh! Opus couldn't show their face. They couldn't show their face at all.[63]

As Lindsay's recollection poignantly demonstrates, competitions were moments in which bands could either win considerable crowd favor or become completely forgotten. The prospects of victory were most acute in large contests such as the government-sponsored National Highlife Competition. The competition, held sporadically from the late 1950s into the 1970s, proceeded in a series of stages. It began in the country's various regions, where local bands contended for notoriety, a monetary prize, and the title of "Regional Champion." From there, winning bands faced off in front of a large audience in Accra for further prizes, extensive press coverage, and the titles of "National Champion" and "Band of the Year."[64]

Since the stakes of these competitions were so high, they occasionally became sites of ill will and even sabotage. Many musicians insisted that certain bands, particularly those with inferior musical abilities, entered competitions not to win, but to carry out devious acts and bring public ruin on rival groups. Calculating bandleaders, for example, sent members to spy on another group's practice sessions so that they could memorize and duplicate their repertoire. On the day of the competition, the mischievous band would take the stage and perform its adversary's songs, effectively forcing the victimized group to abandon their well-rehearsed playlist and perform a set of less-polished tunes. Malicious bandleaders also bribed nightclub owners so that they would fix a competition's outcome or suddenly remove a particular band from the lineup hours before the start. Allegations of witchcraft were fairly rare among highlife dance bands, but guitar band musicians insisted that opposing groups invoked the supernatural to bring bad weather, cut off electricity, spoil instruments and equipment, damage transportation, or cause illness to group members immediately prior to their ascension onstage.[65]

Legitimate or not, these claims of sabotage illustrate bands' conviction that they had to navigate a professional environment that was inherently unpredictable and dangerous. In fact, musicians recalled that their dependence on public engagements, competitions, and limited opportunities exposed them to a number of risks that they could not afford to avoid. Fearful bands, for example, still had to mount the stage if they were going to receive future engagements or win audience favor. Since they were essentially obligated to take part in events that carried the potential for both opportunity and ruin, bands made concerted efforts to mitigate and eliminate potential pitfalls. The most common means of self-preservation concerned their internal structure, rules, and operating procedures. Many dance bands upheld a strict hierarchy that allocated rights, responsibility, and status to each individual member. The principal authority was the bandleader, usually the person who founded the group and recruited others into its fold. Leaders oversaw nearly all of the band's activities. They directed rehearsals, booked engagements, and organized travels and tours. They also exercised substantial authority over other bandsmen and took responsibility for the group's collective reputation. To facilitate their management of internal and external affairs, many leaders created a set of rules that all bandsmen were expected to follow. These rules varied from group to group, but most required members to attend daily rehearsals, display punctuality, maintain their instruments and equipment, and perfect their individual parts. Others mandated that members don particular clothing or uniforms, refrain from smoking or consuming alcohol, and attend to strict curfews while traveling out of town. Band members who broke these rules suffered a range of penalties, including fines, pay cuts, or even suspension from the group.[66]

After the leader, remaining bandsmen enjoyed various positions and benefits. High-ranking members, such as assistant bandleaders and section heads, could allocate tasks, contribute ideas, and earn competitive pay. Lower-status members, including novice musicians and those who had recently joined, often had to complete laborious jobs such as packing equipment or running errands, follow directives, and make do with smaller earnings and remunerations. Band hierarchies did not, however, simply replicate the generational or social conventions observed in urban areas. Instead of positioning members according to their age, background, educational level, or economic status, dance bands employed a meritocratic system that awarded individuals for their musical talent, hard work, and composition skills.[67] When such qualifications corresponded to age and experience, older bandsmen exercised authority over their younger counterparts, much as they might have in the other spheres of daily life. When they did not, the dynamics changed. Because leaders greatly valued bandsmen who could read music, arrange songs, or perform impressive instrumental solos, many groups had structures that placed young men in positions of authority over adults, even those who had several years of musical experience. In such cases, conventional power dynamics held little sway and junior men reaped greater benefits and pay than their senior counterparts.[68] While leaders unapologetically promoted talented youth in order to foster the band's success and enduring appeal, this practice often became a source of tension offstage. Bandleaders and members alike recalled instances when discrepancies—real or perceived—in pay, privilege, or punishment caused jealousy, disdain, and open argument within their group. At such moments, leaders had to do their best to resolve disputes and ensure that offended members did not compromise rehearsals, smear the band's reputation, or leave the group short-staffed for an upcoming engagement.[69]

Individual musicians dealt with this structure and set of rules in complex, and often inconsistent, ways. Ultimately, most agreed that a clear hierarchy and set of behavioral guidelines were necessary components of a successful dance band. After all, these regulations allowed a group to hold efficient rehearsals, divide responsibilities, and cooperate to avoid mishaps and garner a positive reputation. At the same time, most admitted that they occasionally attempted to undermine such policies in order to meet individual aspirations or fulfill personal needs. Younger musicians eager to capitalize on their burgeoning notoriety, newfound independence, and pseudo-adult status often viewed band dictates with indifference or disdain. As a result, most bandleaders made it a point to supervise young musicians and keep them out of situations that could harm the group.[70] Older musicians, particularly those who had responsibilities as husbands, fathers, and family figures, proved problematic in different ways. Since bandsmen hoped to use music to fulfill the expectations that marked them as adult men, they could prove exceptionally obstinate in times of personal hardship or familial duress. Most bandleaders willingly accommodated those who had to miss rehearsals to attend to domestic needs, but they also recalled that older musicians sometimes imposed their troubles on the group at large. Because nearly all of the members of the Pelikans Dance Band were married and had children, Kofi Lindsay insisted that he could not organize performances outside of Cape Coast without first attending to their needs:

> When it came to traveling for an engagement, then the trouble started. Let's say we were travelling the next day. We had arranged to set off by 10:00 AM, we had loaded our instruments and prepared everything. When I went to the first man, "Oh I'm ready"; the second man, "Oh I'm attending to my child, my child is not feeling well, I have to take him or her to the hospital." Another, "I have no money for my child's school fees." These men came up with lots of things before we traveled. If I was not able to help them, I would have been in a fix. So I had to go round and round to satisfy everybody before we left.[71]

Ultimately, bandleaders insisted that it was talented musicians, young or old, who tended to place a group's rules, hierarchy, and collective aims at peril for individual gain.[72] Because bands wanted to solidify a glowing reputation and obtain lucrative contracts, they universally pursued skilled artists who could bring energy and talent to their live performances. At the same time, the relatively loose professional structure of Ghana's popular musical environment, in which individual bandsmen did not sign formal contracts and were free to move to another group at any point in time, granted these musicians considerable clout. Knowing full well that other bands would welcome them with open arms, talented individuals often asked bandleaders for more pay, demanded additional rights, or openly transgressed established rules. Many leaders, meanwhile, remained reluctant to reprimand such artists for fear that they would leave or—even worse—join a rival band and disclose closely guarded songs and musical arrangements. As a result, such musicians were able to enjoy liberties regarding drinking, smoking, and women that were unavailable to their less-adept band mates.[73]

In the annals of popular memory, the 1960s were dance band high-life's apex years. Newspapers and magazines of the period recount how talented artists, enthusiastic audiences, and supportive government officials transformed the music into a vital component of urban life. These same sources frame the era's dance band musicians as public icons, prominent stars, and successful celebrities. From the perspective of these men, however, the decade was more often one of considerable professional challenge and personal hardship. As they attempted to fulfill the expectations that defined being successful musicians as well as successful men, they struggled to overcome risky situations, endure stints of financial insecurity, and carry out consistent and productive relationships with the other members of their band. Many also attempted to use song lyrics to communicate their aspirations and tip the scales in their personal and professional favor.

THE CONTESTED DOMAIN OF
SONG LYRICS, 1950s–1960s

When I spoke to the men and women who flocked to urban nightclubs to hear their favorite dance bands in the years surrounding independence, most recalled that they liked the music for its danceable rhythm, modern cosmopolitan sound, and status as a site of self-expression. Many also said that they enjoyed highlife for its lyrical content and messages. Over the course of our conversations about the music, men and women often burst into song and vividly recounted the lyrics to some of their favorite tunes of the Saturday Nights of old. When pressed to explain their ability to remember such songs roughly fifty years later, they explained how highlife musicians had captured the essence of past lived realities. Recalling their favorite songs was not, they explained, a matter of conjuring up a set of appealing or catchy words; it was an act of remembering their own emotions, problems, and pressing concerns.[74]

Musicians concurred that they approached lyrics as a vital component of their overall performance and efforts to win audience admiration. They attempted to write moving songs that addressed contemporary urban life, offered advice, and reflected on a number of themes, including migration, wealth and poverty, politics and nationalism, social stratification, familial relationships, love and romance, generational tensions, and changing gender norms.[75] Particularly memorable songs, musicians noted, could win them lasting acclaim. A few tunes became so popular that they inspired the creation of additional cultural phenomena, such as cloth designs, dance styles, or idiomatic expressions.[76] Other artists, particularly those who were prolific composers, published written compilations of their song lyrics so that audiences could learn their contents, consult their messages, and sing along during performances.[77] While musicians endeavored to write songs that could resonate with audiences, they also wanted to compose tunes that could enhance their reputation as respectable men. As they mounted the stage, they sang songs that challenged common stereotypes about popular musicians, addressed the tensions that connected Saturday Nights to social change, and encouraged listeners to reflect on their own behaviors and relationships.[78] Lyrics were a means for them to applaud, condemn, and evaluate the actions of others and, in the process, cement their own stature as upstanding adults.

Artists composed songs in various languages, including Twi, Fante, Ga, Ewe, Hausa, Yoruba, and English, so that they could reach diverse listeners. Most bands, however, wrote and sang primarily in Twi. In part, they did so because Twi was the country's most widely spoken and commonly understood language. Yet many artists preferred to sing in Twi because it enabled them to employ a number of communicative strategies directly related to the gendered and generational hierarchies that governed urban life. In conversational settings, Twi often requires its participants to recognize one another's rank and relative social position. The offering and response of everyday greetings, for example, vary according to the age, gender, and stature of the persons involved. By directing individuals to communicate with others in ways that uphold social difference, Twi places people into asymmetrical positions of power. These links between language and rank are most salient in Twi's more specialized styles of speech, including *adehye kasa* (the speech of royals), *mmaa kasa* (the speech of women), and *mmpanyin kasa* (the speech of elders), that are associated with particular groups of people. As its name suggests, *mmpanyin kasa*—a form of speech characterized by the appropriate use of indirection, metaphor (*kasakoa*), and proverbs (*ɛbɛ*)—is the domain of individuals who have gained wisdom and considerable command over a repertoire of communicative tools. While it is not necessarily the exclusive preserve of established elders, it is a form of speech associated with senior, and thereby powerful, men.[79]

For highlife musicians struggling to claim a stable position in both their professional and personal environments, *mmpanyin kasa* was an especially attractive mode of songwriting and self-presentation. Many

recalled that they attempted to employ linguistic tools, such as metaphors, euphemisms, allegories, proverbs, and code-switching (alternating between various languages), to create memorable and controversial
tunes that encouraged audiences to discuss their significance and meaning. Importantly, they also maintained that using such tactics enabled
them to present themselves as persons deserving of respect and admiration. For those adept at language, the employment of *mmpanyin kasa*
could be an especially effective means of enhancing one's reputation
as both a musician and a man. Nana Ampadu, the young leader of the
African Brothers Band, was one artist who used his knowledge of Twi
to acquire great public acclaim. As his earlier recollection revealed, his
well-written songs were critical to the band's emergence, record sales,
and efforts to obtain lucrative contracts and enduring benefits. In 1973,
the African Brothers rode Ampadu's lyrics to victory in the National
Highlife Competition, and Ampadu, at the tender age of twenty-eight,
was crowned Ghana's *odwontofoohene* (singer in chief) and given the
honorary title of "Nana" to indicate his status as a recognized "elder" by
the nation at large.[80]

While many musicians used metaphors, proverbs, and indirect
speech to accentuate their social and professional reputations, others
hoped to employ such elements to safely address controversial topics,
challenge authorities, or intentionally spark social controversy. In the
1950s and 1960s, recording studios, radio broadcasters, and government
officials occasionally censored songs that addressed sensitive or profane
topics—including courtship, sexual relationships, and male-female tensions—relevant to the broader realm of Saturday Nights.[81] Since such
subjects were important to listeners, many artists sought to address them
in discreet and covert ways. They used metaphors and proverbs to sing
about generational and gendered relationships, celebrate or lament individual freedoms, and offer social commentary on the immorality of
men, women, and youth. These allegorical methods enabled musicians
to address obscene topics and, if confronted, insist that their song was
about something much more straightforward or benign.[82] The ability to
address the contentious through indirect means also enabled artists to
comment on or critique the actions of powerful political figures. While
highlife artists used metaphors to discuss leaders or political authorities, they also employed the conventions of *akutia*, a form of indirect
Akan verbal assault, to articulate social injustices and lampoon those
who abused power. Nana Ampadu's 1967 song, *"Ebi Te Yie"* (Some are
favorably positioned), for example, used an imaginary animal world to

highlight the tyrannical behaviors of the National Liberation Council, the government that replaced the CPP after the 1966 military coup that ousted Kwame Nkrumah from power.[83] For musicians eager to win accolade among urban residents, repudiate stereotypes about their own demeanor, and gain respect, carefully crafted lyrics were an important, and potentially powerful, tool.

So how did dance band musicians attempt to capitalize on lyrics' profound potential? What kinds of messages did they forward through their song lyrics? More specifically, what did they have to say about urban Ghana's wider trajectory of social change? In recent years, many scholars have suggested that highlife artists wrote songs that privileged a "male point of view" and unabashedly critiqued women as a source of social and moral trouble.[84] Oftentimes, highlife songs lived up to this assertion. The Tempos' early 1950s song "Don't Mind Your Wife" advised men to be wary of giving their spouses "chop money" (periodic monetary allowances for food and household necessities), because women were inherently untrustworthy, deceitful, and individualistic. Years later, Kyeremateng Stars' "Woman No Good" wove audiences a similar tale of female greed and disloyalty:

ɛbere a mehyiaa ɔbaa no	When I met this woman
Na me ho wɔ bi pa ara	I was resourceful
Manhunu deɛ ɛyɛeɛ	I can't imagine what happened
Sika nyinaa saeɛ	All the money got finished
Sika yi saeɛ a	When the money was finished
Afei deɛ aka me nko ara	Now I'm left alone
Aka me nko ara o	Oh! I'm left alone
Aka me nko ara o	Oh! I'm left alone
Saa deɛ ɛmma nyɛ	Really, women are bad

While such examples certainly forward male concerns about women and romantic relationships, the vast majority of highlife songs provided more nuanced commentaries on urban Ghana's gendered and generational landscape. Many songs that criticized women actually championed the concerns of existing patriarchal figures, chiefs, and CPP officials. In the 1950s, the Tempos' "*Weeya Weya*" [a prostitute] (PURL 5.3) and Oppong's Band's "*Anadwo Baa*" (A nocturnal lady) echoed official assertions about the dangers of prostitutes and worked to convince listeners of the importance of the police raids and state legislation that targeted such women.[85] Shortly after President Nkrumah's call for Ghanaian women to adopt the African Personality, the Ramblers Dance Band released "*Ewuraba Artificial*" (Artificial lady), a song that satirically targeted women who altered their appearance through wigs, makeup, and other foreign tricks (PURL 5.4):

Ewuraba artificial e	Em, artificial lady
Gyae nna nyimpa ndwen o	Oh, give us a break
Ewuraba artificial e	Em, artificial lady
Ndɛ yeehu w'ekyir o	Today we have unearthed your secret
Sɛɛ nna wo dede pii a	For all these noises
Eyɛ kyerɛ hɛn yi	You make before us
Bebrebe yi, people's shop	And for all the bragging it is
adaworoma	the people's shop
Nna oedzi wo eyginamu o	That has bailed you out
W'enyim yi a, sɛɛ nna astra	You have bleached your face with astra soap
W'ekyir yi a	And your behind
Sɛɛ nna ɔnnyɛ hwee, tam nko	It's nothing but a bundle of clothes
Akoko yi, mohu a,	These breasts that make me crazy
Nna morowu yi, asaaba nko	I see they are nothing but bales of cotton wool

"*Ewuraba Artificial*" undoubtedly resonated with official concerns and patriarchal perspectives, but audiences, male and female, appreciated the song as a critique of only a small group of women who were materialistic, boastful, and un-Ghanaian in character.[86] Elizabeth Amonoo considered the song to be an attempt not to lampoon such women, but to convince them to set aside such unscrupulous practices:

> We had some ladies that looked like old women and they wanted to look younger. Because of that, you saw that they went to stores to buy some artificial things. If they went to these stores, men wouldn't know. They would see the back and its fine. See the breasts, and its fine. But these women, they would try to act like they were somebody. They wanted to present themselves as high-class so that they would be rewarded or find a man. This song discusses one of these girls who went with a man and he found out that everything was artificial.... The Ramblers sang this song to change that woman's character. [The band] wanted those who had been doing the artificial thing to hear the song and then stop doing them.[87]

Many other songs directed their attention toward men, especially the young urban men who had garnered so much consternation on Saturday Nights. In the early 1960s, the Professional Uhuru Dance Band responded to "*Ewuraba Artificial*" by composing "*Krakye Brokeman*" (Impoverished gentleman), a song that criticized a man who invested heavily in material items, urban recreation, and sociability in an effort to accelerate his maturity and gain social status. As it chronicled the man's lavish practices and eventual demise as a poor and indebted dependent, the song warned young men about the dangers of using such methods to obtain personal mobility.[88] Another popular highlife, *"Gyae Nsanom na Kuro Wo Dan"* (Stop drinking and put a roof on your house), provided male listeners with a potent declaration about the costs of squandering one's money on alcohol and leisure instead of the essential markers of adulthood such as a home and family life.[89] *"Akpeteshi"* [a type of locally distilled gin], a song composed by the Stargazers in 1959, forwarded a similar critique toward men who consumed alcohol in abundance. Ebo Taylor, the guitarist for the Stargazers, recalled that while the song conveyed the perspective of its male culprit, the band composed it in order to convince young men about the dangers of frequent drinking:[90]

Menya me sika, medze atɔ nsa	This is my own money that I have spent on drinks
Menya me sika, medze atɔ nsa	This is my own money that I have spent on drinks
Ewo tse ekyir, wobo efuw wo ho daa	You are sitting behind, and you always are angry with yourself
Akpeteshi no good o	Akpeteshi no good o
Akpeteshi no good o	Akpeteshi no good o
No good o, no good o daa	No good o, no good at all

While such songs made a point to target the errors of wayward young men and women, others looked to discourage youth from attempting to start life outside the conventions erected by elders and authorities. Throughout the 1950s and 1960s, many highlife musicians—themselves young men—joined forces with members of the press, chiefs and elders, welfare officers, and CPP officials to express alarm about youths' brazen behaviors, budding romances, and unsightly dress. Songs that distanced musicians from rebellious youth and immoral activities helped them to rebut common prejudices and claim prominence as conscientious artists and respectable men. In their song, *"Asɛm a Woakɔfa Aba"* (The trouble you have caused), the singer for the High Class Diamonds positioned himself as an elder who could do little to assist a young couple whose exploits had brought peril and distress:

ɛnnɛ mmaa moaba	You present day women
Mo so mmarima ara na aba yi	You have men who can match you
Asɛm a woakɔfa aba	The trouble you have caused
Onua, mentumi nka ho hwee	My sister, I cannot handle it
ɛnnɛ akorɔmfo a moaba	You thieves of today
Mo so polisi na aba yi	You have police that can handle you
Asɛm a woakɔfa aba yi onua	The trouble you have caused, brother

Mentumi nka ho hwee	I cannot handle it
Sɛantie nyɛ o, na da bi nso na wobɛhu	Disobedience is not good; you will regret in future
Asɛm a woakɔfa aba yi onua	The trouble you have caused, brother
Mentumi nka ho hwee	I cannot handle it
Kwadwo Amoako ɔhoɔfɛni	Kwadwo Amoako the handsome man
Mmaa nim no o	Indeed women know you
Na ɛmmaa pɛ no oo	Indeed women love you
Na asɛm a woakɔfa aba yi, onua	But the trouble you have caused, brother
Mentumi nka ho hwee	I cannot handle it

Although the High Class Diamonds' song never disclosed the exact nature of the trouble at hand, audiences understood its central assertion: that illicit romances and youthful transgressions were means not to start life, but to create unwanted pregnancies, mental anguish, familial strife, or financial hardship.[91] The Ramblers' *"Afotusɛm"* (Advice) reinforced such warnings by encouraging young men to extol hard work, financial security, and civic responsibility—not drinking and womanizing—as staples of their personal maturation (PURL 5.5):[92]

Aber a yɛbotu kwan yi	Before we embarked on our journey
Afotusɛm a awofo de ma yɛn	The following pieces of advice were given to us by our parents
Wɔkaa nsa ho asɛm	They talked about drunkenness
Na mmaapɛ ho asɛm	And womanizing
Tɛkrɛma bɔne ne ayɔnko dodoɔsɛ	Foul language and bad company
Saa noɔma yi wode bɔ ɔbra a	If you start life with these things
Ensi wo yiye	It never augurs well for you

While musicians endeavored to write lyrics that could accentuate their prominence as artists and men, they could not always dictate how audiences received their messages, interpreted their meaning or overall significance, or incorporated them into their own activities.[93] This was especially true of songs that employed metaphors, proverbs, and indirection to discuss the dynamics of urban life. As they engaged elements of *mmpanyin kasa*, artists enabled audiences to speculate about their songs' hidden messages and true intentions. In fact, many audiences proved eager not to passively accept musicians' offerings, but to use them to give meaning to their actions or validate their own worldview. Oftentimes, my conversations about song lyrics, with both musicians and audience members, demonstrated that individual tunes generated various, even conflicting, sets of meaning.[94] Although musicians framed lyrical ambiguity as a strategy they employed to attract and engage audience interest, some admitted that they were often surprised to learn about the interpretations their songs fostered among urban residents.[95] Others recognized that their strategic efforts to use indirection were easily lost on listeners who wanted to imbue songs with alternative meanings. Song lyrics, like so many other aspects of Saturday Nights, were frequently sites of difference and disagreement.

While several songs fostered divergent interpretations among listening publics, few sparked discussions as lively or controversial as those concerning *"Nkatie"* (Groundnuts), a tune performed and recorded by E. T. Mensah's Tempos in the early 1950s (PURL 5.6):

Nkateɛ yi yɛ dede [dɛ dɛ]	This groundnut is nice
Nkyene wɔ mu dogo [do do]	It is too salty
Nkateɛ yi yɛ dede [dɛ dɛ]	This groundnut is nice
Nkyene wɔ mu dogo [do do]	It is too salty
Panin bɛdi, abɔfra bɛdi	The elderly will eat it, the young will eat it
ɔnyɛ akɔnno	It is not appetizing
Nkateɛ yi yɛ dede [dɛ dɛ]	This groundnut is nice
Nkyene wɔ mu dogo [do do]	It is too salty

Many of the men and women who remembered this song insisted that its simple Twi lyrics were readily clear and transparent. The singer, they explained, pronounced that groundnuts were delicious (*"Nkateɛ yi yɛ de dɛ"*) and that large numbers of Ghanaians, young and old, liked to eat them (*"Panin bɛdi, abɔfra bɛdi"*). When asked why a dance band might compose and perform such an innocuous song, men and women vividly recalled how the buying, selling, and eating of groundnuts was an event common to everyday urban life in the years of its composition. For them, it was a straightforward portrayal of a communal activity that was open to individuals of various ages and social positions.[96]

Others, meanwhile, remembered *"Nkateɛ"* as a song that had a deep or hidden meaning that the Tempos wanted to strategically disguise from young people, officials, or casual listeners. A large number of people suggested that the song was not about the buying or eating of groundnuts, but that it used such actions to indirectly discuss a completely different topic. This conviction stemmed from a careful dissection of the song's lyrical content and structure. Many people took issue with the verb *"di,"* which appears in the song's fifth line. In its most conventional form, *di* means "to eat," which explains why so many upheld the song to be a literal and direct discussion of groundnuts. *Di* is not, however, the appropriate verb for the consumption of all foods. As many men and women pointed out, the correct verb for the intake of rougher foods, including groundnuts, is *"we"* ("to chew"). Since Twi-speakers would correctly communicate the eating of groundnuts by using *we* rather than *di* (as in *"Panin bɛwe, abɔfra bɛwe"* instead of *"Panin bɛdi, abɔfra bɛdi"*), many listeners found the phrase to be a clue about the song's hidden or real meaning.[97]

Ultimately, the men and women who highlighted this lyrical discrepancy interpreted its importance in drastically different ways. Some remarked that the use of *di* was little more than an inadvertent mistake. Since the male singer mispronounced other Twi words (*"do do"* as *"do go"*), they claimed that he was likely Ga and had used the verb because he was not singing in his first language.[98] Others, meanwhile, insisted that the use of *di* was no accident. While the principal meaning of *di* is "to eat," the verb is polysemous, meaning that it can be used to characterize a multitude of actions depending on its connected object.[99] When attached a person, as in *"ɔdii no"* ("he ate her"), *di* refers to sexual intercourse ("he had sex with her"). *"Nkateɛ,"* many insisted, was not a song about eating groundnuts, but one that discussed sexual intercourse and male-female relationships.

Those who adamantly claimed that the song discreetly discussed sex offered three distinct arguments about its overall message. Many older men insisted that the song was, like *"Weeya Weya"* and *"Anadwo Baa,"* a clear lamentation about the salty behaviors of sexually autonomous young women who defied parental authority. As Nii Adgen Tettey explained:

> The song was about a young woman who went here and there. This woman, excuse me to say, when a man got ahold of her, she was not satisfied: she went and found another man. But instead of talking about this woman directly, the song spoke about a groundnut. A groundnut is sweet until you put too much salt on it. When you put the salt on it, it is spoiled. When it is sweet, any man will taste it. But with the salt, no one will take it! That was the song's message—as a young woman, you needed to be respectful, you didn't need to go looking for men here and there.[100]

The men who agreed with Tettey often recalled the behaviors that certain women, especially prostitutes, adopted on Saturday Nights of the 1950s and 1960s. In other words, these men placed their own attitudes and concerns at the forefront of the song's ambiguous meaning.[101]

Others explained that *"Nkateɛ"* was a criticism not of the period's problematic women, but of the young men who boldly refused to respect family authorities and elders. Specifically, they argued that the song targeted the behaviors of brazen youth who insistently chased women while ignoring more conventional markers of maturation such as hard work, stable employment, or the acquisition of property. For James Thompson, the song was a treatise that bemoaned the falling moral standards of young men and implored urban audiences to recognize that sexual endeavors were the exclusive domain of mature adults:

JT: Do you understand the gist of that song?

NP: Can you explain it to me?

JT: If you go to a place [here in Ghana] will you see young men eating with adults?

NP: No, you won't see it.

JT: Exactly! Young people cannot eat with adults—they have to eat with others who have not grown! You understand? So if adult men are going for women, how can a younger person do the same?

NP: So it's not talking about groundnuts (*laughing*)?

JT: No (*laughing*)![102]

While Thompson framed the song as a validation of urban areas' gendered and generational hierarchies, others insisted that the Tempos' song actually intended to target irresponsible older men who carried out behaviors unbefitting their adult stature. Recalling instances in which older, married men attended nightclubs not with their wives, but with young girlfriends, some men and women argued that the song was written to protect young people and, like newspaper articles of the period, criticize such men as unappetizing and corrupt persons who abused the advantages of money and age.[103]

As these varied interpretations of the Tempos' apparently benign song indicate, lyrics were a highly contested component of Saturday Nights. Musicians endeavored to write songs that would capture public imagination, garner professional repute, and facilitate their recognition as men. They used metaphors, indirection, and other aspects of *mmpanyin kasa* to comment on controversial behaviors, align themselves with established authorities, and advise audiences how to best navigate existing hierarchies. Oftentimes, however, the songs that represented these efforts enabled audiences to identify ambiguity, speculate about hidden meanings, and effectively target the people that they found problematic or unacceptable. In the end, songs were not necessarily a straightforward or convenient means of developing consensus or collective opinion. They were, like so many other facets of Saturday Nights, a way for individual Ghanaians to pursue a wide array of different, and sometimes conflicting, aims.

CONCLUSION

This chapter opened with a vignette of C. K. Mann, a highlife musician who used his career to acquire widespread fame, financial prominence, and recognition as a successful Ghanaian man. Subsequent discussion of the promises and pitfalls of being a bandsman, however, demonstrates why so few of Mann's contemporaries were able to match his accomplishments. In the decades surrounding independence, Ghana's highlife musicians enjoyed a number of opportunities and advantages that remained out of reach for many of their nonmusical peers. They were extremely visible, widely recognizable, and lauded as celebrities and national stars. Many got to travel, meet and perform for influential leaders, and have their photographs grace the pages of newspapers and magazines. At the same time, these exceptional opportunities led many Ghanaians to believe that all highlife musicians lived lives of uncommon comfort and favor. Despite the considerable fanfare that accompanied their successes, most musicians found that the period of highlife's prominence was one of rather limited gains. Professionally, they endured intense competition, occupational hazards, infrequent performances, and interband turmoil. Most musicians also faced less public, but no less pressing, challenges. Like other Ghanaian men, highlife artists sought to purchase homes, start a family, and meet the expectations that marked their passage into adulthood and potential elderhood. Unfortunately, even successful musicians found that their professional stature did little to help them navigate their private life, secure a steady income, or come to terms with the fact that they possessed an empty name.

Throughout the postwar period, highlife musicians invoked a wide range of strategies to help them thrive as artists and men. Young musicians used their talent to become known, interact with women, and accelerate their personal maturation, by either fostering an identity as exceptional young people or fulfilling the conventions of adulthood. As they advanced in age and stature on and off the stage, musicians formulated different tactics to advance their occupational and personal interests. Established bands looked to cultivate positive reputations and eschew professional hazards by erecting a system of rules and ranks that could facilitate efficient rehearsals and cooperation between individual members. Older musicians often supported such measures, but occasionally exploited them to bring relief to their families. Talented artists, meanwhile, openly navigated the country's loose professional environment in ways that advanced their own needs and desires. Prolific composers turned to well-crafted lyrics and *mmpanyin kasa* to solidify their stature and obtain professional and personal repute.

In the end, the complex confluence of realities that made being a musician such an incredibly difficult venture included many of the same factors that made highlife music such an important part of urban life. Musicians' struggles stemmed from the fact that their music mattered to audiences, political officials, and the wider dynamics of social change. While many musicians recalled highlife's popularity as a positive, they also insisted that the actions and interests of urban residents and government officials did much to impact their professional agency and personal prospects. To be a bandsman in the years surrounding independence was, in essence, to be part of an ongoing and multifaceted debate about understandings of gender, generational strife, and the allocation of power in urban areas. It was also to fully and inescapably enmesh oneself in the shifting terrain of possibilities and limitations that characterized Saturday Nights.

Epilogue

Highlife dancing? The real forms are disappearing.
The movements of the old days are being lost.

—KWADWO DONKOH, September 16, 2005

If I hear highlife right now, it will remind me of the past. . . .
But highlife can't come to change Ghana again. We can't play
it like before because life is different now. The things that
they used to sing about would change peoples' lives!

—FELICIA KUDIAH, June 19, 2009

On July 2, 2005, the Apex-Dansoman Keep Fit Dancing Club held a Ballroom Dancing Soiree at Osu Presbyterian Church in Accra. The club, which aimed to "promote and popularize the art of ballroom dance," had formed nine years earlier and attracted a small but dedicated membership. Having received an invitation to attend the event, I, in the company of a few friends and my wife, spent the Saturday night watching a nostalgic recreation of a dance band highlife affair. The program consisted of a variety of events: speeches by well-dressed club officials, demonstrations in waltz, cha-cha-cha, and rumba, open dances in highlife, quickstep, slow foxtrot, rumba, and tango, musical interludes, refreshments, and the awarding of certificates to individual club members. Despite all its pomp and pageantry, the function was a clear indication that Ghana's once flourishing highlife scene had practically perished. Throughout the evening, men and women moved to recorded music rather than a live band, idle onlookers wandered about the church interior rather than paying strict attention to the happenings on the dance floor, and everyone departed when the event came to an end at the relatively early hour of 10:30 PM.[1]

A few weeks earlier, I had set out from Kwame Nkrumah Circle in order to locate the Tip-Toe nightclub, a prominent venue that had been a favorite destination of many musical enthusiasts in the 1950s and 1960s. Although I had heard that the nightclub had closed years ago, I wanted to walk through its entrance, see its stage, and imagine the place full of music, dancing, and a large boisterous crowd. Finding the club proved to be a bit of a challenge—many people had no idea about its location—but within an hour I stood before its entrance. As I made my way inside, I happily noticed that the gates, stage, and walls were all intact. At the same time, there was little evidence that the place had ever been a hot spot on Saturday Nights. As I turned toward the central floor space that had once been filled with men and women dancing, my eyes quickly fell on the numerous rows of benches set up to face the cement stage. It did not take long to realize that the venue that had long been one of Accra's most prominent nightclubs was now an open-air church.[2]

Today, the Tip-Toe's fate is hardly unique. During the 1970s and 1980s, the vast majority of Accra's nightclubs were closed, torn down, or converted for other uses (PURL 6.1). Most met their demise because the music that had fueled their emergence and prominence, dance band highlife, had also started to disappear. For the musicians, audiences, and officials who had flocked to such venues decades earlier, the music's decline was an unimaginable prospect. Over the course of the twentieth century, highlife was Ghana's most recognizable musical form, a principal medium of urban recreation, and a sphere of indubitable fun. The music essentially defined Saturday Nights: the moments when city residents abandoned the confines of home and work to gather with friends, enjoy refreshments, and enthusiastically hit the dance floor to the sounds of some of their favorite bands. Such activities, moreover, had been integral to the wider dynamics of urban life. Few, if any, cultural forms better encapsulated the opportunities and constraints that marked the colonial era, the march toward independence, and the years that followed Ghana's birth as an autonomous nation. From the vintage point of the 1960s, when major towns supported roughly five hundred popular bands and Accra alone had over sixty nightclubs, there was little reason to believe that the music would ever suffer a precipitous decline.[3]

Beneath this façade of prosperity, however, a number of factors began to chip away at the music's viability as a medium of enjoyment and social change. While the actions of the CPP government diminished urban residents' ability to freely engage the music, the latter half of the 1960s, particularly the years following Nkrumah's ousting as a result of the National Liberation Council's (NLC) 1966 coup, were even more restrictive. Shortly after the coup, the NLC forcibly dissolved the Ghanaian Musicians' Union—an organization that aimed to improve musicians' benefits, social respectability, and economic plight—because of its alleged proximity to the ousted CPP government.[4] A few years later, following the initiation of the Second Republic in 1969, Ghana's new prime minister, Kofi Abrefa Busia, passed the Aliens Compliance Order: a measure that intended to protect Ghanaians from the threats of "unemployed strangers" and foreign "criminals." Over the next year, the order resulted in the expulsion of over 100,000 individuals, including a substantial number of Nigerian musicians, patrons, and nightclub owners. In Accra, the order had immediate impacts on Saturday Nights. Many of the city's most prominent nightclubs, including the Weekend-in-Havana, Holiday Inn, Weekend-in-Miami, and Tip-Toe, fell into new ownership, mismanagement, and irreversible disrepair.[5]

Over the course of the 1970s, the country's Saturday Nights took a number of additional hits. The decade was one of tremendous economic hardship for most Ghanaians. It began with a devalued cedi, increased import prices, high levels of debt, and an estimated unemployment rate of 50 percent.[6] With Ghana on the brink of bankruptcy and urban residents struggling to adjust to ever-falling standards of living, Colonel Ignatius Acheampong led the "13th January Revolution" of 1972 and overthrew Busia's Progress Party government. Acheampong's National Redemption Council (NRC) initiated its own set of interventionist policies, but they did little to alleviate the country's financial woes. By 1975, Ghana was in the midst of an economic collapse. Forced to manage expanding unemployment, food shortages, and the second-highest rate of inflation in the world, relatively few people proved able or willing to invest in popular musical activities. Many of the urban residents who had long fueled the nation's highlife scene, including youth, workers, and middle-class residents, turned their backs on Saturday Nights. While the music continued, largely at the hands of a small number of prominent dance bands that performed at state-owned hotels for affluent and foreign audiences, its live performances became an elitist phenomenon reserved for special, rather than regular, occasions.[7]

For the country's popular musicians, such developments were particularly distressing. As performing opportunities dried up, so did chances to record at one of the nation's musical studios, including Ambassador Records, Ghana Film Studios, and Polygram Records. Following the OPEC oil increases of 1973, the price of vinyl in Ghana skyrocketed, and by 1978, its importation was all but impossible. Local record production effectively ceased, and, because only 5 percent of studio sessions eventually reached the market as commercial products, record sales rapidly plummeted.[8] Faced with the prospects of a defunct nightlife scene and dysfunctional record industry, many highlife musicians began to explore the prospects of leaving the country to secure personal and professional success. In the late 1970s and early 1980s, many of Ghana's most prominent highlife artists, including George Darko, Rex Gyamfi, and Pat Thomas, recorded, performed, and lived outside of the country. In 1983 alone, highlife musicians recorded thirty-five albums outside Ghana, many of which became as popular in European cities such as London and Hamburg as they did in Accra and Kumasi.[9] The bandsmen who remained in Ghana, meanwhile, moved to redress their profession's dire circumstances. On May 21, 1979, roughly a thousand artists organized by the Musicians' Union of Ghana (MUSIGA) conducted a march of protest through the streets of Accra in an effort to convince the government to rekindle its support, foster awareness for their diminishing opportunities, and remind the city's residents that they were not mere "band boys," but professional men of stature and significance (PURL 6.2).[10]

A few weeks after the MUSIGA march, Ghana underwent another tumultuous transition. On June 4, 1979, military officials carried out a coup, removed the government, and promoted a young flight lieutenant, Jerry Rawlings, as head of state. After leading Ghana back into a brief period of civilian rule, Rawlings reclaimed government control on December 31, 1981, and declared his intention to revamp the country's broken political and economic scene. In its efforts to ensure order, his government imposed an evening curfew that prevented Ghanaians, especially those in urban areas, from leaving their homes after dark. In essence the curfew put an end to the country's Saturday Nights. It forced existing bands to dissolve, remaining clubs and recreational venues to close, and individuals to carry out their musical recreation within the confines of their own homes. The private consumption of music prompted a rapid demand for cassette recordings and opened the door for musical piracy, a phenomenon that struck a further blow to the local music industry, transferred profits from musicians to street vendors, and ushered in a new wave of foreign music, particularly from the United States. When the curfew finally lifted in the mid-1980s, dance band highlife had effectively become a thing of the past.[11]

In the decades following dance band highlife's demise, the music has become a focal point not of a revived popular musical scene—that position belongs to more contemporary highlife offshoots such as gospel highlife and hiplife—but of varied, and rather ambiguous, memories about the nation's past. For many individuals now advanced in age, the music offers a convenient lens through which to contrast recollections of personal prosperity, maturation, and accomplishment with more mundane realities, contemporary hardship, and perpetual marginalization. Nearly all of the urban residents I spoke with insisted that the period of dance band highlife's prominence—the decades surrounding independence—was a "better time," an era when optimism filled the air, now-worn infrastructure glistened, and occasions of enjoyment were much easier to exploit. While the music has become entangled in many residents' personal nostalgia, it has also become a focal point for a public remembering of Ghana's golden age. Many outlets, including newspapers, popular publications, radio shows, and government-sponsored cultural events not unlike those that marked the fiftieth anniversary of independence, frame highlife as a symbol of long-lost optimism, economic vitality, and feelings of self-accomplishment. In the process, the music has become a sonic embodiment of a collective "Ghanaian" ethos and moment of collective triumph that gradually gave way to a present-day climate of disappointment and hardship.

The problem with such assertions is not that they inflate the music's overall importance to Ghana's recent past, but that they undermine its variability and complexity as a form of consensus and conflict. At a basic level, narrating highlife as a national medium forces us to miss how remarkably diverse groups of people fueled the music's emergence, ongoing transformations, and privileged place as a form of urban recreation. While "everybody," as the old song title asserts, "liked Saturday Nights," they liked them for drastically different reasons and in drastically different ways. Instead of using the music to facilitate widely shared forms of consciousness, men and women used it to draw lines of inclusion and exclusion, reallocate power, and transform cities' gendered and generational landscape. People used dance band highlife to situate themselves into communities that were smaller, and often more intimate, than the nation as well as to navigate challenges and uncertainties that were different from, but no less daunting than, those of today.

Charting highlife's history outside a convenient nationalist storyline also helps us recover some fundamental truths about Ghana's recent past. While much of the country's recent historiography privileges the transformations of the colonial and postcolonial periods, a music-focused lens enables us to see the ongoing processes that connected the years preceding Ghana's 1957 independence to those that followed it.[12] From 1890 to 1970, the nation's Saturday Nights were occasions marked by an ever-shifting array of possibilities and limitations as well as continuities and changes. At times, they enabled otherwise marginalized groups to make significant personal and public transformations. In the early decades of the twentieth century, song, dance, and merriment enabled migrant wage laborers to challenge their junior status, legitimize new gendered models, and claim autonomy from chiefs and elders. In the 1920s and 1930s, another unprecedented urban group—the *akrakyefoɔ*—used popular music to carve out their own social position and situate themselves alongside the newly erected colonial state. Decades later, in the 1950s and early 1960s, young men and women exploited dance band highlife's new performance setting—the nightclub—and growing links to jazz, calypso, and rock 'n' roll to start life, obliterate what they considered to be outdated practices, and mediate between their personal liberation and that of the nation at large. In this same period, young bandsmen found that the popular musical stage was a place where they could earn money, meet influential personalities, and attract wide recognition as exceptional figures and adult men.

Despite these many openings, there were also times when Saturday Nights enabled established authorities to enforce the status quo, revive past arrangements, or even expand their power into new places. After unsuccessfully attempting to use music to instill discipline, order, and a sense of European superiority over Ghanaian publics, the colonial state partnered with chiefs and elders to pass a number of laws targeting "dangerous" popular musical forms as well as their young participants. Over the course of the 1920s and 1930s, the criminalization of Saturday Nights helped reinforce the social, gendered, and generational order conducive to the emerging system of indirect rule. In the 1930s and 1940s, British officials also lent considerable support to the *akrakyefoɔ*, who they hoped would use highlife to spread the merits of Western education, hard work, and civilization to less-established young men and women. In the 1950s and 1960s, a new group of authorities—the CPP—used popular music to legitimize their power, garner support, and pursue a distinct program of nation-building. Although the CPP's initial efforts to control Saturday Nights proved untenable, it leaned particularly hard on the music as a means of outlining what it meant to be "Ghanaian" in the decades after national independence. In the process, the new government, much like its traditional and colonial predecessors, worked to ensure that long-marginalized publics, including women and youth, abided by rather than challenged its directives.

Packaged together, this trajectory of fluctuating openings and closures reveals that to live in twentieth century urban Ghana was to live in a place marked by complex negotiations about gender, generation, and power. Cities were places where age was not immutable, gender was far from fixed, and hierarchies of power were neither stable nor absolute. At the same time, they were never places where these modes of difference could be completely unmade or transformed. Over the long term, the basic social and political structures of many towns remained remarkably durable, even amid the large-scale transformations that marked the imposition of colonial rule, the nationalist period, and the initiation of a newly independent government. Following Saturday Nights demonstrates that the hierarchies that govern contemporary Ghana's urban contexts are not products of persistent continuities or inevitable transformations; they are the result of generations of Ghanaians' efforts to actively reshape their lived realities, often in a climate defined by music, dance, and a great deal of fun.

Glossary

Most of the words in the glossary are in Twi, the language of the Akan people, and appear below with Asante spelling.

ababawa (pl. *mmabawa*)	a young woman who has achieved puberty but not yet given birth or become a recognized adult
aberanteɛ (pl. *mmeranteɛ*)	a young man who has achieved puberty but not become a recognized adult
aberewa (pl. *mmerewa*)	old woman or female elder
abofra (pl. *mmofra*)	child, boy, girl
abusua (pl. *mmusua*)	matrilineage
adaha	"dance here"; proto-highlife musical style that was popular in coastal cities during the first decades of the twentieth century
adowa	funeral dance from Asante region
akrampa	a Fante asafo company located in Cape Coast and comprised of individuals of European-African descent
akutia	insinuation; a strategic form of verbal assault that employs innuendo and roundabout method
asafo	military company organized within a particular residential area
Asante/Ashanti	an Akan people who live in Ghana and the Ivory Coast
asantehene	the king of Asante
ashawo (Yoruba)	"moneychanger"; prostitute
ashiko	proto-highlife musical style that likely emerged in Sierra Leone or Liberia, but became popular in southern Ghana during the early twentieth century
awuraa (pl. *nwuraanom*)	lady or woman of social status and repute
cedi	the currency of Ghana; replaced the Ghanaian pound in 1965

231

Ewe	people who live in southeast Ghana and Togo and speak the Ewe language
Fante	Akan people who live in southern Ghana; dialect of Akan language
fugu	smock shirt endorsed as form of national Ghanaian dress in the late 1950s–early 1960s; also called *batakari*
Ga	people who live in Accra plains and speak the Ga language
homowo	annual harvest festival held by Ga people each May
kente	silk and cotton fabric made from woven strips; endorsed as form of national Ghanaian dress in the late 1950s–early 1960s
konkoma	proto-highlife musical style popular in southern towns during the late 1920s and 1930s
krakye (pl. *akrakyefoɔ*)	"clerk"; educated gentleman
mantse (Ga, pl. *mantsemei*)	"father of the town," leading office holder of town and residential area in Accra
mmpanyin kasa	"the speech of elders," a style of speech that denotes wisdom and experience
ntama	cloth; often used by women to compose a blouse, skirt, or head scarf
nkwankwaa	young men
ɔbaa (pl. *mmaa*)	adult woman
ɔbarima (pl. *mmarima*)	adult man
ɔbirɛmpɔn (pl. *abirɛmpɔn*)	big man
ɔhene (pl. *ahene*)	chief
ɔpanyin (pl. *mmpanyinfoɔ*)	elder
osibi	recreational musical style of Fante fishermen along the central coast of Ghana; likely precursor to *osibisaaba*; also proposed as a new name for highlife by Kwame Nkrumah in 1960.
osibisaaba	proto-highlife musical style that emerged in Fante areas of southern Ghana in the early twentieth century; often referred to as *patsinkyrren/patsintering*, *ɔdɔ*, and *antekodiwo* in British colonial documents.
safohene	a divisional captain of an *asafo* company
small boy	socially insignificant or marginal male person
stool	important symbol of a chief's political and religious authority
tufuhene	commander of an *asafo* company

Notes

Introduction

1. For a list of nearly fifty advertised dances that took place in various cities that night, see *Daily Graphic,* March 2, 1957.

2. For more on the Ghana@50 celebrations see Carola Lentz and Jan Budniok, "Ghana@50—Celebrating the Nation: An Eyewitness Account from Accra," Working Paper no. 83, Department of Anthropology and African Studies, University of Mainz, March 2007. Also see http://www.ghana50.gov.gh/events/index.php?op=anniversary.

3. Terence Ranger, *Dance and Society in Eastern Africa, 1890–1970: The Beni Ngoma* (Berkeley: University of California Press, 1975); John Miller Chernoff, *African Rhythm and African Sensibility: Aesthetics and Social Action in African Musical Idioms* (Chicago: University of Chicago Press, 1979); David Coplan, *In Township Tonight!: South Africa's Black City Music and Theatre* (London: Longman, 1985); Thomas Turino, *Nationalists, Cosmopolitans, and Popular Music in Zimbabwe* (Chicago: University of Chicago Press, 2000); Kelly Askew, *Performing the Nation: Swahili Music and Cultural Politics in Tanzania* (Chicago: University of Chicago Press, 2002); Marissa Moorman, *Intonations: A Social History of Music and Nation in Luanda, Angola, from 1945 to Recent Times* (Athens: Ohio University Press, 2008); Bob W. White, *Rumba Rules: The Politics of Dance Music in Mobutu's Zaire* (Durham, N.C.: Duke University Press, 2008).

4. George Lipsitz asserts that while popular music is not history in and of itself, it "can be read historically, dialogically, and symptomatically to produce valuable evidence about change over time": *Footsteps in the Dark: The Hidden Histories of Popular Music* (Minneapolis: University of Minnesota Press, 2007), vii–xxv.

5. In the pages that follow, I use the capitalized version of this conceptualization (Saturday Night) to distinguish it from the particular weekend occasion (Saturday night).

6. Felicia Kudiah, June 19, 2009.

7. Bill Freund, *The African City: A History* (Cambridge: Cambridge University Press, 2007), 65–67; David M. Anderson and Richard Rathbone, "Urban Africa: Histories in the Making," in *Africa's Urban Past,* ed. David M. Anderson and Richard Rathbone (Portsmouth: Heinemann, 2000), 8–9; Ghana, *1960 Population Census of Ghana,* vol. 3: *Demographic Characteristics* (Accra: Census Office, 1964).

8. John Parker, *Making the Town: Ga State and Society in Early Colonial Accra* (Portsmouth: Heinemann, 2000); T. C. McCaskie, *Asante Identities: History and Modernity in*

an African Village (Bloomington: Indiana University Press, 2000); S. S. Quarcoopome, "Urbanisation, land alienation, and politics in Accra," *University of Ghana Research Review* 8, nos. 1 & 2 (1992): 40–54.

9. Frederick Cooper, "Urban Space, Industrial Time, and Wage Labor in Africa," in *Struggle for the City: Migrant Labor, Capital, and the State in Urban Africa*, ed. Frederick Cooper (Beverly Hills: Sage Publications, 1983), 7–50; Paul Maylam and Iain Edwards, ed., *The People's City: African Life in Twentieth-Century Durban* (Pietermaritzburg: University of Natal Press, 1996); Andrew Burton, *African Underclass: Urbanisation, Crime, and Colonial Order in Dar es Salaam* (Athens: Ohio University Press, 2005).

10. Richard Jeffries, *Class, Power and Ideology in Ghana: The Railwaymen of Sekondi* (Cambridge: Cambridge University Press, 1978); Jeff Crisp, *The Story of an African Working Class: Ghanaian Miners' Struggles, 1870–1980* (London: Zed Books, 1984); David Kimble, *A Political History of Ghana: The Rise of Gold Coast Nationalism, 1850–1928* (Oxford: Clarendon Press, 1963); Raymond Dumett, *El Dorado in West Africa: The Gold Mining Frontier, African Labor, and Colonial Capitalism in the Gold Coast, 1875–1900* (Athens: Ohio University Press, 1998).

11. In recent decades, available literature on leisure and popular culture has flourished. For a few important works, see Karin Barber, "Popular Arts in Africa," *African Studies Review* 30, no. 3 (1987): 1–78, 104–11; Phyllis Martin, *Leisure and Society in Colonial Brazzaville* (Cambridge: Cambridge University Press, 1995); Emmanuel Akyeampong, *Drink, Power and Cultural Change: A Social History of Alcohol in Ghana, c. 1800 to Recent Times* (Portsmouth: Heinemann, 1996); Laura Fair, *Pastimes and Politics: Culture, Community, and Identity in Post-Abolition Zanzibar, 1890–1945* (Athens, Ohio University Press, 2001); Paul Tiyambe Zeleza, "The Creation and Consumption of Leisure: Theoretical and Methodological Considerations," in *Leisure in Urban Africa*, ed. Paul Tiyambe Zeleza and Cassandra Rachel Veney (Trenton: Africa World Press, 2003), vii–xli.

12. Stephan F. Miescher, *Making Men in Ghana* (Bloomington: Indiana University Press, 2005); Jean Allman and Victoria Tashjian, *"I Will Not Eat Stone": A Women's History of Colonial Asante* (Portsmouth: Heinemann, 2000); Sjaak van der Geest, "ɔpanyin: The Ideal of Elder in the Akan Culture of Ghana," *Canadian Journal of African Studies* 32, no. 3 (1998): 449–93; Stephan F. Miescher, "Becoming an ɔpanyin: Elders, Gender, and Masculinities in Ghana since the Nineteenth Century," in *Africa after Gender*, ed. Catherine M. Cole, Takyiwaa Manuh, and Stephan F. Miescher (Bloomington: Indiana University Press, 2007), 253–69.

13. Akyeampong, *Drink, Power, and Cultural Change*, 157; Miescher, *Making Men*, 11, 17–33, and 160–67; Allman and Tashjian, *I Will Not Eat* Stone, xxi–xxiv.

14. Miescher, *Making Men*; Allman and Tashjian, *I Will Not Eat Stone*; Lisa A. Lindsay and Stephan F. Miescher ed., *Men and Masculinities in Modern Africa* (Portsmouth: Heinemann, 2003); Claire C. Robertson, *Sharing the Same Bowl: A Socioeconomic History of Women and Class in Accra, Ghana* (Ann Arbor: University of Michigan Press, 1984); Christine Oppong, ed., *Female and Male in West Africa* (London: Allen and Unwin, 1983).

15. Dorothy L. Hodgson and Sheryl A. McCurdy, eds. *"Wicked" Women and the Reconfiguration of Gender in Africa* (Portsmouth: Heinemann, 2001); Jean Allman, "'Let Your Fashion Be in line with Our Ghanaian Costume': Nation, Gender, and the Politics of Cloth-ing in Nkrumah's Ghana," in *Fashioning Africa: Power and the Politics of Dress*, ed. Jean Allman (Bloomington: Indiana University Press, 2004), 144–65; Takyiwaa Manuh, "Doing Gender Work in Ghana," in *Africa After Gender?*, 129–31.

16. Emmanuel Akyeampong, *Drink, Power, and Cultural Change;* "Wo pe tam won pe ba (You like cloth but you don't want children): Urbanization, Individualism and Gender Relations in Colonial Ghana, 1900–1939," in *Africa's Urban Past,* 222–34; and "Sexuality and Prostitution among the Akan of the Gold Coast c. 1650–1950," *Past and Present,* no. 156 (1997): 144–73. Also see Jean Allman, "Rounding up Spinsters: Unmarried Women and Gender Chaos in Colonial Asante," *Journal of African History* 37, no. 2 (1996): 195–214.

17. Richard Waller, "Rebellious Youth in Colonial Africa," *Journal of African History* 47, no. 1 (2006): 77–92; Mamadou Diouf, "Engaging Postcolonial Cultures: African Youth and Public Space," *African Studies Review* 46, no. 2 (2003): 1–12; Jay Straker, *Youth, Nationalism and the Guinean Revolution* (Indiana University Press, 2009), 19–55; G. Thomas Burgess and Andrew Burton, "Introduction" in *Generations Past: Youth in East African History,* ed. Andrew Burton and Hélène Charton-Bigot (Athens: Ohio University Press, 2010), 1–24. Like the scholars listed here, I attempt to portray "youth" as a constructed social category whose membership was fluid rather than stable and whose characteristics were open to revision over time. To that end, the pages that follow employ the term "youth" to refer to a group of young men and women who both were young in age and lacked the social standing and rights allocated to adults. I use the terms "young people" and "young men and women" in a similar fashion, both to avoid the monotony of using the same term repeatedly and to reflect the actual terms that people used to describe themselves in the course of our conversations.

18. Jean Allman, *The Quills of the Porcupine: Asante Nationalism in an Emergent Ghana* (Madison: University of Wisconsin Press, 1993), 28–36; Akyeampong, *Drink, Power, and Cultural Change,* 117–38.

19. Michel Foucault, *Power/Knowledge: Selected Interviews and Other Writings, 1972–77* (New York: Pantheon Books, 1980), 89; Askew, *Performing the Nation,* 289–93; White, *Rumba Rules,* 196.

20. Emmanuel Akyeampong and Pashington Obeng, "Spirituality, Gender, and Power in Asante History," *International Journal of African Historical Studies* 28, no. 3 (1995): 481–508; T. C. McCaskie, *State and Society in Pre-colonial Asante* (Cambridge: Cambridge University Press, 1995), 1–23; Dennis Austin, *Politics in Ghana: 1946–1960* (London: Oxford University Press, 1964); David E. Apter, *Ghana in Transition* (Princeton, N.J.: Princeton University Press, 1972); Allman, *Quills of the Porcupine.*

21. Akyeampong, *Drink, Power, and Cultural Change,* 47–69; McCaskie, *Asante Identities,* 201–40; Stephanie Newell, *Literary Culture in Colonial Ghana: How to Play the Game of Life* (Bloomington: Indiana University Press, 2002), 27–52.

22. Akyeampong, *Drink, Power, and Cultural Change,* 21–44; Akyeampong and Obeng, "Spirituality, Gender, and Power in Asante History," 481–508.

23. McCaskie, *Asante Identities,* 124–35.

24. Ibid., 142–71; Akyeampong, *Drink, Power, and Cultural Change,* 44–53; Roger Gocking, *History of Ghana* (Westport: Greenwood Press, 2005), 37–48.

25. Roger Gocking, *Facing Two Ways: Ghana's Coastal Communities under Colonial Rule* (New York: University Press of America, 1999); Parker, *Making the Town;* Akyeampong, *Drink, Power, and Cultural Change.*

26. Quarcoopome, "Urbanisation," 47; Jeffrey S. Ahlman, "Living with Nkrumahism: Nation, State, and Pan-Africanism in Ghana" (PhD diss., University of Illinois, 2011), 78.

27. The pivotal work here is Richard Bauman, *Verbal Art as Performance* (Prospect Heights, Ill.: Waveland Press, 1977).

28. Victor Turner, *Dramas, Fields, and Metaphors: Symbolic Action in Human Society* (Ithaca: Cornell University Press, 1974); Erving Goffman, *The Presentation of Self in Everyday Life* (Garden City, N.Y.: Doubleday, 1959): Richard Schechner, *Between Theater and Anthropology* (Philadelphia: University of Pennsylvania Press, 1985).

29. Johannes Fabian, *Power and Performance: Ethnographic Explorations through Proverbial Wisdom and Theater in Shaba, Zaire* (Madison: University of Wisconsin Press, 1990), 13; Askew, *Performing the Nation*, 18–24; Veit Erlmann, *Nightsong: Performance, Power, and Practice in South Africa* (Chicago: University of Chicago Press, 1996), 18–23.

30. The overall history of Ghana's popular music scene still needs to be written, but readers interested in an introduction to highlife should consult the many important works of John Collins, including *Highlife Time* (Accra: Anansesem Publications, 1996); "The Early History of West African Highlife Music," *Popular Music* 8, no. 3 (1989): 221–30; "The Ghanaian Concert Party: African Popular Entertainment at the Cross Roads," (PhD diss., State University of New York at Buffalo, 1994). Other useful introductions include Wolfgang Bender, *Sweet Mother: Modern African Music* (Chicago: University of Chicago Press, 1991), 74–117; David Coplan, "Go to My Town, Cape Coast!: The Social History of Ghanaian Music," in *Eight Urban Music Cultures*, ed. Bruno Nettl (Urbana: University of Illinois Press, 1978), 96–114; Ronnie Graham, *Stern's Guide to Contemporary African Music* (London: Zed, 1988). For highlife's musical structure, see John Collins, *African Musical Symbolism in Contemporary Perspective (Roots, Rhythms, and Relativity)*, online at http://www.bapmaf.com/books.html; Robert Sprigge, "The Ghanaian Highlife: Notation and Sources," *Music in Ghana, Record of the Ghana Music Society* 2 (1961): 70–94. For its popularity elsewhere, see Sonny Oti, *Highlife Music in West Africa* (Lagos: Malthouse Press, 2009); Markus Coester, "Localising African Popular Music Transnationally: 'Highlife-Travellers' in Britain in the 1950s and 1960s," *Journal of African Cultural Studies* 20, no. 2 (2008): 133–44.

31. Kwadwo Donkoh, September 16, 2005.

32. For nuanced discussions of world music, see Steven Feld, "Notes on 'World Beat'" and "From Schizophonia to Schismogenesis: On the Discourse and Commodification Practices of 'World Music' and 'World Beat,'" in Charles Keil and Steven Feld, *Music Grooves: Essays and Dialogues* (Chicago: University of Chicago Press, 1994), 238–46 and 257–89; Reebee Garofalo, "Whose World, What Beat: The Transnational Music Industry, Identity, and Cultural Imperialism," *World of Music* 35, no. 2 (1993): 16–32.

33. The first written evidence of the term "highlife" comes from a program for a Grand Ball held by the Cape Coast Literary and Social Club in 1922. There is, however, good reason to believe that the term was in use for years prior to this date: "Clubs," PRAAD-Cape Coast, ADM 23/1/298.

34. For an intimate look into hiplife's history and recent prominence, see Jesse Shipley's excellent film, *Living the Hiplife: Musical Life on the Streets of Accra* (New York: Third World Newsreel, 2007).

35. John Collins, "Ghanaian Highlife," *African Arts* 10, no .1 (1976): 62–68, 100; J. H. Kwabena Nketia, "Modern Trends in Ghana Music," *African Music Society Journal* 1, no. 4 (1957): 13–17.

36. J. H. Kwabena Nketia, "Changing Traditions of Folk Music in Ghana," *Journal of the International Folk Music Council* 11 (1959): 31–36; Daniel Avorgbedor, "The Place of the 'Folk' in Ghanaian Popular Music," *Popular Music and Society* 9, no. 2 (1983): 35–44.

37. Owusu Brempong, "Highlife: An Urban Experience and Folk Tradition," *Journal of Performing Arts* 2, no. 2 (1996): 17–29.

38. Coplan, "Go to My Town, Cape Coast!," 97.

39. Barber, "Popular Arts in Africa," 4 and 17–18.

40. Jerry Hansen, October 3, 2005.

41. Kwadwo Donkoh, September 16, 2005.

42. Ebo Taylor, August 24, 2005; Kwadwo Donkoh, September 16, 2005; Nana Ampadu, September 24, 2005; Jerry Hansen, October 3, 2005.

43. Throughout this book, English in parentheses following a song title is a translation, and English in square brackets following a song title is an explanation of the meaning.

44. Collins, *Highlife Time*, 1–42; Rob Boonzajer Flaes, *Brass Unbound: Secret Children of the Colonial Brass Band* (Amsterdam: Royal Tropical Institute, 2000); Roger Rumbolz, "'A Vessel for Many Things': Brass Bands in Ghana" (PhD diss., Wesleyan University, 2000).

45. Collins, *Highlife Time*, xii–xv; and "The Ghanaian Concert Party," 1–18.

46. For more on the history and character of concert parties, see Catherine M. Cole, *Ghana's Concert Party Theatre* (Bloomington: Indiana University Press, 2001); Kwabena N. Bame, *Come to Laugh: African Traditional Theater in Ghana* (New York: L. Barber Press, 1985).

47. John Collins, "Popular Performance and Culture in Ghana: The Past 50 Years," *Ghana Studies* 10 (2007): 9–64. For a particularly revealing look at how one group of Ghanaian musicians embraced a range of cultural influences and dabbled in a cosmopolitan outlook, see Steven Feld, *Jazz Cosmopolitanism in Accra: Five Musical Years in Ghana* (Durham, N.C.: Duke University Press, 2012).

48. Aside from the many works of John Collins, see Akyeampong, *Drink, Power, and Cultural Change* and "Wo pe tam won pe ba"; Kofi E. Agovi, "The Political Relevance of Ghanaian Highlife Songs since 1957," *Research in African Literatures* 20, no. 2 (1989): 194–201; Sjaak van der Geest, "The Image of Death in Akan Highlife Songs of Ghana," *Research in African Literatures* 11, no. 2 (1980): 145–74; Nimrod Asante-Darko and Sjaak van der Geest, "The Political Meaning of Highlife Songs in Ghana," *African Studies Review* 25, no. 1 (1982): 27–35; Owusu Brempong, "Akan Highlife in Ghana: Songs of Cultural Transition" (PhD diss., Indiana University, 1986).

49. Christopher Waterman, *Jùjú: A Social History and Ethnography of an African Popular Music* (Chicago: University of Chicago Press, 1990), 6.

50. Fair, *Pastimes and Politics*, 9; Askew, *Performing the Nation*; Moorman, *Intonations*; White, *Rumba Rules*; Erlmann, *Nightsong*; Waterman, *Jùjú*; Turino, *Nationalists, Cosmopolitans, and Popular Music*; Moses Chikowero, "'Our People Father, They Haven't Learned Yet': Music and Postcolonial Identities in Zimbabwe, 1980–2000," *Journal of Southern African Studies* 34, no. 1 (2008): 145–60; Mwenda Ntarangwi, *Gender, Identity, and Performance: Understanding Swahili Cultural Realities through Song* (Trenton, N.J.: Africa World Press, 2003).

51. Ray Pratt, *Rhythm and Resistance: Explorations in the Political Uses of Popular Music* (New York: Praeger, 1990), 6; Eric Zolov, *Refried Elvis: The Rise of Mexican Counterculture* (Berkeley: University of California Press, 1999), 10; Pete Daniel, *Lost Revolutions: The South in the 1950s* (Chapel Hill: University of North Carolina Press, 2000): 121–173; Anthony Macias, *Mexican American Mojo: Popular Music, Dance, and Urban Culture in Los Angeles, 1935–1958* (Durham, N.C.: Duke University Press, 2008).

52. Gage Averill, *A Day for the Hunter, A Day for the Prey: Popular Music and Power in Haiti* (Chicago: University of Chicago Press, 1997); Peter Wade, *Music, Race, and Nation: Musica Tropical in Colombia* (Chicago: University of Chicago Press, 2000); Hermano Vianna, *The Mystery of Samba: Popular Music and National Identity in Brazil* (Chapel Hill: University of North Carolina Press, 1999).

53. Moorman, *Intonations*, 108.

54. Brempong, "Akan Highlife in Ghana"; Agovi, "The Political Relevance"; van der Geest, "The Image of Death"; Asante-Darko and van der Geest, "The Political Meaning"; Nimrod Asante-Darko and Sjaak van der Geest, "Male Chauvinism: Men and Women in Ghanaian Highlife Songs," in *Female and Male in West Africa*, ed. Christine Oppong (London: George Allen and Unwin, 1983), 242–55; Kwesi Yankah, "The Akan Highlife Song: A Medium of Cultural Reflection or Deflection?," *Research in African Literatures* 15, no. 4 (1984): 568–82, and "Nana Ampadu, the Sung-Tale Metaphor, and Protest Discourse in Contemporary Ghana," in *African Words, African Voices: Critical Practices in Oral History*, ed. Luise White, Stephan F. Miescher, and David William Cohen (Bloomington: Indiana University Press, 2001), 227–45.

55. Asante-Darko and van der Geest, "The Political Meaning," 34.

56. Yankah, "Nana Ampadu"; Asante-Darko and van der Geest, "The Political Meaning," 32–33; John Collins, "One Hundred Years of Censorship in Ghanaian Popular Performance," in *Popular Music Censorship in Africa*, ed. Michael Drewett and Martin Cloonan (Burlington, Vt.: Ashgate, 2006), 171–86.

57. Agovi, "The Political Relevance"; Jerry Hansen, October 3, 2005.

58. White, *Rumba Rules*, 166.

59. Esi Sylvia Kinney, "Urban West African Music and Dance," *African Urban Notes*, Winter 1970, 3–15; Judith Lynne Hanna, "The Highlife: A West African Urban Dance," in *Dance Research Monograph One: 1971–1972*, ed. Patricia A. Rowe (New York: Committee on Research in Dance, 1973), 139–52.

60. John Collins, October 13, 2005; Kwadwo Adum-Attah, April 1, 2005; Samuel Nyamuame, July 20, 2005; Hanna, "The Highlife," 140–42.

61. Judith Lynne Hanna, *To Dance is Human: A Theory of Nonverbal Communication* (Chicago: University of Chicago Press, 1987), 201–20.

62. Wade, *Music, Race, and Nation*, 22–23. My assertion that men and women could use dance to upset preexisting understandings of gender as well as to outline new ones counters that of Judith Butler, who upholds performative acts to be means of cementing established understandings of masculinity and femininity: Butler, *Gender Trouble: Feminism and the Subversion of Identity* (New York: Routledge, 1990), 152.

63. Martin, "Afterword" in *Fashioning Africa*, 227.

64. Phyllis M. Martin, "Contesting Clothes in Colonial Brazzaville," *Journal of African History* 35, no. 3 (1994): 401–26; White, *Rumba Rules*, 141; Waterman, *Jùjú*, 55–81; Marissa Moorman, "Putting on a Pano and Dressing Like Our Grandparents: Nation and Dress in Late Colonial Luanda," in *Fashioning Africa*, 84–103.

65. Allman, "Let Your Fashion," 158.

66. Stephen Ellis, "Writing Histories of Contemporary Africa," *Journal of African History* 43, no. 1 (2002): 3.

67. This collection is currently available due to the initiative and efforts of Catherine Cole, Lawrence Cudjoe, and Joseph Justice Turton Mensah: see Cole, *Ghana's Concert Party Theatre*, 174.

68. One of the most utilized newspapers for this project, the *Daily Graphic,* was founded and operated as a privately owned newspaper in 1951, eleven years prior to its acquisition by Nkrumah's government in 1962.

69. These endeavors were hampered by a lack of time, the unavailability of desired sources, and other logistical obstacles.

70. Though excellent, most of the images in the Information Services Photo Library had little accompanying information about the subject matter, the date of the photograph, or the photographer who took it. It is also not clear how or why such images were procured. Although the government clearly sponsored their collection, I found only one that was reproduced in a government publication. This impressive collection deserves its own historical inquiry, but it is possible that these images were collected with the intention of preservation rather than the dissemination of official ideas.

71. David William Cohen, Stephan F. Miescher, and Luise White, "Introduction: Voices, Words and African History," in *African Words, African Voices,* 1–27.

72. Of these 110 interviews, 33 were conducted with women (alone, with other women, or with men) and 30 were conducted with popular musicians (two of whom were female). A complete listing of these interviews appears in the bibliography.

73. Tragically, a prominent musician, Oscarmore Ofori, and the manager of a well-known dance band, Kofi Lindsay, passed away just prior to the completion of my research in 2005. In 2009, I returned to Ghana only to find that several of the individuals I had befriended, including Kofi Ghanaba (Guy Warren), Daniel Kinful Sam, Comfort Sarpong, Josephine Ayitey, and Margaret Acolatse, had also died. Sadly, Jerry Hansen passed away as I was putting the final touches on this book.

74. For a perspective that validates such caution, see Yankah, "The Akan Highlife Song," 568–82.

1. Popular Music, Political Authority, and Social Possibilities in the Southern Gold Coast, 1890–1940

1. *"Mantse"* (pl. *"mantsemei"*) translates as "father of the town" or chief. The Ga *mantse* was the leading officeholder in Accra, a city established by the Ga people in the seventeenth century. By the early twentieth century, Accra consisted of several "quarters" (*akutso*), each of which had their own *mantse* who oversaw local affairs. For more on the structure of Ga authority in Accra, see John Parker, *Making the Town: Ga State and Society in Early Colonial Accra* (Portsmouth: Heinemann, 2000), 1–25.

2. "Byelaws made by Ga Manche suppressing certain native dances," PRAAD-Accra, ADM 11/1/316; "Immoral Dances, Byelaws for Suppression of in Accra," PRAAD-Accra, ADM 11/1/884.

3. Parker, *Making the Town,* 1.

4. For more on the need to move beyond this "rebellious" label, see Richard Waller, "Rebellious Youth in Colonial Africa," *Journal of African History* 47, no. 1 (2006): 80–82. It is important to note that there are not, to my knowledge, any existing recordings of many of the proto-highlife musical styles discussed in this chapter, including *adaha, osibisaaba, ashiko,* and *konkoma.* This chapter employs both oral testimony and song lyrics to inform its claims, but it relies primarily on written and archival evidence compiled by urban authorities.

5. Ashanti is the British spelling of Asante. For a comprehensive introduction to Asante's history, see Ivor Wilks, *Asante in the Nineteenth Century: The Structure and Evolu-*

tion of a Political Order (Cambridge: Cambridge University Press, 1975); T. C. McCaskie, *State and Society in Pre-colonial Asante* (Cambridge: Cambridge University Press, 1995).

6. For more on the infrastructure that facilitated these relationships, see Wilks, *Asante in the Nineteenth Century*, 1–79. For a few examples of cultural exchange within the region, see Sandra Greene, *Gender, Ethnicity and Social Change on the Upper Slave Coast: A History of the Anlo-Ewe* (Portsmouth: Heinemann, 1996), 32–43; J. H. Kwabena Nketia, "History and the Organization of Music in West Africa," in *Essays on Music and History in Africa*, ed. Klaus P. Wachsmann (Evanston: Northwestern University Press, 1971), 18–21; and "On the Historicity of Music in African Cultures," *Journal of African Studies* 9, no. 3 (1982): 90–100.

7. Kwame Arhin, "Rank and Class among the Asante and Fante in the Nineteenth Century," *Africa: Journal of the International African Institute* 53, no. 1 (1983): 2–22; McCaskie, *State and Society*, 85–99.

8. Arhin, "Rank and Class," 13–19; Parker, *Ga State and Society*, 18; Greene, *Ethnicity and Social Change*, 24–32.

9. Stephan F. Miescher, *Making Men in Ghana* (Bloomington: Indiana University Press, 2005), 115–52; Jean Allman and Victoria Tashjian, *"I Will Not Eat Stone": A Women's History of Colonial Asante* (Portsmouth: Heinemann, 2000), 45–84; Emmanuel Akyeampong, *Drink, Power and Cultural Change: A Social History of Alcohol in Ghana, c. 1800 to Recent Times* (Portsmouth: Heinemann, 1996), 30–39.

10. Stephan F. Miescher, "Becoming an ɔpanyin: Elders, Gender, and Masculinities in Ghana since the Nineteenth Century," in *Africa after Gender*, ed. Catherine M. Cole, Takyiwaa Manuh, and Stephan F. Miescher (Bloomington: Indiana University Press, 2007), 254–59; Miescher, *Making Men*, 8–11; Kwesi Yankah, *The Proverb in Context of Akan Rhetoric: A Theory of Proverb Praxis* (Bern: Peter Lang, 1989).

11. Arhin, "Rank and Class," 17; Roger Gocking, *Facing Two Ways: Ghana's Coastal Communities under Colonial Rule* (New York: University Press of America, 1999), 23–52. For more on the emergence of a coastal mercantile class, see Raymond E. Dumett, "John Sarbah, the Elder, and African Mercantile Entrepreneurship in the Gold Coast in the Late Nineteenth Century," *Journal of African History* 14, no. 4 (1973): 653–79; and "African Merchants of the Gold Coast, 1860–1905—Dynamics of Indigenous Entrepreneurship," *Comparative Studies in Society and History* 25, no. 4 (1983): 661–93. Roger Gocking also effectively argues that native authorities had lost much of their authority in coastal areas such as Cape Coast by the late nineteenth century, and that individuals with access to wealth and Western education increasingly sought to take part in the operation of the "native state" supported by British indirect rule: see *Facing Two Ways*, 147–76; and "Indirect Rule in the Gold Coast: Competition for Office and the Invention of Tradition," *Canadian Journal of African Studies* 28, no. 3 (1994): 421–46.

12. Akyeampong, *Drink, Power, and Cultural Change*, xvii; McCaskie, *State and Society*, 42–49.

13. Stephan Miescher convincingly demonstrates that Akan societies recognized multiple notions of masculinity in the nineteenth century: adult masculinity signified by marriage, senior masculinity signified by an ɔpanyin, and the previously mentioned ɔbirɛmpɔn: Miescher, *Making Men*, 11.

14. For more on the relationship between gun ownership, warfare, and male status, see McCaskie, *State and Society*, 85; Miescher, *Making Men*, 8–11; Parker, *Making the Town*, 47–53; Akyeampong and Obeng, "Spirituality, Gender, and Power in Asante History."

15. Allman and Tashjian, *"I Will Not Eat Stone,"* 45–84.

16. Akyeampong, *Drink, Power, and Cultural Change*, 21–46; Arhin, "Rank and Class," 7–10; McCaskie, *State and Society*, 42–58.

17. Frank Gunderson, "Kifungua Kinywa, or 'Opening the Contest with Chai,'" in *Mashindino!: Competitive Music Performance in East Africa*, ed. Frank Gunderson and Gregory Barz (Dar es Salaam: Mkuku na Nyota Publishers, 2000), 15; J. H. Kwabena Nketia, *African Music in Ghana* (Evanston, Ill.: Northwestern University Press, 1963), 4–10.

18. See several publications by J. H. Kwabena Nketia, including *Drumming in Akan Communities of Ghana* (London: Thomas Nelson and Sons, 1963), 119–51; *African Music of Ghana*, 10–21; "History and the Organization of Music in West Africa," 17; "Changing Traditions in Folk Music in Ghana," *Journal of the International Folk Music Council* 11 (1959): 31–36.

19. Nketia, *African Music*, 12–19; John Miller Chernoff, *African Rhythm and African Sensibility: Aesthetics and Social Action in African Musical Idioms* (Chicago: University of Chicago Press, 1979), 153–72; Kwesi Ampene, *Female Song Tradition and the Akan of Ghana: The Creative Process of Nnwonkorɔ* (Burlington, Vt.: Ashgate, 2005).

20. John Collins, "The Generational Factor in Ghanaian Music," in *Playing with Identities in Contemporary Music in Africa*, ed. Mai Palmberg and Annemette Kirkegaard (Uppsala: Nordiska Afrikainstitutet, 2002), 60–74; Nketia, *Drumming in Akan Communities*, 67–68.

21. Roger Gocking, *History of Ghana* (Westport: Greenwood Press, 2005), 46–47.

22. In 1918, 1,823 Europeans lived in the Gold Coast colony, but only 515 of these were affiliated with the colonial government. By 1931, only 3,182 "Non-Africans" (a category that also included many non-Europeans) lived in the Gold Coast. In 1948 this population had more than doubled to 6,770, but Europeans remained a vast minority as the colony's total population was 4,118,450 persons: Gold Coast, *The Gold Coast Census of Population, 1948: Report and Tables* (Accra: Government Printing Office, 1950). For more on the conditions of the colonial service in the Gold Coast, see Allister MacMillan, *The Red Book of West Africa: Historical and Descriptive, Commercial and Industrial Fact, Figures and Resources* (London: F. Cass, 1920), 165; Henrika Kuklick, *The Imperial Bureaucrat: The Colonial Administrative Service in the Gold Coast, 1920–1939* (Stanford, Calif.: Hoover Institution Press, 1978); A. H. M. Kirk-Greene, "The Thin White Line: The Size of the British Colonial Service in Africa," *African Affairs* 79 (1980): 25–44.

23. Parker, *Making the Town*, 116–53; David Kimble, *A Political History of Ghana: The Rise of Gold Coast Nationalism, 1850–1928* (Oxford: Clarendon Press, 1963), 304–306 and 460–61.

24. Phyllis Martin, *Leisure and Society in Colonial Brazzaville* (Cambridge: Cambridge University Press, 1995), 173.

25. Terence Ranger, *Dance and Society in Eastern Africa, 1890–1970: The Beni Ngoma* (Berkeley: University of California Press, 1975), 13. For more on the history of these ensembles in the Gold Coast/Ghana, see John Collins, "The Ghanaian Concert Party: African Popular Entertainment at the Cross Roads," (PhD diss., State University of New York at Buffalo, 1994), 233; Rob Boonzajer Flaes, *Brass Unbound: Secret Children of the Colonial Brass Band* (Amsterdam: Royal Tropical Institute, 2000), 9–21 and 32–57; Rumbolz, "'A Vessel for Many Things,'" 40–45 and 49–64.

26. "Holidays and Celebrations," PRAAD-Kumasi, ARG 7/1/1; "Empire Day Celebrations," PRAAD-Kumasi, ARG 6/1/4; "Public functions attended by the Governor,"

PRAAD-Accra, ADM 11/1/1430; "Empire Day, 1934–49," PRAAD-Sekondi, WRG 15/1/149. For a recollection of such events, see Thomas Kyei, *Our Days Dwindle: Memories of My Childhood Days in Asante* (Portsmouth: Heinemann, 2001), 106–10.

27. "Public Functions Attended by the Governor, 1923," PRAAD-Accra, ADM 11/1430/47; "Empire Day," PRAAD-Cape Coast, ADM 23/1/665; "Central Club, Sekondi," PRAAD-Accra, CSO 25/1/71; "Income Tax: Sir F. Guggisberg," PRO, CO 923/956/9.

28. The pioneering work on the importance of these "invented traditions" in colonial Africa is Terence Ranger, "The Invention of Tradition in Colonial Africa," in *The Invention of Tradition,* ed. Eric Hobsbawm and Terence Ranger (New York: Cambridge University Press, 1983), 211–62. For more on their application and impacts in the Gold Coast, see Gocking, *Facing Two Ways,* 14–15.

29. Ranger, "The Invention of Tradition," 215–20; Robert Morrell, "Of Boys and Men: Masculinity and Gender in Southern African Studies," *Journal of Southern African Studies* 24, no. 4 (1998): 616–17. For more on the European efforts to cement new hierarchies based on these three axes in various colonial contexts, see Ann Laura Stoler, *Carnal Knowledge and Imperial Rule: Race and the Intimate in Colonial Rule* (Berkeley: University of California Press, 2002); Anne McClintock, *Imperial Leather: Race, Gender, and Sexuality in the Colonial Contest* (London: Routledge, 1995); Mrinalini Sinha, *Colonial Masculinity: The "Manly Englishman" and "Effeminate Bengali" in the Late Nineteenth Century* (Manchester: Manchester University Press, 1995).

30. "Central Club, Sekondi," PRAAD-Sekondi, CSO 25/1/71; "Gold Coast Dinner Club," PRAAD-Accra, CSO 25/1/41; "Accra Club," PRAAD-Accra, CSO 25/1/13; "Kumasi European Club," PRAAD-Kumasi, ARG 1/10/42–45; "Hill Club, Cape Coast," PRAAD-Cape Coast, ADM 23/1/840. For a critique of the Accra Club's policy, see Henry Ofori, "You'll See Me at the Club," *Daily Graphic,* June 9, 1955.

31. Heather J. Sharkey, *Living with Colonialism: Nationalism and Culture in the Anglo-Egyptian Sudan* (Berkeley: California University Press, 2003), 138. The literature on popular culture in Africa is quite large, but two critical, if somewhat dated, starting points are Karin Barber, "Popular Arts in Africa," *African Studies Review* 30, no. 3 (1987): 1–78, 104–11; and the various chapters in Karin Barber, ed., *Readings in African Popular Culture* (Bloomington: Indiana University Press, 1997).

32. Cocoa's large historiography is too expansive to engage here, but for a few important works on its impacts on Gold Coast communities see Polly Hill, *Migrant Cocoa-Famers of Southern Ghana: A Study in Rural Capitalism* (Cambridge: Cambridge University Press, 1963), especially 170–76; Gwendolyn Mikell, *Cocoa and Chaos in Ghana* (New York: Paragon House, 1989); Allman and Tashjian, *I Will Not Eat Stone.*

33. For more on the expansion of various trades within the Gold Coast, see MacMillan, *The Red Book of West Africa,* 160–64; Kimble, *A Political History of Ghana,* 40–60; Raymond Dumett, *El Dorado in West Africa: The Gold Mining Frontier, African Labor, and Colonial Capitalism in the Gold Coast, 1875–1900* (Athens: Ohio University Press, 1998).

34. For more on the history of colonial Accra, see Parker, *Making the Town;* S. S. Quarcoopome, "A History of the Urban Development of Accra: 1877–1957," *University of Ghana Research Review* 9, nos. 1 & 2 (1993): 20–32; Frederick A. Abloh, "Growth of Towns in Ghana: A Study of the Social and Physical Growth of Selected Towns in Ghana" (PhD diss., University of Science and Technology, Kumasi, Ghana, 1967); Jean Rouch, "Notes on Migrations into the Gold Coast—First Report of the Mission Carried out in the Gold Coast from March to December, 1954" (unpublished paper in author's possession, n.d.).

35. Ioné Acquah, *Accra Survey: A Social Survey of the Capital of Ghana, Formerly Called the Gold Coast, Undertaken for the West African Institute of Social and Economic Research, 1953–1956* (London: University of London Press, 1958), 31; K. A. Busia, *Report on a Social Survey of Sekondi-Takoradi* (London: Hazell, Watson and Viney, 1950); *Gold Coast, Appendices: Containing Comparative Returns and General Statistics of the 1931 Census* (Accra: Government Printer, 1932), 6. Male-female ratios varied from town to town. Though fairly balanced in Accra and Kumasi, men outnumbered women by five to one in Takoradi, Tarkwa, and Obuasi: Emmanuel Akyeampong, "Wo pe tam won pe ba (You like cloth but you don't want children): Urbanization, Individualism and Gender Relations in Colonial Ghana, 1900–1939," in *Africa's Urban Past*, 222–34.

36. In many urban areas, occupation became an important means of establishing urban gendered relations; see Acquah, *Accra Survey*, 63–91; Frederick Cooper, "Industrial Man Goes to Africa," in *Men and Masculinities in Modern Africa*, ed. Lisa A. Lindsay and Stephan F. Miescher (Portsmouth: Heinemann, 2003), 128–37; Claire C. Robertson, *Sharing the Same Bowl: A Socioeconomic History of Women and Class in Accra, Ghana* (Ann Arbor: University of Michigan Press, 1984); Miescher, *Making Men*, 84–114.

37. "Daily Rates of Pay for Artisans and Labourers, Accra, 1920," PRAAD-Accra, ADM 11/1/778; David Killingray, "Repercussions of World War I in the Gold Coast," *Journal of African History* 19, no. 1 (1978): 53.

38. Kwadwo Adum-Attah, April 1, 2005.

39. T. C. McCaskie, *Asante Identities: History and Modernity in an African Village, 1850–1950* (Bloomington: Indiana University Press, 2000), 75. While the expansion of the colonial cash economy expanded trade and other activities to individuals outside the mechanism of the state, Gareth Austin has effectively demonstrated that ordinary men and women consumed and exchanged commodities in Ashanti prior to the twentieth century: "'No Elders Were Present': Commoners and Private Ownership in Asante, 1807–96," *Journal of African History* 37, no. 1 (1996): 1–30. For more on the impact of cash in Asante communities, see Kwame Arhin, "Monetization and the Asante State," in *Money Matters: Instability, Values and Social Payments in the Modern History of West African Communities*, ed. Jane Guyer (Portsmouth: Heinemann, 1995), 97–110; and "The Pressures of Cash and Its Political Consequences in Asante in the Colonial Period," *Journal of African Studies* 3, no. 4 (1976): 453–68.

40. Akyeampong, *Drink, Power, and Cultural Change*, 58–67, 101–109, and 112–15; Philip Bartle, "African Rural Urban Migration: A Decision-Making Perspective" (MA thesis, University of British Columbia, 1971); Jean Allman, "Rounding up Spinsters: Unmarried Women and Gender Chaos in Colonial Asante," *Journal of African History* 37, no. 2 (1996): 195–214. Also see Waller, "Rebellious Youth," 80–82; Andrew Burton and Hélène Charton-Bigot ed., *Generations Past: Youth in East African History* (Athens: Ohio University Press, 2010).

41. John Collins, October 5, 2005. In the 1840s, John Beecham reported the presence of a "native band" that performed popular European tunes in the Cape Coast Castle: *Ashantee and the Gold Coast* (London: Dawsons of Pall Mall, 1968 [1841]), 168. Charles Alexander Gordon, who visited the Gold Coast 1847–48, confirmed Beecham's observation and noted that dances such as quadrilles and polkas were frequent entertainments at dinner parties within the Castle, where music was provided by either "a drummer and fifer of the West Indian Regiment in the Castle" or the "band of the Gold Coast militia": *Life on the Gold Coast* (London: Bailliere, Tindall and Coe, 1874), 76.

42. For more on the influence of British military music see Rumbolz, "A Vessel for Many Things," 53–55; Kofi Agawu, *Representing African Music: Postcolonial Notes, Queries, Positions* (London: Routledge, 2003), 5–10.

43. For more on the history of *asafo* companies in coastal areas, see Ansu Datta and R. Porter, "The Asafo System in Historical Perspective," *Journal of African History* 12, no. 2 (1971): 279–97.

44. J. C. De Graft Johnson, "The Fanti Asafu," *Africa: Journal of the International African Institute* 5, no. 3 (1932): 309–10. Also see Collins, "The Ghanaian Concert Party," 1994; Flaes, *Brass Unbound*, 35.

45. Kwadwo Donkoh, September 16, 2005; John Collins, October 5, 2005; Flaes, *Brass Unbound*, 37. One should, however, note that Roger Rumbolz's informants at Agona Kwanyako claimed that local brass bands "preceded colonial rule": "A Vessel for Many Things," 61.

46. John Collins, October 5, 2005; Rumbolz, "A Vessel for Many Things," 60; Kyei, *Our Days Dwindle*, 38. For more on *beni ngoma*, see Ranger, *Dance and Society*; Stephen H. Martin, "Brass Bands and the Beni Phenomenon in Urban East Africa," *African Music* 7, no. 1 (1991): 72–81.

47. A. Turkson, "Effutu Asafo: Its Organization and Music," *Journal of International Library of African Music* 6, no. 2 (1982): 10. For more on *asafo* music, see Nketia, *Drumming in Akan Communities of Ghana*, 103–18.

48. John Collins, October 5, 2005; Jerry Hansen, October 13, 2005.

49. Collins, "The Ghanaian Concert Party," 240–41; Flaes, *Brass Unbound*, 39.

50. Gocking, "Indirect Rule in Cape Coast," 428; John Collins, October 5, 2005; "Clubs," PRAAD-Cape Coast, ADM 23/1/298.

51. John Collins, "The Early History of West African Highlife Music," *Popular Music* 8, no. 3 (1989): 221–30.

52. Elizabeth Amonoo, June 20, 2009; James Matthew Thompson, June 23, 2009; "Suppression of Patsintering, Ankademmu and Odo Dances," PRAAD-Accra, ADM 11/1/1506.

53. For more on the emergence of a seven-day work/rest rhythm that demarcated clear time for leisure and recreation in the Gold Coast and elsewhere, see Miescher, *Making Men*, 44–45; Keletso Atkins, *The Moon Is Dead! Give Us Our Money!: The Cultural Origins of an African Work Ethic, Natal, South Africa, 1843–1900* (Portsmouth: Heinemann, 1993), 86–99; Martin, *Leisure and Society*, 71–98.

54. John Collins, October 5, 2005; "Suppression of Patsintering, Ankademmu and Odo Dances," PRAAD-Accra, ADM 11/1/1506.

55. Jerry Hansen, October 13, 2005, and July 21, 2009; Miescher, *Making Men*, 43–45; John Collins, *Highlife Time* (Accra: Anansesem Publications, 1996), xii–xiii.

56. F. Cobbina, "Konkoma Music and Dance" (Diploma paper in Dance, University of Ghana, n.d.), 26.

57. Collins, "The Ghanaian Concert Party," 257–60; Rumbolz, "A Vessel for Many Things," 63.

58. Cobbina, "Konkoma Music," 48–50.

59. Ibid., 6, 17, and 21–22; Akyeampong, *Drink, Power and Cultural Change*, 47–69.

60. Cobbina, "Konkoma Music," 26, 52–53, and 62. For a comparable example in the Congo, see Ch. Didier Gondola, "Popular Music, Urban Society, and Changing Gender Relations in Kinshasa, Zaire (1950–1990)," in *Gendered Encounters: Challenging Cultural*

Boundaries and Social Hierarchies in Africa, ed. Maria Grosz-Ngate and Omari H. Kokole (New York: Routledge Press, 1997), 65–84.

61. Kwadwo Adum-Attah, April 1, 2005; Elizabeth Amonoo, October 18, 2005; Miescher, *Making Men,* 122–24.

62. Cobbina, "Konkoma Music," 46; Kyei. *Our Days Dwindle,* 140–41.

63. Elizabeth Amonoo, June 21, 2009; Collins, *Highlife Time,* 7–11; Akyeampong, "Wo pe tam won pe ba," 227–30.

64. Cobbina, "Konkoma Music," 21–22 and 46. For more on the use of scandal in competitive music performance, see Gunderson, "Kifungwa Kinywa," 12–13.

65. *"Abrentsie"* is a derivation of *"aberantɛɛ."* The song's usage of the term, however, is one that accords these self-proclaimed *"abrentsie"* rights beyond those sanctioned by the community at large. For more on the distinctions between the *aberantɛɛ* and *ɔpanyin,* see Miescher, "Becoming an *ɔpanyin,*"254–59; Sjaak van der Geest, "ɔpanyin: The Ideal of Elder in Akan Culture of Ghana," *Canadian Journal of African Studies* 32, no. 3 (1998): 449–93.

66. Kwadwo Adum-Attah, April 1, 2005. Young men claimed a similar status in South Africa: see Mac Fenwick, "'Tough Guy, Eh?': The Gangster Figure in Drum," *Journal of Southern African Studies* 22, no. 4 (1996): 617–32; Clive Glaser, "Swines, Hazels and the Dirty Dozen: Masculinity, Territoriality and the Youth Gangs of Soweto, 1960–1976," *Journal of Southern African Studies* 24, no. 4 (1998): 719–36.

67. For more on female strategies of empowerment in the colonial Gold Coast, see Robertson, *Sharing the Same Bowl;* Allman and Tashjian, *"I Will Not Eat Stone";* Emmanuel Akyeampong, "Sexuality and Prostitution among the Akan of the Gold Coast c. 1650–1950," *Past and Present* 15, no. 6 (1997): 144–73; and "Wo pe tam, won pe ba," 222–34.

68. Rumbolz, "A Vessel for Many Things," 49–63.

69. Flaes, *Brass Unbound,* 42.

70. Wesleyan Methodist Missionary Society (WMMS) Archive, SOAS, London, West Africa Synod Minutes Box 248, Synod Minutes from 1937, No. 494, Minutes of the Social Welfare Committee; WMMS, West Africa Synod Minutes Box 253, Synod Minutes Gold Coast 1942, No. 507 Minutes and Recommendations of the Social Welfare Committee, 1942.

71. Many missionaries passed this quandary onto local converts: Miescher, *Making Men,* 64–71.

72. Collins, "One Hundred Years of Censorship in Ghanaian Popular Performance," 171–75; Flaes, *Brass Unbound,* 42.

73. Collins, "One Hundred Years," 171–75; Miescher, *Making Men,* 123.

74. "Obnoxious Customs," PRAAD-Accra, ADM 11/1/64.

75. Miescher, *Making Men,* 123. Similar efforts to legislate popular musical performance continued into the 1930s, when the district commissioner of the Volta Region also oversaw a series of legal proceedings accusing the Alavanyo brass band of corrupting the town's young men and women: Flaes, *Brass Unbound,* 43.

76. "District Magistrate's Court (Nsawam), 1909–1911, Police vs. Kwamini Antwi and Oblamawuo," PRAAD-Accra, SCT 38/5/1. Also cited in Akyeampong, *Drink, Power, and Cultural Change,* 61.

77. Rumbolz, "A Vessel for Many Things," 65–66.

78. "Suppression of Patsintering, Ankademmu, and Odo Dances," PRAAD-Accra, ADM 11/1/1506.

79. "Assistance to Native Chiefs for the Suppression of Objectionable Customs," PRAAD-Accra, ADM 11/1/279.

80. "Native Ceremonies in Connection with the Death of his Majesty King Edward VII," PRAAD-Accra, ADM 11/1/235.

81. K. A. Busia, *The Position of the Chief in the Modern Political System of Ashanti* (London: Oxford University Press, 1951), 104–10; "Asafo," PRAAD-Accra, ADM 11/1/378; Parker, *Making the Town*, 210.

82. Obili himself was all too aware of growing unrest, as he was destooled in 1918 amidst popular demand: Parker, *Making the Town*, 210–13.

83. "Assistance of Native Chiefs for Suppression of Objectionable Customs," PRAAD-Accra, ADM 11/1/279.

84. Gocking, *Facing Two Ways*, 104. For more on the legal codification of "tradition" and "customary law," see Kristin Mann and R. Roberts, eds., *Law in Colonial Africa* (London: James Currey, 1991); Martin Chanock, *Law, Custom and Social Order* (Cambridge: Cambridge University Press, 1985).

85. "Letter from Ga Mantse to Accra Chief of Police, 9 June 1924," PRAAD-Accra, ADM 11/1/884.

86. "Immoral Dances, Byelaws for the Suppression of in Accra," PRAAD-Accra, ADM 11/1/884. For similar concerns about the youthful consumption of alcohol in Mampong, see "Gold Coast Despatches, 1919," PRO, CO 96/601/45430.

87. Parker, *Making the Town*, 210–14.

88. "Winneba Native Affairs," PRAAD-Cape Coast, ADM 23/1/675.

89. "Enquiry at Bekwai into charges brought against Kwame Pokoo by elders," PRAAD-Accra, ADM 11/1/773; Akyeampong, *Drink, Power, and Cultural Change*, 62.

90. "Riot between Leggu and Tantum," PRAAD-Cape Coast, ADM/23/1/377.

91. Ibid.

92. "Assistance to Native Chiefs for the suppression of objectionable customs," PRAAD-Accra, ADM 11/1/279; "Immoral Dances, Byelaws for Suppression of in Accra," PRAAD-Accra, ADM 11/1/884; "Cape Coast and Sekondi Disturbances of 1931," PRAAD-Accra, ADM 11/1/1724.

93. "Permits for Street Processions, 1923," PRAAD-Accra, ADM 11/1/924.

94. These permits continued up to independence in 1957: "Passes, Bonds, etc. for Native Drumming (Saltpond Area)," PRAAD-Cape Coast, ADM 23/1/1653; "Asafo Companies and Drumming Permit," PRAAD-Cape Coast, RG 1/3/33; Letter to the editor, *Gold Coast Times*, June 22, 1929.

95. "Censoring of Gramophone Records, 1930," PRAAD-Accra, CSO 15/8/2. The records in question were Zonophone E.Z 1025, Numbers 2-44305 and 2-44306 respectively.

96. "Letter from Office of the Colonial Secretary to Commissioner of the Central Province, Cape Coast, 9th April, 1930," PRAAD-Accra, CSO 15/8/2.

97. "The company system in the Gold Coast with special reference to the faction fight at Appam in 1930," PRAAD-Accra, ADM 11/1/1439; "Riot at Cape Coast," *West Africa Times*, April 21, 1931.

98. Peter Manuh, July 23, 2005. For similar statements, see Isaac Amuah, March 30, 2005; Bob Biney, April 1, 2005; Stan Plange, June 29, 2005. Importantly, these attitudes

were not unique to the Gold Coast as parents in other African contexts issued similar restrictions within their households: Collins, "The Ghanaian Concert Party," 400–401; David Coplan, "The Urbanisation of African Music: Some Theoretical Observations," *Popular Music* 2 (1982): 120–21.

99. Kofi Lindsay, March 31, 2005. Jacob Sam was one of Ghana's pioneer guitarists and was a founding member of the "Kumasi Trio," which was one of the first guitar bands to record with London's Zonophone label and received widespread acclaim for their pioneering hit *"Yaa Amponsah"* [a woman's name]: Collins, *Highlife Time*, 7, and "The Ghanaian Concert Party," 11.

100. Comfort Sarpong, September 9, 2005; Emmanuel Quao, June 23, 2005; Stan Plange, June 29, 2005; Kwadwo Donkoh, September 16, 2005; C. K. Mann, September 19, 2005. For more on concerns about this gendered chaos, see Allman, "Rounding up Spinsters," 195–214.

2. The Making of a Middle Class

1. "Clubs," PRAAD-Cape Coast, ADM 23/1/298/12.

2. "Clubs," PRAAD-Cape Coast, ADM 23/1/298/11–17.

3. Benjamin N. Lawrance, Emily Lynn Osborn, and Richard L. Roberts, "Introduction," in *Intermediaries, Interpreters, and Clerks: African Employees in the Making of Colonial Africa,* ed. Benjamin N. Lawrance, Emily Lynn Osborn, and Richard L. Roberts (Madison: University of Wisconsin Press, 2006), 23–26. According to Gwendolyn Mikell, during the first few decades of the twentieth century, "educated members of an *abusua* were sometimes resented by their own families": *Cocoa and Chaos in Ghana* (New York: Paragon House, 1989), 66. For more on these men, see Stephan F. Miescher, *Making Men in Ghana* (Bloomington: Indiana University Press, 2005), 64–71, 77–82.

4. Allister MacMillian, *The Red Book of West Africa: Historical and Descriptive, Commercial and Industrial Fact, Figures and Resources* (London: F. Cass, 1920), 169.

5. Throughout the duration of this chapter, I use the term "middle class" to refer to these men's socioeconomic status, shared consciousness, and intermediary position in colonial society. In other words, I use it in ways similar to a number of scholars who have embraced the terms "middle" or "intermediary" in reference to more than economic status. For more on these terms, as well as the actions and importance of such communities in various African contexts, see Lawrance et al., *Intermediaries, Interpreters, and Clerks;* Derek Peterson, *Creative Writing: Translation, Bookkeeping, and the Work of Imagination in Colonial Kenya* (Portsmouth: Heinemann, 2004); Nancy Rose Hunt, *A Colonial Lexicon of Birth Ritual, Medicalization, and Mobility in the Congo* (Durham, N.C.: Duke University Press, 1999); Michael O. West, *The Rise of an African Middle Class: Colonial Zimbabwe, 1898–1965* (Bloomington: Indiana University Press, 2002); Carol Summers, *Colonial Lessons: Africans' Education in Southern Rhodesia, 1918–1940* (Portsmouth: Heinemann, 2002); Thomas Turino, *Nationalists, Cosmopolitans, and Popular Music in Zimbabwe* (Chicago: University of Chicago Press, 2000), 119–57.

6. Philip Foster, *Education and Social Change in Ghana* (Chicago: University of Chicago Press, 1965), 50; F. Kumi Dwamena, "Missionary Education and Leadership Training at Presbyterian Training College, Akropong: An Historical Study of Presbyterian Mission Educational Activities in Ghana, 1848–1960" (PhD diss., Columbia University,

1982); C. K. Graham, *The History of Education in Ghana: From the Earliest Times to the Declaration of Independence* (Accra: Ghana Publishing Corporation, 1976), 13–18; Miescher, *Making Men*, 48–83.

7. Foster, *Education and Social Change*, 57–63; Miescher, *Making Men*, 1–16. For more on the formation and operation of the Aborigines' Rights Protection Society, see David Kimble, *A Political History of Ghana: The Rise of Gold Coast Nationalism, 1850–1928* (Oxford: Clarendon Press, 1963), 330–57.

8. Kimble, *A Political History of Ghana*, 72–78 and 120; Foster, *Education and Social Change in Ghana*, 80–86; Graham, *The History of Education in Ghana*, 35–40. The government's consolidation of education in the Gold Coast began during World War I, when it ousted Basel missionaries and took control over their schools. In the process, the government came to oversee the education of a large percentage of the colony's African students—from 8% in 1914 to 60% in 1919: David Killingray, "Repercussions of World War I in the Gold Coast," *Journal of African History* 19, no. 1 (1978): 43. For a detailed description of the isolation male students experienced in 1920s Kwawu, see Miescher, *Making Men*, 56–72.

9. C. C. Reindorf, *The History of the Gold Coast* (Basel: Missionsbuchhandlung, 1895), 229; Miescher, *Making Men*, 85.

10. Miescher, *Making Men*, 85; Kimble, *A Political History of Ghana*, 41–45; Richard Jeffries, *Class, Power and Ideology in Ghana: The Railwaymen of Sekondi* (Cambridge: Cambridge University Press, 1978), 13.

11. Kimble, *A Political History of Ghana*, 62; Miescher, *Making Men*, 87 and 111; Audrey Gadzekpo, "Public but Private: A Transformational Reading of the Memoirs and Newspaper Writings of Mercy Ffoulkes-Crabbe," in *Africa's Hidden Histories: Everyday Literacy and Making the Self*, ed. Karin Barber (Bloomington: Indiana University Press, 2006), 316–17.

12. "An African Middle Class," *Crown Colonist* 9 (1939): 448–49.

13. Kimble, *A Political History of Ghana*, 134. In Ashanti, these material markers were also adopted by an illiterate "intermediary" group of successful merchants, known as the *akonkofo*. According to Kwame Arhin, the *akonkofo* were retailers who had spent time in southern towns before moving back to Ashanti after the exile of Prempeh I. In addition to adopting distinct styles of dress and material consumption, the *akonkofo* saw themselves as leading a "civilized" lifestyle, though few had received any type of missionary or colonial schooling: "A Note on the Asante Akonkofo: A Non-Literate Sub-Elite, 1900–1930," *Africa: Journal of the International African Institute* 56, no. 1 (1986): 25–31; Akyeampong, *Drink, Power, and Cultural Change*, 55–58.

14. Kimble, *A Political History of Ghana*, 140; Major G. St. J. Orde Browne, O.B.E, "Labor Conditions in West Africa: A Report Presented by the Secretary of State for the Colonies to Parliament by Command of his Majesty, May 1941" (London: His Majesty's Stationary Office, 1941), 22–24; Isaac Amuah, March 31, 2005.

15. Kofi Lindsay, March 30, 2005; Miescher, *Making Men*, 84–114; Gadzekpo, "Public but Private," 316.

16. Kwa Hagan, "The Literary and Social Clubs of the Past: Their Role in National Awakening in Ghana," *ɔkyeame* 4, no. 2 (1969): 81; Catherine M. Cole, *Ghana's Concert Party Theatre* (Bloomington: Indiana University Press, 2001), 66; Stephanie Newell, *Literary Culture in Colonial Ghana: How to Play the Game of Life* (Bloomington: Indiana University Press, 2002), 29.

17. Hagan, "The Literary and Social Clubs of the Past," 81–82; Kimble, *A Political History of Ghana*, 90–98 and 146–47; Augustus Casely-Hayford and Richard Rathbone, "Politics, Families, and Freemasonry in the Colonial Gold Coast," in *People and Empires in African History: Essays in Memory of Michael Crowder*, ed. J. F. Ade Ajayi and J. D. Y. Peel (London: Longman, 1992), 147–51.

18. Newell, *Literary Culture*, 39; Hagan, "The Literary and Social Clubs of the Past," 84. For a more exhaustive list of these clubs, see Newell, *Literary Culture*, 33–35.

19. "Optimism Club, 1926," PRAAD-Sekondi, WRG 44/1/2. One Mr. Isaac Abrahams, who was denied membership in the Optimism Club, claimed that his rejection had resulted in a number of "unfavorable results" on his good name: "Receiver, 1933," PRAAD-Sekondi, WRG 44/1/15.

20. For works that frame clubs as conduits of "European culture," see Kimble, *A Political History of Ghana*, 133 and 148; Foster, *Education and Social Change*, 69. For the latter, see K. A. Busia, *Report on a Social Survey of Sekondi-Takoradi* (London: Hazell, Watson and Viney, 1950), 77–83; Ioné Acquah, *Accra Survey: A Social Survey of the Capital of Ghana, Formerly Called the Gold Coast, Undertaken for the West African Institute of Social and Economic Research, 1953–1956* (London: University of London Press, 1958), 153–63; Gold Coast Government, "Report on Enquiry with Regard to Friendly and Mutual Benefit Groups in the Gold Coast" (Accra: Government Printer, 1955).

21. Newell, *Literary Culture*, 3–8 and 42–46; Miescher, *Making Men in Ghana*, 84–85.

22. The Optimism Club explicitly encouraged its members to set aside "petty jealousies and misunderstandings" in order to promote their common interest: "Literary Work, Lectures, Addresses, Essays to Members," PRAAD-Sekondi, WRG 44/1/24. While clubs worked toward shared interests, their lack of historical writing makes them somewhat different from other African figures who engaged in acts of written composition: Derek Peterson and Giacomo Macola, eds., *Recasting the Past: History Writing and Political Work in Modern Africa* (Athens: Ohio University Press, 2009). Although such clubs overwhelmingly excluded women from their membership ranks, there are examples of Gold Coast women forming their own social clubs: Newell, *Literary Culture*, 32.

23. Karin Barber, ed., *Africa's Hidden Histories: Everyday Literacy and the Making of the Self* (Bloomington: Indiana University Press, 2006). This chapter makes extensive use of club records, particularly those of the Sekondi Optimism Club available at PRAAD-Sekondi and catalogued under the WRG 44/1/ prefix.

24. "Syllabus for Sekondi Literary and Social Club, July-December 1924," PRAAD-Sekondi, WRG 24/1246; "Clubs," PRAAD-Cape Coast, ADM 23/1/298/108. For more on Coker, see Roger Gocking, *Facing Two Ways: Ghana's Coastal Communities under Colonial Rule* (New York: University Press of America, 1999), 67–69.

25. "Despatcher, 1933–34," PRAAD-Sekondi, WRG 44/1/14; "Letters Received, 1934," PRAAD-Sekondi, WRG 44/1/17; "African Clubs," PRAAD-Sekondi, WRG 24/1/246/40 and 94. For more on the club's wall, see Akyeampong, *Drink, Power, and Cultural Change*, 58.

26. "Letters, 1925," PRAAD-Sekondi, WRG 44/1/1; "Literary Work, Lectures, Addresses, Essays by Members," PRAAD-Sekondi, WRG 44/1/24.

27. "Clubs," PRAAD-Cape Coast, ADM 23/1/298/22, 32, and 40.

28. "Clubs," PRAAD-Cape Coast, ADM 23/1/298/60, 64, and 88.

29. Turino, *Nationalists, Cosmopolitans, and Popular Music*, 8–9 and 146–48.

30. Elizabeth Amonoo, October 18, 2005; John Iliffe, *Honour in African History* (Cambridge: Cambridge University Press, 2005), 261–62 and 298–99.

31. "The First Orchestra Seen in Ghana," *Sunday Mirror,* February 15, 1959; "Letters, 1925," PRAAD-Sekondi, WRG 44/1/1.

32. John Collins, *Highlife Time* (Accra: Anansesem Publications, 1996), xiii; Atta Mensah, "Highlife" (Unpublished paper, BAPMAF Archives, 1969/70), 1.

33. During the 1920s–1930s, Lagos had a number of African dance ensembles, like the Lagos City Orchestra and the Triumph Club Dance Orchestra, that played ballroom, light classical, and "imported stock dance music arrangements." These dance orchestras, however, did not incorporate local musical elements into their repertoire. In fact, such synthesis occurred only after Ghanaian dance orchestras visited Lagos, which spurred Nigerian dance bands to play highlife and experiment with local musical sensibilities: John Collins, October 13, 2005. Also see Christopher Waterman: *Jùjú: A Social History and Ethnography of an African Popular Music* (Chicago: Chicago University Press, 1990), 43–44. For similar musical events in Sierra Leone, see Naomi Ware, "Popular Music and African Identity in Freetown, Sierra Leone" in *Eight Urban Musical Cultures: Tradition and Change,* ed. Bruno Nettl (Urbana: University of Illinois, 1978), 299–300; Abner Cohen, *The Politics of Elite Culture: Explorations in the Dramaturgy of Power in a Modern African Society* (Berkeley: University of California Press, 1981), 23–29.

34. Kwadwo Donkoh, September 16, 2005; Jerry Hansen, October 3, 2005; Robert Sprigge, "The Ghanaian Highlife: Notation and Sources," *Music in Ghana* 2 (1961): 70–94; Judith Lynn Hanna, "The Highlife: A West African Urban Dance," in *Dance Research Monograph One: 1971–1972,* ed. Patricia A. Rowe (New York: Committee on Research in Dance, 1973), 147–51.

35. Kwadwo Donkoh, September 16, 2005. For a similar account, see John Collins, *E. T. Mensah: King of Highlife* (Accra: Anansesem Publications, 1996), 2.

36. John Collins, October 5, 2005.

37. "Clubs," PRAAD-Cape Coast, ADM 23/1/298. While highlife likely emerged prior to the early 1920s, this dance program is the first written record of its existence under that name in the Gold Coast or elsewhere; John Collins, October 5, 2005.

38. "Programme of the Cape Coast Literary and Social Club 11th Anniversary Celebration; 1914–1925," PRAAD-Cape Coast, ADM 23/1/298/90 and 92.

39. "Clubs," PRAAD-Cape Coast, ADM 23/1/298; Kimble, *A Political History of Ghana,* 134; Miescher, *Making Men,* 90; Lawrance et al., "Introduction," 4; Turino, *Nationalists, Cosmopolitans,* 9.

40. "Tarkwa District Administration, African Clubs, Games, Sports, Bands, Pastimes," PRAAD-Sekondi, WRG 15/1/399/60 and 262. For one such complaint regarding the behavior of members of the Optimism Club Orchestra, see "Letters, 1925," PRAAD-Sekondi, WRG 44/1/1.

41. *West African Times,* March 23, 1931; April 8, 1931; May 2, 1931. For more on these ladies, real and aspirant, see LaRay Denzer, "Gender and Decolonization: A Study of Three Women in West African Public Life," in *People and Empires in African History: Essays in Memory of Michael Crowder,* ed. J. F. Ade Ajayi and J. D. Y. Peel (London: Longman, 1992); Gadzekpo, "Public but Private," 316–17; Newell, *Literary Culture,* 61.

42. "Receiver, 1931," PRAAD-Sekondi, WRG 44/1/11. Such apparel was standard for most *nwuraanom* who, like the *akrakyefoɔ,* largely shunned local attire. David Kimble reports that one Sekondi women's organization, the Lady's Mutual Club, established a

rule that members who wore native dress in public would be subject to fines: Kimble, *A Political History of Ghana*, 134.

43. "Annual Reports, 1926–41," PRAAD-Sekondi, WRG 44/1/29; Iliffe, *Honour in African History*, 246–61.

44. "Receiver, 1931," PRAAD-Sekondi, WRG 44/1/11. Also see *Gold Coast Leader*, July 20, 1918; *West African Times*, February 18, 1932. For similar efforts in Zimbabwe, see West, *African Middle Class*, 73–80.

45. "Letters, 1925," PRAAD-Sekondi, WRG 44/1/1; "Letters Despatched, 1926," PRAAD-Sekondi, 44/1/4; "Literary Work, Lectures, Addresses, Essays by Members," PRAAD-Sekondi, WRG 44/1/24; "Letters Received, 1926," PRAAD-Sekondi, WRG 44/1/3.

46. "Clubs," PRAAD-Cape Coast, ADM 23/1/298/105.

47. Koo Nimo, October 7, 2005; Jerry Hansen, October 13, 2005; "Annual Reports, 1926–1941," PRAAD-Sekondi, WRG 44/1/29; "Receiver, 1930," PRAAD-Sekondi, WRG 44/1/7; "Minutes Book, 1934," PRAAD-Sekondi, WRG 44/1/19; Mensah, "Highlife," 1, 11–12; Collins, *E. T. Mensah*, 1–3.

48. Henrika Kuklick, *The Imperial Bureaucrat: the Colonial Administrative Service in the Gold Coast, 1920–1939* (Stanford, Calif.: Hoover Institution Press, 1979), 19–42.

49. Paula Jones, "The United Africa Company in the Gold Coast/Ghana, 1920–1965" (PhD diss., School of Oriental and African Studies, 1983), 66–68; David Killingray, "Repercussions of World War I in the Gold Coast," *Journal of African History* 19, no. 1 (1978): 39–59.

50. Gold Coast Government, "Further Correspondence Relating to the Revision of the Initial Rates of Salary in the African Civil Service" (Accra: Government Printing Office, 1931), 4; Kimble, *A Political History of Ghana*, 90 96 and 101–103.

51. "Clubs," PRAAD-Cape Coast, ADM 23/1/298/44.

52. "Clubs," PRAAD-Cape Coast, ADM 23/1/298/45, 90–92, and 104.

53. "List of Members of the Starlite Club," PRAAD-Cape Coast, ADM 23/1/298. Portions in italics indicate the officer's hand-written evaluations. Commissioner Atterbury also directed existing clubs, such as the Cape Coast Literary and Social Club, to provide his office with written assessments of their membership and activities.

54. Kimble, *A Political History of Ghana*, 105–24; Newell, *Literary Culture*, 64–68. For more on Achimota College, see Shoko Yamada, "Global Discourse and Local Response in Educational Policy Process: The Case of Achimota School in Colonial Ghana (Gold Coast)" (PhD diss., Indiana University, 2003). For a comprehensive overview of Guggisberg's time in the colonial service, including his position as governor, see R. E. Wraith, *Guggisberg* (London: Oxford University Press, 1967).

55. Newell, *Literary Culture*, 65.

56. "Africa Clubs," PRAAD-Sekondi, WRG 24/1/246/40a; WRG 24/1/246; "Letters, 1925," PRAAD-Sekondi, WRG 44/1/1.

57. "African Clubs," PRAAD-Sekondi, WRG 24/1/246/84, 94, 109, and 114.

58. "Despatcher 1931," PRAAD-Sekondi, WRG 44/1/10; Miescher, *Making Men*, 105–106.

59. In the Colonial Office the buzzword of technology took particular hold. Throughout the 1930s, the British Advisory Committee on Education proposed that all British colonies adopt gramophone records as a means of teaching English to Africans. Little action was ever taken on the project, but many officials insisted that modern technology

was the ideal tool for civilizing "backwards peoples"; see "Educational Films," PRO, CO 323/1421/17; L. A. Notcutt and G. C. Latham, *The African and the Cinema: An Account of the Work of the Bantu Educational Cinema Experiment during the Period March 1935 to May 1937* (London: Edinburgh House Press, 1937). For more on this use of film, see Charles Ambler, "Popular Films and Colonial Audiences: The Movies in Northern Rhodesia," *American Historical Review* 106, no. 1 (2001): 81–105; J. M. Burns, *Flickering Shadows: Cinema and Identity in Colonial Zimbabwe* (Athens: Ohio University Press, 2002); Mark Nash, "The Modernity of African Cinema," in *The Short Century: Independence and Liberation Movements in Africa 1845–1994*, ed. Okwui Enwezor (New York: Prestel, 2001), 339–46.

60. "Engagement of the Gold Coast Regimental Band," PRAAD-Sekondi, WRG 15/1/399/71. For more on the Regimental Band, see A. Haywood and F. A. S. Clarke, *The History of the Royal West African Frontier Force* (Aldershot: Wellington Press, 1964), 5–7, 40, and 43.

61. "Police Band," PRO, CO 96/673.

62. "Police Band, 1931–36," PRAAD-Accra, CSO 25/1/49. Although the motivation for these performances was reformist in nature, it also had an economic impetus, as the band cost the department an estimated £2,797 per year.

63. John Collins, "The Ghanaian Concert Party: African Popular Entertainment at the Cross Roads" (PhD diss., State University of New York at Buffalo, 1994), 235.

64. "Broadcasting Police Band Music, 1936," PRAAD-Accra, CSO 25/1/49.

65. "Police Band, 1931–36," PRAAD-Accra, CSO 25/1/49; "Police Band Concerts in Accra," PRAAD-Accra, CSO 15/1/299.

66. "African Clubs, Games, Sports, Bands, Pastimes," PRAAD-Sekondi, WRG 15/1/399/60; 73a; 88; 110a; 125, 226 and 303; *West Africa Times*, April 7, 1931; May 1, 1931; May 9, 1931; October 15, 1932; October 26, 1932.

67. Isaac Amuah, March 30, 2005; Kwadwo Donkoh, September 16, 2005; Kofi Ghanaba (Guy Warren), October 19, 2005; *West African Times*, April 13, 1931, and May 29, 1931.

68. "Functions: Social, Library and Sports," PRAAD-Sekondi, WRG 44/1/31; "Letters Miscellaneous," PRAAD-Sekondi, WRG 44/1/30.

69. "Annual Reports, 1926–41," PRAAD-Sekondi, WRG 44/1/29. Also see "Letters Despatched, 1926," PRAAD-Sekondi, WRG 44/1/4; "Receiver 1930," PRAAD-Sekondi, WRG 44/1/7; "Sender, 1930," PRAAD-Sekondi, WRG 44/1/8; "Despatcher 1936," PRAAD-Sekondi, WRG 44/1/23; "Despatcher 1937," PRAAD-Sekondi, WRG 44/1/26; "Clubs," PRAAD-Cape Coast, ADM 23/1/298.

70. For concise overviews of the Depression era in the Gold Coast, see Roger Gocking, *History of Ghana* (Westport, Conn.: Greenwood Press, 2005), 63–71; A. Adu Boahen, *Ghana: Evolution and Change in the Nineteenth and Twentieth Centuries* (London: Longman, 1975), 136–48.

71. "The General Condition of Labour in West Africa (1930)," PRAAD-Accra, ADM 11/1068; G. B. Kay, ed., *The Political Economy of Colonialism in Ghana: A Collection of Documents and Statistics, 1900–1960* (Cambridge: Cambridge University Press, 1972), 318–21; Jones, "The United Africa Company in the Gold Coast/Ghana," 131.

72. Kwadwo Adum-Attah, February 18, 2005; Kwadwo Donkoh, September 16, 2005.

73. The Optimism Club sponsored a dance in October 1930 for which it offered reserved seats (4s. single, 6s. 6d. double), first seats (3s. single, 5s. double), and second

seats (2s. single): "Receiver, 1930," PRAAD-Sekondi, WRG 44/1/7. Also see "Clubs," PRAAD-Cape Coast, ADM 23/1/298.

74. The Optimism Club kept strict budgets of their dances, which were compiled by the master of ceremonies. Following a dance in December 1933, J. E. Ayewa compiled a dance report, which listed the following expenses for the dance: "Ice 4s., Pkt. Candles 6d., 5 pkts. of Envelopes 1s. 3d., Conveyance of Tarpaulins 6s. 6d., Dash to boys and Sundry 4s., Police 7s. 6d., Refreshment to Bandmaster and Bandsmen 16s., Carpenter 2s., Church Press 13s. 6d., Hope Stores Press 10s., Lights 11s., Band, £6 6s." for a total cost of £10 12s. 3d. The club covered these costs by selling 25 "tickets" at 5s. each for a total of £6 5s. as well as an additional £6 10s. worth of tickets at the door. In this case, therefore, the club's profits (£12 15s.) exceeded its expenses: "Receiver, 1933," PRAAD-Sekondi, WRG 44/1/14.

75. "Despatcher, 1931," PRAAD-Sekondi, WRG 44/1/10; "Receiver, 1933," WRG 44/1/15; "Letters Received, 1934," PRAAD-Sekondi, WRG 44/1/17; "Letters Received, 1935," PRAAD-Sekondi, WRG 44/1/18.

76. "Functions, Social, Library, and Sports," PRAAD-Sekondi, WRG 44/1/31; "Receiver, 1932," PRAAD-Sekondi, WRG 44/1/13; "Report of December Dance Committee," "Receiver, 1933," PRAAD-Sekondi, WRG 44/1/15.

77. K. A. B. Jones-Quartey, *A Summary History of the Ghana Press, 1822–1960* (Accra: Ghana Information Services Department, 1974), 17 and 22; *Gold Coast Independent,* April 22, 1933.

78. "Brilliant Dance at the Palladium: The Yacca Club," *West African Times,* April 7, 1931. For others from that year, see "Entertainments and Personnel," *West African Times,* April 16, 1931; "The Congress Dance at Rodger Club," *West African Times,* May 1, 1931; "Diary of a Man About Town," *West African Times,* May 1, 1931; "Select Party Dance," *West African Times,* May 22, 1931; "Dance and Music at Nsawam," *West African Times,* June 12, 1931; "A Concert at Tarkwa," *West African Times,* June 15, 1931; "Society and Personnel," *West African Times,* October 28, 1931.

79. "Optimism Dancing Club," "Play and Dance at the Merry Villas," and "Rodger Club Dance," *West African Times,* April 13, 1931; "Two Dances in Akuapem" *West African Times,* April 14, 1931; "The Congress Dance at Rodger Club," *West African Times,* May 1, 1931; "Ladies Musical Society Dance: The Very Select," *West African Times,* May 9, 1931; "The Chu Chin Chow Orchestra at the Rodger Club," *Gold Coast Independent,* March 4, 1933; "The Forthcoming Co-Optimists Dance," *Gold Coast Independent,* May 20, 1933. J. Kitson Mills was headmaster of the Royal School in Accra; T. Hutton-Mills was a lawyer, chairman of the 1920 British African Conference, and runner-up to Kwame Nkrumah in the 1951 election for the Accra Municipality; and E. C. Quist became the president of the 1949 Gold Coast Legislative Council and speaker of the 1951 Gold Coast General Assembly: Allister MacMillan, *The Red Book of West Africa: Historical and Descriptive, Commercial and Industrial Fact, Figures and Resources* (London: F. Cass, 1920), 208; Dennis Austin, *Politics in Ghana: 1946–1960* (London: Oxford University Press, 1964), 103–14 and 154.

80. "African Clubs, Games, Sports, Bands, Pastimes," PRAAD-Sekondi, WRG 15/1/399/27; "Town Bands Competition in Sekondi," *West African Times,* April 17, 1931; "Dance and Music at Nsawam," *West African Times,* June 12, 1931; "Another Orchestra," *West African Times,* October 8, 1932; "The Chu Chin Chow Orchestra at the Rodger Club," *Gold Coast Independent,* March 4, 1933.

81. Collins, *E. T. Mensah,* 2–4; "Functions, Social, Library, and Sports," PRAAD-Sekondi, WRG 44/1/31.

82. Even members of this second wave of orchestras were salaried clerks, civil servants, or government employees: Stan Plange, June 29, 2005; Ebo Taylor, August 24, 2005. One revealing, if negative, example of how bandsmen became known from their affiliation with such ensembles is a newspaper article about one "Mr. King" who lost his job at Kingsway Drug Store: "Winneba Orchestra Man Loses His Job," *West African Times,* October 14, 1932.

83. Kofi Lindsay, June 22, 2005; Jerry Hansen, October 13, 2005.

84. "Letters Received, 1935," PRAAD-Sekondi, WRG 44/1/18, "Receiver, 1936," PRAAD-Sekondi, WRG 44/1/20, and "Functions, Social, Library, and Sports," PRAAD-Sekondi, WRG 44/1/31. For more on the Cape Coast Light Orchestra's tours of Nigeria, see Waterman, *Jùjú,* 44–45; Mensah, "Highlife," 11; John Collins, May 13, 2005.

85. "Receiver, 1933," PRAAD-Sekondi, WRG 44/1/15; "African Clubs, Games, Sports, Bands, Pastimes," PRAAD-Sekondi, WRG 15/1/399/6, 28, and 187. Another club, "the Humorous Entertainers," formed in 1931 in order to provide concerts and shows in Tarkwa: "A Concert at Tarkwa," *West African Times,* June 15, 1931.

86. "Clubs," PRAAD-Cape Coast, ADM 23/1/298/255; "Dance Competition in Mamfe" and "Optimism Dancing Club," *West African Times,* April 13, 1931.

87. "Letters Received, 1935," PRAAD-Sekondi, WRG 44/1/18; "African Clubs, Games, Sports, Bands, Pastimes," PRAAD-Sekondi, WRG 15/1/399/73.

88. Cole, *Ghana's Concert Party Theatre,* 72–74; MacMillan, *The Red Book of West Africa,* 176 and 203; *Gold Coast Leader,* May 3, 1924.

89. *Gold Coast Independent,* January 2, 1932. For other articles about these venues, see *West African Times,* October 1, 1932; *Gold Coast Independent,* October 15, 1932; *Gold Coast Independent,* November 5, 1932; *West African Times,* June 22, 1933; *Gold Coast Independent,* December 24, 1932.

90. *Gold Coast Independent,* April 22, 1933; *West African Times,* May 29, 1933; July 12, 1933; and August 29, 1934.

91. For more on the terrain of Christian marriages, see Miescher, *Making Men,* 133–37.

92. "Letters Received, 1934," PRAAD-Sekondi, WRG 44/1/17; Achimota College, "Marriage and Debt: The Report of a Discussion Group of the Teachers' Refreshers Course, Achimota, 1938" (Achimota: Achimota Press, 1938), 1–8; Alice Ioné Crabtree, "Marriage and Family Life among the Educated Africans in the Urban Areas of the Gold Coast" (MA thesis, University of London, 1950), 54–67, and 79–89. For social pressures of obtaining a marriage under Ordinance, see *Gold Coast Independent,* December 2, 1933. For the state's concerns, see "Minutes of the Proceedings of the 15th Session of the Provincial Council, Central Province, 6th February 1930," "Native Marriage," PRAAD-Cape Coast, ADM 23/1/446.

93. Crabtree, "Marriage and Family Life," 79; Miescher, *Making Men,* 119–22.

94. Kwadwo Adum-Attah, February 18, 2005; Isaac Amuah, March 30, 2005; Elizabeth Amonoo, October 18, 2005.

3. The Friction on the Floor

1. Alex Bakpa Moffatt, May 21, 2005.

2. For the political impact of the Second World War, see Frederick Cooper, *Decolonization and African Society: The Labor Question in French and British Africa* (Cambridge: Cambridge University Press, 1996); Michael Crowder, "The 1939–45 War and West

Africa," in *History of West Africa*, vol. 2, ed. J. F. I. Ajayi and Michael Crowder (London: Longman, 1974), 596–621; and "World War II and Africa," *Journal of African History* 26, no. 4 (1985): 287–88. For its impact on civilian populations, see David Killingray and Richard Rathbone, eds., *Africa and the Second World War* (New York: St. Martin's Press, 1986); David Killingray, "African Civilians in the Era of the Second World War, c. 1935–50," in *Daily Lives of Civilians in Wartime Africa*, ed. John Laband (Westport, Conn.: Greenwood Press, 2007), 139–68.

3. Meyer Fortes, "The Impact of the War on British West Africa," *International Affairs* 21, no. 2 (1945): 209.

4. In this sense, popular music worked rather differently than it did in Luanda, where it became a place of a new "Angolaness": Marissa Moorman, *Intonations: A Social History of Music and Nation in Luanda, Angola from 1945 to Recent Times* (Athens: Ohio University Press, 2008).

5. Wendell Holbrook, "The Impact of the Second World War on the Gold Coast, 1939–45," (PhD diss., Princeton University, 1978), 113–28, 136–41, 266, and 317; and "British Propaganda and the Mobilization of the Gold Coast War Effort, 1939–45," *Journal of African History* 26, no. 4 (1985): 347–61. Also see Crowder, "The 1939–45 War and West Africa," 610–11; Steven J. Salm, "The Bukom Boys: Subcultures and Identity Transformation in Accra, Ghana" (PhD diss., University of Texas, 2003), 109–15.

6. Holbrook, "The Impact of the Second World War," 198–211, 266–68, and 283–300; Gold Coast, *The Gold Coast Census of Population, 1948: Report and Tables* (Accra: Government Printing Office, 1950).

7. "Grand Hotel (Hotel Metropole), Accra 1936," PRAAD-Accra, CSO 25/1/77/10a, 17a, and 17b.

8. John Collins, *E. T. Mensah: King of Highlife* (Accra: Anansesem Publications, 1996), 6.

9. "In the Beginning Was the Metropole," *Sunday Mirror,* January 9, 1955.

10. Kofi Ghanaba, October 19, 2005.

11. Collins, *E. T. Mensah,* 6–7; "Blow Man Blow," *Daily Graphic,* December 27, 1954.

12. "Nigerians in the Gold Coast," PRAAD-Sekondi, WRG 24/1/250; Salm, "The Bukom Boys," 76; Ioné Acquah, *Accra Survey* (London: University of London Press, 1958), 72–74.

13. Henry Ayawovie, May 30, 2005; "Pilot Boys," PRAAD-Sekondi, WRG 35/1/49; "Pilot Boys in Takoradi Area," PRAAD-Sekondi, WRG 24/1/323; "Nigerians in the Gold Coast," PRAAD-Sekondi, WRG 24/1/250; "Takoradi: The 'Pilot Boys' Menace," *Gold Coast Observer,* December 17, 1948; K. A. Busia, *Report on a Social Survey of Sekondi-Takoradi* (London: Hazell, Watson and Viney, 1950), 96–100.

14. Ebo Taylor, August 24, 2005; Jerry Hansen, October 3, 2005; John Collins, "King of the Black Beat: The Story of King Bruce and the Black Beats, Highlife Dance Band of Ghana" (Unpublished Manuscript, 1987/89), 20; and *E. T. Mensah,* 6.

15. Ebo Taylor, a guitarist for the Stargazers Dance Band, Broadway Dance Band, and Pelikans Dance Band, purchased jazz records throughout the 1940s: Ebo Taylor, August 24, 2005, and September 1, 2005. Also see Saka Acquaye, September 7, 2005; Daniel Kinful Sam, September 19, 2005; Jerry Hansen, October 3, 2005; J. H. Kwabena Nketia, "The Gramophone and Contemporary African Music in the Gold Coast," *Proceedings of the Fourth Annual Conference of the West African Institute of Economic Social Research* (Ibadan, 1955), 194–96. For an insightful look into the impacts of jazz on a small number

of Ghanaian musicians, see Steven Feld, *Jazz Cosmopolitanism in Accra: Five Musical Years in Ghana* (Durham, N.C.: Duke University Press, 2012).

16. "Why She Was Surprised," *Gold Coast Observer,* August 9, 1946.

17. Saka Acquaye, August 24, 2005; Kofi Ghanaba, October 19, 2005.

18. Daniel Kinful Sam, September 19, 2005; Jerry Hansen, October 3, 2005; Collins, "King of the Black Beat," 25–26; *Gold Coast Observer,* January 2, 1948, and January 16, 1948.

19. Kofi Ghanaba, October 19, 2005; Collins, "King of the Black Beat," 20–27.

20. Collins, *E. T. Mensah,* 4–7.

21. Kofi Ghanaba, October 19, 2005; Collins, *E. T. Mensah,* 6–9.

22. John Collins, *Highlife Time* (Accra: Anansesem Publications, 1996), 47–49; *E. T. Mensah,* 11–12; and "King of the Black Beat," 35–36. The Tempos were so popular that they formed and trained a second ensemble, the Tempos No. 2 Band (also known as the "Star Rockets"), who could perform the Tempos' songs in Gold Coast cities while the group traveled abroad. For more on the Tempos' influence on highlife's popularity in Nigeria, see Michael Veal, *Fela: The Life and Times of an African Musical Icon* (Philadelphia: Temple University Press, 2000), 36–38.

23. Stan Plange, June 29, 2005; Ebo Taylor, August 24, 2005; Saka Acquaye, August 24, 2005.

24. Isaac Amuah, March 30, 2005; "African Clubs," PRAAD-Sekondi, WRG 24/1/246; "Clubs," PRAAD-Cape Coast, ADM 23/1/298.

25. "These Modern Girls," *Gold Coast Observer,* July 2, 1943; "Anecdotes from Accra: Concerning Prostitutes," *Gold Coast Observer,* July 9, 1943; "The Dress of Our School Girls," *Gold Coast Observer,* May 3, 1947; *Gold Coast Observer,* August 8, 1947; *Gold Coast Observer,* March 5, 1948; *Gold Coast Observer,* March 26, 1948; "Takoradi: The 'Pilot Boys' Menace," *Gold Coast Observer,* December 17, 1948; Mabel Dove, *Selected Writings of a Pioneer West African Feminist,* ed. Stephanie Newell and Audrey Gadzekpo (Nottingham: Trent Editions, 2004), 4–5, 22–23, 36–37, 38, and 59–90.

26. "Research into Social Conditions in Urban Areas in Gold Coast," PRAAD-Sekondi, WRG 24/1/324"; "Rev. Taylor and the Dances," *Gold Coast Observer,* May 7, 1943.

27. For more on the history of juvenile delinquency in colonial Africa, see John Iliffe, *The African Poor: A History* (Cambridge: Cambridge University Press, 1987), 188–92; Laurent Fouchard, "Lagos and the Invention of Juvenile Delinquency in Nigeria, 1920–1960," *Journal of African History* 47, no. 1 (2006): 115–37; Andrew Burton, "Raw Youth, School-Leavers, and the Emergence of Structural Unemployment in Late-Colonial Urban Tanganyika," *Journal of African History* 47, no. 3 (2006): 363–87; Andrew Burton and Paul Ocobock, "The 'Travelling Native': Vagrancy and Colonial Control in British East Africa," in *Cast Out: Vagrancy and Homelessness in Global and Historical Perspective,* ed. A. L. Beir and Paul Ocobock (Athens: Ohio University Press, 2008), 270–301.

28. "Juvenile Delinquency and Welfare," PRAAD-Accra, CSO 15/3/340/5 and 123; "Address Given By Governor Burns, 1945," in "Gold Coast: Legislative Council Minutes and Sessional Papers, 1944–45," PRO, CO 98/87; "Nigerians in the Gold Coast," PRAAD-Sekondi, WRG 24/1/250; "Juvenile Offenders," PRAAD-Cape Coast, ADM 23/1/297.

29. Holbrook, "The Impact of the Second World War," 142.

30. Fortes, "The Impact of the War," 209; "Jim-Crow Suffers Defeat in London; British Parliament May Enact Law against Race Prejudice; Coloured American Actress and African Professor Victims of Racism," *Gold Coast Observer*, May 14, 1948.

31. For more on the formation and nature of the UGCC, see Dennis Austin, *Politics in Ghana: 1946–1960*, (London: Oxford University Press, 1964), 49–92; David E. Apter, *Ghana in Transition* (Princeton, N.J.: Princeton University Press, 1972), 167–74; Richard Rathbone, "Businessmen in Politics: Party Struggle in Ghana, 1949–1957," *Journal of Development Studies* 9, no. 3 (1973): 391–402.

32. "Central Committee to Formulate a Scheme for the Demobilisation and Resettlement of Gold Coast Troops," PRAAD-Accra, ADM 11/1/1893; "Employment of Ex-Servicemen," PRAAD-Sekondi, WRG 15/1580; Austin, *Politics in Ghana*, 49–92. In 1944, swollen shoot struck cocoa farms in the eastern and western portions of the colony. By 1946, it had spread to the Ashanti region. To counter its spread, the colonial administration implemented a forced "cut-out campaign" that evoked considerable controversy and opposition: Gwendolyn Mikell, *Cocoa and Chaos in Ghana* (New York: Paragon, 1989), 145–46.

33. "Railway African Club Sekondi: Resumption of Public Literary Activities after the Rains," *Gold Coast Observer*, August 18, 1944.

34. "Reflections and Reactions," *Gold Coast Observer*, March 5, 1943; "Sekondi," *Gold Coast Observer*, March 19, 1943; "Sekondi," *Gold Coast Observer*, March 26, 1943; "Concert and Evening Dress Dance, Railway African Club Sekondi," *Gold Coast Observer*, April 16, 1943; "Churchill Bar 1st Anniversary Dance," *Gold Coast Observer*, July 2, 1943; "Committee of Three Hold Gala Day Dance in Cape Coast Town Hall," *Gold Coast Observer*, January 20, 1945; "Wenchi-Ashanti, Successful Dance Staged," *Gold Coast Observer*, November 1, 1946; "Fancy Dress Competition," *Gold Coast Observer*, June 4, 1948.

35. "Optimism Club, Sekondi," PRAAD-Sekondi, WRG 24/1/140; "Clubs and Recreations," PRAAD-Sekondi, WRG 24/1/249; "Clubs and Culture," *Gold Coast Observer*, December 13, 1946; "Open Letter to the President of the Cape Coast Literary and Social Club," *Gold Coast Observer*, April 18, 1947; "A Warning," *Gold Coast Observer*, June 20, 1947; "Letter to the President of the Optimism Club," *Gold Coast Observer*, July 4, 1947.

36. "Letter to Cape Coast Literary and Social Club," *Gold Coast Observer*, September 12, 1947; letter to the editor, *Gold Coast Observer*, June 2, 1948; "Literary Clubs," *Gold Coast Observer*, July 11, 1948.

37. John Collins, May 13, 2005.

38. Other early Accra nightclubs included the King's Bar, Happy Days, Holiday Inn, Christmas in Egypt, Hawaii Nightclub, and Miami in Heat: James Allotey, April 27, 2005; Harry Amenumey, May 3, 2005; J. O. Mills, May 6, 2005; Rebecca Torshie Adja and Diana Ojoko Adja, May 6, 2005; J. J. Sarpong, June 7, 2005. The names of these nightclubs provide another example of the influence American servicemen had on the city's recreational scene. The Kalamazoo nightclub, for example, may have taken its name from a Glen Miller song, "I've Got a Gal in Kalamazoo" that topped the Billboard charts in the United States in 1942: personal communication, Wesley Dick, February 23, 2007.

39. Acquah, *Accra Survey*, 40–42.

40. Georgina Okanee Acei, May 19, 2005; Diana Oboshilay and Margaret Akosua Acolatse, May 24, 2005. A "tro-tro" was a privately owned minibus that carried passengers along set routes in the city for a small fee. In the 1940s, these vehicles charged passengers

three pence and, since "tro" is "three" in the Ga language, they earned the popular name: Jennifer Hart, "Suffer to Gain: Citizenship, Accumulation, and Motor Transportation in Late-Colonial and Postcolonial Ghana" (PhD diss., Indiana University, 2011), 197–99.

41. Abdul Rahim Dixon, Ahmed Tettey Dixon, and Mohammed Mensah Dixon, May 22, 2005.

42. While weekend dances often started at 8 PM, preparations for the evening began in the afternoon. Bands would arrive at the nightclubs at 3 PM or 4 PM in order to set up their instruments, and the dance organizer and staff would begin setting up tables and decorations around 6 PM. By 7 PM regular nightclub staff would arrive, so that they could review everything before beginning to sell tickets: J. J. Sarpong, June 7, 2005; James Matthew Thompson, May 3, 2005; Diana Oboshilay and Margaret Akosua Acolatse, May 24, 2005.

43. Grershon Gaba, April 29, 2005; Justina and Edna Fugar, April 29, 2005; Alex Bakpa Moffatt, May 21, 2005; Benny Amakudzie, June 1, 2005; J. J. Sarpong, June 7, 2005. For a detailed look at the music's appeal among the ethnically diverse residents of Nima, see K. A. Darkwa, "Migrant Music and Musicians: The Effect of Migration on Music, pt. 1: Nima Opinion Survey" (PhD diss., University of Ghana, Institute of African Studies, 1971).

44. Mr. Mexico, April 18, 2005; J. O. Mills, May 6, 2005; Margaret Akosua Acolatse, May 19, 2005.

45. J. J. Sarpong, June 7, 2005. Happy Gaba was denied entrance to an Accra nightclub when she was eighteen years old: Happy Gaba, April 27, 2005.

46. Nightclubs charged higher rates on holidays as well as evenings in which they featured dance competitions, numerous bands, beauty pageants, or special guests: Mr. Mexico, April 18, 2005; James Matthew Thompson, May 3, 2005.

47. John Collins, May 13, 2005; James Allotey, April 27, 2005; Benny Amakudzie, April 27, 2005; Justina and Edna Fugar, April 29, 2005; James Thompson, May 3, 2005; J. O. Mills, May 6, 2005.

48. Acquah, *Accra Survey,* 63–91.

49. Gold Coast, "1953 Survey of Accra Household Budgets" (Accra: Government Printer, 1953). The survey was first administered to 4,898 households, after which collected data was examined for 200 "households" consisting of "one wage-earning head," at least one other working adult, and not more than nine children.

50. Diana Oboshilay and Margaret Akosua Acolatse, May 24, 2005. Also see: James Allotey, April 27, 2005; Justina and Edna Fugar, April 29, 2005; Josephine Ayitey, May 19, 2005; Albert Aflakpui, May 20, 2005; Alex Bakpa Moffatt, May 21, 2005.

51. "Night Life in Christiansborg," *Daily Graphic,* November 1, 1953; Gloria Ocloo, May 24, 2005. Over the course of many interviews, men and women insisted that nightclubs were spaces that did not privilege or emphasize ethnicity.

52. James Matthew Thompson, May 3, 2005; Grershon Gaba, April 29, 2005; Georgina Acei May 19, 2005; Alex Bakpa Moffatt, May 21, 2005; J. J. Sarpong, June 7, 2005. I learned that most nightclubs were owned by Lebanese, Ghanaian, and Nigerian businessmen, but I was unable to speak with any owners during the course of my research.

53. Josephine Ayitey, May 19, 2005; Justina and Edna Fugar, April 29, 2005; James Matthew Thompson, May 3, 2005; Albert Aflakpui, May 20, 2005.

54. Grershon Gaba, April 29, 2005. For a comparable practice in colonial Brazzaville, see Phyllis Martin, "Contesting Clothes in Colonial Brazzaville," *Journal of African*

History 35, no. 3 (1994): 417–18. For more on Accra's department stores, see Paula Jones, "The United Africa Company in the Gold Coast/Ghana, 1920–1965" (PhD diss., School of Oriental and African Studies, 1983); Bianca Murillo, "'The Modern Shopping Experience': Kingsway Department Store and Consumer Politics in Ghana," *AFRICA: Journal of the International African Institute* 82, no. 3 (forthcoming).

55. Charity Agbenyega, April 27, 2005; Justina and Edna Fugar, April 29, 2005; Diana Oboshilay and Margaret Akosua Acolatse, May 24, 2005.

56. Grershon Gaba, April 29, 2005; Alex Bakpa Moffat, May 21, 2005; Benny Amakudzie, June 1, 2005.

57. J. J. Sarpong, June 7, 2005.

58. Josephine Ayitey, May 19, 2005.

59. James Allotey, April 27, 2005. Men, meanwhile, could attend nightclubs alone: Benny Amakudzie, April 27, 2005; Charity Agbenyega, April 27, 2005; Elizabeth Amonoo, October 18, 2005.

60. J. O. Mills, May 6, 2005; Benny Amakudzie, April 27, 2005; Albert Aflakpui, May 20, 2005; "If I Were Your Dancing Partner," *Sunday Mirror,* November 14, 1954.

61. Acquah, *Accra Survey,* 159; *Daily Graphic,* April 3, 1960, and August 7, 1960. Similar schools operated in Takoradi and Cape Coast: Kwadwo Adum-Attah, February 18, 2005; Bob Biney, April 1, 2005; "Sports, Societies, Clubs, and Recreations," PRAAD-Sekondi, WRG 32/1/174.

62. Benny Amakudzie, April 27, 2005; J. J. Sarpong, June 7, 2005; "Dancing Is an Exercise with Rhythmic Steps to Music," *Daily Graphic,* March 7, 1954; "Dancing Is an Art," *Daily Graphic,* September 5, 1954.

63. Dance lessons at the Seaview were run by Mr. Appley, who held classes there 5–7 PM twice a week: Charity Agbenyega, April 27, 2005; Harry Amenumey, May 3, 2005; Josephine Ayitey, May 19, 2005; J. J. Sarpong, June 7, 2005.

64. James Allotey, April 27, 2005; Margaret Akosua Acolatse, May 19, 2005, and May 24, 2005; Benny Amakudzie, April 27, 2005, and June 1, 2005. Several schools advertised their services and events in newspapers during the 1950s and 1960s: see *Daily Graphic,* July 4, 1959; July 25, 1959; November 26, 1959; January 23, 1960.

65. Benny Amakudzie, April 27, 2005; Grershon Gaba, April 29, 2005.

66. Josephine Ayitey, May 19, 2005.

67. Charity Agbenyega, April 27, 2005; Josephine Ayitey, May 19, 2005; Georgina Okanee Acei, May 19, 2005.

68. "Sports, Societies, Clubs, and Recreations," PRAAD-Sekondi, WRG 32/1/174; "Moses Harding and Partner Demonstrate the Calypso," *Sunday Mirror,* January 3, 1954; "Some Dancing Hints," *Sunday Mirror,* October 31, 1954; "Ballroom Dancing," *Sunday Mirror,* December 19, 1954; "Dance Notes: Try This Foxtrot Variation," *Sunday Mirror,* January 16, 1955; "Classifications of Ballroom Dancing," *Sunday Mirror,* January 23, 1955.

69. "Correct Timing Is Essential," *Sunday Mirror,* October 3, 1954.

70. Justina and Edna Fugar, April 29, 2005; Harry Amenumey, May 3, 2005; Georgina Acei, May 19, 2005; Albert Aflakpui, May 20, 2005.

71. "Nightlife in Christiansborg," *Sunday Mirror,* November 1, 1953; "Kill This Zoot Fashion," *Sunday Mirror,* July 24, 1955; Salm, "The Bukom Boys," 153–60. For a comparative framework, see Robin D. G. Kelly, *Race Rebels: Culture, Politics, and the Black Working Class* (New York: Free Press, 1994), 161–81.

72. Grershon Gaba, April 29, 2005; Albert Aflakpui, May 20, 2005.

73. James Matthew Thompson, May 3, 2005; J. O. Mills, May 6, 2005; Josephine Ayitey, May 19, 2005; Albert Aflakpui, May 20, 2005; Alex Bakpa Moffatt, May 21, 2005. Stephan Miescher notes that 1930s school graduates used a similar phrase—"entering the world"—in reference to their emergence: *Making Men in Ghana* (Bloomington: Indiana University Press, 2005), 85–86.

74. Mamadou Diouf, "Engaging Postcolonial Cultures: African Youth and Public Space," *African Studies Review* 46, no. 2 (2003): 6.

75. Kwadwo Adum-Attah, February 18, 2005; Isaac Amuah, March 30, 2005; Vincent Mensah, May 18, 2005; Elizabeth Amonoo, October 18, 2005. This was also true elsewhere in Africa, see Richard Waller, "Rebellious Youth in Colonial Africa," *Journal of African History* 47, no. 1 (2006): 77–92.

76. Nii Armah, May 22, 2005.

77. Elizabeth Amonoo, October 18, 2005.

78. Elizabeth Amonoo, October 18, 2005; James Matthew Thompson, May 3, 2005; Vincent Mensah, May 18, 2005.

79. Ghana Broadcasting Corporation, "Golden Jubilee Lectures: Broadcasting and National Development" (Tema: Ghana Broadcasting Corporation, 1985): 1–6; Ghana Broadcasting Corporation, "GBC" (Accra: GBC Publications Department, 1973): 4–5; "Broadcasting—Gold Coast," PRO, CO 875/1/12.

80. Ghana Broadcasting Corporation, *The Story of Radio Ghana* (Accra: Ministry of Information and Broadcasting, 1965), 4–6; Salm, "The Bukom Boys," 129–31.

81. Diouf, "Engaging Postcolonial Cultures," 2; G. Thomas Burgess and Andrew Burton, "Introduction," in *Generations Past: Youth in East African History,* ed. Andrew Burton and Hélène Charton-Bigot (Athens: Ohio University Press, 2010), 11–13.

82. Emmanuel Akyeampong, *Drink, Power, and Cultural Change* (Portsmouth: Heinemann, 1996), 117–38; Austin, *Politics in Ghana.* The National Liberation Movement also targeted youth; see Jean Allman, *Quills of the Porcupine: Asante Nationalism in an Emergent Ghana* (Madison: University of Wisconsin Press, 1993).

83. *Daily Graphic,* January 29, 1954; May 11, 1954; July 18, 1954; Thomas Turino, *Nationalists, Cosmopolitans, and Popular Music in Zimbabwe* (Chicago: University of Chicago Press, 2002), 190; John Collins, "The Ghanaian Concert Party: An African Popular Entertainment at the Cross Roads" (PhD diss., State University of New York at Buffalo, 1994), 491.

84. Alex Bakpa Moffatt, May 21, 2005; Bob Biney, April 1, 2005; James Allotey, April 27, 2005; James Matthew Thompson, May 3, 2005; J. O. Mills, May 6, 2005.

85. Rebecca Torshie Adja and Diana Ojoko Adja, May 6, 2005 and May 18, 2005.

86. Georgina Okanee Acei, May 19, 2005; Happy Gaba, April 29, 2005.

87. Bob Biney, April 1, 2005; Alex Bakpa Moffatt, May 21, 2005; Collins, *E. T. Mensah,* 3; Catherine M. Cole, *Ghana's Concert Party Theatre* (Bloomington: Indiana University Press, 2002), 99.

88. Rebecca Torshie Adja, May 6, 2005; Vincent Mensah, May 18, 2005; Margaret Acolatse, May 19, 2005; Alex Bakpa Moffatt, May 21, 2005; Abdul Rahim Dixon, Ahmed Tettey Dixon, and Mohammed Mensah Dixon, May 22, 2005.

89. James Matthew Thompson, May 3, 2005.

90. James Matthew Thompson, May 3, 2005; Rebecca Torshie Adja and Diana Ojoko Adja, May 6, 2005; Albert Aflakpui, May 20, 2005; Alex Bakpa Moffatt, May 21, 2005; Nii

Armah, May 22, 2005; Diana Oboshilay and Margaret Acolatse, May 24, 2005; Phyllis Lamptey, July 28, 2005.

91. Kwadwo Adum-Attah, February 18, 2005; Samuel Nyamuame, July 20, 2005.

92. James Allotey, April 27, 2005; James Matthew Thompson, May 3, 2005. For more on the importance of nicknames in young male peer culture, see Charles Ambler, "Popular Films and Colonial Audiences: The Movies in Northern Rhodesia," *American Historical Review* 106, no. 1 (2001): 81–105; Mac Fenwick, "'Tough Guy, eh?': The Gangster-figure in Drum," *Journal of Southern African Studies* 22, no. 4 (1996): 617–32.

93. Charity Agbenyega, April 27, 2005; Harry Amenumey, May 3, 2006; Margaret Acolatse, May 19, 2005.

94. "Messengers Dance Band Activities," PRAAD-Accra, RG 3/7/68/1; Mama Adjoa, July 5, 2005. Mama Adjoa is not her real name, but a pseudonym used at her request.

95. James Allotey, April 27, 2005; James Matthew Thompson, May 3, 2005; Harry Amenumey, May 3, 2005; Benny Amakudzie, April 27, 2005 and June 1, 2005. Nightclubs, moreover, often encouraged such perceptions. A 1958 newspaper advertisement for Nima's Harlem Café enticed readers by stating, "Good time assured, well-stocked bar. Ladies Galore": *Daily Graphic,* May 1, 1958.

96. Benny Amakudzie, April 27, 2005, and June 1, 2005.

97. Josephine Ayitey, August 30, 2005; Aeshitu Zinabo, September 7, 2005; Adjoa and Akua Opoku, September 10, 2005.

98. Margaret Acolatse, May 19, 2005; Diana Oboshilay and Margaret Acolatse, May 24, 2005; Aeshitu Zinabo and Victoria Quaidoo, June 12, 2009.

99. Elizabeth Amonoo, October 19, 2005; James Allotey, April 27, 2005; Kwadwo Adum-Attah, April 1, 2005.

100. Abdul Rahim Dixon, Ahmed Tettey Dixon, and Mohammed Mensah Dixon, May 22, 2005.

101. Gloria Ocloo, May 24, 2005.

102. James Allotey, April 27, 2005.

103. Henry Ayawovie, May 30, 2005; Adjoa and Akua Opoku, September 10, 2005; Lucy Ansah, September 7, 2005.

104. Kwadwo Adum-Attah, April 1, 2005; James Allotey, April 27, 2005; James Matthew Thompson, May 3, 2005; Alex Bakpa Moffatt, May 21, 2005; Abdul Rahim Dixon, Ahmed Tettey Dixon, and Mohammed Mensah Dixon, May 22, 2005. For women, see Justina and Edna Fugar, April 29, 2005; Rebecca Torshie Adja and Diana Ojoko Adja, May 6, 2005; Gloria Ocloo, May 24, 2005; Phyllis Lamptey, July 28, 2005.

105. Ghana, *1960 Population Census of Ghana,* vol. 3: *Demographic Characteristics* (Accra: Census Office, 1964); Philip Bartle, "African Rural-Urban Migration: A Decision Making Perspective," (MA Thesis, University of British Columbia, 1971), 98–105.

106. Gold Coast, *Ten Year Plan for the Economic and Social Development of the Gold Coast* (Accra: Government Printer, 1950); "Slum Clearance in Ussher Town," (Accra: Town Planning Department, 1954); and "Town and Country Planning in the Gold Coast" (Accra: Government Printing Department, 1954).

107. Nate Plageman, "Accra Is Changing, Isn't It?": Urban Infrastructure, Independence, and Nation in the Gold Coast's *Daily Graphic,* 1954–57," *International Journal of African Historical Studies* 43, no. 1 (2010): 137–59.

108. Phillip Foster, *Education and Social Change in Ghana* (Chicago: University of Chicago Press, 1965), 130, 137–42, and 179–209.

109. Salm, "The Bukom Boys," 23–28 and 88–115. For more on the Ga Shifimo Kpee, see Austin, *Politics in Ghana,* 44 and 373–76.

110. Gloria Ocloo, May 24, 2005; Bob Biney, April 1, 2005; Happy Gaba, April 29, 2005; Vincent Mensah, May 18, 2005. Also see Steve Salm, "Rain or Shine We Gonna' Rock: Dance Subcultures and Identity Construction in Accra, Ghana," in *Sources and Methods in African History: Spoken, Written, Unearthed,* ed. Toyin Falola and Christian Jennings (Rochester, N.Y.: University of Rochester Press, 2003), 361–65; Salm, "The Bukom Boys," 160–64.

111. Frankie Laine, June 3, 2009; Salm, "The Bukom Boys," 188; and "Rain or Shine," 365–68. For a few fine looks at rock 'n' roll's impact elsewhere, see Eric Zolov, *Refried Elvis: The Rise of Mexican Counterculture* (Berkeley: University of California Press, 1999), 10; Pete Daniel, *Lost Revolutions: The South in the 1950s* (Chapel Hill: University of North Carolina Press, 2000), 121–73.

112. Vincent Mensah, May 18, 2005.

113. Vincent Mensah, May 18, 2005; Henry Ayawovie, May 30, 2005; J. O. Mills, May 6, 2005; Frankie Laine, June 3, 2009; S. S. Quarcoopome, "Urbanisation, Land Alienation, and Politics in Accra," *University of Ghana Research Review* 8, nos. 1 & 2 (1992): 47; Salm, "The Bukom Boys," 190–202.

114. Vincent Mensah, May 18, 2005; Henry Ayawovie, May 30, 2005.

115. Nii Adgin Tettey, September 11, 2005.

116. Bob Biney, April 1, 2005; Frankie Laine, June 3, 2009.

117. Josephine Ayitey, May 19, 2005. For more on rock 'n' rollers' use of American slang, see Salm, "The Bukom Boys," 208–12.

118. Jerry Hansen, October 3, 2005; Frankie Laine, June 3, 2009; Francis Laryea, June 6, 2009; Salm, "The Bukom Boys," 197.

119. Vincent Mensah, May 18, 2005; Henry Ayawovie, May 30, 2005.

120. Vincent Mensah, May 18, 2005; Diana Oboshilay, May 24, 2005; Henry Ayawovie, May 30, 2005; Frankie Laine, June 3, 2009.

121. James Allotey, April 27, 2005; Bob Biney, April 1, 2005; Vincent Mensah, May 18, 2005.

122. Grace Yawa Aye, May 18, 2005; Salm, "The Bukom Boys," 213–16.

123. Benny Amakudzie, June 1, 2005; "The Rock 'N' Roll Music and Dancing: Is It Good or Bad?," *Sunday Mirror,* March 1, 1959.

124. Maureen Mahon, "Black Like This: Race, Generation, and Rock in the Post–Civil Rights Era," *American Ethnologist* 27, no. 2 (2000): 283–311; Zolov, *Refried Elvis,* 53–61; Daniel, *Lost Revolutions,* 121–73.

125. For more on these connections, in Accra and elsewhere, see: Salm, "The Bukom Boys" and "Rain or Shine We Gonna' Rock"; Mathia Diawara, "The Sixties in Bamako: Malick Sidibé and James Brown," in *Black Cultural Traffic: Crossroads in Global Performance and Popular Culture,* ed. Harry J. Elam Jr. and Kennell Jackson (Ann Arbor: University of Michigan Press, 2005), 242–65.

126. "How Folks Behave in Ballrooms," *Daily Graphic,* August 7, 1960.

127. "Better Dresses at Nightclubs," *Daily Graphic,* March 28, 1956; "Enforce Drink Ban on the Teen-Agers," *Sunday Mirror,* October 12, 1958; "Youths Face Temptation," *Daily Graphic,* January 8, 1959; "Take a Tip Parents: Let's Save Our Teenagers from Bad Practices," *Sunday Mirror,* January 18, 1959; "The Rock 'N' Roll Music and Dancing: Is It Good or Bad?," *Sunday Mirror,* March 1, 1959.

4. "The Highlife Was Born in Ghana"

1. "'Highlife' Takes on a New Name," *Sunday Mirror,* July 1, 1960; "'Osibi' Is New Name," *Sunday Mirror,* September 4, 1960; David Coplan, "Go to My Town, Cape Coast!: The Social History of Ghanaian Music," in *Eight Urban Music Cultures,* ed. Bruno Nettl (Urbana: University of Illinois Press, 1978), 108; John Collins, "The Ghanaian Concert Party" (PhD diss., State University of New York at Buffalo, 1994), 436.

2. Subsequent newspaper articles continually refer to the music as "highlife": see "Osagyefo Does the High life," *Daily Graphic,* December 13, 1960.

3. For works that address popular music's importance to nation-building, see Marissa Moorman, *Intonations: A Social History of Music and Nation in Luanda, Angola, from 1945 to Recent Times* (Athens: Ohio University Press, 2008); Thomas Turino, *Nationalists, Cosmopolitans, and Popular Music in Zimbabwe* (Chicago: University of Chicago Press, 2000); Kelly Askew, *Performing the Nation: Swahili Music and Cultural Politics in Tanzania* (Chicago: University of Chicago Press, 2002).

4. Moorman, *Intonations,* 181.

5. Askew, *Performing the Nation,* 292.

6. John Iliffe, *The African Poor: A History* (Cambridge: Cambridge University Press, 1987), 201–208.

7. Peter Du Sautoy, *Community Development in Ghana* (London: Oxford University Press, 1958), 2–3 and 25–26; "Meeting of the Central Welfare Committee Held at Government House, Accra, on Friday 14th December, 1945," PRO, CO 859/124/6; Gold Coast, *Annual Report of the Department of Social Welfare and Community Development for the Year 1953* (Accra: Government Printing Department, 1954), 1–2.

8. Gold Coast, *Report of the Department of Social Welfare and Community Development 1946–51* (Accra: Government Printing Department, 1953), 11–17. Also see "Juvenile Delinquency and Welfare," PRAAD-Accra, CSO 15/3/340/88; "Department of Social Welfare and Housing," PRAAD-Sekondi, WRG 24/1/232/47; "Case No. 2898, James Town Police," PRAAD-Sekondi, WRG 47/1/15/221.

9. "Life at Night Clubs—Girls and Drinks Galore," *Sunday Mirror,* June 1, 1958; "Youths Face Temptation," *Daily Graphic,* January 8, 1959; "Take a Tip Parents: Let's Save Our Teenagers from Bad Practices," *Sunday Mirror,* January 18, 1959; "The Rock 'N' Roll Music and Dancing: Is It Good or Bad?," *Sunday Mirror,* March 1, 1959; "Girls Who Are Learning Nightclub Ways," *Sunday Mirror,* July 16, 1959.

10. M. L. Clarkson, "Juveniles in Drinking Bars and Nightclubs: A Report on Conditions Observed in Accra, Kumasi, and Takoradi" (Accra: Department of Social Welfare, 1955); Gold Coast, *Problem Children of the Gold Coast* (Accra: Government Printer, 1955).

11. "Drinking Bars in Accra Will Now Close at 8 P.M.," *Daily Graphic,* January 26, 1955; "Bars," *Daily Graphic,* January 28, 1955; Clarkson, "Juveniles in Drinking Bars and Nightclubs," 5–6.

12. "Ban on Drinking Bars," *Daily Graphic,* February 14, 1955; "Drinking Bars to Operate Up to 11 P.M.," *Daily Graphic,* April 14, 1955.

13. "Social Centres," PRAAD-Sekondi, WRG 15/1/642; "Community Centre, Tarkwa," PRAAD-Sekondi, WRG 24/1/105; "Community Centre, Axim," PRAAD-Sekondi, WRG 40/1/39; "Department of Social Welfare," PRAAD-Sekondi, WRG 34/1/22;

"Ashanti—Community Development," *Advance* 1 (1954): 4; "Activities Worth Considering," *Advance* 24 (1959): 23–4.

14. Mr. Mexico, April 18, 2005; Edna and Justina Fugar, April 29, 2005; Georgina Okanee Acei, May 19, 2005.

15. "Ashanti—Community Development," *Advance* 1 (1954): 4; "Course for Bandsmen," *Daily Graphic,* November 22, 1956; "Reports from Field Officers," PRAAD-Sekondi, WRG 47/1/37.

16. Dennis Austin, *Politics in Ghana, 1946–1960* (London: Oxford University Press, 1964), 49–53; David E. Apter, *Ghana in Transition* (Princeton, N.J.: Princeton University Press, 1972), 148–50 and 166–68; Richard Rathbone, "Businessmen in Politics: Party Struggle in Ghana, 1949–1957," *Journal of Development Studies* 9, no. 3 (1973): 391–402. The 1946 Burns Constitution formalized the creation of a new legislative council comprised of the governor (president), six government officials, six nominated members, and eighteen elected members, but also continued to provide the governor with the power to veto any bill approved by its majority.

17. Austin, *Politics in Ghana,* 56–58; Allman, *The Quills of the Porcupine: Asante Nationalism in an Emergent Ghana* (Madison: University of Wisconsin Press, 1993), 28–34.

18. Kwame Nkrumah, *Revolutionary Path* (New York: Panaf Books, 1973), 51. For more on Kwame Nkrumah, see Basil Davidson, *Black Star: A View of the Life and Times of Kwame Nkrumah* (London: Allen Lane, 1973); David Birmingham, *Kwame Nkrumah: The Father of African Nationalism* (Athens: Ohio University Press, 1990).

19. For more on the emergence and aims of the CPP, see Kwame Nkrumah, *Axioms of Kwame Nkrumah* (New York: International Publishers, 1967), 76; Austin, *Politics in Ghana,* 81–102; Apter, *Ghana in Transition,* 202–18; Takyiwaa Manuh, "Women and Their Organizations during the Convention Peoples' Party Period," in *The Life and Work of Kwame Nkrumah,* ed. Kwame Arhin (Accra: Sedco Publishing, 1991), 108–34.

20. Austin, *Politics in Ghana,* 87–90; Manuh, "Women and Their Organizations," 114.

21. Austin, *Politics in Ghana,* 103–52.

22. *Daily Graphic,* May 3, 1954.

23. Margaret Esi Andrews, June 12, 2009; Felicia Kudiah, June 19, 2009; Elizabeth Amonoo, June 20, 2009; George Hagan, "Nkrumah's Leadership Style: An Assessment from a Cultural Perspective," in *The Life and Work of Kwame Nkrumah,* ed. Kwame Arhin (Accra: Sedco Publishing, 1991), 180–210.

24. Collins, "The Ghanaian Concert Party," 491–95; Kofi E. Agovi, "The Political Relevance of Ghanaian Highlife Songs since 1957," *Research in African Literatures* 20, no. 2 (1989): 195–96; *Daily Graphic,* November 28, 1956.

25. Agovi, "The Political Relevance," 194; J. H. Kwabena Nketia, "Modern Trends in Ghana Music," *African Music Society Journal* 1, no. 4 (1957): 14; Daniel Kodzo Avorgbedor, "The Place of the 'Folk' in Ghanaian Popular Music," *Popular Music and Society* 9, no. 2 (1983): 40–41.

26. Elizabeth Amonoo, June 20, 2009.

27. Hagan, "Nkrumah's Leadership Style," 195, emphasis mine; Austin, *Politics in Ghana,* 219.

28. Birmingham, *Kwame Nkrumah,* 311; Austin, *Politics in Ghana,* 132 and 171; *Daily Graphic,* March 29, 1951, January 29, 1954, and May 11, 1954. For Nkrumah's praise of dance, see Kwame Nkrumah, *Africa Must Unite* (London: Heinemann, 1963), 14. For his

efforts to patronize highlife, see *Daily Graphic,* April 11, 1951, March 9, 1954, and December 13, 1960.

29. For more on E. K. Nyame, see "His Music Fits Different Moods," *Sunday Mirror,* May 1, 1960; "He's Successful but Not Yet Rich," *Sunday Mirror,* May 8, 1960.

30. Agovi, "The Political Relevance," 196; Collins, "The Ghanaian Concert Party," 498, 486, and 505. Another example was Kojo Bio's *"Kɔ hwe CPP Assembly ho"* (Go and look at the CPP in the Legislative Assembly): Emmanuel Akyeampong, *Drink, Power, and Cultural Change: A Social History of Alcohol in Ghana, c. 1800 to Recent Times* (Portsmouth: Heinemann, 1996), 126. For a more detailed examination of concert party exploits during the 1950s, see Catherine M. Cole, *Ghana's Concert Party Theatre* (Bloomington: Indiana University Press, 2002), 133–58.

31. "Africa's Man of Destiny" was a title strategically given to Nkrumah in an effort to replace another popular CPP maxim, the demand for "self-government now": Austin, *Politics in Ghana,* 200 and 214.

32. *Daily Graphic,* March 6, 1951; Collins, "The Ghanaian Concert Party," 497–98; Austin, *Politics in Ghana,* 88.

33. *Daily Graphic,* December 10, 1956; Agovi, "The Political Relevance," 196; John Collins, *E. T. Mensah: King of Highlife* (Accra: Anansesem Publications, 1996), 21–23; "Ghana Song of Freedom," PRO, CO 554/595.

34. *Daily Graphic,* July 18, 1954; John Collins, *Highlife Time* (Accra: Anansesem Publications, 1996), 14.

35. "Independence Celebrations," PRAAD-Cape Coast, ADM 23/1/1602; "Independence Day Celebrations—General," PRAAD-Cape Coast, RG 1/11/16. For a schedule of celebration events, see "Ghana Independence Celebrations: Official Programme: Saturday March 2–Saturday March 9, 1957," PRAAD-Accra, ADM 14/6/91.

36. Felicia Kudiah, June 19, 2009.

37. "Independence Celebrations," PRAAD-Cape Coast, ADM 23/1/1602.

38. Advertisements for the numerous dances that celebrated the occasion of independence may be found in *Daily Graphic,* March 1–5, 1957. Also see "Independence Day—General," PRAAD-Cape Coast, RG 1/11/16. For descriptions and accounts of the State Ball, see *Daily Graphic,* March 5, 1957, and March 8, 1957.

39. "Independence Day—General," PRAAD-Cape Coast, RG 1/11/16.

40. "Independence Celebrations, Ballroom Dances," PRAAD-Cape Coast, RG 1/11/22. A few years later, the members of the Association included D. Y. Annan, Adelaide Gbedemah (wife of Komla Gbedemah, the minister of finance), George L. Vroom, Mary Edusei (wife of Krobo Edusei, the minister of transport and communication), Moses Harding, J. F. Augustt, V. V. K. Tamakloe, Julius Schandorf, Eddie Amoo, E. T. Mensah, T. K. Tawiah, Hannah Cudjoe, and Prince Agbodjan; "Highlife Takes a New Name," *Sunday Mirror,* July 1, 1960.

41. "Gold Coast Independence Celebrations," PRAAD-Sekondi, WRG 15/1/216; "Independence Day—General," PRAAD-Cape Coast, RG 1/11/16.

42. "Independence Day—General," PRAAD-Cape Coast, RG 1/11/16. Pre-independence estimates of the number of foreign visitors who would attend Ghana's independence celebrations varied, but the government expected that "about 250 foreign envoys" containing two to eight representatives each and 250,000 Gold Coasters would attend events in Accra: *Daily Graphic,* May 29, 1955, and November 9, 1956.

43. The full text of Nkrumah's independence speech is available in William H. Worger, Nancy L. Clark, and Edward A. Alpers, eds., *Africa and the West: A Documentary History,* vol. 2: *From Colonialism to Independence, 1875 to the Present* (Oxford: Oxford University Press, 2010), 128–29.

44. Nkrumah was not the only newly appointed African leader who held this view: see Askew, *Performing the Nation,* 171– 91; Turino, *Nationalists, Cosmopolitans, and Popular Music,* 177– 84; Bob White, *Rumba Rules: The Politics of Dance Music in Mobutu's Zaire* (Durham, N.C.: Duke University Press, 2008), 69–79.

45. Kwame Nkrumah, *Ghana: The Autobiography of Kwame Nkrumah* (New York: International Publishers, 1957), 198–200; *Revolutionary Path,* 205–208; and *Flower of Learning: Some Reflections on African Learning, Ancient and Modern* (Accra: Government Printer, 1961), 10. Also see "Osagyefo's Speech at the Drama Studio, Saturday 21st October 1961," PRAAD-Accra, RG 3/7/33; George P. Hagan, "Nkrumah's Cultural Policy," in *The Life and Work of Kwame Nkrumah: Papers of a Symposium Organized by the Institute of African Studies,* ed. Kwame Arhin (Accra: Sedco Publishing, 1991), 1–26; Kwame Botwe-Asamoah, *Kwame Nkrumah's Politico-Cultural Thought and Policies: An African-Centered Paradigm for the Second Phase of the African Revolution* (New York: Routledge, 2005), 47–87; Cati Coe, *Dilemmas of Culture in African Schools* (Chicago: University of Chicago Press, 2005), 60–65.

46. James Allotey and Alex Bakpa Moffatt, July 19, 2009; Felicia Kudiah, July 19, 2009; Elizabeth Amonoo, June 20, 2009.

47. Hagan, "Nkrumah's Cultural Policy," 6–8; Austin, *Politics in Ghana,* 371–81. For more on Nkrumah's plans for economic development, see Government of Ghana, *Second Development Plan, 1959–64* (Accra: Government Printer, 1959); Republic of Ghana, *Seven-Year Development Plan* (Accra: Government Printer, 1965).

48. Coe, "Dilemmas of Culture," 65–70; Jeffrey S. Ahlman, "Living with Nkrumahism: Nation, State, and Pan-Africanism in Ghana" (PhD diss., University of Illinois, 2011), 79–94; Jean Allman, "Let Your Fashion Be in Line with Our Ghanaian Costume," in *Fashioning Africa: Power and the Politics of Dress,* ed. Jean Allman (Bloomington: Indiana University Press, 2004), 144–65.

49. Saka Acquaye, August 24, 2005, and September 6, 2005; "The Brigade Drama Group and Band Proposals," PRAAD-Accra, RG 3/7/221; "Material for Consideration by the Ghana Delegation Leader for Inclusion in His Speech to the UNESCO General Conference," PRAAD-Accra, RG 3/7/199; Botwe-Asamoah, *Kwame Nkrumah's Politico-Cultural Thought,* 149–52; Jay Straker, *Youth, Nationalism and the Guinean Revolution* (Bloomington: Indiana University Press, 2009), 84–85; J. H. Kwabena Nketia, "National Development and the Performing Arts of Africa," in *The Muse of Modernity: Essays on Culture as Development in Africa,* ed. Phillip G. Altbach and Salah M. Hassan (Trenton: Africa World Press, 1996), 117–49.

50. Felicia Kudiah, June 19, 2009.

51. Gold Coast, "Legislative Assembly Debates, Issue No. 3, 26th October–9th November 1954" (Accra: Government Printer, 1954), 553.

52. For more on idealized notions of gender, see R. W. Connell, *Masculinities* (Berkeley: University of California Press, 1995), 67–86; Lisa A. Lindsay and Stephan F. Miescher, "Introduction: Men and Masculinities in Modern African History," in *Men and Masculinities in Modern Africa,* ed. Lisa A. Lindsay and Stephan F. Miescher (Portsmouth: Heinemann, 2003), 1–29.

53. "Ghana Republic Is Born," "To the Students of Ghana College, Tamale," "On Home Affairs," "The Noble Task of Teaching," and "Visit to Sunyani," in Kwame Nkrumah, *Selected Speeches of Kwame Nkrumah*, vol. 1, compiled by Samuel Obeng (Accra: Afram Publications, 1979), 93, 203–204, 206–11, 226–30, and 251–54; "Building a Socialist State," in Kwame Nkrumah, *Selected Speeches of Kwame Nkrumah*, vol. 2, compiled by Samuel Obeng (Accra: Afram Publications, 1979), 81–92; "These Moral Wreckers," *Sunday Mirror*, April 11, 1965; "Don't Give Chance Men," *Sunday Mirror*, May 5, 1963.

54. Isaac Amuah, March 30, 2005; Diana Oboshilay, May 24, 2005; "Three Ways to Elegance," *Sunday Mirror*, October 20, 1963; Ghana, *Parliamentary Debates: The Fifth Session of the First Parliament of the Republic of Ghana*, vol. 38 (Accra: State Publishing Corporation, 1965): 381–84. An exhaustive listing of all newspaper articles addressing the appearance of the "new woman" is untenable here, but see the following issues of the 1965 *Sunday Mirror:* January 3, 24, and 31; February 7 and 14; March 28; April 11, 18, and 25; May 2, 9, and 16; June 13, 20, and 27; July 4 and 18; August 15 and 22; September 5, 12, 19, and 26; October 3, 10; and 31; November 7, 14, and 21.

55. For accounts of the Miss Ghana pageant during the 1960s, see *Sunday Mirror,* July 3, 1960, and March 28, 1965. For similar competitions, see "Nkrumah Crowns a Queen," *Daily Graphic*, June 15, 1959; and the following editions of the *Sunday Mirror,* March 13, 1960; April 17, 1960; July 3, 1960; March 17, 1963; May 5, 1963; and December 26, 1963.

56. "Ghana's Republic Is Born," and "To Ghana Women and Women of African Descent," in Nkrumah, *Selected Speeches*, 1:94 and 116–21; "The Fight on Two Fronts," in Nkrumah, *Selected Speeches*, 2:93–104; "Wanted: Ghana's New Girl," *Sunday Mirror,* March 1, 1964.

57. "Motherhood," *Advance*, April 1964; "My Ideal Girl," *Sunday Mirror*, March 29, 1964; "Keep Those Looks But . . .," *Sunday Mirror*, January 3, 1965; "Fall for the Right Men Girls," *Sunday Mirror*, January 10, 1965; "Serve Country with Love and Courage," *Sunday Mirror*, May 2, 1965; "Women's Work in an Urban Community," *Advance*, October 1965.

58. "Things Aren't What We Expect from Our Women," *Daily Graphic*, September 4, 1953; "Moral Weakness in Modern Girls," *Sunday Mirror*, August 8, 1954; "Check This Social Menace," *Daily Graphic*, March 14, 1955; "Why Do Some Men Refuse to Marry?," *Daily Graphic*, November 16, 1957; "Life at Night Clubs—Girls and Drinks Galore!," *Sunday Mirror*, June 1, 1958; "Girls Who Are Learning Night Club Ways," *Sunday Mirror,* July 16, 1959; "Street Girls Are Trying New Plans," *Sunday Mirror,* January 17, 1960; "Sugar Daddy," *Sunday Mirror*, May 22, 1960.

59. Charity Agbenyega, April 27, 2005; Harry Amenumey, May 3, 2005; J. O. Mills, May 6, 2005; Vincent Mensah, May 18, 2005; Joesphine Ayitey, May 19, 2005; Albert Aflakpui, May 20; 2005; Abdul Rahim Dixon, Ahmed Tettey Dixon, and Mohammed Mensah Dixon, May 22, 2005.

60. J. J. Sarpong, June 7, 2005; Aeshitu Zinabo, Comfort Kwame, and Victoria Quainoo, June 12, 2009; "SWOOP!: Police Raids to Stop 'Street Girls' in Ghana," *Sunday Mirror*, October 18, 1955; *Daily Graphic*, April 5, 1957; "Police Round Up Idlers in Accra," *Daily Graphic*, May 18, 1957; "Good Time Girls," *Daily Graphic*, November 25, 1958; "Let Us Move More Freely," *Sunday Mirror*, October 18, 1959; "50 Girls Hold Talks in Accra," *Sunday Mirror*, October 25, 1959; "Men! Stop Taking These Girls Home," *Sunday Mirror*, October 25, 1959; "Stop This Menace in Ghana," *Daily Graphic*, December 22, 1959.

61. J. O. Mills, May 6, 2005.

62. James Allotey, April 27, 2005; *Daily Graphic,* April 4, 1957; "Cape Coast Takes the Lead . . . 'Fish' Skirts Now Banned," *Sunday Mirror,* June 19, 1963; "Must We Ban Such Dresses," *Sunday Mirror,* June 30, 1963.

63. Ahlman, "Living with Nkrumahism," 78–79; "Police Round Up Idlers in Accra," *Daily Graphic,* May 18, 1957; *Sunday Mirror,* June 1, 1958. Coincidentally, Tokyo Joes was also the name of an Accra rock 'n' roll club.

64. In 1961, the Censorship Board banned two films, *Love Me Tender* and *Rock Pretty Baby,* for their musical contents; "Censored Films," PRAAD-Sekondi, WRG 34/1/12. Also see "Too Western?," *Daily Graphic,* September 28, 1957; "Youths Facing Temptation," *Daily Graphic,* January 8, 1958; "Urban Conditions Lead to Juvenile Delinquency," *Daily Graphic,* November 25, 1958; "Ghana Today," *Ghanaian,* January 1961.

65. Ahlman, "Living with Nkrumahism," 79–82; Peter Hodge, "The Ghana Workers Brigade: A Project for Unemployed Youth," *British Journal of Sociology* 15, no. 2 (1964): 114–21; "Builders' Brigade Is to Curb Love for White-Collar Jobs," *Ghana Times,* October 3, 1958; "Work and Workers Page: Nothing Is More Hopeful in Ghana Than the Builder's Brigade Camps," *Ghanaian,* June 1960.

66. Hodge, "The Ghana Workers Brigade," 115 and 124; "The Achievements of the Workers Brigade," *Ghana Pictorial,* September 1962, 14.

67. Margaret Esi Andrews, June 12, 2009; Hodge, "The Ghana Workers Brigade," 119–22; "The Achievements of the Workers Brigade," *Ghana Pictorial,* September 1962, 14; "New Sporting Era in West Africa" and "Sports and African Unity," in Nkrumah, *Selected Speeches,* 1:26–29.

68. "Builders' Brigade Band," *Ghana Times,* April 11, 1959; "No. 1 Builders' Brigade Band," *Sunday Mirror,* July 5, 1959; "Tops of the Pops: Harvest of Discs," *Sunday Mirror,* October 11, 1959.

69. Many Brigade songs, such as *"Hedzole (Freedom) aha Brigades,"* actively espoused pro-government messages: John Collins, "The Importance of African Popular Music Studies for Ghanaian/African Students," paper presented at CODESRIA's 30th Anniversary Humanities Conference, Accra, September 17–19, 2003. For more on the band's performances, see "Spike and Tommy the Winners," *Daily Graphic,* July 10, 1959; "9 Will Play in Accra August 1," *Sunday Mirror,* July 26, 1959; "'Graphic' Goes to Town Tonight," *Daily Graphic,* October 3, 1959.

70. Republic of Ghana, "Report on the Commission Appointed to Enquire into the Functions, Operation and Administration of the Worker's Brigade" (Accra: Government Printer, 1968), 1. The cedi replaced the pound as Ghana's national currency in 1965. In 1967 it was reissued at the rate of 2 cedis=1 pound. It is unclear when this report derived its figures, but exchange rates of the period suggest that 1,903.76 cedis would have been roughly equivalent to £950 or $1,900.

71. G. Thomas Burgess, "Cinema, Bell Bottoms, and Miniskirts: Struggles over Youth Citizenship in Revolutionary Zanzibar," *International Journal of African Historical Studies* 35, nos. 2–3 (2002): 287–313.

72. "Interim Committee for an Arts Council," PRAAD-Accra, RG 3/7/212.

73. In the 1950s, the term "jaguar" referred to individuals who exhibited modern appeal: Collins, "The Ghanaian Concert Party," 371; "Interim Committee for an Arts Council, 1957–59," PRAAD-Accra, RG 3/7/212; Botwe-Asamoah, *Kwame Nkrumah's Politico-Cultural Thought,* 158–59.

74. Botwe-Asamoah, *Kwame Nkrumah's Politico-Cultural Thought,* 159–61; Coe, *Dilemmas of African Schools,* 70–74.

75. "Arts Council, General Matters: 1959–60," PRAAD-Accra, RG 3/7/31; "Arts Council, General Matters: 1959–1962," PRAAD-Accra, RG 3/7/33; "Arts Council Regional Reports, 1961–64," PRAAD-Accra, RG 3/7/243. For a similar case in Tanzania, see Askew, *Performing the Nation,* 172–76.

76. "Brong-Ahafo Region Arts Committee Monthly Report for May, 1961," and "Monthly Report Eastern Region Arts Committee, August 1961," PRAAD-Accra, RG 3/7/243.

77. "Report on the Black Star Troupe—'Un-Ghanaian Dancing,'" PRAAD-Accra, RG 3/7/57/1; "Osagyefo's Speech at the Drama Studio, Saturday 21st October 1961," PRAAD-Accra, RG 3/7/33.

78. "Monthly Report Eastern Regional Arts Committee, April 1961," PRAAD-Accra, RG 3/7/243/3; "Minutes of the First Meeting of the Dance Panel," PRAAD-Accra, RG 3/7/156/5.

79. "Arts Council General Matters and Policies," PRAAD-Accra, RG 3/7/33; "Monthly Report Eastern Regional Arts Committee, April 1961," PRAAD-Accra, RG 3/7/243/3; "Minutes of the First Meeting of the Dance Panel," PRAAD-Accra, RG 3/7/156/5.

80. Hagan, "Nkrumah's Cultural Policy," 14–16.

81. Stan Plange, October 5, 2005; "The Ghana Institute of Art and Culture: Drumming and Dancing," PRAAD-Accra, RG 3/7/57/121; "Interim Committee for an Arts Council," PRAAD-Accra, RG 3/7/212; J. H. Kwabena Nketia, "Changing Traditions of Folk Music in Ghana," *Journal of the International Folk Music Council* 11 (1959): 35.

82. "Local Government Dance Band," PRAAD-Accra, RG 3/7/57; "Messengers Dance Band Activities," PRAAD-Accra, RG 3/7/68; "Globemasters Dance Band, General Correspondence," PRAAD-Accra, RG 3/7/193.

83. "Dance Band General Matters," PRAAD-Accra, RG 3/7/197.

84. "The Ghana Institute of Art and Culture: Drumming and Dancing," PRAAD-Accra, RG 3/7/57/121; "Messengers Dance Band Activities," PRAAD-Accra, RG 3/7/68.

85. "Local Government Dance Band," PRAAD-Accra, RG 3/7/57; "Messengers Dance Band Activities," PRAAD-Accra, RG 3/7/68; "Globemasters Dance Band, General Correspondence," PRAAD-Accra, RG 3/7/193. In his second quarterly report of 1963, Opoku Ware reported that he taught the Workers Brigade Dance Band a pro-government highlife entitled "*Nkrumah Wo Ho Yɛhu*"; "Report: From April-July, 1963," PRAAD-Accra, RG 3/7/57.

86. Henry Ayawovie, May 30, 2005; Ebo Taylor, September 1, 2005. For more on the impacts of government-sponsored dance bands, see Collins, *E. T. Mensah,* 35–37.

87. "Dance Band General Matters," PRAAD-Accra, RG 3/7/197/ 13, 18, 21 and 46; "Messengers Dance Band Activities," PRAAD-Accra, RG 3/7/68/92; "Globemasters Dance Band, General Correspondence," PRAAD-Accra, RG 3/7/193.

88. Stan Plange, October 5, 2005.

89. Stan Plange, June 29, 2005, and October 5, 2005; "Globemasters Dance Band, General Correspondence," PRAAD-Accra, RG 3/7/193.

90. "Ghanaian Writes Special Hi-Life," *Ghana Times,* February 10, 1959; "Role of Musician Envoys," *Daily Graphic,* May 16, 1967; "National Drama Company," PRAAD-

Accra, RG 3/7/171/165, 177, 211, and 317; "Interim Committee for an Arts Council," PRAAD-Accra, RG 3/7/212.

91. "Dance Band General Matters," PRAAD-Accra, RG 3/7/197/ 13, 18, 21 and 46; "Messengers Dance Band Activities," PRAAD-Accra, RG 3/7/68/92; "Report on My Staff—Drumming and Dancing Section," PRAAD-Accra, RG 3/7/57; "Globemasters Dance Band, General Correspondence," PRAAD-Accra, RG 3/7/193.

92. "Show of 18/7/62—Messengers," PRAAD-Accra, RG 3/7/57/121; "Messengers Dance Band Activities," PRAAD-Accra, RG 3/7/68.

93. Entire script taken from "Messengers Dance Band Activities," PRAAD-Accra, RG 3/7/68/1. Although the council created other versions of the scripted performance, this is the final and most polished effort available. "George" is George Lee, the bandleader.

94. "Deep Purple" was originally published in the early 1930s as a piano composition, after which it became a common standard in many jazz circles. The script's other Western number, "Answer Me," was originally written and composed in German and was likely included to appeal to German audiences.

95. "The Modernaires," *Sunday Mirror,* July 26, 1959; "Modernaires Dance Band Is Reborn," *Ghana Pictorial,* September 1962.

96. Jerry Hansen, October 3 and October 13, 2005; "Encore Ramblers!," *Sunday Mirror,* February 2, 1964; "Work and Happiness," *Sunday Mirror,* February 16, 1964. The song's title corresponds to that of a speech given by Kwame Nkrumah on May 5, 1962: "Work and Happiness: Ghana's Seven-Year Development Plan," in *Selected Speeches of Kwame Nkrumah,* vol. 3, compiled by Samuel Obeng (Accra: Afram Publications, 1997), 65–70.

97. "The Spots—Ten Years Old," *Sunday Mirror,* April 3, 1963; "Joe Mensah—A Singer with Vibrant Voice," *Sunday Mirror,* September 8, 1963; "Who Earns More Fame for Ghana: Sportsmen or Musicians?," *Sunday Mirror,* February 9, 1964; "Star Who Blends His Artistry with Folklore," *Sunday Mirror,* April 12, 1964. For one that decried particular band practices, see "Four Bandsmen Go to Jail," *Daily Graphic,* May 13, 1960.

98. "Outline Program for the Fourth Republic Anniversary Celebrations in 1964," PRAAD-Accra, RG3/7/9/31 and 43–5; "Two Bands to Play at 'Royal' Dance," *Daily Graphic,* June 10, 1959; "They Are Selected Best Bands," *Daily Graphic,* July 13, 1959; "Music Festivals and Competitions," PRAAD-Accra, RG 3/7/148.

99. "The National Dance Bands Competition," RG 3/7/197/84; "Minutes of Meeting Held between the Arts Council Members and the Bandsmen," RG 3/7/197/100–104; "The National Dance Bands Competition—Round 3, Western Region," RG 3/7/197/158.

100. "Regional Music Activities," PRAAD-Accra, RG 3/7/154; "Arts Council of Ghana," PRAAD-Sekondi, WRG 34/1/11; "Drumming and Dancing," PRAAD-Accra, RG 3/7/145.

101. *Daily Graphic,* September 28, 1960.

102. "The Origin of the Highlife: Graphic Readers Have Their Say," *Daily Graphic,* October 22, 1960.

5. "We Were the Ones Who Composed the Songs"

1. From 1931 to 1948, Takoradi's population increased from 5,478 residents to 17,327: Gold Coast, *The Gold Coast Census of Population 1948: Report and Tables* (Accra: Government Printer, 1950), 94.

2. For more on Kakaiku's Band and its role in the concert-party genre, see Catherine M. Cole, *Ghana's Concert Party Theatre* (Bloomington: Indiana University Press, 2001), 144–49.

3. C. K. Mann, September 19, 2005; Daniel Kinful Sam, September 19, 2005.

4. James Allotey, April 27, 2005.

5. C. K. Mann, September 19, 2005. A more recent visit in June 2009 revealed that the street had later been renamed "C. K. Mann Avenue."

6. "Clubs," PRAAD-Cape Coast, ADM 23/1/298/233; "The Eureka Literary and Social Club and the Schools," *Gold Coast Observer,* February 5, 1943; "Empire Day at Cape Coast," *Gold Coast Observer,* June 18, 1943; "An Omission in School Curriculum," *Gold Coast Observer,* June 25, 1948.

7. Oscarmore Ofori, October 20, 2005; Desmond Ababio, July 27, 2005; Jerry Hansen, October 3 and October 13, 2005.

8. John Collins, May 13, 2005; Saka Acquaye, August 24, 2005; Jerry Hansen, October 3, 2005 and October 13, 2005.

9. Isaac Amuah, March 30, 2005; Kwadwo Adum-Attah, April 1, 2005; John Collins, "The Generational Factor in Ghanaian Music," in *Playing with Identities in Contemporary Music in Africa,* ed. Mai Palmberg and Annemette Kirkegaard (Uppsala: Nordiska Afrikainstitutet, 2002), 60–74.

10. In 1953, E. T. Mensah became the Gold Coast's first professional highlife musician, leaving his work as a pharmacist in order to pursue music as his sole source of income. In the years that followed, growing numbers of highlife musicians dabbled with the challenges and prospects of being professional musicians: Bob Biney, April 1, 2005; John Collins, *E. T. Mensah: King of Highlife* (Accra: Anansesem Publications, 1996), 13.

11. Peter Manuh, July 23, 2005; John Collins, "The Ghanaian Concert Party: African Popular Entertainment at the Cross Roads" (PhD diss., State University of New York at Buffalo, 1994), 64.

12. Abdul Rahim Dixon, Ahmed Tettey Dixon, and Mohammed Mensah Dixon, May 22, 2005. Such attitudes were not unique to Ghana: Collins, "The Ghanaian Concert Party," 400–401; David Coplan, "The Urbanisation of African Music: Some Theoretical Observations," *Popular Music* 2 (1982): 120–21; Bob White, *Rumba Rules: the Politics of Dance Music in Mobutu's Zaire* (Durham, N.C.: Duke University Press, 2008), 136.

13. When Y. B. Bampoe, the leader of the Jaguar Jokers, a well-known concert party troupe during the 1950s–1970s, informed an enquirer that he was married and had a family he met stubborn disbelief, largely on the widespread conviction that no married man would agree to spend large periods of time away from home: Collins, "The Ghanaian Concert Party," 130.

14. Stan Plange, June 29, 2005.

15. Desmond Ababio, July 27, 2005; Collins, "The Ghanaian Concert Party," 296–300.

16. Oscarmore Ofori, October 20, 2005.

17. Desmond Ababio, July 27, 2005; Kwadwo Adum-Attah, February 18, 2005; George Nanabanyin Johnson, September 21, 2005; "Profile of a Top Singer," *Ghana Radio Review and TV Times,* September 25, 1965. Steven Feld reveals how similar attitudes impacted a group of Ghanaian jazz musicians: *Jazz Cosmopolitanism in Accra: Five Musical Years in Ghana* (Durham, N.C.: Duke University Press, 2012).

18. Vincent Mensah, May 18, 2005. For more on education's importance to shaping young men, see Stephan F. Miescher, *Making Men in Ghana* (Bloomington: Indiana University Press, 2005), 48–83.

19. Ebo Taylor, August 24, 2005.

20. Kwadwo Donkoh experienced similar opposition for his decision to leave the diplomatic service in order to found Ghana's Agoro Records in the 1960s: September 16, 2005. Also see George Nanabanyin Johnson, September 21, 2005; Nana Ampadu, September 24, 2005; Collins, "The Ghanaian Concert Party," 93 and 442–46.

21. Kwadwo Adum-Attah, February 18, 2005; Aeshitu Zinabo, May 20, 2005; Stan Plange, June 29, 2005; Peter Manuh, July 23, 2005; Saka Acquaye, August 24, 2005; C. K. Mann, September 19, 2005.

22. Agnes Ayitey and Julie Okine performed with E. T. Mensah's Tempos, while Charlotte Dada joined the Builder's Brigade Dance Band and later the Professional Uhuru Dance Band. For more on women's exclusion from highlife performance, see Stan Plange, June 29, 2005; Collins, "The Ghanaian Concert Party," 459–85; K. M. Ashaley, "Radio Ghana Annual Dance: It Was a Gala Night," *Ghana Radio Review and TV Times*, January 7, 1966.

23. Comfort Sarpong, September 9, 2005; Emmanuel Quao, June 23, 2005; Stan Plange, June 29, 2005; Kwadwo Donkoh, September 16, 2005; C. K. Mann, September 19, 2005. Margaret Quainoo informed me that many people labeled her a prostitute after she decided to become a concert party actress: Margaret Quainoo, September 12, 2005.

24. Because there were relatively few female highlife musicians, locating and interviewing them was an extremely difficult venture. I was able to conduct brief interviews with two female popular musical performers, Margaret Quainoo and Comfort Sarpong, in 2005, but both passed away prior to my second research trip in 2009.

25. A copy of this song is not currently available, but Okine's lyrics can be found in John Collins, *Highlife Time* (Accra: Anansesem Publications, 1996), 179.

26. J. H. Kwabena Nketia, *Drumming in Akan Communities of Ghana* (London: Thomas Nelson and Sons, 1963), 71–73.

27. Collins, "The Ghanaian Concert Party," 464–65; Kwabena Nketia, "The Instrumental Resources of African Music," *Papers in African Studies 3* (1968): 1–23.

28. Kofi Lindsay, March 31, 2005; Collins, "The Ghanaian Concert Party," 461–64.

29. Kofi Lindsay, March 31, 2005. Also see Henry Ayawovie, May 30, 2005; Peter Manuh, July 29, 2005.

30. Daniel Kinful Sam, September 19, 2005.

31. Stan Plange, June 29, 2005.

32. Daniel Kinful Sam, September 19, 2005.

33. Kofi Lindsay, March 31, 2005; Peter Manuh, July 23, 2005; Daniel Kinful Sam, September 19, 2005. For more on musicians' embrace of female attention in Luanda and Kinshasa, see Marissa Moorman, *Intonations: A Social History of Music and Nation in Luanda, Angola, from 1945 to Recent Times* (Athens: Ohio University Press, 2008), 93–101; White, *Rumba Rules*, 132–41.

34. Charity Agbenyega, April 27, 2005; Josephine Ayitey, May 19, 2005; Alex Bakpa Moffatt, May 21, 2005; Nii Armah, May 22, 2005; Gloria Ocloo, May 24, 2005; Henry Ayawovie, May 30, 2005; J. J. Sarpong, June 7, 2005; Elizabeth Amonoo, October 18, 2005.

35. "Form 4" was a stage of secondary education, equivalent to the tenth year of schooling.

36. "Small boy" is the opposite of a "big man" and is a term used to refer to an insignificant person of little consequence to community affairs. Here, the charge that John-

son was a "small boy" suggests that he was too young to have any musical knowledge or ability and, hence, had no right approaching the stage. For more on the "big man" / "small boy" paradigm in the realm of Ghanaian politics, see Robert Prince, "Politics and Culture in Contemporary Ghana: The Big-Man Small-Boy Syndrome," *Journal of African Studies* 1, no. 2 (1974): 173–204; Paul Nugent, *Big Men, Small Boys, and Politics in Ghana: Power, Ideology, and the Burden of History, 1982–1994* (London: Pinter, 1995).

37. "Blue Moon" was an American ballad originally written and performed by Richard Rodgers and Lorenz Hart in 1934. In subsequent decades, it became popular among groups that played jazz standards.

38. George Nanabanyin Johnson, September 21, 2005.

39. For other examples, see Clive Glaser, *Bo-Tsotsi: The Youth Gangs of Soweto, 1935–1976* (Portsmouth: Heinemann, 2000), 67–71; James Ferguson, *Expectations of Modernity: Myths and Meanings of Urban Life on the Zambian Copperbelt* (Berkeley: University of California Press, 1999), 82–112; Moorman, *Intonations*, 204; White, *Rumba Rules*, 102–10; G. Thomas Burgess, "Cinema, Bell Bottoms and Miniskirts: Struggles over Youth and Citizenship in Revolutionary Zanzibar," *International Journal of African Historical Studies* 35, nos. 2–3 (2002): 287–313.

40. Kwadwo Adum-Attah, February 18, 2005; Isaac Amuah, March 30, 2005; Elizabeth Amonoo, October 18, 2005.

41. George Nanabanyin Johnson, September 21, 2005.

42. Yamoah's Band was a guitar band that performed throughout the 1960s and 1970s. Ampadu first performed with the band when he was only fifteen years old.

43. Despite the prevalence of local drums, most highlife dance bands relied primarily on Western drum sets. In the 1950s, Kofi Ghanaba, then a member of the Tempos, began to use imported congas and bongos alongside the drum kit, which proved to be an instant success. These imported drums remained instruments of choice for many dance bands throughout the 1950s and 1960s. Unable to afford such drums, Ampadu's group had to use a "Ghana-made conga," or *kpanlogo,* instead.

44. This was the same year that the Organization of African Unity was formed, largely with Nkrumah's support.

45. In Ghanaian English, the repetition of an adjective implies emphasis. Thus, "small small" means "very small."

46. While HMV and Zonophone recorded Gold Coast musicians during the 1930s and 1940s, a local record industry did not blossom until after independence. Decca opened a recording studio in Accra in 1947, but other recording companies only made annual or semiannual trips to West African cities in order to record local artists. Even Phillips, which established two studios in Nigeria during the late 1950s and early 1960s, continued to send agents to Accra in order to record artists on an occasional basis. As a result, highlife musicians had limited studio time until the 1960s, when local recording studios, such as Ghana Films Corporation (Accra), Ambassador Records (Kumasi), and Polygram Records (Accra), were established: Collins, "The Ghanaian Concert Party," 247–49 and 267–68.

47. This is not the name of the actual band but a pseudonym used at the author's discretion.

48. Nana Ampadu, September 24, 2005.

49. Ampadu's recollection of looking for musicians inside the gramophone player is another instance that reveals his unfamiliarity with the recording process instrumental

to the profession. Ampadu, however, was not alone in this assumption: Kwame Sarpong, April 1, 2005.

50. For more on the ways in which musical big men fostered political and social power in Mobutu's Zaire, see White, *Rumba Rules,* 195–221.

51. Kwadwo Adum-Attah, April 1, 2005; Kofi Lindsay, June 1, 2005; Comfort Sarpong, September 9, 2005; C. K. Mann, September 19, 2005; King Onyina, October 9, 2005. For an overview of the expansion of the Ghana Broadcasting System, see Ghana Broadcasting Corporation, *GBC* (Accra: New Times Corporation, 1973). One weekly journal that reflected musicians' growing prominence in 1960s Ghana was the *Ghana Radio Review and TV Times,* which was published by the Ghana Radio and Television Corporation. In addition to featuring articles highlighting individual artists, the *Times* featured the upcoming schedule for what the Ghana Broadcasting Corporation would play on air.

52. Ebo Taylor, August 24, 2005; George Nanabanyin Johnson, September 21, 2005; King Onyina, October 9, 2005.

53. Bob Biney, April 1, 2005; Emmanuel Quao, June 23, 2005; Desmond Ababio, July 27, 2005; Ebo Taylor, September 1, 2005; Nana Ampadu, September 24, 2005; Jerry Hansen, October 5, 2005; King Onyina, October 9, 2005.

54. For more on this maxim, "being a man is hard," see Miescher, *Making Men in Ghana,* 1.

55. C. K. Mann, September 19, 2005; Stan Plange, June 29, 2005; Ebo Taylor, September 1, 2005; Daniel Kinful Sam, September 19, 2005; Nana Ampadu, September 24, 2005; Koo Nimo, October 7, 2005.

56. Kofi Lindsay, June 22, 2005; Stan Plange, June 29, 2005; Ebo Taylor, August 24, 2005; Jerry Hansen, October 3, 2005; Collins, *Highlife Time,* 65.

57. Desmond Ababio, July 27, 2005; Ebo Taylor, August 24, 2005.

58. Ebo Taylor, August 24, 2005. Also see Stan Plange, June 29, 2005; "He's Successful but Not Yet Rich," *Sunday Mirror,* May 8, 1960.

59. Kofi Lindsay, June 22, 2005; Saka Acquaye, August 24, 2005; Jerry Hansen, October 3, 2005; C. K. Mann, June 26, 2009. The styles Lindsay mentioned included tango, waltz, slow foxtrot, *pachanga,* blues, quick-step, bolero, smoochy highlife, calypso, reggae, highlife, *adowa, kolomashie, asafo beat,* apostolic songs, and *karakaara.*

60. Ebo Taylor, July 26, 2005; Saka Acquaye, August 24, 2005; Jerry Hansen, October 3, 2005; Collins, "The Ghanaian Concert Party," 103–104.

61. Stan Plange, June 29, 2005; Ebo Taylor, August 24, 2005.

62. "Bolga" is short for Bolgatanga, the present-day capital of Ghana's Upper East Region.

63. Kofi Lindsay, March 31, 2005.

64. "Arts Council, Regional Reports, 1961–64," NAG-Accra, RG 3/7/243; "Dance Bands, General Matters, 1970–72," NAG-Accra, RG 3/7/197; *Sunday Mirror,* December 31, 1967.

65. Kofi Lindsay, March 31, 2005; Peter Manuh, July 23, 2005; Nana Ampadu, September 24, 2005; Jerry Hansen, October 3, 2005.

66. Emmanuel Quao, June 23, 2005; Desmond Ababio, July 27, 2005; Ebo Taylor, August 24, 2005; Daniel Kinful Sam, September 19, 2005; Jerry Hansen, October 3, 2005; Koo Nimo, October 7, 2005. For the rules of the Jaguar Jokers Band, see Collins, "The Ghanaian Concert Party," 110–11.

67. Kofi Lindsay, June 22, 2005; Stan Plange, June 29, 2005; Peter Manuh, July 23, 2005.

68. Kofi Lindsay, June 22, 2005; Emmanuel Quao, June 23, 2005; Stan Plange, June 29, 2005; Peter Manuh, July 23, 2005; Saka Acquaye, August 24, 2005; Nana Ampadu, September 24, 2005; Jerry Hansen, October 3, 2005.

69. Stan Plange, June 29, 2005.

70. Kofi Lindsay, March 31, 2005; Peter Manuh, July 23, 2005; Saka Acquaye, August 24, 2005; Daniel Kinful Sam, September 19, 2005. Also see Collins, "The Ghanaian Concert Party," 450; and *E. T. Mensah*, 41–42.

71. Kofi Lindsay, March 31, 2005, and June 22, 2005.

72. C. K. Mann, September 19, 2005; Stan Plange, October 5, 2005; Koo Nimo, October 7, 2005.

73. Stan Plange, June 29, 2005; Saka Acquaye, August 24, 2005; Jerry Hansen, October 3, 2005.

74. Grershon Gaba, April 29, 2005; Elizabeth Amonoo, September 10, 2005; K. Ampom Darkwa, "Migrant Music and Musicians: The Effect of Migration on Music, pt. 1: Nima Opinion Survey" (PhD diss., University of Ghana, Institute of African Studies, 1971). For parallel observations about lyrics in Congolese popular music, see White, *Rumba Rules*, 165–67.

75. Nana Ampadu, September 24, 2005; Jerry Hansen, October 3, 2005. For more on the lyrical content and character of highlife songs, see Owusu Brempong, "Akan Highlife in Ghana: Songs of Cultural Transition" (PhD diss., Indiana University, 1986); Atta Annan Mensah, "The Popular Song and the Ghanaian Writer," *Okyeame* 4, no. 1 (1968): 110–19.

76. Several highlife songs gave way to particular cloth designs, including "*Yaw Berku*" [a man's name], "*Aku Sika*" (Golden money), "*Aban Nkaba*" (Handcuffs), and "*Afie Bɛ Yɛ Asan*" (Some years are full of trouble): Collins, "The Ghanaian Concert Party," 176.

77. Africander Stores, *Sensational Gramophone Record Song Book* (Accra: Africander Stores, 1953); E. K. Nyame, *E. K.'s Band Song Book* (Accra: H. Teymani, 1955); Koo Nimo and J. L. Latham, *Ashanti Ballads* (Kumasi: Published by authors, 1969); Atta Annan Mensah, *Sing, Sing, Sing: Forty Ghanaian Songs You Enjoy* (Accra: Anowuo Educational Publications, 1968).

78. Kwadwo Adum-Attah, February 18, 2005; Ebo Taylor, July 26, 2005; Comfort Sarpong, September 9, 2005; Kwadwo Donkoh, September 16, 2005; Daniel Kinful Sam, September 19, 2005.

79. Koo Nimo, October 7, 2005; Kwesi Yankah, *Speaking for the Chief: Okyeame and the Politics of Akan Royal Oratory* (Bloomington: Indiana University Press, 1995), 45–67; J. H. Kwabena Nketia, "The Linguistic Aspect of Style in African Languages," in *Current Trends in Linguistics: Linguistics in Sub-Saharan Africa*, vol. 7, ed. Thomas Sebeok (The Hague: Mouton Press, 1971), 733–57.

80. Nana Ampadu, September 24, 2005; Jerry Hansen, October 3, 2005; Koo Nimo, October 7, 2005. For more on Ampadu's lyrical eminence, see Kwesi Yankah, "Nana Ampadu, the Sung-Tale Metaphor, and Protest Discourse in Contemporary Ghana," in *African Words, African Voices: Critical Practices in Oral History*, ed. Luise White, Stephan F. Miescher, and David William Cohen (Bloomington: Indiana University Press, 2001), 227–45; Nimrod Asante-Darko and Sjaak van der Geest, "The Political Meaning of Highlife Songs in Ghana," *African Studies Review* 25, no. 1 (1982): 27–35.

81. Stan Plange, June 29, 2005; Kwadwo Donkoh, September 16, 2005; John Collins, "One Hundred Years of Censorship in Ghanaian Popular Performance," in *Popular Music Censorship in Africa,* ed. Michael Drewett and Martin Cloonan (Burlington, Vt.: Ashgate, 2006), 178–81.

82. Jerry Hansen, October 3, 2005; Nimrod Asante-Darko and Sjaak van der Geest, "Male Chauvinism: Men and Women in Ghanaian Highlife Songs," in *Female and Male in West Africa,* ed. Christine Oppong (London: George Allen and Unwin, 1983), 242–55; Anna Oppong, "The Use of English in Ghanaian Highlife Music" (Diploma paper, Department of English, University of Ghana, Legon, 1979).

83. Nana Ampadu, September 24, 2005; Edward Apenteng-Sackey, October 5, 2005; Asante-Darko and van der Geest, "The Political Meaning"; Kofi Agovi, "The Political Relevance of Ghanaian Highlife Songs Since 1957," *Research in African Literatures* 20, no. 2 (1989): 194–201; Yankah, *Speaking for the Chief,* 51–52; and "Nana Ampadu," 227–45.

84. Asante-Darko and van der Geest, "Male Chauvinism"; Samuel Gyasi Obeng, "Language and Gender: Women in Akan Highlife Discourse" (unpublished paper in author's possession, 1997); Kwabena Bame, "Domestic Tensions Reflected in the Popular Theatre in Ghana," in *Domestic Rights and Duties in Southern Ghana,* ed. Christine Oppong (Legon: University of Ghana Institute of African Studies, 1974), 145–61.

85. James Matthew Thompson, August 29, 2005; J. J. Sarpong, August 24, 2005; Ebo Taylor, September 1, 2005; Abdul Rahim Dixon, Ahmed Tettey Dixon, and Mohammed Mensah Dixon, September 4, 2005; Lucy Ansah, September 7, 2005.

86. Several newspaper articles voiced similar concerns. See the following issues of the *Daily Graphic:* March 1, 1963; March 29, 1963; July 4, 1965; January 12, 1967. Also see the following issues of the *Sunday Mirror:* February 17, 1963; January 3, 1965; May 2, 1965; March 27, 1966; September 11, 1966; January 4, 1967.

87. Elizabeth Amonoo, September 10, 2005. Also see Henry Ayawovie, May 30, 2005; J. J. Sarpong, August 24, 2005; Josephine Ayitey, August 29, 2005; James Matthew Thompson, August 29, 2005; James Allotey and Linda Botchway, August 30, 2005; Edna Fugar, August 31, 2005; Abdul Rahim Dixon, Ahmed Tettey Dixon, and Mohammed Mensah Dixon, September 4, 2005; Alice Amakoa, September 9, 2005; Jerry Hansen, October 3, 2005.

88. Stan Plange, October 5, 2005.

89. Isaac Amuah, March 30, 2005.

90. Ebo Taylor, August 24, 2005, and September 1, 2005.

91. J. J. Sarpong, August 24, 2005; Kofi Ofori, August 30, 2005; Lucy Efia Ansah, September 7, 2005; Akua Danso, September 9, 2005; Alice Amakoa, September 9, 2005; Adjoa and Akua Opoku, September 10, 2005.

92. J. J. Sarpong, August 24, 2005; Josephine Ayitey, August 29, 2005; James Matthew Thompson, August 29, 2005; James Allotey and Linda Botchway, August 30, 2005; Edna Fugar, August 31, 2005; Ebo Taylor, September 1, 2005; Abdul Rahim Dixon, Ahmed Tettey Dixon, and Mohammed Mensah Dixon, September 4, 2005; Aeshitu Zinabo, September 7, 2005; Alice Amakoa, September 9, 2005; Elizabeth Amonoo, September 10, 2005; Adjoa and Abena Opoku, September 10, 2005.

93. Stan Plange, October 5, 2005; Collins, "The Ghanaian Concert Party," 305–308.

94. Vincent Mensah and Juliana Yeboah, August 30, 2005; Kofi Ofori, August 30, 2005; Ato and Matilda Ray, July 17, 2009. For similar practices in Zanzibar, see Laura

Fair, "Voice, Authority, and Memory: The Kiswahili Lyrics of Siti binti Saadi," in *African Words, African Voices: Critical Practices in Oral History,* ed. Luise White, Stephan F. Miescher, and David William Cohen (Bloomington: Indiana University Press, 2001), 246–63; and *Pastimes and Politics: Culture, Community, and Identity in Post-Abolition Urban Zanzibar, 1890–1945* (Athens: Ohio University Press, 2001), 169–225.

95. Jerry Hansen, October 3, 2005; Stan Plange, October 5, 2005; Saka Acquaye, September 7, 2005.

96. Godwin Azameti, August 28, 2005; Josephine Ayitey, August 29, 2005; James Allotey and Linda Botchway, August 30, 2005; Edna Fugar, August 31, 2005; Ebo Taylor, September 1, 2005; Lucy Ansah, September 7, 2005; Alice Amakoa, September 9, 2005.

97. Saka Acquaye, September 7, 2005; Jerry Hansen, October 3, 2005; Elizabeth Amonoo, September 10, 2005.

98. Abdul Rahim Dixon, Ahmed Tettey Dixon, and Mohammed Mensah Dixon, September 4, 2005; Aeshitu Zinabo, September 7, 2005; Akua Danso, September 9, 2005. Although not the singer, E. T. Mensah was indeed Ga.

99. For example, "*di holidays*" (eat or spend holidays), *di sika* (eat or spend money), and "*di nkɔmɔ*" (eat conversation or chat).

100. Nii Adgin Tettey, September 11, 2005.

101. J. J. Sarpong, August 24, 2005; Nii Adgin Tettey, September 11, 2005; Willie Darko, September 13, 2005. For similar concerns about young women's sexual autonomy in the 1950s and 1960s, see the following issues of the *Daily Graphic:* August 12, 1952; September 4, 1953; March 14, 1955; January 13, 1960; November 9, 1960. Also see the following issues of the *Sunday Mirror:* July 18, 1954; August 8, 1954; January 3, 1955; June 1, 1958.

102. James Thompson, August 28, 2005. Also see Akua and Abena Opoku, September 10, 2005; Emmanuel Ashie Nukwuani, September 11, 2005. For similar critiques in newspapers of the period, see the *Daily Graphic:* July 17, 1953; September 22, 1953; January 28, 1955; May 14, 1955; October 16, 1957; November 16, 1957. Also see the *Sunday Mirror:* January 30, 1955.

103. Vincent Mensah and Juliana Yeboah, August 31, 2005; Margaret Quainoo, September 12, 2005; Abu Bakr and Ellen Bratema, September 12, 2005. For similar critiques in newspapers of the period, see the *Daily Graphic,* February 9, 1963; *Sunday Mirror:* May 22, 1960; April 11, 1965.

Epilogue

1. Apex Dancing Club, "Program for the Apex-Dansoman Keepfit Dancing Club Ballroom Dancing Soiree, 2 July 2005"; Musicians and Music Lovers Association, "10th Anniversary Program, 1987–1997."

2. My attempt to photograph the venue's transformation in July 2009 was thwarted by various church employees as well as the groundskeeper. The church, it seems, wants little to do with the venue's past.

3. John Collins, May 13, 2005; Kwesi Yankah, "The Future of Highlife," *Glendora Review: African Quarterly on the Arts* 1, no. 3 (1996): 108–10.

4. Ebo Taylor, September 1, 2005; John Collins, *E.T. Mensah* (Accra: Anansesem Publications, 1996), 43; and *Highlife Time* (Accra: Anansesem Publications, 1996), 251.

5. John Collins, May 13, 2005; J. J. Sarpong, June 7, 2005; Margaret Peil, "The Expulsion of West African Aliens," *Journal of Modern African Studies* 9, no. 2 (1971): 205–22.

6. A. Adu Boahen, *Ghana: Evolution and Change in the Nineteenth and Twentieth Centuries* (London: Longman, 1975), 234–35; Roger Gocking, *History of Ghana* (Westport, Conn.: Greenwood, 2005), 156–57.

7. Kofi Ghanaba, October 19, 2005; Gocking, *History of Ghana,* 173.

8. Kwadwo Donkoh, September 16, 2005; Collins, *Highlife Time,* 247 and 257–58; and "King of the Black Beat: The Story of King Bruce and the Black Beats, Highlife Dance Band of Ghana" (Unpublished manuscript, 1987/89), 47.

9. Kwabena Fosu-Mensah, Lucy Duran, and Chris Stapleton, "On Music in Contemporary Africa," *African Affairs* 86, no. 343 (1987): 230; Collins, *Highlife Time,* 247; Nana Budjei and Amma Biney, "The Thinking Person's Musician," *West Africa* 3792 (1990): 745–46; Nii Laryea Korley, "Burgher Highlife," *West Africa* 3586 (1986): 1114; Jon Offei-Ansah, "The Golden Voice," *West Africa* 3604 (1986): 2026.

10. For more on MUSIGA, see Collins, "King of the Black Beat," 49–52; and *Highlife Time,* 251–56.

11. Emmanuel Quao, June 23, 2005; Nanabanyin Dadson, July 14, 2005; Desmond Ababio, July 27, 2005; Collins, *Highlife Time,* 247; John Duke, "New Look to Night Life," *West Africa* 3714 (1988): 1945; Kojo Krante, "Singing the Heavy Blues," *West Africa* 4112 (1996): 1286–87.

12. Frederick Cooper, "Possibility and Constraint: African Independence in Historical Perspective," *Journal of African History* 49, no. 2 (2008): 169.

Discography

This discography is neither a comprehensive catalogue of Ghanaian popular music nor an exhaustive list of the highlife recordings that men and women enjoyed in their homes, heard on their radios, or purchased in their efforts to prepare for Saturday Nights. In recent decades, many original highlife recordings, issued primarily on gramophone records, have been lost. In the early decades of the twentieth century, the few artists who landed recording opportunities with European agencies released their music on 78 rpm shellac discs, which were quite fragile and easily broken. In the 1940s, these brittle discs were replaced with sturdier vinyl 45 rpm singles. In the early 1960s, most recordings began to appear on full-length 12-inch 33⅓ rpm records. Although these vinyl records were much more durable, they too have now suffered the test of time. High temperatures, casual storing practices, and uninterested heirs have all played their part in making high-quality copies of such records difficult to procure.[1] Since similar challenges have also had adverse effects on the master reels for many original records, recent reissues, on both cassette and compact disc, provide only a glimpse into what was an expansive offering of recorded highlife music.[2]

The following discography focuses on two collections of Ghanaian popular music. The first consists of commercially available recordings that readers can find and purchase with relative ease. This section is organized into three component subsections: (1) Proto and Early Highlife Recordings (which includes some brass band and choral recordings); (2) Dance Band Highlife (which focuses largely on recordings released in the 1950s and 1960s); and (3) Guitar Band and Other Highlife (which includes recordings from the 1950s through 1980s). The contents of each section are listed alphabetically according to the art-

---

[1] In 2005, I attempted to procure original recordings on gramophones (45 rpm or 33⅓ rpm format), either by asking informants, approaching musicians and producers, or simply scouring musical markets in Accra and other towns. Eventually, I was able to obtain a collection of eighty-one 45 singles and seventeen full-length LPs. I have not, however, incorporated many of these recordings into this work.

[2] A glimpse of this impressive corpus of recordings may be found at the Gramophone Records Museum and Research Centre of Ghana, which is located in Centre for National Culture office directly opposite the University of Cape Coast in Cape Coast, Ghana. For more information on the Centre as well as its expansive collection, see Kwame Sarpong, "Ghana's Highlife Music: A Digital Repertoire of Recordings and Pop Art at the Gramophone Records Museum," *History in Africa* 31 (2004): 455–461; or visit the Centre's website at http://ghana.icom.museum/24008_e.html.

ist's first name, except for compilations, which appear according to their title. Each entry includes the album title, recording company, and, where available, catalogue number. While the temporal focus of this discography centers around the timeframe examined in the preceding text, I have included a few highlife recordings from the 1970s and 1980s so that readers may discover additional components of the music's development, evolution, and status as a fluid musical genre.

The second section, which is organized into three subsections, lists most of the cassette and compact disc recordings I obtained and consulted during my research stints in Ghana. I have arranged the first two subsections according to media type, and entries appear according to the alphabetical format outlined above. Many of these recordings stem from the period covered by this book, but a few also come from the 1970s and 1980s. The third and final subsection lists the 115 songs that I, in conjunction with those mentioned in the introduction, worked to translate and transcribe during the course of my research for this project.[3] This catalogue, organized alphabetically according to the artist, also contains translated versions of individual song titles.

Since this discography is by no means exhaustive, I would encourage readers interested in accessing recordings to seek out additional sources, including Ronnie Graham's still important *Stern's Guide to Contemporary African Music* and John Gray's excellent *African Music: A Bibliographical Guide to the Traditional, Popular, Art, and Liturgical Musics of Sub-Saharan Africa*.

COMMERCIALLY AVAILABLE RECORDINGS

Proto and Early Highlife

Delta Dandies: Dance Bands in Nigeria, 1936–1941. Savannahphone, AFCD011. (Includes a few songs by the Gold Coast Police Band.)
Early Guitar Music from West Africa. Heritage, HTCD33.
Ghana: Ancient Ceremonies—Dance Music and Songs. Nonesuch.
Ghana: High-Life and Other Popular Musics. Nonesuch.
Ghana Funk from the 70s. Hippo Records, HIPPO012.
Ghana Popular Music, 1931–1957. Arion, ARN64564.
Jacob Sam and Kumasi Trio. *Volume 2: 1928.* Heritage, HTCD28.
Kumasi Trio. *1928.* Heritage Music, HTCD22.
Living Is Hard: West African Music in Britain, 1927–28. Honest Jon's Records, HJRCD33.
Music in Ghana. Pam/Ap, PAMAP601.
Vintage Palmwine Highlife. Otrabanda, OTB02.
West African Instrumental Quintet. *1929.* Heritage, HTCD16.

Dance Band Highlife

African Music: The Glory Years. Original Music, OMCD024.
Classic Highlife: The Best of Ghanaian Highlife Music. AIM Records, AIM1053.

---

[3] Each song title is accompanied by either an English translation, which appears in parentheses, or an explanation of the meaning, which appears in brackets. All song titles appear as offered on their original formats.

E. T. Mensah and the Tempos. *All For You*. RetroAfric, RETRO1XCD.
———. *Day By Day*. RetroAfric, RETRO 3CD.
E. T. Mensah and Victor Olaiya. *Highlife Souvenir Volume 1: Highlife Giants of Africa*.
    Polygram, POLP 102.
Electric Highlife: Sessions from the Bookor Studios. Naxos World, 76030–2.
Ghana Special: Modern Highlife, Afro-Sounds and Ghanaian Blues, 1968–81. Soundway,
    SNDWCD016.
Golden Oldies of Ghana Volume 1. Kinswat Music, GHA300.
Highlife: High Ups: La Musique du Gold Coast des Années 60 (2-Disc Set). Night and Day,
    NDCD025.
Highlife Time: Nigerian and Ghanaian Sound from the 60s and Early 70s. Vampi, CD101.
Ignance De Souza. *The Great Unknowns*. Original Music, OMCD026.
King Bruce and the Black Beats. *Gold Highlife Classics from the 1950s and 1960s*. Ret-
    roAfric, RETRO 13CD.
Kings of Highlife Volume 1. No. 1 Records, GHA454.
*London Is the Place for Me Part Two: Calypso and Kwela, Highlife and Jazz from Young
    Black London*. Honest Jon's Records.
Marvellous Boy: Calypso from West Africa. Honest Jon's Records, HJRCD38.
Ramblers Dance Band. *The Hit Sound of the Ramblers Dance Band*. Flame Tree,
    FLTRCD526.
Rough Guide to Highlife. World Music Net, RGNET1102CD.
Super Sweet Talks International. *The Lord's Prayer*. Stern's, STCD 3009.
Sweet Talks. *Adam and Eve*. Ashanti Records, ASHR2001.
———. *Hollywood Highlife Party*. PAM/ADC, ADC301.
———. *The Kusum Beat*. Soundway, SNDWCD014.
The Best of High-Life Volume 1. Joe Etti Productions, 41078–2.
The Highlife Allstars: Sankofa. Network, 37.992.

Guitar Band and Other Highlife

A. B. Crentsil. *Menba Bio*. Nakasi Records, CDNAK0771.
African Brothers International. *Abena Fosua Wuo*. Afrisong, 72400.
———. *Agatha*. Benoka Nig Ltd.
———. *Greatest Hits Volume 2*. Music Makers, GHA231.
Afro Tropical Soundz Volume 1. Soundway, SNDWCD024.
Blay Ambolley. *Son of Ghana*. Simigwa Records.
Bookor Beats: Vintage Afro-Beat, Afro-Rock and Electric Highlife from Ghana. Otrabanda,
    OTB08.
City Boys Band. *Nya Asem Hwe*. C-Meks Music Ltd.
Eric Agyeman. *Highlife Safari*. Stern's STCD 3002.
Ghana Soundz: Afro-Beat, Funk, and Fusion in 70s Ghana. Soundway, SNDWCD001.
Ghana Soundz: Afro-Beat, Funk, and Fusion in 70s Ghana Volume 2. Soundway,
    SNDWCD003.
Guy Warren / Ghanaba. *The Divine Drummer: Odumankuma*. RETROAFRIC,
    RETRO16CD.
Joe Mensah. *Efua: Friday Girl*. JMint, MINT1000.
King Onyina. *King Onyina's Guitar Highlife*. Popular African Music, PAM AG 702.

Koo Nimo. *Osabarima*. Adasa (Fosu), ADCD102.
Kwabena Awkaboa. *Evergreen: the Best of Volume 1*. Monsu Music, GHA022.
Kwabena Nyama. *Sunday Monday: Palm Wine Music*. Buda, 1979352.
Nana Tuffour. *Sankofa*. G Money, GHA073.
———. *Genesis*. Black M Sounds, BMS353CD.
Okukuseku International Band of Ghana. *Yellow Sissi / Hits Volume 2*. RAS, RASCD019.
———. *Suffer Suffer*. RAS, RASCD026.
Paapa Yankson. *Nenyina Ye (It Is Well)*. Flying Elephant, FE7783CD.
———. *Osode in Perspective: Abam Kofi*. Gapophone, SDGA0898.
Pat Thomas. *Back to the 70s*. Back in Business, GMMCD2000/8.
———. *In Retrospect: Sika Ye Mogya*. Tropic Vibe, GHA328.
———. *The Best of Pat Thomas, Volume 1*. Joks African, JOK8238.
———. *Woba Nye Nti Wo Beku No*. Jass Records, PAT2007CD.
Roadmaster and Agyemang. The Old Highlife. Art Hurts, ARTHURTS001.
The Guitar and the Gun: Highlife Music From Ghana. Earthworks, STEW50CD.
The Rough Guide to Nigeria and Ghana. World Music Net, RGNET1075CD.
Voices of Africa: High-Life and Other Popular Music. Nonesuch, H72026.
Western Diamonds. *Agor: Hi-life Splash*. Westline, CDWR003.
———. *Passenger / Hi-life Boogie*. Westline, WL004.

RECORDINGS OBTAINED AND CONSULTED IN GHANA

Compact Discs

A. B. Crenstil. *Landlord Abodwese*. Afriko, AML198.
———. *Naana*. Tropic Vibe Productions.
Adadamu: A Tribute to K. Gyasi. Ekɔoba Records.
Adlib Young Anim. *The Best of Adlib Young Anim of Stargazers Fame*. S Records,
    SRCD012.
African Brothers Band International. *Greatest Hits Volume 1*. Savanna, 02020291.
———. *Evergreen Volume 1*.
Alhaji K. Frimpong. *Kyenkyen bi Adi Mawu*. Regency Music, R105.
Broadway Dance Band and Stargazers Dance Band. *Nkae*. Tropic Vibe Productions,
    13013.
C. K. Mann. *Timeless Highlife*. Sikafutro, AVL95144.
———. *Party Time with CeeKay*. Tropic Vibe Productions.
———. *The Legendary C. K. Mann: The Singles Volume 1*. Essiebons, EBCD 708.
———. *The Legendary C. K. Mann: The Singles Volume 2*. Essiebons, EBCD 707.
C. K. Mann and His Carousel 7. *Funky Highlife*. Tropic Vibe Productions.
Chief Abiriekyiera Kofi Sammy. *Odo Bra*. Icha Strong, 02.0109.
CST Amankwah. *M'abusua Yi Mu: The Best of CST Amankwah*. COMPUDISC,
    MR1003.
Dr. K. Gyasi and His Noble Kings. *Sikyi Highlife Volume 1*. Ekɔoba
———. *Sikyi Highlife Volume 2*. Ekɔoba.
E.K.'s Band. *Akwankwaahiani*. A Solid State Ride Away Music Production.
———. *Owuo Busue Ni*. A Solid State Ride Away Music Production.
Essiebons Music Presents REPPAGH One: Best Ghana Hi-Life Hits. Essiebons.

From Bamaya to Bosoe: Roots of Highlife. Faisal Helwani Productions.
Golden "Hits" of Ghana Volume 1. Essiebons, EBCD701.
Golden "Hits" of Ghana Volume 2. Essiebons, EBCD711.
Happy Stars of Ghana. *Meko Magya Fie.* A Solid State Ride Away Music Production.
Hedzoleh Soundz. *Rekpete.* Faisal Helwani Productions.
Hilife Oldtimers Volume 1: Master Kwabena Akwaboa. Adonten, ADTCD1051.
Hilife Oldtimers Volume 2: The Best of Kakaiku's Band and Master Akwaboa's Band. Adonten, ADTCD1052.
Jerry Hansen and the Ramblers Dance Band. *Best of Jerry Hansen and the Ramblers Dance Band.* Tropic Vibe Productions.
———. *Best of Jerry Hansen and the Ramblers Dance Band Volume 2.* Tropic Vibe Productions.
———. *Best of Jerry Hansen and the Ramblers Dance Band Volume 3.* Tropic Vibe Productions.
———. *Best of Jerry Hansen and the Ramblers Dance Band Volume 4.* Tropic Vibe Productions.
Joe Mensah. *Bɔsoe, Bonsue, and More.* JMINT.
K. Gyasi Guitar Band. *Timeless Highlife Classics.* S Records, SRCD023.
K.K.'s No. 2 Band. *Anthology Volume 1.* Tropic Vibe Productions.
———. *Anthology Volume 2.* Tropic Vibe Productions.
King Bruce and the Black Beats. *Golden Highlife Classics from the 1950s and 1960s, Volume 2.* ARFLAG, ARFLAG CD1.
Kofi Ani Johnson. *M'admfo pa bɛkɔ.* Regency Music.
Kyeremateng Stars. *Susu Ka.* A Solid State Ride Away Music Production.
Paapa Yankson. *Wiadzi Mu Nsem.* Flying Elephant, FE7796.
Professional Uhuru Dance Band. *Osibi.* Tropic Vibe Productions, 13006.
———. *Freedom Tour in U.K.* Tropic Vibe Productions.
———. *Wɔfa Wɔhɔ.* Tropic Vibe Productions, 10073.
———. *Kwadwo Donkoh Presents the Professional Uhuru Dance Band: Sound of Africa.* Agoro Records.
Smart Nkansah. *The Best of Smart Nkansah and the Sunsum Band.* San Music, SAN 002CD.
The Stargazers Band. *Those Days in (Gold Coast) Ghana* (2 Discs). Evergreen Musical Company.
Tony Mensah. *Tony Mensah Sings Oscarmore: It's More Oscarmore.* Afriko Music International, AML 298.
Western Diamonds. *Diamonds Forever.* Westline, CDWC002.
Yamoah's Band. *Back to 60s Volume 1.* Akosua Ba Yaw Production, RDRCD2793.

Cassettes

A. B. Crenstil. *Moses.*
———. *Atea Special.*
Abirekyieba Kofi Sammy. *Agyenka Due: The Best of Okukuseku.* U Name It Records.
Adadam Paa Ni. *San Kɔ Da Wa Mena Mu.*
Aflao Brass Band. *Kale Hawo.* Jawahdada Productions.
———. *Akofa Hawo.* Jawahdada Productions.

Akwaboa. *Fidie Wura.*

Alex Konadu and His International Band. *Agyatawuo.*

C. K. Mann. *Highlife Salsa: Dance Time '88.*

City Boys International Band. *Dada So Volume 1.* White Stone Music Productions.

———. *Yaa Dufie Wo Tan Me A.*

———. *Mischa: Rettet Das Weihnachtsfest.* Family Frost.

Dr. K. Gyasi and His Noble Kings. *African "High Life" Beat Goes Sky-High-U.S.A.*
   Ekɔoba.

———. *Best of Volume 1.* Citirock Serengeti.

———. *Best of Volume 2.* Citirock Serengeti.

E.K.'s Band. *Evergreen Tunes Volume 5.* A Solid State Ride Away Music Production.

———. *Evergreen Tunes Volume 7.* A Solid State Ride Away Music Production.

———. *Evergreen Tunes Volume 10.* A Solid State Ride Away Music Production.

———. *Evergreen Tunes Volume 15.* A Solid State Ride Away Music Production.

Hi-Life Stars. *Live 2003.* Easyway.

K.K.'s Executive Band. *Akyinkyin Akyinkyin.* Ambassador Records.

Kakaiku's Band. *Volume 1.* Mercury.

———. *Volume 2.* Mercury.

———. *Volume 3.* Mercury.

King Onyina. *Volume 1.* Citirock Serengeti.

———. *Volume 2.* Citirock Serengeti.

———. *Volume 3.* Citirock Serengeti.

———. *Volume 5.* Citirock Serengeti.

Koo Nimo. *Tete Wobi Ka.* Human Songs Records.

———. *Ohia Ye Ya.* Bibini.

Kwaa Mensah. *Alive and Well.* Bombiribi.

Nana Ampadu and His African Brothers Band. *Agatha.* Nana Ampadu I Ent.

———. *Ebi Te Yie.* Nana Ampadu I Ent.

Nana Tuffour. *Abeiku.* Owusek Productions.

Obuobu J. A. Adofo. *Live.* Easyway.

S. K. Oppong. *Abusua Bɔne Special.* J.J.T.T. Production.

Starlets Band. *Rock of Ages.* Lino Digitals, GMC005.

Uhuru Hilife Classics Volume 1: The Big Band Africa Sounds. Bibini Music.

Yamoah's Band. *The Best of Yamoah Volume 1.* Yemoah's Production.

———. *The Best of Yamoah Volume 2.* Yemoah's Production.

———. *The Best of Yamoah Volume 3.* Yemoah's Production.

SONGS TRANSCRIBED, TRANSLATED, AND CONSULTED

Akompi's Guitar Band
"*Meremma Bio*" (I won't come back again)
"*Ose Obeko*" (If she insists she will go)
B. E. Sackey Band
"*Nkyrinna*" (This generation)
E. K. Anang's Band
"*Fa me 'Back Pay' ma me*" (Give me my "back pay")
E. K. Nyame and EK's Band

"*Amane a Mahu*" (I have suffered a disappointment)
"*Ao! Me Nua*" (Oh! My sibling)
"*Dadada mete hɔ*" (I've been living peacefully)
"*Ɛnnɛ mmaa a aba so*" (Women of today)
"*Gyae o, Ahoɔfɛ Ntua Ka*" (Physical beauty is nothing)
"*Ka Nokware Kyerɛ Me*" (Tell me the truth)
"*Kaa bi reba o*" (There's a car approaching)
"*Kɔbɔ Awesa*" (For excitement)
"*Kwame Nkrumah ayɛ*" (Kwame Nkrumah has done it)
"*Mayɛ Mayɛ Mannya Ayɛ*" (I have done my best but to no avail)
"*Mede me ho aba*" (It's my fault)
"*Nea woka biara*" (Whatever you say)
"*Ɔda mpatia ahyɛ me nsa*" (He has put a ring on my finger)
"*Ɔdɔ a medɔ wo*" (It is all because of the love I have for you)
"*Onimdifoɔ*" (Learned one)
"*Onipa a ɔde n'ade*" (The owner of an item)
"*Small Boy Nnyɛ Me Bia*" (It is not my fault young man)

E. T. Mensah and the Tempos
"*205*"
"*Abele*" (Corn)
"*Daavi Loloto*" (My dear lady)
"*Don't Mind Your Wife*"
"*Essie Nana*" [a woman's name]
"*Fom Fom*" [type of kenkey common in Ahanta area of Ghana's Western Region]
"*Gbaa Anokwale*" (Tell me the truth)
"*Medzi Medzi*" (I will enjoy)
"*Mee Bei Obaba*" (My "jolly" has gone abroad)
"*Munsuro*" (I am not afraid)
"*Nkatie*" (Groundnuts)
"*Odo Anigyina*" (Love sickness)
"*Odofo*" (My darling)
"*Wiadzi*" (The world)

Frimpong
"*Nkonkohweree Mmienu*" (Two wood hens)

Gyak's Guitar Band
"*Kumasi E.D.*" [ED was a large store in the town of Kumasi]

High Class Diamonds
"*Kae Me*" (Remember me)
"*Asɛm a Woakɔfa Aba*" (The trouble you have caused)

Ignance de Souza
"*Augustina*" [A woman's name]

Kakaiku's Band
"*Driver ni*" (The driver)
"*Mayen Nkantem*" (Let us take a vow)
"*Na Minim*" (I didn't know)
"*Obiaa Ho Woasem*" (Everybody is fallible)
"*Odo Yede Sen Sika*" (Love is more pleasant than money)

"*Offie Nifie*" (*Home sweet home*)
King Bruce and the Black Beats
"*Aban Kaba*" (Handcuffs)
"*Agodzi*" (Money)
"*Anokwa Edomi*" (It's really pained me)
"*Dear Si Abotar*" (My darling, be patient)
"*Enya Wo Do Fo*" (You have got your lover)
"*Medaho Mao*" (I am there for you)
"*Menenam*" (I'm on my rounds)
"*Mikuu Mise Mbaa Dal*" (I won't return again)
"*Nantsew Yie*" (Good-bye)
"*Nibii Bibii Babaoo*" (Many small things)
"*Odor fofor*" (New love)
"*Srotoi Ye Mli*" (There are varieties)
"*Suomô Gboo Ke Moo Shi*" (Love doesn't die completely)
"*Misumo Bo Tamo She*" (I love you like sugarcane)
King Onyina
"*Ahoofe San Bra*" (Beautiful darling come back)
"*Baako Yɛ Yaw*" (It is sad to be lonely)
"*Obaa ahoofe*" (Pretty woman)
"*Ɔbaa Frema*" (Frema my woman)
"*Ɔdɔ yɛ Anwanwade*" (Love is strange)
Kofi Ani Johnson
"*Me Dofo*" (My darling)
"*Su Nkwa*" (Pray for life)
Kpagon Band
"*Gbele Wa*" (Death is painful)
Kumasi Trio
"*Yaa Amponsah Part I*" [a woman's name]
"*Yaa Amponsah Part II*" [a woman's name]
Kyeremateng
"*Omama Ho Yɛ Ahi*" (A distinguished man is always a victim of hatred)
"Woman No Good"
Mexico Rhythm Band
"*Nana Kwasi Wade Kwahu*" (Nana Kwesi what have you done for me)
Oscarmore Ofori
"*Ahye Wo*" (You are hurt)
"*Nkaeɛ*" (Remembrance)
"*Oburoni Wawu*" (Second-hand clothes)
Oppong's Guitar Band
"*Anadwo Baa*" (A nocturnal lady)
Osu Selected Union
"*Homowo Ese*" (Hômôwô is here)
Professional Uhuru Dance Band
"*Betu Me Ho Awɔw*" (Come and keep me warm)
"*Medzi Me Sigya*" (I prefer to be a bachelor)
Ramblers Dance Band

"*Agbo Ayee*" (All work and no play makes Jack a dull boy)
"*Afotusɛm*" (Advice)
"Auntie Christie" [a woman's name]
"*Broni Wewu*" (Second-hand clothing)
"*Ewuraba Artificial*" (Artificial lady)
"*Kae Dabi*" (Don't forget the past)
"*Mala Haleluya*" (I'll sing Alleluia)
"*Mi Tee Momo*" (I've already gone)
"*Owu Nye*" (It is death)
"No Parking"
"*Ɔbaa Ahoɔfɛ*" (Beautiful woman)
"*Yiadom Boakye*" [a man's name]
Red Spots
"Essie Attah" [a woman's name]
"*Owu Adaadaa Me*" (Death has deceived me)
Smart Nkansah and the Sunsum Band
"*Emma Bekum Mmarima*" (Women will ruin men)
"*Gye Wani*" (Enjoy life)
"*Mpena Twi*" (Concubinage)
"*Odo*" (Love)
"*Yei Nti*" (Because of this?)
Stargazers Band
"*Akpeteshi*" [a type of locally distilled gin]
"*Gyae Me Haw*" (Don't worry me)
"*Mbaa Bekum Hɛn*" (Women will ruin us)
"*Mɛsan makɔ ɔdɔ*" (I will go back darling)
"*Ɔbra Ayɛ Me Pasaa*" (My life is devastated)
"*Owu Na Mewu*" (I will certainly die)

Bibliography

ARCHIVES AND LIBRARIES

Ghana:

Balme Memorial Library, University of Ghana, Legon
Bookor African Popular Music Archives Foundation (BAPMAF), Accra
Department of Linguistics Library, University of Ghana, Legon
George Padmore Research Library, Accra
Gramophone and Records Museum and Research Centre of Ghana, Cape Coast
Information Services Department Photograph Library, Ministry of Information, Accra
Institute of African Studies Library, University of Ghana, Legon
International Center for African Music and Dance (ICAMD) Audio Visual Archive, University of Ghana, Legon
International Center for African Music and Dance (ICAMD) Library, University of Ghana, Legon
Public Records and Archives Administration Department (PRAAD)--Accra, Cape Coast, Kumasi, and Sekondi Depositories
TV3 Video Archive, Accra
W. E. B. Du Bois Library, Accra

United Kingdom:

British Library, London
British Library Sound Archive, London
Public Records Office (PRO), Kew
Rhodes House Library, Oxford
School of Oriental and African Studies (SOAS) Library, London
Wesleyan Methodist Missionary Society (WMMS) Archive, SOAS, London

ORAL INTERVIEWS

In 2005 and 2009, I conducted 110 oral interviews in several Ghanaian towns. What follows is the complete list of oral interviews that informed this book. Each individual I interviewed appears in alphabetical order (by surname), and I have included the date and location of each. All interviews were recorded, except those marked with an asterisk, and were conducted in English, Twi, Ga, or Ewe. Interviews in Twi, Ga, and Ewe were conducted, transcribed, and translated with the assistance of Apetsi Amenuney or, in a few cases, Francis Akotua.

Ababio, Desmond. Osu, Accra, July 27, 2005.

Acei, Georgina Okanee. Accra New Town, May 19, 2005.

Acolatse, Margaret Akosua. Accra New Town, May 19, 2005.

Acquaye, Saka. Korle Gonno, Accra, August 24, 2005.

———. Korle Gonno, Accra, September 7, 2005.

Adja, Rebecca Torshie, and Diana Ojoko. La Paz, Accra, May 6, 2005.

Adum-Attah, Kwadwo. Cape Coast, February 18, 2005.

———. Cape Coast, April 1, 2005.

Aflakpui, Albert. Accra New Town, May 20, 2005.

Agbenyega, Charity. Accra New Town, April 27, 2005.

Agyepong, J. K. Takoradi, June 30, 2009.

Akotua, Francis. Madina, Accra, January 25, 2005.

Allotey, James. Accra New Town, April 27, 2005.

Allotey, James, and Linda Botchway. Accra New Town, August 30, 2005.

Allotey, James, and Alex Bakpa Moffatt. Abose Okai, June 19, 2009.

Amakoa, Alice. Nima, Accra, September 9, 2005.

Amakudzie, Benny Baten Kofi. Lartebiokorshie, Accra, April 27, 2005.

———. Lartebiokorshie, Accra, June 1, 2005.

Amakwa, Kwaku, and Yao Mensah. Accra New Town, June 22, 2009.

Amenumey, Harry. Chokor, Accra, May 3, 2005.

Amonoo, Elizabeth. La Paz, Accra, September 10, 2005.

———. La Paz, Accra, October 18, 2005.

———. La Paz, Accra, June 20, 2009.

Ampadu, Nana Kwame. La Paz, Accra, September 24, 2005.

———. La Paz, Accra, July 20, 2009.*

Amuah, Dr. Isaac R. Cape Coast, March 30, 2005.

Andrews, Margaret Esi. Accra New Town, June 12, 2009.

Ansah, Lucy Efia. Accra New Town, September 7, 2005.

Apenteng-Sackey, Edward. Legon, Accra. October 5, 2005.

Armah, "Captain" Nii. Accra New Town, May 22, 2005.

Ayawovie, Henry. Accra New Town, May 30, 2005.

Aye, Grace Yawa. Accra New Town, May 18, 2005.

Ayitey, Josephine Nafisatu. Accra New Town, May 19, 2005.

———. Accra New Town, August 30, 2005.

Azameti, Godwin. Madina, Accra, August 28, 2005.

Bakr, Abu, and Ellen Bratema. Accra New Town, September 12, 2005.

Biney, Bob. Cape Coast, April 1, 2005.

Binla, Kwesi. Adabraka, Accra, June 23, 2009.

Collins, John. Legon, Accra, May 13, 2005.

———. Legon, Accra, October 5, 2005.

Dadson, Kojo. Kanda Estates, Accra, October 18, 2005.

Dadson, Nanabanyin. Korle Dudor, Accra, July 14, 2005.*

Danso, Akua. Accra New Town, September 9, 2005.

Darko, Willie. Legon, Accra, September 13, 2005.

Dixon, Abdul Rahim, Ahmed Tettey, and Mohammed Mensah. Alajo, Accra, May 22, 2005.

———. Alajo, Accra, September 4, 2005.

Donkoh, Kwadwo. Accra Arts Centre, September 16, 2005.

———. Kaneshie, Accra, June 21, 2009.*

Eshun, Isaac. Airport Residential Area, Accra, October 27, 2005.

Essilfie Bondzie, Dick. Ridge, Accra, June 14, 2009.

Frimpong, Kofi, and Justina Yaaba Martin. Accra New Town, September 16, 2005.

Fugar, Edna. Accra New Town, August 31, 2005.

Fugar, Edna and Justina. Accra New Town, April 29, 2005.

Gaba, Grershon. Lartebiokorshie, Accra, April 29, 2005.

Gaba, Happy. Lartebiokorshie, Accra, April 29, 2005.

Ghanaba, Kofi (Guy Warren). Medie, Accra, October 19, 2005.*

Gyasi, K. (with Koo Nimo). Kumasi, October 9, 2005.*

Hansen, Jerry. North Kaneshie, Accra, October 3, 2005.

———. North Kaneshie, Accra, October 13, 2005.

———. North Kaneshie, Accra, July 20, 2009.*

Johnson, Cole. Takoradi, July 12, 2009.

Johnson, George Nanabanyin. Sekondi, September 21, 2005.

Kudiah, Felicia. Accra New Town, June 19, 2009.

Lamptey, Phyllis Odartey. Osu, Accra, July 28, 2005.

Laine, Frankie. James Town, Accra, June 3, 2009.

Laryea, Francis. Mamprobi, Accra, June 6, 2009.

Lindsay, Kofi. Cape Coast, March 31, 2005.

———. Cape Coast, June 22, 2005.

Mama Adjoa. Pig Farm, Accra, July 5, 2005.*

Mann, Charles Kofi (C. K.). Takoradi, September 19, 2005.

———. Takoradi, June 26, 2009.

Manuh, Peter. Legon, Accra, July 23, 2005.

Mensah, Vincent. Accra New Town, May 18, 2005.

Mensah, Vincent, and Juliana Yeboah. Accra New Town, August 30, 2005.

Mexico, Mr. Adrabraka, Accra, April 18, 2005.*

Mills, J. O. La Paz, Accra, May 6, 2005.

Moffatt, Alex Bakpa. Abose Okai, Accra, May 21, 2005.

Nimo, Koo. Kumasi, October 7, 2005.

Nukwuani, Emmanuel Ashie. Alajo, Accra, September 11, 2005.

Nyamuame, Samuel. Madina, Accra, July 20, 2005.

Oboshilay, Diana, and Margaret Akosua Acolatse. Accra New Town, May 24, 2005.

Ofori, Henry. Osu, June 19, 2005.

———. Osu, June 29, 2005.

Ofori, Kofi. Accra New Town, May 30, 2005.

———. Accra New Town, August 30, 2005.

Ofori, Oscarmore. Odumase Krobo, October 20, 2005.

Ocloo, Gloria. Pig Farm, Accra, May 24, 2005.

Onyina, King (with Koo Nimo). Kumasi, October 9, 2005.

Opoku, Adjoa and Akua. La Paz, Accra, September 10, 2005.

Plange, Stan. Airport Residential Area, Accra, June 29, 2005.
———. Osu, Accra, October 5, 2005.
Quao, Emmanuel. Cape Coast, June 23, 2005.
Quainoo, Margaret (Araba Stamp). Accra Arts Centre, September 12, 2005.
Ray, Ato and Matilda. Accra New Town, July 17, 2009.
Sackey, Emmanuel. Achimota, Accra, July 17, 2009.
Sam, Daniel Kinful. Takoradi, September 19, 2005.
Sarpong, Comfort. Takoradi, September 20, 2005.
Sarpong, J. J. James Town, Accra, June 7, 2005.
———. James Town, Accra, August 24, 2005.
Sosu, Emmanuel Quist. La Paz, Accra, June 20, 2009.
Taylor, Ebo. La Paz, July 26, 2005.
———. Legon, Accra, August 24, 2005.
———. Legon, Accra, September 1, 2005.
Tettey, Nii Adgin. Alajo, Accra, September 11, 2005.
Thompson, James Matthew. Adabraka, Accra, May 3, 2005.
———. Adabraka, Accra, August 29, 2005.
———. Adabraka, Accra, June 23, 2009.
Zinabo, Aeshitu. Accra New Town, May 20, 2005.
———. Accra New Town, September 7, 2005.
Zinabo, Aeshitu, Comfort Kwame, and Victoria Quainoo. Accra New Town, June 12, 2009.

GOVERNMENT REPORTS AND DOCUMENTS

Clarkson, M. L. "Juveniles in Drinking Bars and Nightclubs: A Report on Conditions Observed in Accra, Kumasi, and Takoradi." Accra: Department of Social Welfare, 1955.
———. "A Report on an Enquiry into Cinema Going among Juveniles Undertaken by the Department of Social Welfare and Community Development in Accra and Kumasi." Accra: Department of Social Welfare, 1954.
Colonial Office. "Report on the Commission of Enquiry into Disturbances in the Gold Coast, 1948." London: His Majesty's Stationery Office, 1948.
Ghana. *1960 Population Census of Ghana.* Vol. 3: *Demographic Characteristics.* Accra: Census Office, 1964.
———. *Parliamentary Debates: The Fifth Session of the First Parliament of The Republic of Ghana.* Vol. 38. Accra: State Publishing Corporation, 1965.
———. "Report on the Commission Appointed to Enquire into the Functions, Operation and Administration of the Worker's Brigade." Accra: Government Printer, 1968.
———. *Second Development Plan, 1959–64.* Accra: Government Printer, 1959.
———. *Seven-Year Development Plan.* Accra: Government Printer, 1965.
Ghana Broadcasting Corporation. *GBC.* Accra: GBC Publications Department, 1973.
———. "Golden Jubilee Lectures: Broadcasting and National Development." Tema: Ghana Broadcasting Corporation, 1985.
———. *The Story of Radio Ghana.* Accra: Ministry of Information and Broadcasting, 1965.
Gold Coast. *Annual Report of the Department of Social Welfare and Community Development for the year 1953.* Accra: Government Printing Department, 1954.
———. *Annual Report of the Department of Social Welfare and Community Development for the year 1954.* Accra: Government Printing Department, 1955.

———. *Annual Report of the Department of Social Welfare and Community Development for the year 1955.* Accra: Government Printing Department, 1956.

———. *Annual Report of the Department of Social Welfare and Community Development for the year 1956.* Accra: Government Printing Department, 1957.

———. *Appendices: Containing Comparative Returns and General Statistics of the 1931 Census.* Accra: Government Printer, 1932.

———. "Further Correspondence Relating to the Revision of the Initial Rates of Salary in the African Civil Service." Accra: Government Printing Office, 1931.

———. *The Gold Coast Census of Population, 1948: Report and Tables.* Accra: Government Printing Office, 1950.

———. "Legislative Assembly Debates, Issue No. 3, 26th October–9th November 1954." Accra: Government Printer, 1954.

———. "1953 Survey of Accra Household Budgets." Accra: Government Printer, 1953.

———. *Problem Children of the Gold Coast.* Accra: Government Printer, 1955.

———. "Report of the Committee of the Legislature Appointed to Consider and Report on Certain Questions Arising from the Effect of the Cost of Living on the Civil Service." Accra: Government Printer, 1950.

———. "Report on Enquiry with Regard to Friendly and Mutual Benefit Groups in the Gold Coast." Accra: Government Printer, 1955.

———. "Report on the Police Department, 1935–36." Accra: Government Printing Department, 1936.

———. "Slum Clearance in Ussher Town." Accra: Town Planning Department, 1954.

———. *Ten Year Plan for the Economic and Social Development of the Gold Coast.* Accra: Government Printer, 1950.

———. "Town and Country Planning in the Gold Coast." Accra: Government Printing Department, 1954.

Orde Browne, Major G. St. J. "Labor Conditions in West Africa: A Report Presented by the Secretary of State for the Colonies to Parliament by Command of his Majesty, May 1941." London: His Majesty's Stationary Office, 1941.

NEWSPAPERS AND PERIODICALS

Advance, 1954–1969
Crown Colonist, 1933–39, 1942–1948
Daily Graphic, 1951–1970, 1996
Foreign Field, 1928–1929
Ghana Pictorial, 1962
Ghana Radio Review and TV Times, 1963–1967
Ghana Today, 1956–1959, 1968
The Ghanaian, 1960–1961, 1965
Gold Coast Independent, 1932–1933
Gold Coast Leader, 1918–1924
Gold Coast Nation, 1914
Gold Coast Observer, 1942–1950
Gold Coast Times, 1926–1929, 1936–1937
Guinea Times (Ghana Times), 1958–1959
Kingdom Overseas, 1940–1946

New Nation, 1956–1957
Sunday Mirror, 1955–1969
West Africa, 1980–1996
West African Times, 1930–1934

SECONDARY WORKS

Abloh, Frederick A. "Growth of Towns in Ghana: A Study of the Social and Physical Growth of Selected Towns in Ghana." PhD diss., University of Science and Technology, Kumasi, Ghana, 1967.

Achimota College. "Marriage and Debt: The Report of a Discussion Group of the Teachers' Refresher Course, Achimota, 1938." Accra: Achimota Press, 1938.

Acquah, Ioné. *Accra Survey: A Social Survey of the Capital of Ghana, Formerly Called the Gold Coast, Undertaken for the West African Institute of Social and Economic Research, 1953–1956.* London: University of London Press, 1958.

Addi-Sundiata, John Hodiak. "Culture and National Development: an African Perspective." Paper presented at the Symposium on the Life and Work of Kwame Nkrumah, University of Ghana, May 27–June 1, 1985.

Adjaye, Joseph K. *Boundaries of Self and Other in Ghanaian Popular Culture.* Westport, Conn.: Praeger Publishers, 2004.

African Academy. *Minutes of the Inaugural Meeting of the African Academy.* Sekondi: Railway Press, 1930.

Africander Stores. *Sensational Gramophone Record Song Book.* Accra: Africander Stores, 1953.

Agawu, Kofi. *Representing African Music: Postcolonial Notes, Queries, Positions.* London: Routledge, 2003.

Agovi, Kofi E. "Black American Dirty Dozens and the Tradition of Verbal Insult in Ghana." *Research Review* 3, no. 1 (1987): 1–23.

———. "The Political Relevance of Ghanaian Highlife Songs since 1957." *Research in African Literatures* 20, no. 2 (1989): 194–201.

Agyeman, D. K. *Ideological Education and Nationalism in Ghana under Nkrumah and Busia.* Accra: Ghana Universities Press, 1988.

Ahlman, Jeffrey S. "Living with Nkrumahism: Nation, State, and Pan-Africanism in Ghana." PhD diss., University of Illinois, 2011.

Akyeampong, Emmanuel. *Drink, Power and Cultural Change: A Social History of Alcohol in Ghana, c. 1800 to Recent Times.* Portsmouth: Heinemann, 1996.

———. "Sexuality and Prostitution among the Akan of the Gold Coast c. 1650–1950." *Past and Present* 156 (1997): 144–73.

———. "Wo pe tam won pe ba (You like cloth but you don't want children): Urbanization, Individualism and Gender Relations in Colonial Ghana, c. 1900–1939." In *Africa's Urban Past,* ed. David M. Anderson and Richard Rathbone, 222–34. Portsmouth: Heinemann, 2000.

Akyeampong, Emmanuel, and Pashington Obeng. "Spirituality, Gender, and Power in Asante History." *International Journal of African Historical Studies* 28, no. 3 (1995): 481–508.

Allman, Jean, ed. *Fashioning Africa: Power and the Politics of Dress.* Bloomington: Indiana University Press, 2004.

———. "'Let Your Fashion Be in line with Our Ghanaian Costume': Nation, Gender, and the Politics of Cloth-ing in Nkrumah's Ghana." In *Fashioning Africa: Power and the Politics of Dress*, ed. Jean Allman, 144–65. Bloomington: Indiana University Press, 2004.

———. *The Quills of the Porcupine: Asante Nationalism in an Emergent Ghana*. Madison: University of Wisconsin Press, 1993.

———. "Rounding up Spinsters: Unmarried Women and Gender Chaos in Colonial Asante." *Journal of African History* 37, no. 2 (1996): 195–214.

Allman, Jean, and Victoria Tashjian. *"I Will Not Eat Stone": A Women's History of Colonial Asante*. Portsmouth: Heinemann, 2000.

Ambler, Charles. "Popular Films and Colonial Audiences: The Movies in Northern Rhodesia." *American Historical Review* 106, no. 1 (2001): 81–105.

Ampene, Kwesi. *Female Song Tradition and the Akan of Ghana: The Creative Process of Nnwonkorɔ*. Burlington, Vt.: Ashgate, 2005.

Anderson, David M., and Richard Rathbone, eds. *Africa's Urban Past*. Portsmouth: Heinemann, 2000.

———. "Urban Africa: Histories in the Making." In *Africa's Urban Past,* ed. David M. Anderson and Richard Rathbone, 1–17. Portsmouth: Heinemann, 2000.

Apex Dancing Club. "Program for the Apex-Dansoman Keepfit Dancing Club Ballroom Dancing Soiree, 2 July 2005."

Apter, David E. *Ghana in Transition*. Princeton, N.J.: Princeton University Press, 1972.

Arhin, Kwame. "Monetization and the Asante State." In *Money Matters: Instability, Values and Social Payments in the Modern History of West African Communities*, ed. Jane Guyer, 97–110. Portsmouth: Heinemann, 1995.

———. "A Note on the Asante Akonkofo: A Non-Literate Sub-Elite, 1900–1930." *Africa: Journal of the International African Institute* 56, no. 1 (1986): 25–31.

———. "The Pressures of Cash and Its Political Consequences in Asante in the Colonial Period." *Journal of African Studies* 3, no. 4 (1976): 453–68.

———. "Rank and Class among the Asante and Fante in the Nineteenth Century." *Africa: Journal of the International African Institute* 53, no. 1 (1983): 2–22.

Asante-Darko, Nimrod, and Sjaak van der Geest. "Male Chauvinism: Men and Women in Ghanaian Highlife Songs." In *Female and Male in West Africa,* ed. Christine Oppong, 242–55. London: Allen and Unwin, 1983.

———. "The Political Meaning of Highlife Songs in Ghana." *African Studies Review* 25, no. 1 (1982): 27–35.

Askew, Kelly. *Performing the Nation: Swahili Music and Cultural Politics in Tanzania*. Chicago: University of Chicago Press, 2002.

Atkins, Keletso. *The Moon Is Dead! Give Us Our Money!: The Cultural Origins of an African Work Ethic, Natal, South Africa, 1843–1900*. Portsmouth: Heinemann, 1993.

Austin, Dennis. *Politics in Ghana: 1946–1960*. London: Oxford University Press, 1964.

Austin, Gareth. "'No Elders Were Present': Commoners and Private Ownership in Asante, 1807–96." *Journal of African History* 37, no. 1 (1996): 1–30.

Averill, Gage. *A Day for the Hunter, a Day for the Prey: Popular Music and Power in Haiti*. Chicago: Chicago University Press, 1997.

Avorgbedor, Daniel Kodzo. "The Place of the 'Folk' in Ghanaian Popular Music." *Popular Music and Society* 9, no. 2 (1983): 35–44.

Bame, Kwabena N. *Come to Laugh: African Traditional Theater in Ghana*. New York: L. Barber Press, 1985.

———. "Domestic Tensions Reflected in the Popular Theatre in Ghana." In *Domestic Rights and Duties in Southern Ghana*, ed. Christine Oppong, 145–61. Legon: University of Ghana Institute of African Studies, 1974.

———. *Profiles in African Traditional Popular Culture: Consensus and Conflict: Dance, Drama, Festival, and Funerals*. New York: Clear Type Press, 1991.

Barber, Karin, ed. *Africa's Hidden Histories: Everyday Literacy and the Making of the Self*. Bloomington: Indiana University Press, 2006.

———. "Popular Arts in Africa." *African Studies Review* 30, no. 3 (1987): 1–78, 104–11.

———, ed. *Readings in African Popular Culture*. Bloomington: Indiana University Press, 1997.

Barber, Karin, John Collins, and Alain Ricard. *West African Popular Theatre*. Bloomington: Indiana University Press, 1997.

Bartle, Philip. "African Rural-Urban Migration: A Decision-Making Perspective." MA thesis, University of British Columbia, 1971.

Bauman, Richard. *Verbal Art as Performance*. Prospect Heights, Ill.: Waveland Press, 1977.

Beecham, John. *Ashantee and the Gold Coast*. London: Dawsons of Pall Mall, 1968 [1841].

Bender, Wolfgang. *Sweet Mother: Modern African Music*. Chicago: University of Chicago Press, 1991.

Bennet, Judith M. *History Matters: Patriarchy and the Challenge of Feminism*. Philadelphia: University of Pennsylvania Press, 2006.

Birmingham, David. *Kwame Nkrumah: The Father of African Nationalism*. Athens: Ohio University Press, 1998.

Blavo, E. Q. "The World Social Situation of Youth: A Survey of the Needs and Aspirations of Youth in Ghana." Unpublished paper, Institute of African Studies, Legon, 1988.

Boahen, A. Adu. *Ghana: Evolution and Change in the Nineteenth and Twentieth Centuries*. London: Longman, 1975.

Botwe-Asamoah, Kwame. *Kwame Nkrumah's Politico-Cultural Thought and Policies: An African-Centered Paradigm for the Second Phase of the African Revolution*. New York: Routledge, 2005.

Brempong, Owusu. "Akan Highlife in Ghana: Songs of Cultural Transition." PhD diss., Indiana University, 1986.

———. "Highlife: An Urban Experience and Folk Tradition." *Journal of Performing Arts* 2, no. 2 (1996): 17–29.

Brooks, George. *The Kru Mariner in the 19th Century: An Historical Compendium*. Liberia Monograph Study Series. Newark: University of Delaware:, 1972.

Burgess, G. Thomas. "Cinema, Bell Bottoms and Miniskirts: Struggles over Youth and Citizenship in Revolutionary Zanzibar." *International Journal of African Historical Studies* 35, nos. 2–3 (2002): 287–313.

———. "Introduction to Youth and Citizenship in East Africa." *Africa Today* 51, no. 3 (2005): vii–xxiv.

Burgess, G. Thomas, and Andrew Burton. "Introduction." In *Generations Past: Youth in East African History*, ed. Andrew Burton and Hélène Charton-Bigot, 1–24. Athens: Ohio University Press, 2010.

Burns, J. M. *Flickering Shadows: Cinema and Identity in Colonial Zimbabwe.* Athens: Ohio University Press, 2002.

Burton, Andrew. *African Underclass: Urbanisation, Crime and Colonial Order in Dar es Salaam.* Athens: Ohio University Press, 2005.

———. "Raw Youth, School-Leavers, and the Emergence of Structural Unemployment in Late-Colonial Urban Tanganyika." *Journal of African History* 47, no. 3 (2006): 363–87.

Burton, Andrew, and Hélène Charton-Bigot, eds. *Generations Past: Youth in East African History.* Athens: Ohio University Press, 2010.

Burton, Andrew, and Paul Ocobock, "The 'Travelling Native': Vagrancy and Colonial Control in British East Africa." In *Cast Out: Vagrancy and Homelessness in Global and Historical Perspective,* ed. A. L. Beir and Paul Ocobock, 270–301. Athens: Ohio University Press: 2008.

Busia, K. A. *The Position of the Chief in the Modern Political System of Ashanti.* London: Oxford University Press, 1951.

———. *Report on a Social Survey of Sekondi-Takoradi.* London: Hazell, Watson and Viney, 1950.

Butler, Judith. *Gender Trouble: Feminism and the Subversion of Identity.* New York: Routledge, 1990.

———. *Undoing Gender.* New York: Routledge, 2004.

Casely-Hayford, Augustus, and Richard Rathbone. "Politics, Families, and Freemasonry in the Colonial Gold Coast." In *People and Empires in African History: Essays in Memory of Michael Crowder,* ed. J. F. Ade Ajayi and J. D. Y. Peel, 143–60. London: Longman, 1992.

Chanock, Martin. *Law, Custom and Social Order.* Cambridge: Cambridge University Press, 1985.

Chernoff, John Miller. *African Rhythm and African Sensibility: Aesthetics and Social Action in African Musical Idioms.* Chicago: University of Chicago Press, 1979.

———. "Music and Historical Consciousness among the Dagbamba of Ghana." In *Enchanting Powers: Music in the World's Religions,* ed. Lawrence Sullivan, 91–120. Cambridge, Mass.: Harvard University Press, 1997.

Chikowero, Moses. "'Our People Father, They Haven't Learned Yet': Music and Postcolonial Identities in Zimbabwe, 1980–2000." *Journal of Southern African Studies* 34, no. 1 (2008): 145–60.

———. "Subalternating Currents: Electrification and Power Politics in Bulawayo, Colonial Zimbabwe, 1894–1939." *Journal of Southern African Studies* 33, no. 2 (2007): 287–306.

Clifford, Hugh. *The Gold Coast Regiment in the East African Campaign.* London: John Murray, 1920.

Cobbina, F. "Konkoma Music and Dance." Diploma paper in Dance, University of Ghana, n.d.

Coe, Cati. *Dilemmas of Culture in African Schools.* Chicago: University of Chicago Press, 2005.

Coester, Markus. "Localising African Popular Music Transnationally: 'Highlife-Travellers' in Britain in the 1950s and 1960s." *Journal of African Cultural Studies,* 20, no. 2 (2008): 133–44.

Cohen, Abner. *The Politics of Elite Culture: Explorations in the Dramaturgy of Power in a Modern African Society.* Berkeley: University of California Press, 1981.

Cohen, David William, Stephan F. Miescher, and Luise White. "Introduction: Voices, Words and African History" In *African Words, African Voices: Critical Practices in Oral History,* ed. Luise White, Stephan F. Miescher, and David William Cohen, 1–27. Bloomington: Indiana University Press, 2001.

Cole, Catherine M. *Ghana's Concert Party Theatre.* Bloomington: Indiana University Press, 2001.

Cole, Catherine M., Takyiwaa Manuh, and Stephan F. Miescher, eds. *Africa after Gender?* Bloomington: Indiana University Press, 2007.

Collins, John. "The Decolonisation of Ghanaian Popular Entertainment." In *Urbanization and African Cultures,* ed. Toyin Falola and Steven Salm, 119–37. Durham: Carolina Academic Press, 2005.

———. *E. T. Mensah: King of Highlife.* Accra: Anansesem Publications, 1996.

———. "The Early History of West African Highlife Music." *Popular Music* 8, no. 3 (1989): 221–30.

———. "The Generational Factor in Ghanaian Music." In *Playing with Identities in Contemporary Music in Africa,* ed. Mai Palmberg and Annemette Kirkegaard, 60–74. Uppsala: Nordiska Afrikainstitutet, 2002.

———. "The Ghanaian Concert Party: African Popular Entertainment at the Cross Roads." PhD diss., State University of New York at Buffalo, 1994.

———. "Ghanaian Highlife." *African Arts* 10, no. 1 (1976): 62–68, 100.

———. "Ghanaian Popular Performance and the Urbanisation Process: 1900–1980." *Transactions of the Historical Society of Ghana* 8 (2009): 203–26.

———. "Ghanaian Women Enter into Popular Entertainment." *Humanities Review Journal* 3, no. 1 (2003): 1–10.

———. *Highlife Time.* Accra: Anansesem Publications, 1996.

———. "The Importance of African Popular Music Studies For Ghanaian/African Students." Paper presented at CODESRIA's 30th Anniversary Humanities Conference, Accra, September 17–19, 2003.

———. "King of the Black Beat: The Story of King Bruce and the Black Beats, Highlife Dance Band of Ghana." Unpublished manuscript, 1987/89.

———. "One Hundred Years of Censorship in Ghanaian Popular Performance." In *Popular Music Censorship in Africa,* ed. Michael Drewett and Martin Cloonan, 171–86. Burlington, Vt.: Ashgate, 2006.

———. "Popular Performance and Culture in Ghana: The Past 50 Years." *Ghana Studies* 10 (2007): 9–64.

———. "The Reasons for Teaching African Popular Music Studies at University." Paper presented as Full Professorship Inaugural Lecture, University of Ghana, November 17, 2005.

———. *West African Pop Roots.* Philadelphia: Temple University Press, 1992.

Connell, R. W. *Gender and Power.* Stanford: Stanford University Press, 1987.

———. *Masculinities.* Berkeley: University of California Press, 1995.

Cooper, Frederick. *Colonialism in Question: Theory, Knowledge, History.* Berkeley: University of California Press, 2005.

———. "Conflict and Connection: Rethinking Colonial African History." *American Historical Review* 99, no. 5 (1994): 1516–45.

———. *Decolonization and African Society: The Labor Question in French and British Africa.* Cambridge: Cambridge University Press, 1996.

————. "Industrial Man Goes to Africa." In *Men and Masculinities in Modern Africa,* ed. Lisa A. Lindsay and Stephan F. Miescher, 128–37. Portsmouth: Heinemann, 2003.

————. "Possibility and Constraint: African Independence in Historical Perspective." *Journal of African History* 49, no. 2 (2008): 167–96.

————. "Urban Space, Industrial Time, and Wage Labor in Africa." In *Struggle for the City: Migrant Labor, Capital, and the State in Urban Africa,* ed. Frederick Cooper, 7–50. Beverly Hills, Calif.: Sage Publications, 1983.

Cooper, Frederick, and Ann Laura Stoler. *Tensions of Empire: Colonial Cultures in a Bourgeois World.* Berkeley: University of California Press, 1997.

Coplan, David. "Go to My Town, Cape Coast!: The Social History of Ghanaian Music." In *Eight Urban Music Cultures* ed. Bruno Nettl, 96–114. Urbana: University of Illinois Press, 1978.

————. *In the Time of Cannibals: The Word Music of South Africa's Basotho Migrants.* Chicago: University of Chicago Press, 1994.

————. *In Township Tonight!: South Africa's Black City Music and Theatre.* London: Longman, 1985.

————. "The Urbanisation of African Music: Some Theoretical Observations." *Popular Music* 2 (1982): 113–29.

Cornwall, Andrea. "To Be a Man Is More than a Day's Work: Shifting Ideals of Masculinity in Ado-Odo, Southwestern Nigeria." In *Men and Masculinities in Modern Africa,* ed. Lisa Lindsay and Stephan Miescher, 230–48. Portsmouth: Heinemann, 2003.

Couzens, Tim. "Moralizing Leisure Time: The Transatlantic Connection and Black Johannesburg 1918–1936." In *Industrialisation and Social Change in South Africa,* ed. Shula Marks and Richard Rathbone, 314 37. London: Longman, 1982.

Crabtree, Alice Ioné. "Marriage and Family Life among the Educated Africans in the Urban Areas of the Gold Coast." MA thesis, University of London, 1950.

Crisp, Jeff. *The Story of an African Working Class: Ghanaian Miners' Struggles, 1870–1980.* London: Zed Books, 1984.

Crowder, Michael. "The 1939–45 War and West Africa." In *History of West Africa,* vol. 2, ed. J. F. I. Ajayi and Michael Crowder, 596–621. London: Longman, 1974.

————. "World War II and Africa: Introduction." *Journal of African History* 26, no. 4 (1985): 287–88.

Daniel, Pete. *Lost Revolutions: The South in the 1950s.* Chapel Hill: University of North Carolina Press, 2000.

Darkwa, K. Ampom. "Migrant Music and Musicians: The Effect of Migration on Music. Pt. 1: Nima Opinion Survey." PhD diss., University of Ghana, Institute of African Studies, 1971.

Datta, Ansu, and R. Porter. "The Asafo System in Historical Perspective." *Journal of African History* 12, no. 2 (1971): 279–97.

Davidson, Basil. *Black Star: A View of the Life and Times of Kwame Nkrumah.* London: Allen Lane, 1973.

De Graft Johnson, J. C. "The Fanti Asafu." *Africa: Journal of the International African Institute* 5, no. 3 (1932): 307–22.

Denzer, LaRay. "Gender and Decolonization: A Study of Three Women in West African Public Life." In *People and Empires in African History: Essays in Memory of Michael Crowder,* ed. J. F. Ade Ajayi and J. D. Y. Peel, 217–36. London: Longman, 1992.

Diawara, Manthia. "The Sixties in Bamako: Malick Sidibé and James Brown." In *Black Cultural Traffic: Crossroads in Global Performance and Popular Culture,* ed. Harry J. Elam Jr. and Kennell Jackson, 242–65. Ann Arbor: University of Michigan Press, 2005.

Dickson, K. B. "Evolution of Seaports in Ghana: 1800–1928." *Annals of the Association of American Geographers* 55, no. 1 (1965): 98–111.

Diouf, Mamadou. "Engaging Postcolonial Cultures: African Youth and Public Space." *African Studies Review* 46, no. 2 (2003): 1–12.

Dirks, Nicholas B., Geoff Eley, and Sherry B. Ortner, eds. *Culture/Power/History: A Reader in Contemporary Social Theory.* Princeton, N.J.: Princeton University Press, 1994.

Dove, Mabel. *Selected Writings of a Pioneer West African Feminist.* Ed. Stephanie Newell and Audrey Gadzekpo. Nottingham: Trent Editions, 2004.

Drewal, Margaret. *Yoruba Ritual: Performers, Play, Agency.* Bloomington: Indiana University Press, 1992.

Dumett, Raymond E. "African Merchants of the Gold Coast, 1860–1905--Dynamics of Indigenous Entrepreneurship." *Comparative Studies in Society and History* 25, no. 4 (1983): 661–93.

———. *El Dorado in West Africa: The Gold Mining Frontier, African Labor, and Colonial Capitalism in the Gold Coast, 1875–1900.* Athens: Ohio University Press, 1998.

———. "John Sarbah, the Elder, and African Mercantile Entrepreneurship in the Gold Coast in the Late Nineteenth Century." *Journal of African History* 14, no. 4 (1973): 653–79.

Du Sautoy, Peter. *Community Development in Ghana.* London: Oxford University Press, 1958.

Dwamena, F. Kumi. "Missionary Education and Leadership Training at Presbyterian Training College, Akropong: An Historical Study of Presbyterian Mission Educational Activities in Ghana, 1848–1960." PhD diss., Columbia University, 1982.

Ebron, Paulla. "Constituting Subjects through Performative Acts." In *Africa After Gender?,* ed. Catherine M. Cole, Takyiwaa Manuh, and Stephen F. Miescher, 171–90. Bloomington: Indiana University Press, 2007.

———. *Performing Africa.* Princeton, N.J.: Princeton University Press, 2002.

Eckhart, Andreas, and Adam Jones. "Introduction: Historical Writing about Everyday Life." *Journal of African Cultural Studies* 15, no. 1 (2002): 5–16.

Ellis, Stephen. "Rumor and Power in Togo." *Africa: Journal of the International African Institute* 63, no. 4 (1993): 462–76.

———. "Writing Histories of Contemporary Africa." *Journal of African History* 43, no. 1 (2002): 1–26.

Enwezor, Okwui, ed. *The Short Century: Independence and Liberation Movements in Africa 1945–1994.* New York: Prestel, 2001.

Erlmann, Veit. *Nightsong: Performance, Power, and Practice in South Africa.* Chicago: University of Chicago Press, 1996.

Fabian, Johannes. *Power and Performance: Ethnographic Explorations through Proverbial Wisdom and Theater in Shaba, Zaire.* Madison: University of Wisconsin Press, 1990.

Fair, Laura. *Pastimes and Politics: Culture, Community, and Identity in Post-Abolition Urban Zanzibar, 1890–1945.* Athens: Ohio University Press, 2001.

———. "Voice, Authority, and Memory: The Kiswahili Lyrics of Siti binti Saadi." In *African Words, African Voices: Critical Practices in Oral History,* ed. Luise White,

Stephan F. Miescher, and David William Cohen, 246–63. Bloomington: Indiana University Press, 2001.

Feld, Steven. "From Schizophonia to Schismogenesis: On the Discourse and Commodification Practices of 'World Music' and 'World Beat.'" In Charles Keil and Steven Feld, *Music Grooves: Essays and Dialogues*, 257–89. Chicago: University of Chicago Press, 1994.

———. *Jazz Cosmopolitanism in Accra: Five Musical Years in Ghana*. Durham, N.C.: Duke University Press, 2012.

———. "Notes on 'World Beat.'" In Charles Keil and Steven Feld, *Music Grooves: Essays and Dialogues*, 238–46. Chicago: University of Chicago Press, 1994.

Fenwick, Mac. "'Tough Guy, eh?': The Gangster Figure in Drum." *Journal of Southern African Studies* 22, no. 4 (1996): 617–32.

Ferguson, James. *Expectations of Modernity: Myths and Meanings of Urban Life on the Zambian Copperbelt*. Berkeley: University of California Press, 1999.

Flaes, Rob Boonzajer. *Brass Unbound: Secret Children of the Colonial Brass Band*. Amsterdam: Royal Tropical Institute, 2000.

Fortes, Meyer. "The Impact of the War on British West Africa." *International Affairs* 21, no. 2 (1945): 206–19.

Foster, Phillip. *Education and Social Change in Ghana*. Chicago: University of Chicago Press, 1965.

Fosu-Mensah, Kwabena, Lucy Duran, and Chris Stapleton. "On Music in Contemporary Africa." *African Affairs* 86, no. 343 (1987): 227–40.

Foucault, Michel. *Power/Knowledge: Selected Interviews and Other Writings, 1972–77*. New York: Pantheon Books, 1980.

Fouchard, Laurent. "Lagos and the Invention of Juvenile Delinquency in Nigeria, 1920–1960." *Journal of African History* 47, no. 1 (2006): 115–37.

Freund, Bill. *The African City: A History*. Cambridge: Cambridge University Press, 2007.

Gadzekpo, Audrey. "Public but Private: A Transformational Reading of the Memoirs and Newspaper Writings of Mercy Ffoulkes-Crabbe." In *Africa's Hidden Histories: Everyday Literacy and Making the Self*, ed. Karin Barber, 314–37. Bloomington: Indiana University Press, 2006.

Garland, Phyl. "Soul to Soul: Music Festival in Ghana Links Black Music to Its Roots." *Ebony*, June 1971, 78–89.

Garofalo, Reebee. "Whose World, What Beat: The Transnational Music Industry, Identity, and Cultural Imperialism." *World of Music* 35, no. 2 (1993): 16–32.

Geiger, Susan. *TANU Women: Gender and Culture in the Making of Tanganyikan Nationalism, 1955–1965*. Portsmouth: Heinemann, 1997.

Gilman, Lisa. "Purchasing Praise: Women, Dancing, and Patronage in Malawi Party Politics." *Africa Today* 48, no. 4 (2002): 42–64.

Glaser, Clive. *Bo-Tsotsi: The Youth Gangs of Soweto, 1935–1976*. Portsmouth: Heinemann, 2000.

———. "Swines, Hazels and the Dirty Dozen: Masculinity, Territoriality and the Youth Gangs of Soweto, 1960–1976." *Journal of Southern African Studies* 24, no. 4 (1998): 719–36.

Gocking, Roger. *Facing Two Ways: Ghana's Coastal Communities under Colonial Rule*. New York: University Press of America, 1999.

———. *History of Ghana*. Westport, Conn.: Greenwood Press, 2005.

———. "Indirect Rule in the Gold Coast: Competition for Office and the Invention of Tradition." *Canadian Journal of African Studies* 28, no. 3 (1994): 421–46.

Goffman, Erving. *The Presentation of Self in Everyday Life*. Garden City, N.Y.: Doubleday, 1959 [1956].

Gondola, Ch. Didier. "Popular Music, Urban Society, and Changing Gender Relations in Kinshasa, Zaire (1950–1990)." In *Gendered Encounters: Challenging Cultural Boundaries and Social Hierarchies in Africa*, ed. Maria Grosz-Ngate and Omari H. Kokole, 65–84. New York: Routledge Press, 1997.

Gordon, Charles Alexander. *Life on the Gold Coast*. London: Bailliere, Tindall and Coe, 1874.

Graham, C. K. *The History of Education in Ghana: From the Earliest Times to the Declaration of Independence*. Accra: Ghana Publishing Corporation, 1976.

Graham, Ronnie. *Stern's Guide to Contemporary African Music*. London: Zed, 1988.

Gray, John. *African Music: A Bibliographical Guide to the Traditional, Popular, Art, and Liturgical Musics of Sub-Saharan Africa*. New York: Greenwood Press, 1991.

Greene, Sandra. *Gender, Ethnicity and Social Change on the Upper Slave Coast: A History of the Anlo-Ewe*. Portsmouth: Heinemann, 1996.

———. "A Perspective from African Women's History: Comment on 'Confronting Continuity.'" *Journal of Women's History* 9, no. 3 (1997): 95–104.

Guilbault, Jocelyne. *Zouk: World Music in the West Indies*. Chicago: University of Chicago Press, 1993.

Gunderson, Frank. "Kifungua Kinywa, or 'Opening the Contest with Chai.'" In *Mashindano!: Competitive Music Performance in East Africa*, ed. Frank Gunderson and Gregory Barz, 7–17. Dar es Salaam: Mkuku na Nyota Publishers, 2000.

Hagan, George P. "Nkrumah's Cultural Policy." In *The Life and Work of Kwame Nkrumah: Papers of a Symposium Organized by the Institute of African Studies*, ed. Kwame Arhin, 1–26. Accra: Sedco Publishing, 1991.

———. "Nkrumah's Leadership Style: An Assessment from a Cultural Perspective." In *The Life and Work of Kwame Nkrumah: Papers of a Symposium Organized by the Institute of African Studies*, ed. Kwame Arhin, 180–210. Accra: Sedco Publishing, 1991.

Hagan, Kwa. "The Literary and Social Clubs of the Past: Their Role in National Awakening in Ghana." *Okyeame* 4, no. 2 (1969): 81–86.

Hanna, Judith Lynne. "The Highlife: A West African Urban Dance." In *Dance Research Monograph One: 1971–1972*, ed. Patricia A. Rowe, 139–52. New York: Committee on Research in Dance, 1973.

———. *To Dance Is Human: A Theory of Nonverbal Communication*. Chicago: University of Chicago Press, 1987.

Hansen, Karen Tranberg. "Dressing Dangerously: Miniskirts, Gender Relations, and Sexuality in Zambia." In *Fashioning Africa: Power and the Politics of Dress*, ed. Jean Allman, 166–85. Bloomington: Indiana University Press, 2004.

Hart, Jennifer. "Suffer to Gain: Citizenship, Accumulation, and Motor Transportation in Late-Colonial and Postcolonial Ghana." PhD diss., Indiana University, 2011.

Hawkins, Sean. *Writing and Colonialism in Northern Ghana: The Encounter between the LoDagaa and the "World on Paper."* Toronto: University of Toronto Press, 2002.

Haywood, A., and F. A. S. Clarke. *The History of the Royal West African Frontier Force*. Aldershot: Gale and Polden, 1964.

Hess, Janet. "Exhibiting Ghana: Display, Documentary, and 'National' Art in the Nkrumah Era." *African Studies Review* 44, no. 1 (2001): 59–77.

Hill, Polly. *Migrant Cocoa-Famers of Southern Ghana: A Study in Rural Capitalism*. Cambridge: Cambridge University Press, 1963.

Hobsbawm, Eric, and Terence Ranger, eds. *The Invention of Tradition*. New York: Cambridge University Press, 1983.

Hodge, Peter. "The Ghana Workers Brigade: A Project for Unemployed Youth." *British Journal of Sociology* 15, no. 2 (1964): 113–28.

Hodgson, Dorothy L., and Sheryl A. McCurdy, eds. *"Wicked" Women and the Reconfiguration of Gender in Africa*. Portsmouth: Heinemann, 2001.

Holbrook, Wendell. "British Propaganda and the Mobilization of the Gold Coast War Effort, 1939–45." *Journal of African History* 26, no. 4 (1985): 347–61.

———. "The Impact of the Second World War on the Gold Coast, 1939–45." PhD diss., Princeton University, 1978.

Hunt, Nancy Rose. *A Colonial Lexicon: Of Birth Ritual, Medicalization, and Mobility in the Congo*. Durham, N.C.: Duke University Press, 1999.

Iliffe, John. *The African Poor: A History*. Cambridge: Cambridge University Press, 1987.

———. *Honour in African History*. Cambridge: Cambridge University Press, 2005.

Jeffries, Richard. *Class, Power and Ideology in Ghana: The Railwaymen of Sekondi*. Cambridge: Cambridge University Press, 1978.

Jones, Paula. "The United Africa Company in the Gold Coast/Ghana, 1920–1965." PhD diss., School of Oriental and African Studies, 1983.

Jones-Quartey, K. A. B. "Press and Nationalism in Ghana." *United Asia* 9, no. 1 (1957): 55–60.

———. *A Summary History of the Ghana Press, 1822–1960*. Accra: Ghana Information Services Department, 1974.

Jopp, Keith. *Ghana: Ten Great Years, 1951–1960*. Accra: Ghana Information Services, 1960.

Kay, G. B., ed. *The Political Economy of Colonialism in Ghana: A Collection of Documents and Statistics, 1900–1960*. Cambridge: Cambridge University Press, 1972.

Keil, Charles, and Steven Feld, eds. *Music Grooves: Essays and Dialogues*. Chicago: University of Chicago Press, 1994.

Kelly, Robin D. G. *Race Rebels: Culture, Politics, and the Black Working Class*. New York: Free Press, 1994.

Killingray, David. "African Civilians in the Era of the Second World War, c. 1935–50." In *Daily Lives of Civilians in Wartime Africa: From Slavery Days to Rwandan Genocide*, ed. John Laband, 139–68. Westport, Conn.: Greenwood Press, 2007.

———. "Military and Labour Recruitment in the Gold Coast During the Second World War." *Journal of African History* 23, no. 1 (1982): 83–95.

———. "The Mutiny of the West African Regiment in the Gold Coast, 1901." *International Journal of African Historical Studies* 16, no. 3 (1983): 441–54.

———. "Repercussions of World War I in the Gold Coast." *Journal of African History* 19, no. 1 (1978): 39–59.

Killingray, David, and Richard Rathbone, eds. *Africa and the Second World War*. New York: St. Martin's Press, 1986.

Kimble, David. *A Political History of Ghana: The Rise of Gold Coast Nationalism, 1850–1928*. Oxford: Clarendon Press, 1963.

Kinney, Esi Sylvia. "Urban West African Music and Dance." *African Urban Notes,* Winter 1970, 3–15.

Kirk-Greene, A. H. M. "The Thin White Line: The Size of the British Colonial Service in Africa." *African Affairs* 79 (1980): 25–44.

Kuklick, Henrika. *The Imperial Bureaucrat: The Colonial Administrative Service in the Gold Coast, 1920–1939.* Stanford, Calif.: Hoover Institution Press, 1979.

Kyei, Thomas. *Our Days Dwindle: Memories of My Childhood Days in Asante.* Portsmouth: Heinemann, 2001.

Lawrance, Benjamin N., Emily Lynn Osborn, and Richard L. Roberts, eds. *Intermediaries, Interpreters, and Clerks: African Employees in the Making of Colonial Africa.* Madison: University of Wisconsin Press, 2006.

Lentz, Carola, and Jan Budniok. "Ghana@50--Celebrating the Nation: An Eyewitness Account from Accra." Working Paper no. 83. Department of Anthropology and African Studies, University of Mainz, March 2007.

Lindsay, Lisa A. "Trade Unions and Football Clubs: Gender and the 'Modern' Public Sphere in Colonial Southwestern Nigeria." In *Leisure in Urban Africa,* ed. Paul T. Zeleza and Cassandra R. Veney, 105–24. Trenton, N.J.: Africa World Press, 2003.

Lindsay, Lisa A., and Stephan F. Miescher, eds. *Men and Masculinities in Modern Africa.* Portsmouth: Heinemann, 2003.

Lipsitz, George. *Footsteps in the Dark: The Hidden Histories of Popular Music.* Minneapolis: University of Minnesota Press, 2007.

Macías, Anthony. *Mexican American Mojo: Popular Music, Dance, and Urban Culture in Los Angeles, 1935–1958.* Durham, N.C.: Duke University Press, 2008.

MacMillan, Allister. *The Red Book of West Africa: Historical and Descriptive, Commercial and Industrial Fact, Figures and Resources.* London: F. Cass, 1920.

Mahon, Maureen. "Black Like This: Race, Generation, and Rock in the Post–Civil Rights Era." *American Ethnologist* 27, no. 2 (2000): 283–311.

Mann, Kristin. *Marrying Well: Marriage, Status and Social Change among the Educated Elite in Colonial Lagos.* Cambridge: Cambridge University Press, 1985.

Mann, Kristin, and Richard L. Roberts, eds. *Law in Colonial Africa.* London: James Currey, 1991.

Manuh, Takyiwaa. "Doing Gender Work in Ghana." In *Africa After Gender?,* ed. Catherine M. Cole, Takyiwaa Manuh, and Stephan F. Miescher, 125–49. Bloomington: Indiana University Press, 2007.

———. "Women and Their Organizations during the Convention Peoples' Party Period." In *The Life and Work of Kwame Nkrumah: Papers of a Symposium Organized by the Institute of African Studies,* ed. Kwame Arhin, 108–34. Accra: Sedco Publishing, 1991.

Martin, Phyllis M. "Afterword." In *Fashioning Africa: Power and Politics of Dress,* ed. Jean Allman (Bloomington: Indiana University Press, 2004). 227–30.

———. "Contesting Clothes in Colonial Brazzaville." *Journal of African History* 35, no. 3 (1994): 401–26.

———. *Leisure and Society in Colonial Brazzaville.* Cambridge: Cambridge University Press, 1995.

Martin, Stephen. "Brass Bands and the Beni Phenomenon in Urban East Africa." *African Music* 7, no. 1 (1991): 72–81.

Maxwell John, ed. *The Gold Coast Handbook, 1928.* London: Whitefriars Press, 1929.

Maylam, Paul, and Iain Edwards, eds., *The People's City: African Life in Twentieth-Century Durban*. Pietermaritzburg: University of Natal Press, 1996.

McBee, Randy D. *Dance Hall Days: Intimacy and Leisure among Working-Class Immigrants in the United States*. New York: New York University Press, 2000.

McCaskie, T. C. "Accumulation: Wealth and Belief in Asante History: II the Twentieth Century." *Africa: Journal of the International African Institute* 56, no. 1 (1986): 3–23.

———. *Asante Identities: History and Modernity in an African Village, 1850–1950*. Bloomington: Indiana University Press, 2000.

———. *State and Society in Pre-colonial Asante*. Cambridge: Cambridge University Press, 1995.

McClintock, Anne. *Imperial Leather: Race, Gender and Sexuality in the Colonial Contest*. London: Routledge, 1995.

Mensah, Atta Annan. "Highlife." Unpublished paper, BAPMAF Archives, 1969/70.

———. "The Popular Song and the Ghanaian Writer." *Okyeame* 4, no. 1 (1968): 110–19.

———. *Sing, Sing, Sing: Forty Ghanaian Songs You Enjoy*. Accra: Anowuo Educational Publications, 1968.

Miescher, Stephan F. "Becoming an *Opanyin*: Elders, Gender, and Masculinities in Ghana since the Nineteenth Century." In *Africa after Gender* ed. Catherine M. Cole, Takyiwaa Manuh, and Stephan F. Miescher, 253–69. Bloomington: Indiana University Press, 2007.

———. *Making Men in Ghana*. Bloomington: Indiana University Press, 2005.

———. "The Making of Presbyterian Teachers: Masculinities and Programs of Education in Colonial Ghana." In *Men and Masculinities in Modern Africa*, ed. Lisa A. Lindsay and Stephan F. Miescher, 89–108. Portsmouth: Heinemann, 2003.

Mikell, Gwendolyn. *Cocoa and Chaos in Ghana*. New York: Paragon House, 1989.

Moorman, Marissa J. *Intonations: A Social History of Music and Nation in Luanda, Angola, from 1945 to Recent Times*. Athens: Ohio University Press, 2008.

———. "Putting on a Pano and Dressing Like Our Grandparents: Nation and Dress in Late Colonial Luanda." In *Fashioning Africa: Power and the Politics of Dress*, ed. Jean Allman, 84–103. Bloomington: Indiana University Press, 2004.

Morrell, Robert. "Of Boys and Men: Masculinity and Gender in Southern African Studies." *Journal of Southern African Studies* 24, no. 4 (1998): 605–30.

Murillo, Bianca. "'The Modern Shopping Experience': Kingsway Department Store and Consumer Politics in Ghana." *AFRICA: Journal of the International African Institute* 82, no. 3 (forthcoming).

Musicians and Music Lovers Association. "10th Anniversary Program, 1987–1997." Unpublished program in author's possession, n.d.

Nash, Mark. "The Modernity of African Cinema." In *The Short Century: Independence and Liberation Movements in Africa 1845–1994*, ed. Okwui Enwezor, 339–46. New York: Prestel, 2001.

Newell, Stephanie. *Literary Culture in Colonial Ghana: How to Play the Game of Life*. Bloomington: Indiana University Press, 2002.

Nimo, Koo, and J. L. Latham. *Ashanti Ballads*. Kumasi: Published by authors, 1969.

Nketia, J. H. Kwabena. *African Music in Ghana*. Evanston, Ill.: Northwestern University Press, 1962.

———. "Changing Traditions of Folk Music in Ghana." *Journal of the International Folk Music Council* 11 (1959): 31–36.

———. *Drumming in Akan Communities of Ghana.* London: Thomas Nelson and Sons, 1963.

———. *Folk Songs of Ghana.* Legon: University of Ghana Press, 1963.

———. *Ghana: Music, Dance and Drama: A Review of the Performing Arts of Ghana.* Accra: Ghana Information Services, 1965.

———. "The Gramophone and Contemporary African Music in the Gold Coast." In *Proceedings of the Fourth Annual Conference of the West African Institute of Economic Social Research,* 189–200. Ibadan, 1955.

———."History and the Organization of Music in West Africa." In *Essays on Music and History in Africa,* ed. Klaus P. Wachsmann, 3–26. Evanston, Ill.: Northwestern University Press, 1971.

———. "The Instrumental Resources of African Music." *Papers in African Studies* 3 (1968): 1–23.

———. "The Linguistic Aspect of Style in African Languages." In *Current Trends in Linguistics: Linguistics in Sub-Saharan Africa,* vol. 7, ed. Thomas Sebeok, 733–57. The Hague: Mouton Press, 1971.

———. "Modern Trends in Ghana Music." *African Music Society Journal* 1, no. 4 (1957): 13–17.

———. "Musical Interaction in Ritual Events." *Concilium* 2, no. 202 (1989): 111–24.

———. "National Development and the Performing Arts of Africa." In *The Muse of Modernity: Essays on Culture as Development in Africa,* ed. Phillip G. Altbach and Salah M. Hassan, 117–49. Trenton, N.J.: Africa World Press, 1996.

———. "On the Historicity of Music in African Cultures." *Journal of African Studies* 9, no. 3 (1982): 90–100.

Nkrumah, Kwame. *Africa Must Unite.* London: Heinemann, 1963.

———. *Axioms of Kwame Nkrumah.* New York: International Publishers, 1967.

———. *Consciencism: Philosophy and Ideology for De-Colonization and Development with Particular Reference to the African Revolution.* London: Heinemann, 1964.

———. *Flower of Learning: Some Reflections on African Learning, Ancient and Modern.* Accra: Government Printer, 1961.

———. *Ghana: The Autobiography of Kwame Nkrumah.* New York: International Publishers, 1957.

———. *I Speak of Freedom: A Statement of African Ideology.* New York: Praeger, 1961.

———. *Revolutionary Path.* New York: Panaf Books, 1973.

———. *Selected Speeches of Kwame Nkrumah.* Vols. 1–5. Compiled by Samuel Obeng. Accra: Afram Publications, 1979–1997.

Nortey, D. N. A. "The Treatment of Juvenile Delinquency in Ghana." *Ghana Journal of Child Development* 2, no. 1 (1969): 30–46.

Notcutt, L. A., and G. C. Latham. *The African and the Cinema: An Account of the Work of the Bantu Educational Cinema Experiment during the Period March 1935 to May 1937.* London: Edinburgh House Press, 1937.

Ntarangwi, Mwenda. *Gender, Identity, and Performance: Understanding Swahili Cultural Realities through Song.* Trenton, N.J.: Africa World Press, 2003.

Nugent, Paul. *Big Men, Small Boys, and Politics in Ghana: Power, Ideology, and the Burden of History, 1982–1994.* London: Pinter, 1995.

Nyame, E. K. *E.K.'s Band Song Book.* Accra: H. Teymani, 1955.

Obeng, Pashington. "Gendered Nationalism: Forms of Masculinity in Modern Asante of Ghana." In *Men and Masculinities in Modern Africa*, ed. Lisa A. Lindsay and Stephen F. Miescher, 192–208. Portsmouth: Heinemann, 2003.

Obeng, Samuel Gyasi. "Language and Gender: Women in Akan Highlife Discourse." Unpublished paper in author's possession, 1997.

Oppong, Anna. "The Use of English in Ghanaian Highlife Music." Diploma paper, Department of English, University of Ghana, Legon, 1979.

Oppong, Christine, ed. *Female and Male in West Africa*. London: Allen and Unwin, 1983.

———. *Marriage among a Matrilineal Elite: A Family Study of Ghanaian Senior Civil Servants*. Cambridge: Cambridge University Press, 1974.

Oti, Sonny. *Highlife Music in West Africa*. Lagos: Malthouse Press, 2009.

Oyĕwumi, Oyèrónké. *The Invention of Women: Making an African Sense of Western Gender Discourses*. Minneapolis: University of Minnesota Press, 1997.

Parker, John. *Making the Town: Ga State and Society in Early Colonial Accra*. Portsmouth: Heinemann, 2000.

Parpart, Jane L. "'Wicked Women' and 'Respectable Ladies': Reconfiguring Gender on the Zambian Copperbelt, 1936–64." In *Wicked Women and the Reconfiguration of Gender*, ed. Dorothy Hodgson and Sheryl McCurdy, 274–92. Portsmouth: Heinemann, 2001.

Peil, Margaret. "The Expulsion of West African Aliens." *Journal of Modern African Studies* 9, no. 2 (1971): 205–29.

Pellow, Deborah. *Women of Accra: Options for Autonomy*. Algonac, Mich.: Reference Publications, 1977.

Peterson, Derek R. *Creative Writing: Translation, Bookkeeping, and the Work of Imagination in Colonial Kenya*. Portsmouth: Heinemann, 2004.

Peterson, Derek R., and Giacomo Macola, eds. *Recasting the Past: History Writing and Political Work in Modern Africa*. Athens: Ohio University Press, 2009.

Plageman, Nate. "Accra Is Changing, Isn't It?: Urban Infrastructure, Independence, and Nation in the Gold Coast's *Daily Graphic*, 1954–57." *International Journal for African Historical Studies* 43, no. 1 (2010): 137–59.

Pratt, Ray. *Rhythm and Resistance: Explorations in the Political Uses of Popular* Music. New York: Praeger, 1990.

Prince, Robert. "Politics and Culture in Contemporary Ghana: The Big-Man Small-Boy Syndrome." *Journal of African Studies* 1, no. 2 (1974): 173–204.

Quarcoopome, S. S. "A History of the Urban Development of Accra: 1877–1957." *University of Ghana Research Review* 9, nos. 1 & 2 (1993): 20–32.

———. "Urbanisation, Land Alienation, and Politics in Accra." *University of Ghana Research Review* 8, nos. 1 & 2 (1992): 40–54.

Ranger, Terence. *Dance and Society in Eastern Africa, 1890–1970: The Beni Ngoma*. Berkeley: University of California Press, 1975.

———. "The Invention of Tradition in Colonial Africa." In *The Invention of Tradition*, ed. Eric Hobsbawm and Terence Ranger, 211–62. New York: Cambridge University Press, 1983.

Rathbone, Richard. "Businessmen in Politics: Party Struggle in Ghana, 1949–1957." *Journal of Development Studies* 9, no. 3 (1973): 391–402.

Reed, Daniel B. *Dan Ge Performance: Masks and Music in Contemporary Cote d'Ivoire*. Bloomington: Indiana University Press, 2003.

Reindorf, C. C. *The History of the Gold Coast.* Basel: Missionsbuchhandlung, 1895.

Robertson, Claire C. *Sharing the Same Bowl: A Socioeconomic History of Women and Class in Accra, Ghana.* Bloomington: Indiana University Press, 1984.

Rohlehr, Gordon. "I Lawa: The Construction of Masculinity in Trinidad and Tobago Calypso." In *Interrogating Caribbean Masculinities: Theoretical and Empircal Analyses,* ed. Rhoda E. Reddock, 326–403. Kingston: University of the West Indies Press, 2004.

Rouch, Jean. "Notes on Migrations into the Gold Coast--First Report of the Mission Carried Out in the Gold Coast from March to December, 1954." Unpublished paper in author's possession, n.d.

Royce, Anya. *The Anthropology of Dance.* Bloomington: Indiana University Press, 1977.

Rumbolz, Roger. "'A Vessel for Many Things': Brass Bands in Ghana." PhD diss., Wesleyan University, 2000.

Salm, Steven J. "The Bukom Boys: Subcultures and Identity Transformation in Accra, Ghana." PhD diss., University of Texas, 2003.

———. "'Rain or Shine We Gonna' Rock': Dance Subcultures and Identity Construction in Accra, Ghana." In *Sources and Methods in African History: Spoken, Written, Unearthed,* ed. Toyin Falola and Christian Jennings, 361–75. Rochester, N.Y.: University of Rochester Press, 2003.

Sarpong, Kwame. "Ghana's Highlife Music: A Digital Repertoire of Recordings and Pop Art at the Gramophone Records Museum." *History in Africa* 31 (2004): 455–61.

Schechner, Richard. *Between Theater and Anthropology.* Philadelphia: University of Pennsylvania Press, 1985.

Sharkey, Heather J. *Living with Colonialism: Nationalism and Culture in the Anglo-Egyptian Sudan.* Berkeley: California University Press, 2003.

Sinha, Mrinalini. *Colonial Masculinity: The "Manly Englishman" and "Effeminate Bengali" in the Late Nineteenth Century.* Manchester: Manchester University Press, 1995.

Sprigge, Robert. "The Ghanaian Highlife: Notation and Sources." *Music in Ghana, Record of the Ghana Music Society* 2 (1961): 70–94.

Stoler, Ann Laura. *Carnal Knowledge and Imperial Rule: Race and the Intimate in Colonial Rule.* Berkeley: University of California Press, 2002.

Straker, Jay. *Youth, Nationalism and the Guinean Revolution.* Bloomington: Indiana University Press, 2009.

Summers, Carol. *Colonial Lessons: Africans' Education in Southern Rhodesia, 1918–1940.* Portsmouth: Heinemann, 2002.

Tampour-Kuupol, Veronica. "The Use of Indirection in Some Contemporary Akan Highlife and Hiplife Songs." BA paper, Department of Linguistics, University of Ghana, 2004.

Tetteh, N. N. "The Ghana Young Pioneer Movement--A Youth Organisation in the Kwame Nkrumah Era." Paper presented at the Symposium on the Life and Work of Kwame Nkrumah, University of Ghana, May 27–June 1, 1985.

Turino, Thomas. *Nationalists, Cosmopolitans, and Popular Music in Zimbabwe.* Chicago: University of Chicago Press, 2000.

Turner, Victor. *Dramas, Fields, and Metaphors: Symbolic Action in Human Society.* Ithaca, N.Y.: Cornell University Press, 1974.

Turkson, A. "Effutu Asafo: Its Organization and Music." *Journal of International Library of African Music* 6, no. 2 (1982): 4–16.

Van der Geest, Sjaak. "The Image of Death in Akan Highlife Songs of Ghana." *Research in African Literatures* 11, no. 2 (1980): 145–74.

———. "*ɔpanyin:* The Ideal of Elder in the Akan Culture of Ghana." *Canadian Journal of African Studies* 32, no. 3 (1998): 449–93.

Veal, Michael E. *Fela: The Life and Times of an African Musical Icon.* Philadelphia: Temple University Press, 2000.

Vianna, Hermano. *The Mystery of Samba: Popular Music and National Identity in Brazil.* Chapel Hill: University of North Carolina Press, 1999.

Wade, Peter. *Music, Race, and Nation: Música Tropical in Colombia.* Chicago: University of Chicago Press, 2000.

Waller, Richard. "Rebellious Youth in Colonial Africa." *Journal of African History* 47, no. 1 (2006): 77–92.

Ward, W. E. F. *My Africa.* Accra: Ghana Universities Press, 1991.

Ware, Naomi. "Popular Music and African Identity in Freetown, Sierra Leone." In *Eight Urban Musical Cultures: Tradition and Change,* ed. Bruno Nettl, 296–320. Urbana: University of Illinois, 1978.

Waterman, Christopher Alan. *Jùjú: A Social History and Ethnography of an African Popular Music.* Chicago: University of Chicago Press, 1990.

West, Michael O. *The Rise of an African Middle Class: Colonial Zimbabwe, 1898–1965.* Bloomington: Indiana University Press, 2002.

White, Bob W. *Rumba Rules: The Politics of Dance Music in Mobutu's Zaire.* Durham, N.C.: Duke University Press, 2008.

Wilks, Ivor. *Asante in the Nineteenth Century: The Structure and Evolution of a Political Order.* Cambridge: Cambridge University Press, 1975.

Wilmer, Valerie. "Soulcd Out in Ghana." *Down Beat,* February 18, 1971, 14–15.

Wolfson, Freda. *Pageant of Ghana.* London: Oxford University Press, 1958.

Worger, William H., Nancy L. Clark, and Edward A. Alpers, eds. *Africa and the West: A Documentary History.* Vol. 2: *From Colonialism to Independence, 1875 to the Present.* Oxford: Oxford University Press, 2010.

Wraith, R. E. *Guggisberg.* London: Oxford University Press, 1967.

Yamada, Shoko. "Global Discourse and Local Response in Educational Policy Process: The Case of Achimota School in Colonial Ghana (Gold Coast)." PhD diss., Indiana University, 2003.

Yankah, Kwesi. "The Akan Highlife Song: A Medium of Cultural Reflection or Deflection?" *Research in African Literatures* 15, no. 4 (1984): 568–82.

———. "The Future of Highlife." *Glendora Review: African Quarterly on the Arts* 1, no. 3 (1996): 108–10.

———. "Nana Ampadu, the Sung-Tale Metaphor, and Protest Discourse in Contemporary Ghana." In *African Words, African Voices: Critical Practices in Oral History,* ed. Luise White, Stephan F. Miescher, and David William Cohen, 227–45. Bloomington: Indiana University Press, 2001.

———. *The Proverb in Context of Akan Rhetoric: A Theory of Proverb Praxis.* Bern: Peter Lang, 1989.

———. *Speaking for the Chief: Okyeame and the Politics of Akan Royal Oratory.* Bloomington: Indiana University Press, 1995.

Zeleza, Paul Tiyambe, and Cassandra Rachel Veney, eds. *Leisure in Urban Africa.* Trenton, N.J.: Africa World Press, 2003.

Zeleza, Paul Tiyambe. "The Creation and Consumption of Leisure: Theoretical and Methodological Considerations." In *Leisure in Urban Africa,* ed. Paul Tiyambe Zeleza and Cassandra Rachel Veney, vii–xli. Trenton, N.J.: Africa World Press, 2003.

Zolov, Eric. *Refried Elvis: The Rise of Mexican Counterculture.* Berkeley: University of California Press, 1999.

Zonophone. *Catalogue of Zonophone West African Records by Native Artists.* Middlesex: British Zonophone Company, 1929.

FILMS

Living the Hiplife: Musical Life on the Streets of Accra. Dir. Jesse Weaver Shipley. New York: Third World Newsreel, 2007.

Stage-Shakers! Ghana's Concert Party Theatre. Dir. Kwame Braun. Bloomington: Indiana University Press, 2001.

Index

NATE PLAGEMAN is Assistant Professor of History at Wake Forest University in Winston Salem, North Carolina. His work has previously appeared in the *International Journal of African Historical Studies*.

.